April 13–15, 2010
Stockholm, Sweden

**Association for
Computing Machinery**

Advancing Computing as a Science & Profession

LCTES'10

Proceedings of the ACM SIGPLAN/SIGBED 2010 Conference on
Languages, Compilers, & Tools
for Embedded Systems

Sponsored by:

ACM SIGPLAN & ACM SIGBED

Supported by:

**The Royal Institute of Technology,
the FP7 Cooperation Work Program,
European Commission through ArtistDesign,
& the National Science Foundation of the USA**

Association for
Computing Machinery

Advancing Computing as a Science & Profession

The Association for Computing Machinery
2 Penn Plaza, Suite 701
New York, New York 10121-0701

ISBN: 978-1-60558-953-4

Additional copies may be ordered prepaid from:

ACM Order Department
PO Box 30777
New York, NY 10087-0777, USA

Phone: 1-800-342-6626 (USA and Canada)
+1-212-626-0500 (Global)
Fax: +1-212-944-1318
E-mail: acmhelp@acm.org
Hours of Operation: 8:30 am – 4:30 pm ET

ACM Order Number 533100

Printed in the USA

Foreword

On the behalf of the program and organizing committees, it is our great pleasure to welcome you to the *ACM SIGPLAN/SIGBED Conference on Languages, Compilers and Tools for Embedded Systems – LCTES 2010*. This year's conference continues its tradition of being the premier forum for presentation of research results on leading edge issues in embedded and cyber-physical systems. LCTES 2010 will join the Cyber-Physical Systems Week for the first time this year; this is an exciting opportunity for the exchange of ideas and results among several closely related conferences at CPS Week.

The call for papers attracted 58 submissions from Asia-Pacific, Europe and the Americas. Each submission was reviewed by at least three program committee members and outside reviewers when necessary. The program committee meeting was held online over a four day period from December 2 to December 5, 2009. Each program committee member could read and discuss each paper and review where he/she did not have a conflict. The papers were thoroughly discussed via a message forum facility in the START Conference Manager system. At the end of the meeting, the program committee selected 18 papers on memory and cache systems, languages and design environments, compiler optimization, synthesis, and timing analysis.

LCTES 2010 was a team effort, and we had an extraordinary team! We thank the authors who submitted their work for consideration to LCTES and the invited speakers for their willingness to talk with the LCTES community. We also thank the program committee and external reviewers for their hard work in reviewing papers and providing suggestions on how to make LCTES 2010 a successful event. In addition, we thank Youtao Zhang, our Publicity Chair, Aviral Shrivastava, our Work-in-Progress Organizer, and José Baiocchi and Ryan Moore, our Web Chairs. Finally, we thank the LCTES Steering Committee for their guidance and our sponsors, ACM SIGPLAN and SIGBED, for their continued support of the conference. We also thank the supporters of CPS Week, including ACM, IEEE, KTH Royal Institute of Technology, NSF, and the European Union Commission.

We hope that you will find this year's program exciting and that the conference will provide many valuable opportunities to share your work with the embedded and cyber-physical systems communities.

Jaejin Lee   **Bruce Childers**
LCTES'10 General Chair   *LCTES'10 Program Chair*
Seoul National University, Korea   *University of Pittsburgh, USA*

Table of Contents

Session 1: Memory Systems

Session 2: Streaming and Synchronous Languages

Session 3: Synthesis, Timing Analysis and Design Exploration

Session 4: Compiler Techniques

Session 5: Design Frameworks and Tools

Session 6: Caching and Buffer Management

LCTES 2010 Conference Organization

General Chair: Jaejin Lee *(Seoul National University, Korea)*

Program Chair: Bruce R. Childers *(University of Pittsburgh, USA)*

Publicity Chair: Youtao Zhang *(University of Pittsburgh, USA)*

Work-in-Progress Chair: Aviral Shrivastava *(Arizona State University, USA)*

Website Chairs: José A. Baiocchi *(University of Pittsburgh, USA)*
Ryan W. Moore *(University of Pittsburgh, USA)*

Steering Committee Chair: Zhiyuan Li *(Purdue University, USA)*

Steering Committee: Koen De Bosschere *(Ghent University, Belgium)*
Kristian Flautner *(ARM Ltd., UK)*
Rajiv Gupta *(University of California Riverside, USA)*
Mary Jane Irwin *(Pennsylvania State University, USA)*
Christoph Kirsch *(Saarland University, Germany)*
Mahmut Kandemir *(Pennsylvania State University, USA)*
Yunheung Paek *(Seoul National University, Korea)*
Santosh Pande *(Georgia Institute of Technology, USA)*
John Regehr *(University of Utah, USA)*

Program Committee: Neven (Nevine) Abou Gazala *(Intel Labs, USA)*
Albert Cohen *(INRIA, France)*
Daniel Connors *(University of Colorado, USA)*
Bjorn De Sutter *(Ghent University, Belgium)*
Alexander Dean *(North Carolina State University, USA)*
Bernhard Egger *(Samsung Advanced Institute of Technology, Korea)*
Jakob Engblom *(Virtutech, Sweden)*
Sebastian Fischmeister *(University of Waterloo, Canada)*
Michael Franz *(University of California Irvine, USA)*
Stephen Hines *(NVIDIA Research, USA)*
Jason Hiser *(University of Virginia, USA)*
Andreas Krall *(Technische Universität Wien, Austria)*
Prasad Kulkarni *(University of Kansas, USA)*
Walid Najjar *(University of California Riverside, USA)*
Michael O'Boyle *(University of Edinburgh, UK)*
Yunheung Paek *(Seoul National University, Korea)*
Paul Pop *(Technical University of Denmark, Denmark)*
Jan Reineke *(Saarland University, Germany)*
Aviral Shrivastava *(Arizona State University, USA)*
Eric Stotzer *(Texas Instruments, USA)*
Zehra Sura *(IBM Research, USA)*
Gary Tyson *(Florida State University, USA)*
Jingling Xue *(University of New South Wales, Australia)*
Youtao Zhang *(University of Pittsburgh, USA)*
Dakai Zhu *(University of Texas at San Antonio, USA)*

Additional reviewers:

David Ashtaralnakhai
Akramul Azim
Peter Backes
Jose Baiocchi
Gergo Barany
Claire Burguiere
Tong Chen
Tom Crick
Nagendra Gulur Dwarakanath
Peter Ehlig
Alexandre E. Eichenberger
Daniel Grund
Todd Hahn
Brett Huber
Alexander Jordan
Sangyeol Kang
Kyungwon Kim
Yongjoo Kim
Gayathri Krishnamurthy
Per Larsen
Byeong Lee
Jongwon Lee
Weijia Li
Philipp Lucas
Roger Moussalli

Vijay Nagarajan
V. Kirshna Nandivada
Samaneh Navabpour
Jianwei Niu
Augusto Oliveira
Gregory S. Parsons
Stavros Passas
Hiren Patel
Viktor Pavlu
Roger Pease
Shaolin Peng
Yi Qian
Morten Sleth Rasmussen
Lakshminaraya Renganarayana
Prabhat Kumar Saraswat
Doruk Sark
Karthik Sundaramoorthy
Ali S. Tosun
Jason Villarreal
Jeffery von Ronne
Peng Wu
Seungjoon Yang
Jonghee Youn
Yuan Zhao
Xiaotong Zhuang

LCTES 2010 Sponsors & Supporters

Sponsors:

In cooperation with:

Hosted by:

Supported by:

Analysis and Approximation for Bank Selection Instruction Minimization on Partitioned Memory Architecture

Minming Li   Chun Jason Xue   Tiantian Liu   Yingchao Zhao

Department of Computer Science, City University of Hong Kong

minmli@cs.cityu.edu.hk, {jasonxue,yingzhao}@cityu.edu.hk, tiantiliu2@student.cityu.edu.hk

Abstract

A large number of embedded systems include 8-bit microcontrollers for their energy efficiency and low cost. Multi-bank memory architecture is commonly applied in 8-bit microcontrollers to increase the size of memory without extending address buses. To switch among different memory banks, a special instruction, Bank Selection, is used. How to minimize the number of bank selection instructions inserted is important to reduce code size for embedded systems.

In this paper, we consider how to insert the minimum number of bank selection instructions in a program to achieve feasibility. A program can be represented by a control flow graph (CFG). We prove that it is NP-Hard to insert the minimum number of bank selection instructions if all the variables are pre-assigned to memory banks. Therefore, we introduce a 2-approximation algorithm using a rounding method. When the CFG is a tree or the out-degree of each node in the CFG is at most two, we show that we can insert the bank selection instructions optimally in polynomial time. We then consider the case when there are some nodes that do not access any memory bank and design a dynamic programming method to compute the optimal insertion strategy when the CFG is a tree. Experimental result shows the proposed techniques can reduce bank selection instructions significantly on partitioned memory architecture.

Categories and Subject Descriptors   C.3 [*SPECIAL-PURPOSE AND APPLICATION-BASED SYSTEMS*]: Real-time and embedded systems; B.3 [*MEMORY STRUCTURES*]: general; D.3.4 [*Programming Languages*]: Processors-Optimization, Code generation

General Terms   Algorithms

Keywords   Bank Selection Instruction Minimization, Partitioned Memory Architecture

1. Introduction

Embedded systems are prevalent in every aspect of our daily lives. A large number of embedded systems apply 8-bit microcontrollers for their energy efficiency, low cost, and smaller chip die-size compared to 16-bit and 32-bit microcontrollers. For example,

8-bit microcontrollers are used in cell phones, barcode readers, hotel card key writers, home appliances, automobiles, etc. About 55% of all CPUs sold in the world are 8-bit microcontrollers and microprocessors. According to Semico research corporation, over 4 billion 8-bit microcontrollers were sold in 2006 [2]. To increase the size of memory for 8-bit microcontrollers, the address space is often partitioned into memory banks so that a smaller address bus can be used. Smaller address buses result in smaller chip die-size, higher clock frequency and lower power consumption. With a partitioned memory architecture, codes and data are distributed into available memory banks. One memory bank will be active and ready to be accessed by CPU at any single moment. A special instruction, Bank Selection, is used to switch among memory banks. While partitioned memory gives a larger address space without extending address buses, inserting bank selection instructions introduces both timing and code size overhead. This paper studies how to minimize the number of bank selection instructions by careful placement of bank selection instructions.

Partitioned memory architecture is common in 8-bit microcontrollers. For example, Freescale [1] 68HC11 8-bit microcontrollers allow multiple 64KB memory banks to be accessed by their 16-bit address registers with only one bank being active at a time. Zilog [3] Z80 also addresses a maximum of 64 KB memory using 16-bit address registers. With multiple 64 KB memory banks, Z80 effectively increases its memory space without extending its address buses. Other examples include Intel 8051 processor family and MOS technology 6502 series microcontrollers. For embedded systems using these 8-bit microcontrollers, how to insert bank selection instructions so that the code size is minimum is an important research topic.

In this paper, we consider how to insert the minimum number of bank selection instructions in the input CFG (control flow graph). The contributions of this paper are as follows:

1. Prove that it is NP-Hard to insert the minimum number of bank selection instructions and introduce a 2-approximation algorithm using a rounding method.

2. When the CFG is a tree or the out-degree of each node in the CFG is at most two, propose algorithms to obtain the optimal solutions in polynomial time.

3. When there are some nodes that do not access any memory banks, propose two heuristic algorithms for general CFGs and a dynamic programming algorithm to obtain the optimal solutions when the CFG is a tree.

The remaining paper is organized as follows. Section 2 gives the related work. We define the models in Section 3. Then we study the model without transparent nodes in Section 4 and obtain a 2-approximation algorithm using a rounding method. In Section 5, we study the model with transparent nodes and give a dynamic programming method to solve the problem on trees. Experimental results are given in Section 6. Finally, we conclude our work in Section 7.

2. Related Work

Most previous efforts on partitioned memory architectures focus on maximizing parallel data accesses to make memory banks simultaneously active [4–8]. By enabling parallel memory accesses in a single instruction, one can increase memory bandwidth and thus improve program performance. Considering sequential accesses to partitioned memory architectures, some work has been done. In [9] [10], Scholz et al. present an optimization technique that minimizes the overhead of bank switching through cost-effective placement of bank selection instructions. The placement is controlled by a number of different objectives, such as runtime, low power, small code size or a combination of these parameters. They formulate the placement of bank selection instructions as a discrete optimization problem that is mapped to a partitioned boolean quadratic programming (PBQP) problem (not polynomial solvable). Yuan et al. in [11] consider using the partitioned memory architecture with a globally shared memory and presents a dynamic programming algorithm to generate the optimal assignment of variables in the shared memory to minimize bank selection instructions.

There are significant research efforts [12–16] on assigning variables into partitioned multiple memory banks for parallel data access. Some of them aim to achieve the maximum instruction level parallelism. Saghir et al. [12] transform the partitioning problem into an Interference Graph (IG), while Zhuge et al. [13] transform the problem into a Variable Independence Graph (VIG) to find the parallelism between variables. Xue et al. [14] explore the variable partitioning further combined with scheduling problem for DSP architectures with multiple cores. Others [15, 16] optimize the energy consumption for architectures with multiple memory banks. They try to determine when to power some banks down to low power mode based on access data pattern analysis.

In this paper, we consider partitioned memory architecture where only one memory bank can be active at a time. Techniques are proposed to minimize the number of bank selection instructions inserted in a program represented by a CFG. We investigate the model where the variables are pre-assigned to memory banks. We analysis the problems in CFGs without or with some nodes that do not access any memory banks. It is proved that both of the two problems are NP-Hard problem. Some approximate algorithms are proposed for the general problems, while some optimal algorithms are proposed for some special cases.

3. Problem Description

In this paper, we assume that each variable accessed by a computation is stored in one of the memory banks and only one copy of each variable is available.

A control flow graph (CFG) $G = (V, E)$ is a representation of all paths that might be traversed through a program during its execution. A basic block is a sequence of statements in which flow of control can only enter from its beginning and leave at its end. Each vertex $v \in V$ represents a basic block and each edge $e \in E$ represents a control flow edge in a CFG.

We mainly consider CFGs which are also DAGs (Directed Acyclic Graph) and further break each basic block in the CFG into an equivalent path so that each node in the path is a single instruction and at most reads or writes one variable.

Now we can formulate our model as follows. The input graph is a DAG $G = (V, E, B)$ where $V = \{v_1, \ldots, v_n\}$ is the set of nodes and E is the set of edges. The set $B = \{1, 2, \ldots, m\}$ represents the set of memory banks. We call a node *bank-sensitive* and associate bank label i to the node if the node accesses a variable in bank i. A node is called *transparent* if it does not read or write any variable. If $(u, v) \in E$, then we say u is v's *parent node*, while v is u's *child node*. The bank selection instruction could be inserted either at the entrance of one node or at the exit of one node. A directed edge (u, v) is called *satisfied* if after the insertion decisions at the exit of u and at the entrance of v, the memory bank which v accesses is activated when the execution flow from u reaches v. If v does not access any variable, then the edge is automatically satisfied. We say an insertion strategy is feasible if all the edges are satisfied. If a bank selection instruction "Activate Bank i" is inserted at the entrance of a node which accesses a variable in bank i, then all the edges coming into this node are satisfied. If a bank selection instruction "Activate Bank j" is inserted at the exit of node u, then no matter which edge the execution goes through after u, the active bank will be bank j when the execution flow leaves u. If no instruction is inserted at the exit of u, then after the flow leaves u, the active memory bank will be j if u accesses a variable in bank j and will be k if u is transparent and the active memory bank is k before the flow enters u.

Now we have formulated our problem, in the following sections, we will first propose solutions for CFGs without transparent nodes. And then, solutions for CFGs with transparent nodes will be analyzed.

4. Insertion in CFGs without transparent nodes

In this section, we study the insertion of bank selection instructions in CFGs without transparent nodes. A transparent node is a node that does not access any variable. First, we prove that the problem for general CFGs is NP-Hard and propose a 2-approximation solution. Second, we present polynomial time optimal algorithms for input graphs as trees. Third, for CFGs whose out-degree is bounded, we give an optimal solution. CFGs with transparent nodes will be studied in the next section.

4.1 General CFGs

When the input CFG is an arbitrary DAG, it is NP-Hard to decide whether the minimum total number of bank selection instructions is within a given number. To prove the NP-Hardness, we make a reduction from *EXACT COVER BY 3-SETS (X3C)*, which is shown to be NP-complete by Karp in 1972 [17].

EXACT COVER BY 3-SETS

INSTANCE: Set X with $|X| = 3q$ and a collection C of 3-element subsets of X.

QUESTION: Does C contain an exact cover for X, i.e., a subcollection $C' \subseteq C$ such that every element of X occurs in exactly one member of C'?

THEOREM 4.1. *When variables have been assigned to memory banks, it is NP-Hard to decide whether the minimum total number of bank selection instructions is within a given number.*

Proof: We prove the NP-Hardness by reduction from the X3C problem. Given an instance of X3C, there are an element set $X = \{e_1, e_2, \ldots, e_{3q}\}$ and a collection $C = \{S_1, S_2, \ldots, S_n\}$ of 3-element subsets of X. We construct the CFG of our instance and the variable assignment as follows.

The CFG is a DAG with $3q + n^3$ nodes, and these nodes are divided into a parent set $A = \{v_1, \ldots, v_{3q}\}$ and n child sets $C_1, \ldots, C_n$ such that $C_i = \{u_{i1}, \ldots, u_{in^2}\}$ for $1 \le i \le n$. Each node v_i in A corresponds to one element e_i in X, and we assume that node v_i accesses variable a_i assigned in memory bank 0. Each child set C_j corresponds to one subset S_j and it contains n^2 nodes all of which access variable b_j assigned in memory bank j. There is an edge from v_i to all the nodes in C_j if S_j contains element e_i and we say v_i is a parent of C_j. Now we show that the X3C instance has a solution if and only if our problem has a solution with the total number of bank selection instructions at most $3q + (n-q)n^2$.

If the X3C instance has a solution $\{S_{\sigma(1)}, \ldots, S_{\sigma(q)}\}$. Then we can insert $3q + (n-q)n^2$ bank selection instructions to achieve the goal as follows. First, add a bank selection instruction "Activate Bank $\sigma(j)$" after node v_i if $e_i \in S_{\sigma(j)}$. Then we add "Activate Bank j" before all the nodes in C_j if j is not in the set $\{\sigma(1), \ldots, \sigma(q)\}$. Notice that we need to add a bank selection instruction before each node in group C_i if and only if at least one parent of C_i does not have a bank selection instruction "Activate Bank i" at the exit. Therefore, it can be seen that this way of adding bank selection instructions can achieve the goal and the total number of instructions added is $3q + (n-q)n^2$.

If our problem has a solution with at most $3q + (n-q)n^2$ bank selection instructions, then it must be true that a bank selection instruction is added at the exit of every node v_i. Otherwise, at most $q - 1$ child sets have all their parents changing the bank selection towards them and therefore need not add any bank selection instruction at the entrance of the nodes inside, which will require at least $(n-q+1)n^2 > 3q + (n-q)n^2$ bank selection instructions at the entrance of the nodes in the child sets to settle the bank differences, a contradiction. Since every parent must change the bank at its exit, we can see that exactly $(n-q)n^2$ bank selection instructions are added at the entrance of nodes in the child sets in the solution. This means exactly q child sets (we call them fortunate child sets) do not need bank selection instructions added and each such child set C_i must have all its parents select bank i at their exit. Because each node in the parent set can only choose one bank at the exit, we can see that subsets corresponding to all these fortunate child sets will be a solution to the instance of the X3C problem.

Since the problem of inserting minimum number of bank switch instructions is NP-Hard, we turn to find approximation algorithms by formulating it as an Integer Linear Program (ILP). For each node a which accesses a variable in bank a_0, suppose that its child nodes access variables from s different banks say $a_1, \ldots, a_s$ besides a_0, then there are $s + 1$ variables $x_{a1}, \ldots, x_{as}, y_a$ associated with a in the ILP.

$$x_{ai} = \begin{cases} 1 & \text{if there is an instruction "Activate bank } a_i\text{"} \\ & \text{at the exit of node } a \\ 0 & \text{otherwise} \end{cases}$$

$$y_a = \begin{cases} 1 & \text{if there is an instruction "Activate bank } a_0\text{"} \\ & \text{at the entrance of node } a \\ 0 & \text{otherwise} \end{cases}$$

The ILP then can be written as follows:

$$\begin{aligned} min \quad & \sum_{a,i} x_{ai} + \sum_a y_a \\ s.t. \quad & y_b + x_{aj} \geq 1 \quad a, b \text{ access different banks} \quad (1) \\ & \qquad\qquad\qquad (b \text{ accesses bank } a_j) \\ & y_b \geq \sum_j x_{aj} \quad a, b \text{ access the same bank} \quad (2) \\ & \sum_i x_{ai} \leq 1 \quad \forall a \quad (3) \\ & x_{ai} \in \{0, 1\} \quad \forall a, i \quad (4) \\ & y_a \in \{0, 1\} \quad \forall a \quad (5) \end{aligned}$$

First, all the edges (a, b) where a and b access different banks are satisfied since "Activate bank a_j" is either added at the entrance of b or at the exit of a by constraints (1). Second, all the edges (a, b) where a and b access the same bank k are satisfied since if there is no instruction inserted at the exit of a then the edge is automatically satisfied while if "Activate bank a_j" is inserted at

the exit of a ($x_{aj} = 1$) then "Activate bank k" will be inserted before b ($y_b = 1$) due to constraints (2). Finally, constraints (3) guarantee that only one instruction is inserted at the exit of each node. Therefore the ILP formulation is correct. Note that this ILP formulation can also be applied to general CFGs.

To obtain an efficient approximation solution, we relax the ILP into the following LP:

$$\begin{aligned} min \quad & \sum_{a,i} x_{ai} + \sum_a y_a \\ s.t. \quad & y_b + x_{aj} \geq 1 \quad a, b \text{ access different banks} \\ & \qquad\qquad\qquad (b \text{ accesses bank } a_j) \\ & y_b \geq \sum_j x_{aj} \quad a, b \text{ access the same bank} \\ & \sum_i x_{ai} \leq 1 \quad \forall a \\ & 0 \leq x_{ai} \leq 1 \quad \forall a, i \\ & 0 \leq y_a \leq 1 \quad \forall a \end{aligned}$$

After getting one optimal solution of the LP above, denoted as $OPT(L)$, we do a rounding to each x_{ai} and y_b in $OPT(L)$ and get an integer solution, denoted as S. The rounding method is as follows.

For each y_b in $OPT(L)$,

- If $y_b \geq \frac{1}{2}$, round y_b to 1;

- If $y_b < \frac{1}{2}$, round y_b to 0.

For each x_{ai} in $OPT(L)$,

- If $x_{ai} > \frac{1}{2}$, then round x_{ai} to 1;

- If $x_{ai} < \frac{1}{2}$, then round x_{ai} to 0;

- If $x_{ai} = \frac{1}{2}$ and there exists no other $x_{aj} = \frac{1}{2}$, then round x_{ai} to 1;

- If $x_{ai} = \frac{1}{2}$ and there exists another $x_{aj} = \frac{1}{2}$, then round x_{ai} to 0.

THEOREM 4.2. *The rounding solution S is 2-approximation of the original ILP.*

Proof: First we show that S is a feasible solution of the ILP. Hence we consider the five classes of constraints of the ILP.

For constraints (1), if $y_b \geq \frac{1}{2}$, then y_b will be rounded to 1 and the inequality holds. Otherwise, we have $x_{aj} > \frac{1}{2}$, then x_{aj} will be rounded to 1 and the inequality also holds. Therefore, constraints (1) are satisfied in the rounding solution S.

For constraints (2), at most one item on the right hand side is rounded to 1 according to constraints (3) and the rules for rounding x_{aj}. Once there is such an item, y_b on the left hand side must have value at least $\frac{1}{2}$ and it will be rounded to 1 and the inequality holds. Therefore, constraints (2) are satisfied in the rounding solution S.

For constraints (3), there are three cases. Case 1, there is no item having value at least $\frac{1}{2}$ on the left hand side, then all these items will be rounded to 0, and the inequality holds. Case 2, there is only one item of value at least $\frac{1}{2}$ on the left hand side, then only this item will be rounded to 1 and the inequality also holds. Case 3, there are two items of value $\frac{1}{2}$ on the left hand side, then both of these items will be rounded to 0 according to the last rule for rounding x_{ai}. Hence the inequality holds. Combining the three cases, constraints (3) are satisfied.

From the rounding process, it is easy to see that constraints (4) and (5) are satisfied.

Since all five classes of constraints are satisfied in S, the rounding solution S is a feasible solution of the ILP.

Next we show that the objective value in the rounding solution S is at most twice of the optimal value of the ILP. Notice that the value of each x_{ai} and y_b after the rounding are at most twice of the original value, therefore the objective value is at most twice of

$OPT(L)$. Since $OPT(L) \leq OPT(I)$ (the optimal solution for the corresponding integer linear programming), we can see that the objective value of the rounding solution S is at most twice of the optimal solution of the ILP. Because we have also shown that the rounding solution is a feasible solution of the ILP, the rounding solution S is a 2-approximation of the ILP.

In the next section, we will analyze inserting bank selection instructions when the CFGs are trees.

4.2 Trees

For each internal node v in the tree, the insertion decision in the subtree rooted at v can be considered separately because after the execution flow goes to v, the active memory bank will definitely be the bank containing the variable accessed by v, which makes the insertion decisions before v and after v independent. Therefore, we can break the tree into subtrees at every internal node and consider the insertions in each subtree separately and every such subtree is a star. A star is a tree with a root and all the children of the root are leaves. It is easy to see that optimal solutions for a star can be obtained as follows.

We group the leaves according to the banks their accessed variables are assigned to. If one of the largest size groups accesses the same bank i as the root, then we insert one bank selection instruction at the entrance of each leaf which accesses a variable not in bank i; Otherwise, suppose that one of the largest size groups access bank j, then we insert one bank selection instruction at the entrance of each leaf which accesses a variable not in bank j and also insert "Activate Bank j" at the exit of the root.

The algorithm for tree is concluded in Algorithm 1.

Algorithm 1 Optimal algorithm for bank selection instruction insertion in trees

---

Require: A CFG which is a tree.
Ensure: An optimal solution of bank selection instruction insertion in this CFG.
  Break the tree into stars at every internal node;
  for each star **do**
    Group the leaves according to the banks their accessed variables are assigned to;
    if one of the largest size groups accesses the same bank i as the root of the star **then**
      (a) Insert one bank selection instruction at the entrance of each leaf which accesses a variable not in bank i;
    else
      Suppose that one of the largest size groups access bank j;
      (a) Insert one bank selection instruction at the entrance of each leaf which accesses a variable not in bank j;
      (b) Insert "Activate Bank j" at the exit of the root;
    end if
  end for

4.3 Out-degree bounded CFGs

In this subsection, we analyze how to insert bank selection instructions if the out-degree of each node in the CFG is bounded by two. We first deal with six cases shown in Figure 1. After we process all six cases, we will show how to find an optimal solution to insert the minimum number of bank switching instructions efficiently in the CFG.

Case 1. The out-degree of the node is one and this node accesses the same memory bank with its child.

Case 2. The out-degree of the node is one and this node accesses a different memory bank with its child.

Case 3. The out-degree of the node is two and this node accesses the same memory bank with its two children.

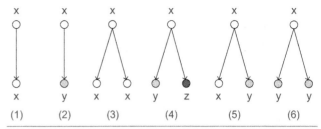

Figure 1. Six cases of the out-degree bounded nodes.

Case 4. The out-degree of the node is two and this node accesses different memory banks with its children. Additionally, the two children access different memory banks from each other.

Case 5. The out-degree of the node is two and this node accesses the same memory bank with one of its children, but different from the other one.

Case 6. The out-degree of the node is two and this node accesses different memory banks with its children. However, the two children access the same memory bank and at least one of the children has only one parent.

Now we show how to deal with the above six cases in the given CFG so that the total number of bank selection instructions is minimum. The high level idea is as follows. Suppose that we are given an optimal solution. Whenever there is a subgraph falling into Case 1 to Case 6, we do a corresponding adjustment of the optimal solution on the subgraph and prove that the new solution is feasible and does not increase the inserted bank selection instructions compared with the optimal solution. This means that we can find an optimal solution where the insertion decisions in the subgraph are the same as our decision. Hence, the inserted instructions (after the adjustment) in this subgraph are finalized in our solution since it maintains the possibility of the optimal solution. Furthermore, we can delete those edges which are satisfied no matter how the insertion decisions are made in the remaining graph. Obviously the remaining graph requires no more insertions than the graph before edge deletion. We keep doing the adjustment and fix the insertion decisions gradually until no pattern satisfies Case 1 to Case 6, then we generate an optimal solution for the remaining graph where each node is either isolated or has exactly two children or has at least two parents.

For Case 1, we can just delete the edge from the parent to the child because no matter what insertions are done in the remaining part of the graph, this edge will always be satisfied. This is because the parent node has no child in the remaining graph and therefore we do not need to insert an instruction at the exit of the parent node. If there is an instruction at the entrance of the child node in the remaining graph, the inserted instruction must be "Activate Bank i", where i is the bank storing the variable in the child node. Therefore, this edge is always satisfied.

For Case 2, we must either insert an instruction at the exit of the parent node or at the entrance of the child node in the optimal solution to keep feasibility because the parent node and the child node access different memory banks. No matter how the optimal solution behaves along this edge, we can always maintain the feasibility and optimality of the solution by inserting a bank selection instruction only at the entrance of the child node along this edge and keep the remaining insertions in the optimal solution unchanged. After we fix this insertion, we can further delete all the incoming edges of this child node because all these edges are always satisfied.

For Case 3, we can just delete the two edges between the parent and the two children. The analysis is similar to that of Case 1.

4

For Case 4, in the optimal solution, we need to insert at least two instructions in the subgraph in order to satisfy the two edges. Therefore, we can guarantee the feasibility and optimality of the solution by keeping the optimal solution in the remaining graph and inserting one instruction at the entrance of each child in this subgraph. After fixing these two insertions, we can delete all the incoming edges of these two children due to similar reasons as in Case 2.

For Case 5, in the optimal solution, we need to insert at least one instruction in the parent-child pair which accesses different memory banks in order to achieve feasibility. Therefore, we can guarantee the feasibility and optimality of the solution by keeping the optimal solution in the remaining graph and inserting an instruction at the entrance of the child (the grey node) which accesses a different memory bank from the parent node. If in the optimal solution, one instruction is inserted at the exit of the parent node, then another instruction must be inserted at the entrance of the other child. Hence our method just moves the instruction from the exit of the parent to the entrance of the grey child, and such a moving does not increase the number of instructions and also maintains the feasibility by satisfying all the edges entering the two children. After fixing this insertion, we can delete the two outgoing edges of the parent and all the incoming edges of the grey child.

For Case 6, in the optimal solution, at least one instruction needs to be inserted in the parent-child pair where the child only has one parent. Therefore, we can guarantee the feasibility and optimality of the solution by keeping the optimal solution in the remaining graph and inserting an instruction "Activate Bank i" at the exit of the parent node, where i is the bank storing the variable accessed by the children. After fixing this insertion, we can delete the two outgoing edges of the parent because they are always satisfied now.

We conclude the rules in Algorithm 2.

Algorithm 2 Pre-processing algorithm for each parent-child pair
---
Require: A parent-child pair.
Ensure: A parent-child pair with bank selection instruction pre-inserted and some edges deleted.
> **For Case 1**:
>> Delete the edge from the parent node to the child node;
> **For Case 2**:
>> (a) Insert a bank selection instruction at the entrance of the child node;
>> (b) Delete all the incoming edges of this child node;
> **For Case 3**:
>> Delete the two edges from the parent node to the child nodes;
> **For Case 4**:
>> (a) Insert a bank selection instruction at the entrance of each child node;
>> (b) Delete all the incoming edges of each child node;
> **For Case 5**:
>> (a) Insert a bank selection instruction at the entrance of the child node whose variable is not in the same bank with the parent node;
>> (b) Delete all the incoming edges of the child node in Step (a);
> **For Case 6**:
>> (a) Inserting an instruction "Activate Bank i" at the exit of the parent node, where i is the bank storing the variable accessed by the child nodes;
>> (b) Delete the two edges from the parent node to the child nodes;

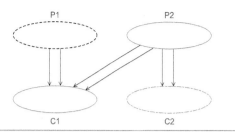

Figure 2. A connected bipartite component.

After repeatedly dealing with subgraphs belonging to the six cases, we construct a graph G' based on the remaining graph G_r as follows. For each node $u \in G_r$, we create two nodes u_{in} and u_{out} in G' accessing the same variable as u. For each edge uv in G_r, we add an edge $u_{out}v_{in}$ in G'. According to the way we add bank selection instructions, the solution for G' directly corresponds to a solution for G_r. Therefore, we focus on G' in the following discussion. It is easy to see that G' consists of some isolated nodes and several connected directed bipartite components, where each component is formed by several parent nodes and child nodes and all the child nodes access the same memory bank which is different from any parent node. Furthermore, each child node has at least two parents and each parent node has exactly two children. Then we can just insert bank selection instructions at the entrance of each child node in the connected component to achieve optimality. The optimality is shown by the following lemma.

LEMMA 4.3. *Inserting bank selection instructions at the entrance of each child node in a connected component of G' is optimal.*

Proof: First, it is easy to see that inserting bank selection instructions at the entrance of each child node could activate the memory bank before variables in this bank are accessed. Hence it is a feasible solution.

Second, we can show that such inserting at the entrance of each child node will use no more instructions than the optimal solution.

Suppose that G' is such a connected component. In G', each parent node has exactly two children and each child node has at least two parents.

Assume that the optimal solution inserts instructions both at the entrance of some selected child nodes and at the exit of some selected parent nodes as shown in Figure 2. We assume that the set of selected parent nodes is P_2 (the set of unselected parent nodes is P_1) and the set of selected child nodes is C_1 (the set of unselected child nodes is C_2). Then we can see that nodes in P_1 only have children in C_1 and the nodes in C_2 only have parents in P_2.

Now we focus on P_2, C_2 and the edges between these two sets. For each parent node in P_2, it has at most two children in C_2 but for each child node in C_2, it has at least two parents in P_2. Hence the number of nodes in C_2 is no more than the number of nodes in P_2 which means that inserting at the entrance of each child node will use no more instructions than the optimal solution.

With the proof for Lemma 4.3, we have an optimal solution for inserting minimum number of bank selection instructions in CFGs with out-degree bounded by two. Algorithm 3 describes how to insert the bank selection instructions.

5. Insertion in CFGs with transparent nodes

In the previous section, we analyze CFGs without transparent nodes. In some CFGs, there are transparent nodes which do not access any variables. Recall that all the incoming edges of a transparent node are satisfied automatically. However, the existence of transparent nodes affects the insertion of bank selection instructions. For example, in Figure 3(a), we have to insert at least two

Algorithm 3 Algorithm for instruction insertion in out-degree bounded CFGs

Require: A CFG with nodes whose out-degree are bound by two.
Ensure: An optimal solution of bank selection instruction insertion in this CFG.
  while there are nodes belonging to the six cases **do**
    Insert instructions and delete satisfied edges according to Algorithm 2;
  end while
  for each bipartite connected component **do**
    (a) Insert bank selection instructions at the entrance of each child node in this component;
    (b) Delete all the edges in this component;
  end for

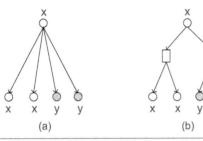

Figure 3. Transparent nodes

bank selection instructions (at the entrance of each child node accessing bank y). However, in Figure 3(b), we only need to insert one bank selection instruction at the entrance of the right transparent node. The existence of transparent nodes makes minimizing the number of bank selection instructions more difficult and complex. Additionally, we cannot consider the insertion of bank selection instructions at the entrance and at the exit of the transparent node separately because of the uncertainty of the activated bank when the execution flows leaves the node.

Since the CFG with transparent nodes are more general, by the result from the previous section, we can see that it is NP-Hard to find an optimal insertion strategy in a CFG with transparent nodes.

5.1 Heuristic Algorithm for general CFGs

In this subsection, we give two heuristic algorithms for general CFG's with transparent nodes.

The first one is Algorithm 4. We first consider those non-transparent nodes and decide the insertions of bank selection instructions for those nodes using the ILP rounding method introduced in Section 4.1. Then we decide how to insert the bank selection instructions for the transparent nodes. Finally we adjust the instruction insertions for the children of transparent nodes.

The second heuristic algorithm (Algorithm 5) first transforms those transparent nodes to non-transparent nodes, then decides how to insert the bank selection instructions in the new CFG without transparent nodes, and finally removes all the redundant instructions.

5.2 Trees

In some special CFGs with transparent nodes, for example, if the given CFG is a tree, then there is an algorithm that can insert bank selection instructions optimally.

To insert the minimum number of bank selection instructions in a CFG which is a tree with transparent nodes, the main idea is to split the tree into disjoint subtrees with every non-transparent internal node as a break point and deal with different subtrees

Algorithm 4 Heuristic Algorithm (A) for a general CFG with transparent nodes

Require: A general CFG with transparent nodes.
Ensure: A solution of bank selection instruction insertion in this CFG.
  delete all the edges incident to transparent nodes and get a new CFG G';
  Use ILP rounding to insert instructions in graph G';
  for each transparent node u **do**
    if all the activated banks are the same (bank x) for u's incoming edges **then**
      Consider u as a node accessing bank x and insert proper memory bank instructions
    else
      Insert "Activate Bank y" at the exit of u, where y is the memory bank accessed most frequently by u's children
    end if
  end for
  for the children of those transparent nodes **do**
    Insert some bank selection instructions if needed;
  end for

Algorithm 5 Heuristic Algorithm (B) for a general CFG with transparent nodes

Require: A general CFG with transparent nodes.
Ensure: A solution of bank selection instruction insertion in this CFG.
  for each transparent node u **do**
    Consider u as a non-transparent node accessing bank x where x is the memory bank accessed most frequently by u's children.
  end for
  Use ILP rounding to decide the instruction insertions in G'.
  for each transparent node u **do**
    if there is an instruction "Activate Bank y" at the exit of u **then**
      Remove the instruction at the entrance of u if any.
    end if
  end for

separately. The reason that we can treat these subtrees separately is that if a node v is not transparent, then we can consider the subtree rooted at v separately to achieve feasibility by a similar argument as that in Section 4.2. Hence, in the following, we only need to deal with trees whose non-root internal nodes are all transparent.

Firstly, for transparent nodes, insertion at the entrance and insertion at the exit have the same effect. Therefore, we only consider insertion at the entrance in this section. In the subtree rooted at node v, if the current activated memory bank before entering node v is bank i, we use $f(v, i)$ to denote the minimum number of bank selection instructions that we need to insert in this subtree to achieve feasibility. To simplify the formula, we define $K_i(u) = 1 + \min_{j \neq i}\{f(u, j)\}$.

If node v is a leaf which accesses a variable in bank j, then function $f(v, i)$ is defined as

$$f(v, i) = \begin{cases} 0 & \text{if } i = j \\ 1 & \text{otherwise} \end{cases} \quad (1)$$

If node v is a non-root internal node (therefore transparent) with children set $C(v)$, then we have two choices.

The first choice is to insert no instructions at the entrance of node v, hence the total number of instructions is the sum of inserted instructions needed in each subtree rooted at a child node of v because the decision in these subtrees are independent. For each child u, it could insert another bank selection instruction "Activate Bank j", which corresponds to the term $K_i(u)$ or insert no instructions, which corresponds to the term $f(u, i)$.

The second choice is to insert an instruction "Activate Bank j" at the entrance of node v, which causes an extra insertion. And the analysis of the children nodes are similar to the first case. We will take a better one out of the two choices.

Therefore the function $f(v, i)$ for any non-root internal node with children set $C(v)$ can be defined as follows.

$$f(v, i) = \min\{\sum_{u \in C(v)} \min\{f(u, i), K_i(u)\},$$
$$1 + \min_{j \neq i} \sum_{u \in C(v)} \min\{f(u, j), K_j(u)\}\} \quad (2)$$

Finally, we need to enumerate all the possibilities at the exit of the root. This is equivalent to adding a new root connecting to the old root (accessing the same memory bank) and changing the old root into a transparent node. we can then decide how to insert the minimum number of bank selection instructions in the whole tree by evaluating the function $f(v, i)$ where i is the bank the root accesses and v is the transparent node connecting to the new root. The algorithm is shown in Algorithm 6.

Algorithm 6 Algorithm of trees with transparent nodes

Require: A CFG which is a tree with transparent nodes.
Ensure: A optimal solution of bank selection instruction insertion in this CFG.
  Split the tree into disjoint subtrees with every non-transparent node as a break point;
  for each subtree without transparent nodes **do**
    Deal with such case as the method in Section 4.2
  end for
  for each subtree with transparent nodes **do**
    /* its non-root internal nodes are all transparent*/
    Add a new root r_n connecting to the old root r_o and change the old root into a transparent node;
    Make a table T for this tree
    while there is a node v which is a leaf or whose children have been calculated **do**
      Calculate $f(v, i)$ value for each i with either (1) or (2);
      The entry $T(v, i)$ contains $f(v, i)$ and the corresponding insertions of v's children set;
    end while
    Find the minimum value of $f(r_o, i)$ among all i, and insert instructions according to the recorded insertion method in the corresponding entry $T(v, i)$;
  end for

---

6. Experiments

This section presents the experimental results to illustrate the effectiveness of the algorithms proposed in this paper. We run the proposed algorithms for CFGs without transparent nodes. The benchmarks used in this section are shown in Table 1. "SQUAR", "FILTER", "EXP", "ROOT", "FFT", "PACKET", "PETRINET" and "RADIO" are benchmarks used in previous studies by various research groups (MRTC [18], SNU [19]), while the others are synthesized graphs using TGFF tool [20]. In Table 1, Columns "Nodes" and "Varis" give the numbers of nodes and variables in each CFG respectively. Column "Prop" presents the properties that each CFG exhibit, where "Tree", "Out<2" and "General" mean that the CFG is a tree, the CFG is a graph with nodes of out-degree bounded by 2 and the CFG is a general CFG respectively. A four-bank memory architecture is used for benchmarks with variables

no more than 30, and an eight-banks memory architecture for the others. For the real benchmarks, each program is compiled to obtain its assembly program and bank-partition information. We ignore all the assembly instructions that do not access memory and construct the others as CFG nodes. Then we create edges between nodes according to the control flow. For the TGFF synthesized graph, for each node we assign the bank it accesses as its attribute.

Table 1. Benchmarks

Real Benchmarks				Constructed CFGs			
Name	Nodes	Varis	Prop	Name	Nodes	Varis	Prop
SQUAR	19	7	Out<2	TREE1	30	8	Tree
FILTER	35	6	Tree	TREE2	50	15	Tree
EXP	50	14	Out<2	TREE3	100	30	Tree
ROOT	65	18	General	GRAPH1	150	20	Out<2
FFT	155	16	General	GRAPH2	200	35	Out<2
PACKET	200	17	General	GRAPH3	360	40	Out<2
PETRINET	365	38	General	GRAPH4	40	20	General
RADIO	505	56	General	GRAPH5	100	30	General

The results of the methods proposed in this paper are shown in Table 2. Column "Original" gives the total number of BSLs inserted in the un-optimized solutions generated by the compiler. For each benchmark, "lp_solve" [21], an ILP tool, is first used to obtain its optimal solution. Column "OptILP" gives the total number of BSLs inserted in the optimal solution. For trees, we run the optimal Algorithm 1 proposed in Section 4.2 and give the number of BSLs in the solutions in column "OptFunc". For graph with nodes of out-degree not bigger than 2, we run the optimal Algorithm 3 proposed in Section 4.3 and also give the results in column "OptFunc". For general CFGs, we run the proposed 2-approximation rounding algorithm and give the results in column "Rounding".

It can be seen from the results that the proposed optimal algorithms for tree and graph are correct. The rounding algorithms obtain the same solutions compared to the optimal solutions.

7. Conclusion

In this paper, we study the problem of inserting the minimum number of bank selection instructions in a program to achieve feasibility, where feasibility means that no matter which path the program follows in a real execution, the variable stored in a bank is always accessed after the bank is activated.

We study the model where all the variables are already assigned to banks. We prove that it is NP-Hard to insert the minimum number of bank selection instructions to achieve feasibility. Then, for graphs without transparent nodes (nodes that do not access any variables), we introduce a 2-approximation algorithm using a rounding method and when the CFG is a tree or the out-degree of each node in the CFG is at most two, we show that the minimum insertions of bank selection instructions can be computed in polynomial time. We also consider the case when some nodes in the graph are transparent and design a dynamic programming method to compute the optimal insertion strategy when the CFG is a tree.

Table 2. Results of the proposed algorithms for CFGs without transparent nodes.

Prop	Name	Nodes	Original	OptILP	OptFunc	Rounding
Tree	FILTER	35	32	28	28	28
	TREE1	30	28	21	21	21
	TREE2	50	45	37	37	37
	TREE3	100	86	72	72	72
Out<2	SQUAR	19	18	17	17	17
	EXP	50	43	40	40	40
	GRAPH1	150	140	128	128	128
	GRAPH2	200	182	167	167	167
	GRAPH3	360	341	329	329	329
General	ROOT	65	60	56	-	56
	FFT	155	146	128	-	128
	PACKET	200	183	163	-	163
	PETRINET	365	345	330	-	330
	RADIO	505	480	453	-	453
	GRAPH4	40	33	30	-	30
	GRAPH5	100	89	82	-	82

Acknowledgement

This work is partially supported by grants from the Research Grants Council of the Hong Kong Special Administrative Region, China [Project No. CityU 117408, CityU 123609].

References

[1] Freescale. *http://www.freescale.com*.

[2] Semico. *http://www.semico.com/*.

[3] Zilog. *http://www.zilog.com*.

[4] Mazen A. R. Saghir, Paul Chow, and Corinna G. Lee. *Exploiting Dual Data-Memory Banks in Digital Signal Processors*, In ASPLOS-VII: Proceedings of the 7th International Conference on Architectural Support for Programming Languages and Operating Systems: 234C243, 1996.

[5] P. R. Panda, F. Catthoor, N. D. Dutt, K. Danckaert, E. Brockmeyer, C. Kulkarni, A. Vandercappelle, and P. G. Kjeldsberg. *Data and Memory Optimization Techniques for Embedded Systems*, ACM Transactions on Design Automation of Electronic Systems, 6(2): 149C206, 2001.

[6] Preeti Ranjan Panda, Nikil D. Dutt, and Alexandru Nicolau. *On-Chip vs. Off-Chip Memory: The Data Partitioning Problem in Embedded Processor-Based Systems*, ACM Transactions on Design Automation of Electronic Systems, 5(3): 682-704, 2000.

[7] Xiaotong Zhuang, Santosh Pande, and John S. Greenland Jr. *A Framework for Parallelizing Load/Stores on Embedded Processors*, In PACT 02: Proceedings of the 2002 International Conference on Parallel Architectures and Compilation Techniques: 68C79, 2002.

[8] Jeonghun Cho, Yunheung Paek, and David Whalley. *Fast Memory Bank Assignment for Fixed-Point Digital Signal Processors*, ACM Transactions on Design Automation of Electronic Systems, 9(1):52C74, 2004.

[9] B. Scholz, B. Burgstaller and J. Xue, *Minimizing Bank Selection Instructions for Partitioned Memory Architectures*, Proceedings of the 2006 international conference on Compilers, architecture and synthesis for embedded systems (CASES2006): 201-211, 2006.

[10] B. Scholz, B. Burgstaller, J. Xue, *Minimal Placement of Bank Selection Instructions for Partitioned Memory Architectures*, ACM Transactions on Embedded Computing Systems (TECS), Vol. 7, No. 2: 1-32, 2008.

[11] M. Yuan, G. Wu, C. Yu, *Optimizing Bank Selection Instructions by Using Shared Memory*, The 2008 International Conference on Embedded Software and Systems (ICESS2008): 447-450, 2008.

[12] M. A. R. Saghir, P. Chow, and C. G. Lee, *Exploiting Dual Data-Memory Banks in Digital Signal Processors*, 7th International Conference on Architectural Support for Programming Languages and Operating Systems: 234-243, 1996.

[13] Q. Zhuge, B. Xiao, E. H.-M. Sha, *Variable Partitioning and Scheduling of Multiple Memory Architectures for DSP*, Proceedings of the 16th International Parallel and Distributed Processing Symposium: 332-339, 2002.

[14] C. J. Xue, T. Liu, Z. Shao, et al, *Address Assignment Sensitive Variable Partitioning And Scheduling For DSPS With Multiple Memory Banks*, ICASSP2008: 1453-1457, 2008.

[15] M. Kandemir, I. Kolcu and I. Kadayif, *Influence of loop optimizations on energy consumption of multi-bank memory systems*, Proceedings of the 11th International Conference on Compiler Construction: 276-292, 2002.

[16] Z. Wang and X. S. Hu, *Energy-aware variable partitioning and instruction scheduling for multibank memory architectures*, ACM Transactions on Design Automation of Electronic Systems, Vol. 10, No. 2: 369-388, 2005.

[17] A.M. Garey and D.S. Johnson, *Computers and intractability: A Guide to the theory of NP-completeness*, Freeman, San Francisco, (1979).

[18] MRTC.*http://www.mrtc.mdh.se/projects/wcet/home.html*.

[19] SNU (Seoul National University). *http://www.useoul.edu/*.

[20] TGFF. *http://ziyang.eecs.umich.edu/ dickrp/tgff/*.

[21] lp_solve. *http://lpsolve.sourceforge.net/5.5/*.

Versatile System-level Memory-aware Platform Description Approach for embedded MPSoCs

Robert Pyka

Informatik Centrum Dortmund ICD,
Dortmund, Germany
pyka@icd.de

Felipe Klein

Computer Systems Laboratory,
University of Campinas, Brazil
klein@ic.unicamp.br

Peter Marwedel

Faculty of Computer Science
12,Technische Universität Dortmund,
Germany
peter.marwedel@tu-dortmund.de

Stylianos Mamagkakis

Interuniversity Micro-electronics Center IMEC, Leuven, Belgium
mamagka@imec.be

Abstract

In this paper, we present a novel system modeling language which targets primarily the development of source-level multiprocessor memory aware optimizations. In contrast to previous system modeling approaches this approach tries to model the whole system and especially the memory hierarchy in a structural and semantically accessible way. Previous approaches primarily support generation of simulators or retargetable code selectors and thus concentrate on pure behavioral models or describe only the processor instruction set in a semantically accessible way, A simple, database-like, interface is offered to the optimization developer, which in conjunction with the MACCv2 framework enables rapid development of source-level architecture independent optimizations.

Categories and Subject Descriptors B3.3 [*Memory Structures*]: Performance Analysis and Design Aids; D.2.2 [*Design Tools and Techniques*]: Computer-aided software engineering; C0 [*General*]: System architectures; C4 [*Performance of Systems*]: Modeling techniques

General Terms Algorithms, Languages, Design, Performance

Keywords Architecture description, component, channel, configuration, definition, energy models, framework

1. Introduction

In the past years, a huge amount of work has been done in the area of optimized program compilation. Especially lots of effort has been spent for optimizations which take particular properties of the memory subsystem into account. Nevertheless, the usual approach in that area is to use optimization-specific memory configuration descriptions, or even incorporate this information into the optimizer code. On the one side, this allows for a compact and simple memory description, on the other side combining various optimizations

becomes difficult, porting them to other architectures even more. Furthermore, a consistent memory model would be beneficial for ensuring comparable results.

Among all the system modeling languages developed recently, some of them incorporate a memory model. In almost all cases, the target application is generation of simulators, transformation to hardware description languages or code generator generation, which does not fit well with source-level optimizations. The first class of languages implement a behavioral model, which can be transformed into executable code on the host platform and thus supporting simulation. Transformations to HDLs require primarily structural information. A fixed set of properties per component is required to interpret the description and translate it to the lower level HDL. Furthermore, due to the fact, that a complete and synthesizable hardware description has to be generated, a high level of detailed information is required right from the beginning of the system specification. In contrast to this, for memory aware optimizations usually a quite abstract system model is sufficient. Finally, models for code generator generators concentrate on the internal structure and instruction set of the processor.

Therefore, we propose a combined structural and semantical description at system level. On the one side, it offers a structural modeling approach for the system designer. But on the other side, a database-like interface is presented to the optimizations designer. It supports model refinement and requires only limited effort for the initial abstract system model.

The structure of this paper is as follows: It starts with an overview of requirements imposed by the intended application field. The next section provides references to related work and puts this approach in relation to these publications. Section 4 describes details of the system model and concentrates on the key feature of this system description, which allows the database-like access to the system model properties. In Section 5 the MaCCv2 framework is introduced. MaCCv2 provides the surrounding infrastructure which incorporates our system description model. Afterwards, an application example is shown in Section 6. This example demonstrates an implementation of the static scratchpad allocation technique. This optimization technique was implemented in a fully architecture independent way.

In the following results section we are going to show that the completely different method of accessing system and memory hierarchy properties does provide same quality results as the simulation based approach in the modeled MPARM SoC.

The paper closes with a conclusion. As a result, we can summarize that our approach qualifies as a viable way for rapid development of memory aware source-level optimization techniques which can adopt to different architectures without the need of developer interaction.

2. Requirements

The memory description proposed in this paper has to fulfill a set of requirements. These requirements were chosen according to the needs of current memory optimization techniques and available architectures. Furthermore, the memory description should be sufficiently generic to be applicable to future memory architectures. For example a fixed set of memory component types would be an unacceptable limitation in this context. Therefore, the proposed modeling approach provides in addition to the predefined components and channels an open API to extend the set of available building blocks. Finally, it has to permit the design of a memory description in a top down approach in terms of complexity and precision, without losing compatibility to optimization techniques which do not require such a high level of details. The refinement of memory models includes the possibility to add aspects of interest as required. The remaining model and the API should not be affected by the amount of aspects (i.e. latencies, energy values etc.) provided by the model for a particular memory device type. Referring to Section 4 this approach does not impose limitations on number or type of provided component properties.

Since the memory description should be accessible from within the optimization techniques, an API has to be provided. An object-oriented representation of the memory model – as used in this approach – fits best the requirements of current programming style. In conjunction with the previously stated requirement for extensibility, this results in a challenging task, which was successfully tackled through the integration into the MaCCv2 framework, shortly described in Section 5. Previous experiences show that beside pure simulation-oriented models a query-oriented database-like interface is also required. Especially for fully compile-time based optimizations, this is the key to a portable implementation. Current MPSoCs are designed in various configurations: Starting from simple shared memory systems consisting of a set of equal computing elements, up to heterogeneous systems with separated address spaces. This requires a model which goes beyond the description of memory devices but also incorporates an interconnection model.

Finally, a graphical user interface which allows for an easy design and modification of memory descriptions would be beneficial for a rapid development process.

3. Related Work

According to the classification of system modeling languages along the abstraction level as shown in Figure 1, the description language presented in this paper can be assigned to the PMS level. Processor-Memory-Switch models were introduced by Bell and Newell in [5]. They describe the system at an abstract level where the main building blocks are the system components (i.e. processors and memories) and the interconnection between them.

Various architecture description languages (ADLs) have been developed in recent years. One comprehensive approach to classify them is by the main application target. A first application target is the automatic transformation into a hardware description language. This helps in automating hardware development as well as in shortening the development cycle, where precise simulators can be derived in advance from the HDL representation of the system. A second main application target is the automatic generation of de-

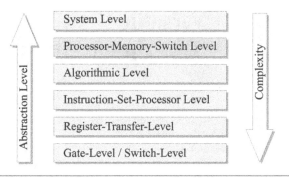

Figure 1. System modeling levels

velopment tools like compilers, assemblers and linkers. Both application targets impose almost disjoint requirements on the ADL. On the one side, hardware description requires precise structural information, on the other side, automatic tool generation requires a behavioral and semantic description of the system.

LISA [12] is an ADL which targets primarily at the automatic generation of application-specific hardware and corresponding simulators and low-level tools. Primary architectural targets are signal processing and generic irregular single processor architectures. The language has been extended later towards automatic compiler generation. To accomplish this task, an additional semantic instruction set model has been added [7]. Since the main target of LISA is the cycle-true description of the DSP, neither a sophisticated system model nor detailed memory models exist. The timing model integrated into LISA concentrates on the specification of the pipeline behavior. There is no energy model incorporated into LISA.

Another ADL developed recently is ArchC [4]. ArchC was designed to support processor architecture description. While the language has evolved also the possibility to design memory hierarchies has been added. Similar to LISA, ArchC also covers the structural and behavioral view of a system model. Since ArchC uses the SystemC language, which provides extensions to C++ for description of timing and concurrency, ArchC models are described in C++ code. On the positive side, this opens a possibility to describe a large scale of different systems, on the negative side, it is really hard to extract any semantic meaning from the model, once it comes to other tasks than simulator generation. The SystemC language offers all the expression possibilities of the C++ language. This is perfect for simulation, since this allows for compiled simulation which is the fastest simulation method available. But even the task of extracting timing information out of such a model in advance without imposing any restrictions to the modeling style is a almost intractable problem. Closely related to ArchC is PDesigner [2]. Basically, it is a graphical editor which can be used for intuitive component based development of ArchC system models.

Another group of system modeling languages are specialized system descriptions targeting mapping of applications on MPSoCs. As examples, references to the ADL used in DEADALUS [8] or the hardware platform description in the CIC based retargetable parallel programming framework for MPSoC [14] are given. In general, these system descriptions are from the structural point of view similar to the one presented in this paper. Nevertheless, significant differences can be observed when it comes to the annotation of component and channel properties. These approaches suffer from the fact that changes to the properties of one component need to be annotated in several places of the system description. An example for such an annotation would be the energy consumption of a memory component. In contrast to our approach, a change of such value will affect the per-access energy values annotated to processing elements. In general this will require user interaction, and in-depth system knowledge to precompute these values.

EXPRESSION has been developed in the late 90's [11]. EXPRESSION aims primarily at automatic generation of software development tools. The motivation for this language was faster design space exploration on a single processor of the SoC. To accomplish this task, EXPRESSION describes the system in a structural and behavioral way. In contrast to the previous languages, EXPRESSION offers an explicit memory model. There is a fixed set of parameters which can be used to describe properties of memories available to the processor. On the downside of this ADL, there is no method to convert the description into an HDL for automatic generation of processor hardware.

A slightly different application scenario is specified for the TDL [13] language. The primary goal of this language is to support retargetable postpass optimizations at assembly level. This is what comes closest to the approach presented in this paper. TDL includes a structural description of the resources present in the system. This includes memories and corresponding cache hierarchies. Furthermore, behavioral description of the instruction set is the second key part of this language. Nevertheless, there are significant differences to our ADL. The semantical information in the resource section does not allow for modeling structural dependencies between memories, furthermore only a single processor based memory hierarchies can be described.

Finally, there exists a vast variety of other ADLs. As examples, references to hardware related ADLs like nML [9], ISDL [10] and MIMOLA [17] are given. All of them do not focus on development of memory hierarchy aware source code transformations. The common goals are simulation, HDL extraction or compiler generation. None of them satisfies all the requirements imposed in the previous section. In a broader scope, the set of software related ADLs also has to be take into account. Examples in this class of ADLs are Wright [3] or Darwin [16]. In contrast to this approach, these ADLs concentrate on description of the architecture of the application instead of the platform the application is being executed on.

4. Model

The novel architecture description model presented in this paper can be classified as a structural PMS model. In contrast to previous ADLs where a detailed model has to be developed in advance, in this approach only high-level structural information has to be provided for a new architecture. Once tools require more details, these can be added to the model without losing backward compatibility. Furthermore, the main application target of this ADL is the development of code optimizations at source-level which leverage the knowledge of the memory hierarchy. This implies the accessibility of the system properties while the optimizations are being executed. In contrast to ADLs with simulation as the main target, system descriptions can contain pure behavioral parts, which are passed through the generator tool without any further semantical analysis. ADLs designed for compiler and development tool generation contain semantical information, but this is usually limited to the description of the instruction set.

The ADL proposed in this paper provides a structural model of the memory hierarchy, enriched with semantical information. This model allows for a database-like access to the system description, where the optimizations can query system properties which are required to apply them on different architectures. The approach presented in this paper has been developed as part of the MaCCv2 compiler framework. Therefore, it smoothly integrates within this framework. The memory description is part of the complete system and application description. The memory description presented here is defined as an object oriented C++ API provided to the op-

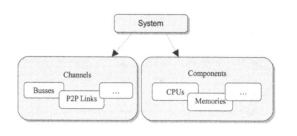

Figure 2. System Model.

timization or analysis tool. The actual format the memory description is stored in, is not part of this specification. Due to the strong relation between the MaCCv2 framework and the ICD-C compiler tools [1], the current implementation uses an XML based storage method. ICD-C is a compiler development platform. It represents C-code as a source-level abstract syntax tree and offers a code selector interface and a wide range of transformation and optimization techniques.

Basically, the system description consists of a set of channels and components. Figure 2 depicts the top-level structure of a system description. Channels represent the interconnections between components. Examples are: Usual busses, point-to-point links or some other kind of abstract direct connections. The last one could be useful in the case the processor register file is also modeled as a memory component. Registers are part of the processor architecture, but they have similar restrictions in terms of maximum number of parallel accesses and delays as usual memories. Therefore, it is a valid model to separate the processing unit and the register file and connect them through a direct link. Components are self-contained parts of the system which have to exchange data with each other. The most common types of components are processing units and various kinds of memories. Additional components like ASIPs or DMA units may be included in the model. In most cases, components will map to particular parts of the on-chip hardware. Nevertheless, this is not required. Also, hard disks or even software-controlled data exchange between processors could be modeled as a virtual memory device.

From the structural point of view, the system models described in our modeling language are similar to the one used in languages for simulator modeling. Therefore, a translation to another system description language is possible. For example, from our system model a SystemC skeleton can be generated. Due to the high-level representation and the missing behavioral information, it is not possible to generate a fully specified SystemC model. Nevertheless, if future tools would require automatic translation to SystemC it is possible to attach behavioral information as user extended data to the system model. A particular translation tool which can handle this data could generate full fledged SystemC models.

A typical architectural example is shown in Figure 3. Multiple processing units with a local memory and dedicated caches are connected to a shared main memory. The basic blocks of this structural view are components, which are equipped with ports that are connected to channels. Components may initiate requests or may be a target for requests initiated by others. Structural memory hierarchies may be modeled as shown for the cache components. In that case, the component has multiple ports which are connected to different channels. On the one side, it is the target for requests on the other side, it issues requests to the next level.

Going deeper into the details, Figure 4 shows the concept of address space translation and mappings. Each component has a set of address spaces. They may have different properties. For

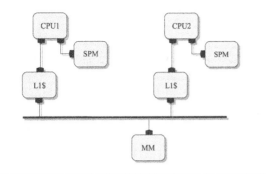

Figure 3. Interconnection Model.

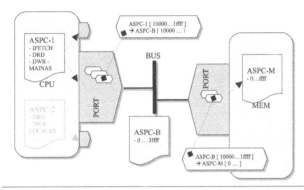

Figure 4. Mapping Model.

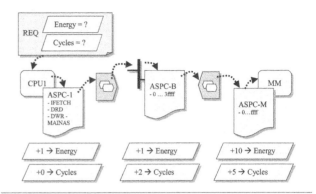

Figure 5. Routing Model.

example, a processing unit having a Harvard architecture will have at least two address spaces; one for instructions and a second one for data. Another example could be a processing unit which has a local memory that is not part of the main address space and has to be accessed through auxiliary instructions.

Address spaces are not limited to be part of access initiating components like processing units, but also target components have at least one address space. In the case of a simple memory, this would be a plain range starting at 0 and going up to the size of this memory.

Besides components, channels have also a set of address spaces assigned to them. They represent which kinds of accesses may be transported over that particular channel. The mapping between address spaces of components and channels is performed at the connection port. Each port has a set of mapping rules which translate between component address spaces and channel address spaces and vice versa. It is possible to have mapping rules for the same address space at different ports. This allows for modeling systems which have a bus based interface to the main memory and a fast dedicated interface to a local scratchpad memory, while both are located in the same address space.

The memory description is presented to the application as an object graph with nodes representing components and channels and edges representing connections. Traversing this graph allows the application to collect structural properties of a system. Each object in this graph may have user defined attributes assigned to it. This resembles the often used approach of direct annotation of required component properties, present in other modeling languages. This is feasible for attributes which are solely related to a particular component. An example would be the number of banks a memory consist of. An example of less suitable value type would be the per-access energy consumption annotated to a processing unit. This value depends on several system properties. On the one side,

in general there will be no single value, but a set of values which depend on the number of memories present in the system. On the other side, when performing design space exploration, the update of these values is a non-trivial task. It requires user interaction and in-depth system knowledge. When exploring the effects of changes in the energy consumption of a particular memory, in general several values across the whole system description may need an update. To avoid this error-prone overhead, the proposed model offers a generic mechanism to collect component and chanel properties. Its basic item is the access-request. It is similar to a database query. The application (i.e. the optimization) issues an access to a component object—usually a processing unit—and the implementation of the model ensures to route the query through the structural description. After the access has reached another component, the target component processes the request and fills in the information it can provide according to the request. Figure 5 shows the access processing scheme built into this memory description model. Which kind of information is being returned depends on the actual implementation of this component. Usually, energy values, latencies or data values will be returned. In the case a memory device can provide its data content for a particular access, this query based approach could resemble also simulation based approaches. But in contrast to them, not only the actual value is being returned, but also information about which kind of additional accesses were required to get this value. For example, an access directed to a cache will provide information about the accesses to the next level caused by a cache miss.

Each request has a basic set of properties which are necessary to route the request through the model:

- Address range.
- Number of bytes.
- Alignment.
- Access mode (e.g. "IFETCH").

These properties are required in each request to ensure that the model can resemble in the routing algorithm the paths the request would have taken in an actual hardware instance.

Further, an arbitrary set of requested aspects may be attached to the access request. In most cases this will be:

- Energy values
- Latencies / Cycle values
- Throughput
- Data values

The implementation of an optimization technique issues an access request to the component which would initiate the access in a physical environment. The access request is targeted for an address range in a particular address space and access mode (i.e. "IFETCH"). In the first step, the port to which the access should be routed is looked up. As mentioned before, each port has a set of mapping rules. Each rule states from which address space to which one the access can be mapped, and for which address range in the ingress address space it is valid for. After an applicable rule has been found, this port is used for further routing. Basically, the access is being translated and issued to the channel the port is connected to. The next step forwards the access to the target port. The procedure is the same as described before for the component. A port with a suitable mapping rule is being searched. After mapping the access to the target component address space, the access request is being forwarded to that component for service.

Throughout that request chain, three places exist where requested properties may be updated; namely at the initiating component, the channel and the targeted component. If at one place, particular properties can not be provided by the implementation, this is visible in the request, too. Assuming the case that each component and channel on the path can provide a particular aspect value, an update operation has to be performed at each place. For cumulative values like cycle counts the update operation will reduces into an addition. Other types of aspects may need other update operations (i.e. for throughput this could be the computation of a minimum value). Since computation of aspect values is performed in reverse order, starting at the target component, even more complex update functions which need knowledge of other aspect values from partial results may be performed. A common example for this kind of complex update functions would be the computation of the energy consumption of a processing unit. A practical example for this complex update function occurs in the energy model for the MPARM processor, used in the evaluation part of this paper. This processor's energy model provides two energy states; namely running and idling. When accessing a memory the processor consumes some energy to setup the access and than idles until the resulting value is available, still consuming energy. Therefore, the computation has to take into account the number of cycles the access will take. Since the values are computed bottom up, the amount of cycles the memory and interconnect requires to perform a particular access has already been computed and is known to the update function at the processor level.

In general, multiple target components will be addressed in an access request. For example, in a system consisting of a main memory and a scratchpad memory, an access request covering a sufficient wide address range could target both memories. Therefore, the reply contains information about every path a request has taken. While the request is posted, the user can choose which path should be the primary result. Currently between best-case or worst-case answers can be choosen. In the example, one path would target the scratchpad, the other would target the main memory. In general, both paths will result in different values for each aspect. Scratchpads require less cycles and less energy than the main memory. Therefore, aspect values of scratchpad would be the best-case answer, while the aspect values of main memory would be the worst-case answer.

Furthermore, in general an access request may exceed the maximal width per access of involved components and channels. Therefore, an access request can be split into an access sequence while being routed through the system description. The model ensures proper accumulation of values in that case. Nevertheless, each step and each transformation involved in the access processing is recorded. Therefore, besides the accumulated values, detailed analysis of the effects which lead to the result can be performed.

The detailed access processing history allows to compute precise values for components with sophisticated aspect models. An example for this kind of components are DRAM memories. In general the access times and energy consumption of DRAM memories vary depending on the sequence of previously performed accesses. At the first view, this may contradict the static approach proposed in this paper. This approach requires the computation of aspect values to be stateless across multiple queries, otherwise the resulting values would depend on the control flow of the optimization algorithm performing the queries. Obviously, resulting in completely unreliable values. To support this kind of memories, the approach presented here exploits the possibility to model explicit access sequences. Either the user (i.e. the optimization algorithm) may place queries which do not consist of a single access, but specify an access sequence. Alternatively, a sequence may be build implicitly, as described in previous paragraph. This would enable a DRAM memory to treat subsequent accesses differently computing more precise value. Furthermore, the knowledge of the purpose of the query may be taken into account to improve the result quality. If the optimization algorithm needs conservative values, it may ask for those worst case results. This case is shown in the Example–Section 6. Another option would be to place a query for the best case values.

Besides DRAMs, other memory types benefit from this approach. Caches will in general take sequences into account. Furthermore, specialized memory types optimized for particular access patterns, like video memories optimized for frame-buffer accesses or memories organized in multiple banks, where accesses can be interleaved, will have the option to provide values with respect to an access sequence.

5. Framework

The system description model is tightly integrated into the MaCCv2 framework. MaCCv2 is intended as a platform for the rapid development of source-level memory aware optimization techniques. The key features are:

- The integration of a scalable structural PMS-level system model.

- Database-like interface to the system model. The properties of the system model are accessible to the optimization developer at runtime.

- Integration of the application code into system model. The ICD-C code representation is used to attach program code to processing units.

- A graphical user interface for system modeling. An Eclipse based plug-in has been developed, which allows to modify the system model from within this widely used IDE.

- A template for optimizations and analysis tool development is provided. This enables the development of interchangeable tools which can be combined and reused in further optimization techniques or upcoming architectures.

- Interface to backend tools (i.e. compilers, linkers, simulators).

- Configuration and event notification interfaces.

The first two features are an integral part of the system model and the corresponding API. They have been presented in the previous section. Furthermore, the structural model can be used to solve the problem of representing program code assignment to particular processors. Among other properties, each processing unit has one or more ICD-C based C program code representations assigned to it. This code is stored in an ICD-C based abstract syntax tree. Any transformation or optimization available for ICD-C can be performed on program code stored in a MACC system model.

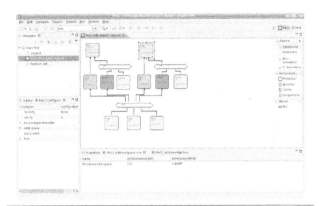

Figure 6. Graphical user interface.

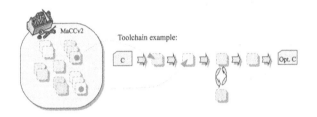

Figure 7. MaCCv2 example optimization chain.

In the context of the MACCv2 framework, a graphical editor has been integrated into the Eclipse IDE. Figure 6 shows the editor. It can be used to define new system models or alter exiting models (e.g. change the scratchpad size or configuration parameters). Furthermore, the framework provides methods for ordered execution of transformation, analysis and optimization techniques. Each implementation may specify requirements which task has to be performed first. The usual application scenario for this feature is shown in Figure 7. The blocks in this figure represent transformation, analysis and optimization tasks which have been combined to form a source-level optimizer. Finally, a rich set of methods is provided which supports rapid development of optimization techniques and provides an abstraction layer which allows for integration of those techniques into a comprehensive graphical user interface.

6. Application Example

The example shows a typical approach of implementing a static scratchpad allocation algorithm in a fully architecture independent way using the memory model and the MACCv2 framework.

To demonstrate the allocation strategy, we choose a system model which describes the MPARM [15] system. Figure 8 shows the model with the default configuration of 4 cores. According to the original setup, caches have been disabled.

The static scratchpad allocation used for demonstration purposes was presented by Steinke et al. in [18]. Further extension toward multiprocessor systems has been done by Verma et al. [19]. Basically the approach solves a knapsack problem for each processor separately using integer linear programming. Without loss of generality, our example targets energy reduction as the objective. A set of input parameters is required per processor to formulate the ILP:

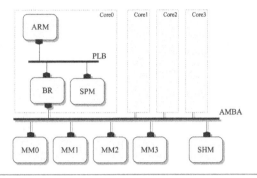

Figure 8. MPARM Model.

- A set of code or data items which can be placed independently in the main memory or the scratchpad memory. These items are identified as memory objects in literature. In our example global variables (i.e. scalars and arrays) and functions are used.
- Size of each memory object.
- Access counts to each memory object.
- Scratchpad size as the limit for the knapsack.
- Energy consumption per main memory access.
- Energy consumption per scratchpad memory access.

The set of movable items can be identified easily in the abstract syntax tree of the C program provided by ICD-C [1]. The processor nodes in the system model incorporate the ICD-C based representation of the program code which is going to be executed at this processor. Iterating over the global symbol table provides the names and references to these objects. Access counts to each of these memory objects are generated via profiling in MACCv2. From the point of view of this example optimization, the access count information is inherent to the system description. Each MACCv2 based optimization can specify its requirements, which processing and analysis steps have to be performed first. In our case, we would specify the requirement to run the access count generator and size estimator. The former in turn would employ profiling and simulation to collect this values. Once static analysis methods become more sophisticated they may replace the profiling step.

In the context of this paper, more interesting are the steps required to find the architectural properties. Determining them is as easy as looking up some predefined values, but with the confidence of always getting precise up to date values without the need for manual adaption to new platforms. Part of the MACCv2 framework is an address space analyzer, which provides a mapping list of address ranges in the address spaces of an initiator component (i.e. an ARM processor) and the final target component. The analysis is performed by default across all memory hierarchy levels, therefore in the mapping the final target component (i.e. Main memory) will be visible.

For the architecture shown in Figure 8, a mapping would look as follows for the first processor:

```
ARM0.[0x0-0xbfffff] -> MM0.[0x0-0xbfffff]
ARM0.[0x19000000-0x190fffff] -> SHM.[0x0-0xffffff]
ARM0.[0x22000000-0x22002fff] -> SPM0.[0x0-0x2fff]
```

Similar mappings exist for other processors. According to the object class in the MACCv2 representation of each target component in that list, the scratchpad memory can be identified easily (i.e. the type of that memory is a derived class of MACC_Scratchpad). In a second step, its size in the processor address space has to be retrieved. Simple arithmetic operations on the address ranges are necessary to compute a size of 12k bytes for our example architecture.

The energy values which are required to compute the gain for each object for the knapsack formulation can be retrieved in a similar way. As described in Section 4, the key feature of this model is to provide system properties on a query based interface. Two sets of queries are required for this optimization. The first one would be placed to the address space range of the main memory, the second one to the range of the scratchpad memory. Each set would collect three values; for data read, data write and instruction fetch. The difference of the corresponding values of each set is the gain factor multiplied by the access counts. All the prerequisites for the ILP formulation are present now. Solving the ILP will result in a set of decision variables indicating which memory object has to be placed on the scratchpad. The final step required in this optimization is to translate these decision variables into linker hints, which will be annotated to this particular memory objects directing them either to the scratchpad or the main memory. The optimization can delegate the actual compiling and linking process to MACCv2.

7. Results

For the application example presented in the previous section, the key value directing the ILP solution is the gain which can be achieved per memory object when moving it to the scratchpad memory. Therefore, we have compared the computed gain values of our model to the ones which are achieved by the whole system simulation in MPARM.

The simulation platform consists of the MPARM SoC simulator extended with the memory hierarchy simulator MEMSIM [20]. The system configuration defines one processing tile with a 12k Bytes scratchpad and a 12M Bytes main memory connected via an AMBA-AHB bus. The energy and latency values for these memories are configured according to the reference design:

- Scratchpad memory read: 0.0241275682 nJ / 0 WS
- Scratchpad memory write: 0.0080780647 nJ / 0 WS
- Main memory read: 10.6813104793 nJ / 10 WS
- Main memory write: 1.0667890999 nJ / 10 WS

The benchmark application chosen for this comparison was a chain of matrix operations. In the first step, a matrix A has to be transposed, and in the second step, a second matrix B is added and the result is stored in another matrix C.

$$\begin{aligned} AT &= A^T \\ C &= AT + B \end{aligned}$$

All matrix values are 32 bit unsigned integers. Two sets of experiments have been performed, one with 10×10 matrices, another with 30×30 matrices.

For our purposes, this benchmark has the advantage that the access counts to each matrix are fixed and can be determined via profiling. Table 1 shows the access counts for 10×10 matrices which have been determined in advance.

Matrix	Reads	Writes
A	100	0
B	100	0
C	0	100
AT	100	100

Table 1. Access counts for 10×10 matrices.

Corresponding values for 30×30 matrices are shown in Table 2.

Matrix	Reads	Writes
A	900	0
B	900	0
C	0	900
AT	900	900

Table 2. Access counts for 30×30 matrices.

For each matrix size, we have run the benchmark with all matrices located in the main memory in the MPARM simulator and retrieved the total energy consumption. This results in an energy value of $27130.266nJ$ for the 10×10 matrix and $231908.203nJ$ for the 30×30 matrix. Afterwards, we have moved each matrix to the scratchpad memory and got total energy reductions according to Table 3. This values are the gain factors which could be used in the ILP formulation presented in previous section.

Matrix	10×10	30×30
A	$1122.741nJ$	$10104.672nJ$
B	$1122.741nJ$	$10104.672nJ$
C	$164.459nJ$	$1480.125nJ$
AT	$1287.202nJ$	$11584.812nJ$

Table 3. Measured gain per matrix.

The next step consists of computing these values using our MACC system model without the need for full system simulation. The model has been designed according to the simulator setup. The energy and latency values for memories are setup to the same default values as used for simulation. The interconnection energy computation is based on work done by Bona et al. [6]. The subsequent values of total energy per access were retrieved with four access queries. Two queries directed to the scratchpad memory and two to the main memory, each one for a 4 bytes read and a 4 bytes write access correspond to the size of the matrix elements.

A typical query consists of only few lines of code; setup, add aspects, perform query and retrieve value:

```
MACC_Access *acc=new MACC_SingleAccess(...);

acc->addData(ASPECT_ENERGY);
acc->addData(ASPECT_CYCLES);
acc->queryAccess(AS_WORSTCASE,ASPECT_ENERGY);

val=acc->getValue(ASPECT_ENERGY);
delete acc;
```

Matrix	10×10	30×30
A	$1120.457nJ$	$10084.114nJ$
B	$1120.457nJ$	$10084.114nJ$
C	$164.238nJ$	$1478.143nJ$
AT	$1284.695nJ$	$11562.258nJ$

Table 4. MACCv2 computed gain per matrix.

Via these queries, we have retrieved total per access energy values of $0.0791284nJ$ per scratchpad read, $0.0630784nJ$ per scratchpad write, $11.2837nJ$ per main memory read and finally $1.70546nJ$ per main memory write. With these values and the access counts, we were able to compute the gain values for each matrix. The values can be found in Table 4. Comparing these values to the ones generated via full system simulation, we can conclude that the system modeling approach presented in this paper has the capability to provide very accurate information about the energy consumption. The computed results were all less than 0.21% off compared to the actual values. Furthermore, the results are stable along the increased number of accesses, even for the bigger matrices with nine times higher access counts, the divergence remains almost the same.

Matrix	Divergence
A	0.203%
B	0.203%
C	0.134%
AT	0.195%

Table 5. Relative divergence to simulation results.

8. Conclusion

We have presented a novel system modeling approach with the primary target in support for developing architecture independent source code optimizations, which can still take advantage of architectural properties to achieve higher gains. Especially the knowledge of properties of the memory subsystem, enables a wide range of code optimization opportunities. Together with the query-based interface of the system model, which is capable of providing instant results, the memory aware optimization techniques can be guided without the need for time consuming simulation. Furthermore, the implementation of these technique can be fully architecture independent. Required architecture information is retrieved from the system model, dependencies on other processing steps may be specified in a generic way, without the need to relay on a architecture dependent implementation of those steps.

As shown for the MPARM system model, even with a high level model which consist only of few building blocks, it is possible to achieve quite precise results. We have demonstrated that our model can provide energy values which are less than 0.21% off to the actual values.

The system modeling approach integrates smoothly into MACCv2 compiler framework which offers a comprehensive infrastructure for compiler development and in particular for architecture-independent source-level transformation development.

References

[1] ICD-C Compiler framework. http://www.icd.de/es/icd-c/icd-c.html, 2008.

[2] PDesigner: Simulator development framework. http://www.cin.ufpe.br/~pdesigner/, 2008.

[3] R. Allen. *A Formal Approach to Software Architecture*. PhD thesis, Carnegie Mellon, School of Computer Science, January 1997. Issued as CMU Technical Report CMU-CS-97-144.

[4] R. Azevedo, S. Rigo, M. Bartholomeu, G. Araujo, C. Araujo, and E. Barros. The ArchC Architecture Description Language and Tools. *International Journal of Parallel Programming*, 33(5):453–484, 2005.

[5] C. G. Bell and A. C. Newell. *Computer structures: Readings and examples (McGraw-Hill computer science series)*. McGraw-Hill Pub. Co., 1971. ISBN 0070043574.

[6] A. Bona, M. Caldari, V. Zaccaria, and R. Zafalon. High-Level Power Characterization of the AMBA Bus Interconnect. In *SNUG*, 2004.

[7] J. Ceng, M. Hohenauer, R. Leupers, G. Ascheid, H. Meyr, and G. Braun. C Compiler Retargeting Based on Instruction Semantics Models. In *Proc. Design, Automation and Test in Europe*, pages 1150–1155, 2005. doi: 10.1109/DATE.2005.88.

[8] C. Erbas, A. D. Pimentel, M. Thompson, and S. Polstra. A framework for system-level modeling and simulation of embedded systems architectures. *EURASIP J. Embedded Syst.*, 2007(1):2–2, 2007. ISSN 1687-3955. doi: http://dx.doi.org/10.1155/2007/82123.

[9] A. Fauth, J. Van Praet, and M. Freericks. Describing instruction set processors using nML. In *Proc. European Design and Test Conference ED&TC 1995*, pages 503–507, 6–9 March 1995. doi: 10.1109/EDTC.1995.470354.

[10] G. Hadjiyiannis, S. Hanono, and S. Devadas. ISDL: An Instruction Set Description Language For Retargetability. In *Proc. 34th Design Automation Conference*, pages 299–302, June 9–13, 1997.

[11] A. Halambi, P. Grun, V. Ganesh, A. Khare, N. Dutt, and A. Nicolau. EXPRESSION: a language for architecture exploration through compiler/simulator retargetability. In *Proc. Design Automation and Test in Europe Conference and Exhibition 1999*, pages 485–490, 9–12 March 1999. doi: 10.1109/DATE.1999.761170.

[12] A. Hoffmann, T. Kogel, A. Nohl, G. Braun, O. Schliebusch, O. Wahlen, A. Wieferink, and H. Meyr. A novel methodology for the design of application-specific instruction-set processors (ASIPs) using a machine description language. *IEEE Transactions on Computer-Aided Design of Integrated Circuits and Systems*, 20(11):1338–1354, Nov. 2001. doi: 10.1109/43.959863.

[13] D. Kästner. TDL: a hardware description language for retargetable postpass optimizations and analyses. In *GPCE '03: Proceedings of the 2nd international conference on Generative programming and component engineering*, pages 18–36, New York, NY, USA, 2003. Springer-Verlag New York, Inc. ISBN 3-540-20102-5.

[14] S. Kwon, Y. Kim, W.-C. Jeun, S. Ha, and Y. Paek. A retargetable parallel-programming framework for MPSoC. *ACM Trans. Des. Autom. Electron. Syst.*, 13(3):1–18, 2008. ISSN 1084-4309. doi: http://doi.acm.org/10.1145/1367045.1367048.

[15] M. Loghi, F. Angiolini, D. Bertozzi, L. Benini, and R. Zafalon. Analyzing on-chip communication in a MPSoC environment. In *Proc. Design, Automation and Test in Europe Conference and Exhibition*, volume 2, pages 752–757, 16–20 Feb. 2004. doi: 10.1109/DATE.2004.1268966.

[16] J. Magee and J. Kramer. Dynamic structure in software architectures. *SIGSOFT Softw. Eng. Notes*, 21(6):3–14, 1996. ISSN 0163-5948. doi: http://doi.acm.org/10.1145/250707.239104.

[17] P. Mishra and N. Dutt, editors. *Processor description languages*, chapter MIMOLA - A Fully Synthesizable Language, pages 35–63. Morgan Kaufmann, 2008.

[18] S. Steinke, L. Wehmeyer, B.-S. Lee, and P. Marwedel. Assigning program and data objects to scratchpad for energy reduction. In *Proc. Design, Automation and Test in Europe Conference and Exhibition*, pages 409–415, 4–8 March 2002. doi: 10.1109/DATE.2002.998306.

[19] M. Verma and P. Marwedel. *Advanced Memory Optimization Techniques for Low-Power Embedded Processors*. Springer, 2007.

[20] L. Wehmeyer and P. Marwedel. *Fast, Efficient and Predictable Memory Accesses*. Springer, 2006.

Operation and Data Mapping for CGRAs with Multi-bank Memory

Yongjoo Kim

School of EECS, Seoul National
University, Korea
yjkim@optimizer.snu.ac.kr

Jongeun Lee *

School of ECE, Ulsan National Institute
of Sci. and Tech. (UNIST), Ulsan, Korea
jlee@unist.ac.kr

Aviral Shrivastava

CML Research Group, Arizona State
University, USA
Aviral.Shrivastava@asu.edu

Yunheung Paek

School of EECS, Seoul National University, Korea
ypaek@snu.ac.kr

Abstract

Coarse Grain Reconfigurable Architectures (CGRAs) promise high performance at high power efficiency. They fulfil this promise by keeping the hardware extremely simple, and moving the complexity to application mapping. One major challenge comes in the form of data mapping. For reasons of power-efficiency and complexity, CGRAs use multi-bank local memory, and a row of PEs share memory access. In order for each row of the PEs to access any memory bank, there is a hardware arbiter between the memory requests generated by the PEs and the banks of the local memory. However, a fundamental restriction remains that a bank cannot be accessed by two different PEs at the same time. We propose to meet this challenge by mapping application operations onto PEs and data into memory banks in a way that avoids such conflicts. Our experimental results on kernels from multimedia benchmarks demonstrate that our local memory-aware compilation approach can generate mappings that are up to 40% better in performance (17.3% on average) compared to a memory-unaware scheduler.

Categories and Subject Descriptors C.3 [*Special-Purpose and Application-Based Systems*]: Real-time and embedded systems; D.3.4 [*Processors*]: Code generation and Optimization

General Terms Algorithms, Design, Performance

Keywords Coarse-grained Reconfigurable Architecture, Compilation, Multi-bank Memory, Bank conflict, Arbiter.

1. Introduction

The need of high performance processing is undeniable, not only in increasing our pace of learning by large-scale simulation of fundamental particle and object interactions, but also to fructify the

---

* Corresponding author.

Category	Processor Name	MIPS	W	MIPS/mW
VLIW	Itanium2	8000	130	0.061
GPP	Athlon 64 Fx	12000	125	0.096
GPMP	Intel core 2 quad	45090	130	0.347
Embedded	Xscale	1250	1.6	0.78
DSP	TI TMS320C6455	9.57	3.3	2.9
MP	Cell PPEs	204000	40	5.1
DSP(VLIW)	TI TMS320C614T	4.711	0.67	7

Figure 1. CGRAs promise the highest levels of power-efficiency in programmable architectures

increasing horizons of possibilities in automation, robotics, ambient intelligence etc. General-purpose high performance processors attempt to achieve this, but pay a severe price in power-efficiency. However, with thermal effects directly limiting achievable performance, *power-efficiency* has become the prime objective in high performance solutions. Figure 1 shows that there is a fundamental trade-off between "performance" and "ease of programmability" and the power-efficiency of operation. It illustrates that special-purpose and embedded systems processors achieve high performance by trading off "performance" and "ease of programming" for higher power-efficiency. While high-performance processors operate at power-efficiencies of 0.1 MIPS/mW, embedded processors can operate at up to two orders of magnitude higher, at about 10 MIPS/mW. Application Specific Integrated Circuits provide extremely high performance, at extremely high power efficiency of about 1000 MIPS/mW, but they are not programmable. Among programmable platforms, CGRAs or Coarse Grain Reconfigurable Architectures come closest to ASICs in simultaneously achieving both high performance and high power-efficiency. CGRA designs have been demonstrated to achieve high performance at power efficiencies of 10-100 MIPS/mW [18].

The simultaneous high performance, and high power efficiency comes with significant challenges. The hardware of CGRAs is extremely simplified, with very little "dynamic effects", and the complexity has been shifted to the software. CGRAs are essentially an array of processing elements (PEs), like ALUs and multipliers, interconnected with a mesh-like network. PEs can operate on the result of their neighboring PEs connected through the interconnection

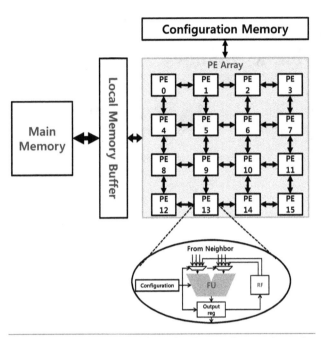

Figure 2. CGRA is just a 2-dimensional array of processing units, like adders and multipliers connection by a mesh-like interconnect. The computation has to be laid out in space and time, and the data routed through the interconnection explicitly in the application code.

we need 128 read ports, and 64 write ports. Even if one row of PEs access one port of the local memory. we need at 16 read and 8 write ports in the local memory. This is still quite large, and a more practical solution is to have multi-bank local memory, in which each bank has two read and one write port on the memory side, and a row of PEs sharing memory access on the PE array side. So that each PE can access data in any bank, a hardware arbiter between the memory requests generated by the PEs and the banks of the memory is used. We call such an architecture, that has arbiters in front of the memory ports of multiple banks, *Multiple Banks with Arbitration* (MBA) architecture, and most existing CGRA designs are MBA architectures [7, 13, 18].

Even in the MBA architecture, a fundamental restriction remains that a bank cannot be accessed by two different PEs at the same time remains. This is the challenge that we meet in this paper. Fundamentally there are two solutions to this. One is hardware solution, i.e., add a request queue in the arbiter, and increase the access latency of the memory operation, or second is to change the application mapping technique to explicitly consider the memory banking architecture, and map memory operations into rows, so that two different rows do not access the same bank simultaneously. We argue for the second technique and develop application data and operation mapping techniques to avoid memory bank conflicts. Our experiments on important multimedia kernels demonstrate that our memory memory aware compilation approach generates mappings that are up 17.3% better than the state-of-the-art memory unaware scheduler. As compared to the hardware approach using arbiters, our technique is on average 8.5% better, and promises to be a good alternative.

2. Background on CGRAs

2.1 CGRA Architecture

The main components of CGRA include the PE (Processing Element) array and the local memory. The PE array is a 2D array of possibly heterogeneous PEs connected with a mesh interconnect, though the exact topology and the interconnects are architecture-dependent. A PE is essentially a function unit (e.g., ALU, multiplier) and a small local register file. Some PEs can additionally perform memory operations (load/store), which are specifically referred to as load-store units. The functionality of each PE and the connections between PEs are controlled by *configuration*, much like the configuration bitstream in FPGAs. However, the configuration for CGRAs is coarser-grained (word level), and can be changed very fast, even in every cycle for some CGRAs [7, 13, 18].

The local memory of a CGRA is typically a high speed, high bandwidth, highly predictable random access memory that provides temporary storage space for array data, which are often input/output of loops that are mapped to CGRAs. To provide high bandwidth, local memories are often organized in multiple banks. For instance the MorphoSys architecture [18] has 16 banks, every two of which may be accessed exclusively by each row of PEs (there are eight rows in total). However, this organization can severely limit the accessibility of the local memory, since a PE can access only its own share of the local memory. This limitation can be relaxed by providing arbiters or muxes at the interface (memory ports) to the local memory; for instance, a mux in front of a memory port allows the bank to be accessed by different load-store units at different cycles. We call such an architecture that has arbiters in front of the memory ports of multiple banks, *MBA (Multiple Banks with Arbitration)* architecture.

Even in MBA architecture, a fundamental restriction remains that a bank cannot be accessed by two different PEs at the same time, if the bank consists of single-port cells. (In the rest of the paper we assume that a bank consist of single-port cells, and thus

network. CGRAs are completely statically scheduled, including the memory operations. One of the main challenges in using CGRAs is that the computation in the application must be laid out explicitly over the PEs, in space and time, and their data routed through the interconnection network. When we program general-purpose processor, the code just contains the "application" expressed in terms of the instruction set, and all this is automatically managed by the processor hardware. In contrast, this has to be explicitly done in the application code for CGRAs, and therefore compilation for CGRAs is quite tough.

A lot of work has been done towards this aspect of application mapping [5, 6, 12, 14–17, 20, 21], however, another aspect of application mapping, i.e., managing application data has been rather left untouched. Caches are an excellent dynamic structures, that ease "programmability" by automatically fetching the data required by the processor "on-demand" in general purpose processors. However, due to their dynamic behavior, high complexity and power consumption, CGRAs do not use caches, and use local memory instead. The local memory is raw memory, in the sense, that it does not store address tags for (or with) the data, and therefore form an separate address space than the main memory. The main challenge in using local memories is that, since there are no address tags, there is no concept of a "hit", or "miss". The application must explicitly bring the data that it will need next into the local memory and after its use, it must write it back and bring the data that will be needed after that.

To minimize the challenge, CGRAs could have large on-chip local memory so that all the required data may fit into the local memory which can be loaded once before the program, and then written back at the end of the program. Clearly this is not always possible, and in reality the on-chip local memories are rather small. Further complications arise, because PEs have to share the local memory especially in large, say 8x8 CGRA. If each PE should be able to read two data and write one data to the local memory, then

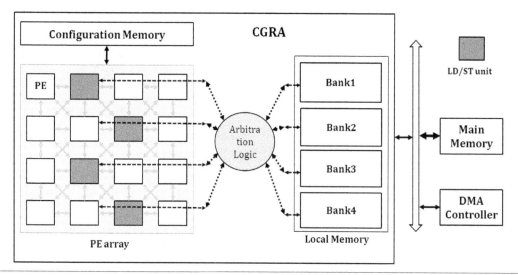

Figure 3. Multi-Bank with Arbitration (MBA) architecture: There is arbitration between the PE array and the memory banks, so that any PE can access data from any bank. However a fundamental limitation still remains: Two PEs cannot access data in the same bank simultaneously. This can be solved either by i) hardware approach of adding a queue to sequentialize the accesses, and ii) compiler approach, where compiler makes sure that this does not happen. This paper develops application operations and data mapping for the second approach and show that it is promising.

has only one port.) In MBA architecture, if two PEs try to access the same bank at the same time, a *bank conflict* occurs. CGRA hardware supporting MBA architecture must detect such a bank conflict and resolve it by generating a stall. Hardware stall ensures that all the requests from different PEs are serviced sequentially, but is very expensive because most of the PEs will be idle during stall cycles.

A solution proposed by [1] uses in front of each bank a hardware queue, called DMQ or DAMQ (Dynamically Allocated, Multi-Queue buffer) [19]. Though adding DMQ of length n ($n > 1$) increases the latency of a load operation by $n - 1$ cycles, it allows up to n simultaneous memory requests to be serviced without a stall.[1] But since adding a queue cannot increase the bandwidth of a memory system, stall must be generated if the request rate exceeds the service rate, or the number of memory ports. We call such a memory architecture *MBAQ (Multiple Banks with Arbitration and Queues)* architecture, an example of which is the ADRES architecture. In this paper we present mapping algorithms for both MBA and MBAQ architectures, and compare them against using hardware solutions only.

2.2 Execution Model and Application Mapping

CGRA is typically used as a coprocessor, offloading the burden of the main processor by accelerating compute-intensive kernels. We assume blocking communication between main processor and CGRA coprocessor (i.e., no parallelism between them). For application mapping, first the loops that are mapped to CGRA are identified. The selected loops are then compiled for CGRA while the rest of the code is compiled for the main processor.

The result of CGRA compilation for selected loops is configuration, which is fed to the PE array at runtime. The other component, the local memory, gets the necessary data through DMA from system memory. After loop execution the output data of the loop may be transferred back to system memory. Such data transfers and

CGRA computation are often interleaved to hide the data transfer latency. For CGRAs with larger local memories, opportunities may exist to reuse data (usually arrays) between different loops, as the output of one loop is often an input to the next loop. For instance, ADRES allows a fairly large local memory of up to 1 Mbytes in total, which can provide input data of 100 Kbytes each for 10 loops. In such a case if the data can be reused between the loops without needing to move the data around on the local memory (e.g., to another bank), it can greatly reduce the runtime as well as energy consumption of CGRA execution.

There are two dominant ways of placing arrays on multiple banks. *Sequential* refers to placing all the elements of an array to an particular bank, whereas *interleaving* refers to placing contiguous elements of an array on different banks. Interleaving can not only guarantee a balanced use of all the banks, but also more or less randomize memory accesses to each bank, thereby spreading bank conflicts around as well. The DMQ used in the MBAQ architecture thus can effectively reduce stalls due to bank conflicts when used with bank-interleaved arrays. However, interleaving makes it complicated for compilers or static analysis to predict bank conflicts. Thus our compiler approach uses sequential array mapping.[2]

3. Related Work

Memory architectures of CGRA can be largely classified into implicit load-store architecture (e.g., MorphoSys [18] and RSPA [7]) and explicit load-store architecture (e.g., ADRES [1, 13]). Whereas implicit load-store architectures have data (array elements) prearranged in the local memory and PEs can only sequentially access them, explicit load-store architectures allow random access of data in the local memory. There are also variations in the connection between banks and PEs. Whereas earlier architectures [7, 18] have assumed one-to-one connection between PE rows and local memory banks, recent architectures like ADRES assume one-to-many connection through muxes or arbiters, and even load queues. Our

---

[1] It works as if the DMQ holds the values of n requests until all of them become available, which requires $n - 1$ additional cycles in a pipelined memory, when all the load values are returned simulataneously.

[2] To be fair, we compare our approach with sequential array mapping against hardware approach (DMQ) with interleaved array mapping.

target architecture assumes explicit load-store with muxes and optionally queues.

Most previous CGRA mapping approaches [5, 6, 9, 10, 12, 14–17, 20, 21] consider computation mapping only, but not data mapping. [21] considers computation mapping as a graph embedding problem from a data flow graph into a PE interconnection graph, and solves the problem using a known graph algorithm. Many others consider mapping as a scheduling problem targeting an array processor, of which a simpler form is VLIW processor. Software pipelining and modulo scheduling is often used. [16] proposes an improved variant of modulo scheduling by considering edges rather than nodes (of input data flow graph) as the unit of scheduling. [14] proposes a scheduling algorithm for loops with recurrence relation (inter-iteration data dependence). In all those approaches, data mapping is only an after-thought, and not included in the optimization framework.

There is little work that considers memory during CGRA mapping. [3] considers a hierarchical memory architecture and presents a mapping algorithm to reduce the amount of data transfer between L1 and L2 local memory. [4] proposes routing reused data through PEs instead of using the local memory, which can reduce the local memory traffic and thus improve performance. Our work is orthogonal to this and the effective is additive when applied together. [4] also considers the data layout with sequential memory. But it is limited as it considers only one loop and is based on simulated annealing; extending it to multiple loops does not seem straightforward. [11] proposes the idea of quickly evaluating memory architectures for CGRA mapping; however, it lacks a detailed mapping algorithm. Our earlier work [8] proposes a mapping algorithm that takes into account data mapping as well as computation mapping. However, the memory architecture assumed in [8] is much simpler, with no arbiter or queues. In this paper we provide a more general framework that considers data and computation mappings together.

4. Problem of Memory Aware Mapping

Given a sequence of loops and the CGRA architecture parameters, the problem of CGRA compilation is to find the optimal mapping of the loops on to the CGRA architecture, which includes the PE array and the local memory. A CGRA mapping must specify two pieces of information; i) **computation mapping:** mapping from each operation of the loops to a specific PE (where) and to which schedule step (when, in cycle), and ii) **data mapping:** mapping from each array in the loops to which bank of the local memory to use. A loop is represented by the data flow graph of the loop body, along with data dependence information and memory reference information (which array is accessed by a memory operation and the access function). We assume that the number of iterations is given at runtime before the loop entry and remains constant during loop execution (hence the actual number may not be available at compile-time). The optimality of mapping is judged by the schedule length of the mapping, which is equivalent to the II (Initiation Interval) in the case of modulo scheduling. For a sequence of loops, we take the average II, assuming equal weights for all loops.

Hence the goal of optimization problem is to minimize the average II. In addition to the usual constraints for computation mapping (e.g., [16]), we have additional constraints for optimal data mapping. One thing to understand to derive the constraints is that assuming sequential array placement and a sufficiently large local memory, the optimal solution should be without any expected stall. If there is an expected stall in the optimal mapping, one can always find a different mapping that has the same schedule length but no expected stall. Simply add a new cycle in the place where a stall is expected and schedule one of the conflicting memory operations at the new cycle, which does not increase the actual schedule length and has no expected stall. Thus we can limit our

search to those with no expected stall, without losing optimality. This no-conflict condition translates into different forms depending on the memory architecture. For a MBA architecture (any load-store PE can access any bank through arbitration), the constraint is that there must be at most one access to each bank at every cycle. For a MBAQ architecture, the memory access latency is slightly increased. If the added latency is n cycle, there must be at most n accesses to each bank in every n consecutive cycles.

5. Our Approach

5.1 Overview

The main challenge of our problem comes from inter-dependence between computation mapping and data mapping; i.e., fixing data mapping creates constraints on computation mapping, and vice versa. Due to the inter-dependence, the optimal solution can only be obtained by solving the two subproblems simultaneously. However solving the two subproblems simultaneously is extremely hard, since even a subproblem alone, i.e., computation mapping, is an intractable problem. In [21], spatial mapping is solved by ILP formulation. In this experiments, ILP solver cannot find a solution within a day, if a node number excesses only 13. Our problem is also intractable, since it can be reduced to the computation temporal mapping problem, which is more intractable than spatial mapping. Hence our heuristic solves them sequentially, first clustering data arrays to balance utilization and access frequency of each bank, and then finding computation mapping through conflict free modulo scheduling.

First we perform a pre-mapping, which is just computation mapping by traditional modulo scheduling without considering data mapping. The II resulting from pre-mapping serves as the minimum II in the ensuing iterative process. We then repeat the two steps of array clustering and conflict free scheduling, incrementing II, until a conflict free mapping is found. Pre-mapping can provide a tighter upper bound for II than traditional minimum II calculation considering resource and recurrence requirements only, and thus reduce the overall time for CGRA compilation.

5.2 Array Clustering

Like other CGRA architectures including ADRES, our target architecture is homogeneous across multiple rows though it may have heterogenous PEs within a row. This makes data mappings position-independent, meaning that the absolute position, or bank, that an array is mapped to is not important as long as the same set of arrays is mapped together.

Array mapping can affect performance (through computation mapping) in at least two ways. First, banks have a limited capacity. If arrays are concentrated in a few banks, not only does it reduce the effective total size of the local memory, but there is a higher chance of having to reload arrays during a loop execution or between loops, diminishing data reuse. And since the size of arrays can be very different from each other especially due to different strides, it is important to balance the utilization of banks and prevent pathological cases. Second, each array is accessed a certain number of times per iteration in a given loop, which is denoted by Acc_A^L for array A and loop L. In both MBA and MBAQ architectures, II cannot be less than the sum of access counts of all the arrays mapped to a bank. In other words, there can be no conflict free scheduling if $\sum_{A \in \mathcal{C}} Acc_A^L > II_L'$, where $\mathcal{C}$ is an array cluster (set of arrays) that will be mapped to a certain bank and II_L' is the current target II of loop L. Thus it is important to spread out accesses (per-iteration access count) across banks. Note that bank utilization balancing is static, or independent of loops, whereas balancing per-iteration access counts is dependent on which loop we are looking at.

We combine the two factors, viz. array size and array access count, into one metric, i.e., priority. Our clustering algorithm takes one array at a time and determines its clustering by assigning a cluster to it. Because of the greedy nature of the algorithm the order of selecting arrays is important. We use priority to determine which array to cluster first. The priority of an array A is defined as:

$$priority_A = Size_A/SzBank + \sum_{\forall L} Acc_A^L/II_L' \quad (1)$$

where $Size_A$ is the size of array A and $SzBank$ is the size of a bank.

Once the priorities of all arrays are calculated, we begin assigning cluster to arrays, starting from the one with the highest priority. To make this decision of which cluster to assign to a given array, we compare the relative costs of assigning different clusters. Similarly to the priority definition, our cost model considers both array size and array access count, and is defined as follows. Given a cluster C and an array A, the relative cost of assigning C to A is,

$$cost(C, A) = Size_A/SzSlack_C + \sum_{\forall L} Acc_A^L/AccSlack_C^L \quad (2)$$

where $SzSlack_C$ and $AccSlack_C^L$ are the remaining space of a cluster (total budget is $SzBank$) and the remaining per-iteration access count of loop L (total budget is II_L'), respectively, and are updated as assignments are made. In this formula, we use the remaining value to calculate cost. If one bank's size or access count is used up too much than other bank, we have to avoid assigning array to this bank for balancing and leaving it to other array which really need this resource. So, to avoid this case, when we calculate cost, we decide to divide by remaining resource. If remaining resources are small, the cost becomes bigger. In a consequence, the balancing is derived. Figure 4 shows the pseudo code of array clustering algorithm. From line 1 to 6, array information is analyzed. From line 7 to 10, priority for each array is calculated. And in the remaining parts, assignment is executed. The array which has high priority is assigned first.(11) Cost for each cluster is calculated(14-17) and then the cluster which shows minimum cost is chosen(19). If the assignment is failed by a lack of access count, increase II and start clustering again. But if the reason of fail is lack of memory size, then we need to reduce the number of loop considered together. After array clustering, we can decide a MII for conflict aware scheduling. In previous modulo scheduling algorithm, resMII and recMII is used to calculate MII. But in our work, we used third factor that is calculated in array clustering step. We define the third factor is MemMII(Memory-constrained minimum II). MemMII is related with the number of access to each bank for one iteration and a memory access throughput per a cycle. The array clustering is calculated with this information. So, the II, the result of array clustering, is MemMII.

Figure 5 illustrates array clustering. Figure 5(a) shows the parts of array analysis result(access frequency analysis). Then after calculating array priority once (Figure 5(b)), the minimum-cost clusters are assigned to arrays, in the decreasing order of array priority (Figure 5(c)). Figure 5(d) lists the number of accesses to each bank (per iteration), which is balanced across different banks and loops.

5.3 Conflict Free Scheduling

With previous memory-unaware scheduling, bank conflicts can occur even if array clustering is first done. It is because array clustering only guarantees that the *total* per-iteration access count to the arrays included in a cluster, or simply, the total (per-iteration) access count of a bank, does not exceed the target II(because it is already reflected by MemMII), which is only a necessary condition for a conflict free mapping. In other words, once array clustering is done, the total access count of a bank does not change because

```
ArrayInfo;      // a data structure that contains a size of array,
                // # access for each loop's iteration
AL;             // a list of arrayInfo
DFGs;           // a list of DFG
CandList;        // a set of candidate cluster

        // array analysis
1.      AL = initArrayList();
2.      for(each DFGs) {
3.          * let dfg be an element of DFGs;
4.          AL = arrayAccessAnalysis(dfg);
5.      }
6.      AL = arraySizeAnalysis();
        // cluster assignment
7.      for(each arrayInfo in AL) {
8.          * let x be an element of AL
9.          calcPriority(x);
10.     }
11.     sortArrayList(AL); // sort in descending order by priority
12.     while(AL ≠ Ø) {
13.         * let x be an element of AL
14.         for(#cluster) {
15.             * let y be a cluster number
16.             candList += calcCost(x, y);
17.         }
18.         if (candList ≠ Ø) {
19.             cl = getMinCostCluster(candList);
20.             assign(x, cl);
21.         }
22.         else {
23.             fail(); // increase II and do clustering again
24.         }
25.     }
```

Figure 4. Array clustering algorithm

of scheduling, but temporary access count can. For instance if two memory operations accessing the same bank are scheduled at the same cycle, spontaneously two load-store units will try to access the same bank, which is a bank conflict. Thus we extend a previous modulo scheduling algorithm [16] developed for CGRAs to generate conflict free mapping.

5.3.1 Base scheduling algorithm

In this paper, we applied a previous scheduling research results to make a base modulo scheduling algorithm. We decide to use EMS(Edge-centric Modulo Scheduling) [16] for our base scheduler. In previous node-centric scheduling, the placements of source node and destination node are decided first. And then it try to find the routing path between these nodes. But in the edge-centric approach, routing from source node is tried first. During routing, if routing path pass through a place that destination node can be placed, then the placement is decided at this time. Figure 6 shows a pseudo code of our base scheduler. In this paper, we use several costs for placement decision, which are widely used in mapping algorithm such as resource cost, routing cost, relativity cost. Resource cost means the cost for using a PE for node placement. Its costs are set to be different according to function of PE. If target PE is expensive PE, such as the PE having memory access unit, the cost is set to higher. Routing cost means the cost for routing data to destination. The cost becomes bigger, if routing path is long or routing path passed by expensive PE. Relativity cost is used for placing related nodes at adjacent PEs. In these basic modulo scheduling environment, we added our approaches.

5.3.2 MBA Architecture

Modulo scheduling for CGRA uses placement and routing (P&R) technique to find feasible scheduling and resource allocation simultaneously. While the resources that are considered in previous mod-

Array name	#Access (per iter)
p	4
u	3
v	3
cu	1
cv	1
z_	1
h_	1

<swim loop1>

Array name	#Access (per iter)
h_	3
z_	3
cv	4
cu	4
uold	1
vold	1
pold	1
unew	1
vnew	1
pnew	1

<swim loop2>

(a) Array access frequency analysis

Array name	Priority
p	1.0
u	0.80
v	0.80
h_	0.90
z_	0.90
cv	1.07
cu	1.07
uold	0.367
vold	0.367
pold	0.367
unew	0.367
vnew	0.367
pnew	0.367

(b) Prioritization

Cluster0	Cluster1	Cluster2	Cluster3
cv, u, uold	h_, z_	p, pnew, pold, unew, vold	cu, v, vnew

(c) Clustering result

	Array	#access (per iter)	Total (per iter)
Bank1	u, cv	3 1	4
Bank2	h_, z_	1 1	2
Bank3	p	4	4
Bank4	cu, v	1 3	4

<swim loop1>

	Array	#access (per iter)	Total (per iter)
Bank1	cv, uold	4 1	5
Bank2	h_, z_	3 3	6
Bank3	pnew, pold, unew, vold	1 1 1 1	4
Bank4	cu, vnew	4 1	5

<swim loop2>

(d) Number of accesses for each loop

Figure 5. Array clustering example.(swim application)

```
DFG G;              // the data flow graph
NodeList N;         // the set of DFG node
CandSpace S;        // the set of mapping candidate
1.      prioritizeEdge(G);
2.      N = getOrderedNodes(G);
3.      while(N ≠ Ø) {
4.          targetN = pop(N);
5.          setSearchSpace(targetN);
                // consider targetN's predecessor
6.          for(searchSpace) {
7.            * let s be a mapping space of searchSpace
                // mapping space consists of a location of PE & time)
8.              if( spaceAvailable(s) && routable(s) ) {
                    // spaceAvailable checks the functionality and availability of PE
                    // routable function checks the routability from source nodes to s
9.                  S += saveCandidate( s, calcCost(s) );
                    // resource, routing and relativity cost are used to calculate cost
10.             }
11.         }
12.         if( S≠ Ø ) {
13.             decision = getMinCostCand( S );
14.             update( decision );
15.         else {
16.             fail();         // increase II & do scheduling again
17.         }
18.     }
```

Figure 6. Base modulo scheduling(implemented based on EMS algorithm)

about to be scheduled. The first candidate for node 8 is cycle 4 on PE2, which has conflict not in terms of computation resources (PE2 was not used in cycle 1 nor 4) but in terms of memory resources (CL1 was already used in cycle 1). Choosing the first candidate thus means bank conflict, or one stall, per every II, effectively increasing II by one. Alternatively node 8 can be scheduled at cycle 6 on PE1 albeit via a longer route. But since this choice does not cause any conflict on computation or memory resources, the effective II is not increased, resulting in much better performance than the first candidate. Thus our extended modulo scheduling can find conflict free mapping, which works well with our array clustering. Moreover our approach can be easily applied to previous work. In EMS algorithm, our clustering aware scheduling approach is implemented in spaceAvailable function which is called Figure 6 line 9. spaceAvailable function checks several conditions to confirm the space is available. Conflict free approach just adds one more condition on these, so there is no hard problems with unifying previous scheduling algorithm with our approach.

5.3.3 MBAQ Architecture

As mentioned before, accesses to the same bank at the same time occur bank conflict. MBA architecture treats this problem by stalling CGRA processor until all requested data are ready. But stalling processor degrade CGRA performance, so some works[1, 2] proposed DMAQ architecture. They designed an arbitration logic have queues for each bank and increase memory operation latency longer than the lowest obtainable memory latency. During this additional cycles, the loaded data is stored in the arbitration logic queue. And at the end of latency, the data is delivered to PE. In this manner, several accesses to the same array can be handled without processor stall by fetching data earlier to give an extra time for fetching other conflicted data. But these previous works assumed interleaving memory architecture. In our case, we can predict bank conflict. So in our case, MBAQ architecture is used for relaxing the mapping constraint. MBA architecture doesn't permit bank conflict, but MBAQ architecture can permit several conflict within a range of added memory operation latency. We distinguish two cases(n is the added memory operation latency cycles by MBAQ approach)

i) $II' \leq n$ (Target II is no greater than the DMQ length): Our array clustering guarantees that there are at most II' accesses per

ulo scheduling include only PEs and interconnects, our extension treats memory banks, or memory ports to the banks, as resources too.[3] This small extension, combined with our array clustering, allows us to find conflict free mapping.

As explained, if two memory accesses to the same bank occur at the same cycle, memory conflict occurs. Then one memory access request cannot be completed on time. But we know the array clustering information, we can prevent memory conflict by saving the time information that memory operation is mapped on. When a memory operation is mapped, update the cluster access information. And by using this information, we can prevent that two memory operations belonging same cluster is mapped on the same cycle.

Figure 7 illustrates our conflict free mapping algorithm through an example shown in Figure 7(b). Suppose that the architecture has four PEs, two of which are load-store units (PE0 and PE2), and it has two banks with arbiters (MBA architecture). Also assume that arrays have been clustered as listed in Figure 7(c) with the target II of 3, and that all the nodes from 1 through 7 have been scheduled as shown in Figure 7(d), and now node 8, a memory operation, is

---

[3] We use bank and cluster interchangeably since clusters are one-to-one mapped to banks.

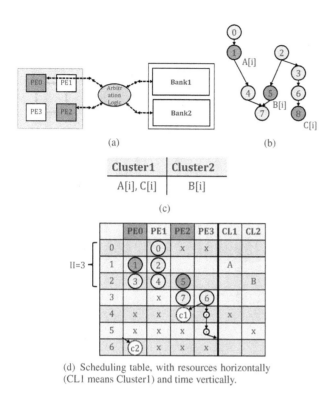

(a)　(b)

Cluster1	Cluster2
A[i], C[i]	B[i]

(c)

	PE0	PE1	PE2	PE3	CL1	CL2
0		⓪	x	x		
1	①	②			A	
2	③	④	⑤			B
3		x	⑦	⑥		
4	x	x	ⓒ1	○	x	
5	x	x	x	○		x
6	ⓒ2	x	x	x		

$II=3$

(d) Scheduling table, with resources horizontally (CL1 means Cluster1) and time vertically.

Figure 7. Conflict free scheduling.

iteration to every bank; if such a clustering cannot be found, the target II is incremented. The worst scheduling of the II' accesses, from the bank conflict point of view, is if they are all scheduled at the same cycle(recollect MemMII)—and none until II' cycles later. But this case cannot generate a bank conflict because the DMQ can absorb at most n simultaneous requests. Therefore if $II' \leq n$, any schedule is conflict free.

ii) $II' > n$ (Target II is greater than the DMQ length): In this case, processor stall can occur if we do not consider data layout. To ensure absence of processor stall, the scheduler checks if the spontaneous request rate exceeds 1 whenever a new memory operation is placed, where the spontaneous request rate can be calculated as the number of memory operations during the last n cycles divided by n. If the request rate doesn't exceed 1, bank conflict can be absorbed by DMAQ memory interface.

6. Experiments

6.1 Setup

For the target architecture we use a CGRA that is very similar to the one illustrated in Figure 3. It has four load-store units in the locations shown in the figure. The local memory has 4 banks, each of which has one read/write port. Arbitration logic allows every load-store unit to access any bank. Similarly to ADRES, we assume that the local memory access latency is 3 cycles without DMQ; with DMQ whose length is 4, the local memory load latency is 7 cycles. We assume that the local memory size is unlimited for our experiments. Our CGRA has no shared register file, but each PE has its own register file whose size is 4 entries. The local registers are used for scalar variables or routing temporary data. A PE is connected to its four neighbor PEs and four diagonal ones.

We use important kernels from multimedia applications. To get performance numbers we run simple simulation on the mapping result as well as array placement, which gives the total number

of execution cycles consisting of stall cycles and useful (non-stall) cycles. Because of randomness in the scheduling algorithm (in the placement and routing) we compile each loop ten times and the average performance is taken as the representative performance of the algorithm for that loop.

6.2 Effectiveness of Our Compiler Approach

To see the effectiveness of our approach, we compare our memory aware scheduling (MAS) with the hardware approach using DMQ to reduce bank conflict. For the hardware approach we use an existing modulo scheduling algorithm [16], which is referred to as memory unaware scheduling (MUS). MUS is also used as the base scheduler for our memory aware scheduling.

Figure 8 compares three architecture-compiler combinations. The first one, which represents the baseline performance, is the combination of MUS with hardware arbiter only. Having no DMQ, a stall occurs whenever there are more than one requests to the same bank. Bank conflict is detected and resolved at runtime. Interleaving array placement is used. The load latency is small (3 cycles) as DMQ is not used. The second case is the hardware approach, using DMQ to absorb some potential bank conflicts. Again, interleaved array placement is used to maximize the effectiveness of DMQ (by distributing bank conflicts). The use of DMQ results in longer load latency (7 cycles). The third case is our compiler approach, using MAS to generate conflict free mapping. Only hardware arbiter is required, but no DMQ or runtime conflict detection/resolution hardware. The load latency is small (3 cycles). Sequential array placement is used. The graph plots the runtimes normalized to that of the baseline. We assume that the clock speed is the same for all the cases.

In the baseline case we observe that about $10 \sim 30\%$ of the total execution time is spent in stalls. Using the DMQ, the hardware scheme can effectively reduce the stall cycles, which now account for a very small fraction of the total execution time. The non-stall times are mostly the same as in the baseline case, with a few exceptions. The notable increase of the non-stall time of hardware scheme in some applications (CopyImg, Init_mbaff) is due to the increase in the load latency. Overall the hardware scheme can reduce the expected CGRA runtime, though not always, by $10 \sim 27\%$ (9.7% on average) compared to the baseline case. With our compiler approach the stall time is completely removed. The increase in the non-stall time is very small to modest in most cases, reducing the total execution time by up to more than 40%. The graph shows that our compilation technique can achieve in most cases far better performance (10 to 40% runtime reduction, 17.3% on average) compared to memory unaware mapping. Also our approach allows the removal of bank conflict resolution hardware, which can contribute to reducing the cost and energy consumption. Further, even compared to the hardware approach using DMQ, our approach can deliver higher performance in most loops (on average 8.5% runtime reduction). Considering that the use of DMQ can reduce the speed of the processor as well as complicate its design and verification, the advantage of our compiler approach is many-fold.

6.3 Effect of Using DMQ in Our Approach

Since DMQ can reduce bank conflicts and increase performance when used with a conventional memory unaware scheduler, it is interesting to know how effective it is with our memory aware compilation flow. Figure 9 compares the II (the average of ten trials) by our memory aware compiler with/without DMQ. Our compiler can generate different mappings for architectures with DMQ, by relaxing the bank conflict condition. Surprisingly, contrary to the significant performance improvement in the case of memory unaware scheduling, DMQ does not really help in the case of our memory

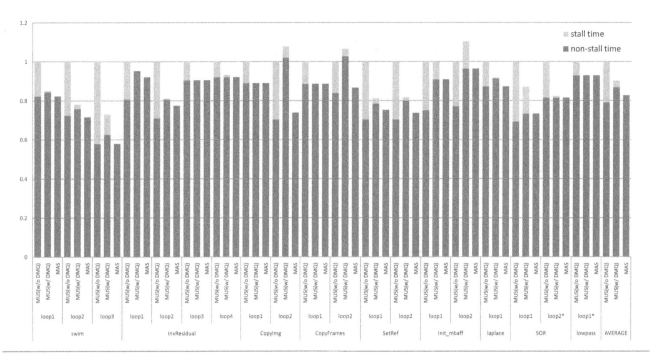

Figure 8. Runtime comparison, normalized to the baseline case (MUS w/o DMQ). Total execution time is the sum of non-stall time and stall time. Our compiler approach (MAS) completely eliminates stall time in all cases and can achieve up to 40% better performance than the baseline. Asterisk (*) indicates the loop has recurrent edge, where non-stall time can be increased due to data dependence

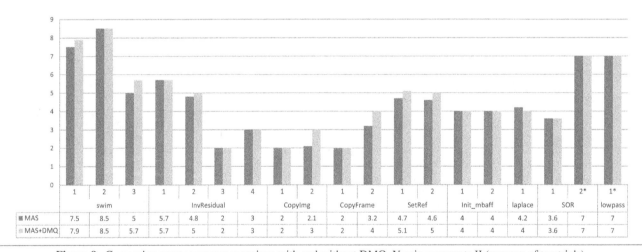

	1	2	3	1	2	3	4	1	2	1	2	1	2	1	2	1	1	2*	1*
		swim			InvResidual				Copylmg		CopyFrame		SetRef		Init_mbaff		laplace		SOR	lowpass
■ MAS	7.5	8.5	5	5.7	4.8	2	3	2	2.1	2	3.2	4.7	4.6	4	4	4.2	3.6	7	7
■ MAS+DMQ	7.9	8.5	5.7	5.7	5	2	3	2	3	2	4	5.1	5	4	4	4	3.6	7	7

Figure 9. Comparing memory aware mappings with and without DMQ. Y-axis represents II (average of ten trials).

aware mapping. Mostly the II is the same, and in some cases the II actually increases if there is DMQ. This is because while DMQ relaxes the bank conflict condition, it also increases the load latency, complicating the job of the scheduler. Thus we conclude that one of the best architecture-compiler combinations is our memory aware mapping plus MBA (multiple bank with arbitration) architecture, which again does not require runtime conflict detection and contributes to reducing the complexity of the memory interface design.

7. Conclusion

We presented a data mapping aspect of CGRA compilation, focusing on how to efficiently and effectively reduce bank conflicts for realistic local memory architectures. Bank conflict is a fundamen-

tal problem and can cause a serious degradation of performance. To reduce or eliminate bank conflicts either hardware approach or compiler approach can be used. We define the mapping problem for compiler approach, and also propose a heuristic approach, since the problem is computationally intractable like many problems in compilation. Our approach is a two-step process, first determining the array mapping considering statically known information, and then finding a computation mapping that is free of any bank conflict. Our experiments demonstrate that our memory memory aware compilation approach can generate mappings that are up to 40% better in performance (on average 17.3%) compared to memory unaware scheduler. Even compared to the hardware approach using DMQ, our technique is on average 8.5% better, and can be a good alternative to the hardware solution. Moreover, our compiler guarantees that all the mappings are free of bank conflict, which can be used to eliminate conflict resolution hardware, which is another advantage of our approach.

Acknowledgments

This work was supported by the Engineering Research Center of Excellence Program of Korea Ministry of Education, Science and Technology(MEST)/ Korea Science and Engineering Foundation(KOSEF)(R11-2008-007-01001-0), Seoul R&BD Program(10560), the IDEC and the Korea Science and Engineering Foundation(KOSEF) NRL Program grant funded by the Korea government(MEST) (No. 2009-0083190), the Korea Research Foundation Grant funded by the Korean Government(MOEHRD) (KRF-2007-357-D00225), 2009 Research Fund of UNIST, and grants from National Science Foundation CCF-0916652, Microsoft Research, Raytheon, SFAz and Stardust Foundation.

References

[1] B. Bougard, B. De Sutter, D. Verkest, L. Van der Perre, and R. Lauwereins. A coarse-grained array accelerator for software-defined radio baseband processing. *IEEE Micro*, 28(4):41–50, 2008.

[2] F. Bouwens. Power and performance optimization for adres. Master's thesis, Delft University of Technology, 2006.

[3] G. Dimitroulakos, M. D. Galanis, and C. E. Goutis. Alleviating the data memory bandwidth bottleneck in coarse-grained reconfigurable arrays. In *ASAP '05: Proceedings of the 2005 IEEE International Conference on Application-Specific Systems, Architecture Processors*, pages 161–168, Washington, DC, USA, 2005. IEEE Computer Society.

[4] G. Dimitroulakos, S. Georgiopoulos, M. D. Galanis, and C. E. Goutis. Resource aware mapping on coarse grained reconfigurable arrays. *Microprocess. Microsyst.*, 33(2):91–105, 2009.

[5] M. Ahn, J. Yoon, Y. Paek, Y. Kim, M. Kiemb, and K. Choi. A spatial mapping algorithm for heterogeneous coarse-grained reconfigurable architectures. In *DATE '06: Proceedings of the conference on Design, automation and test in Europe*, pages 363–368, 3001 Leuven, Belgium, Belgium, 2006. European Design and Automation Association.

[6] A. Hatanaka and N. Bagherzadeh. A modulo scheduling algorithm for a coarse-grain reconfigurable array template. In *Parallel and Distributed Processing Symposium, 2007. IPDPS 2007. IEEE International*, pages 1–8, March 2007.

[7] Y. Kim, M. Kiemb, C. Park, J. Jung, and K. Choi. Resource sharing and pipelining in coarse-grained reconfigurable architecture for domain-specific optimization. In *DATE '05: Proceedings of the conference on Design, Automation and Test in Europe*, pages 12–17, Washington, DC, USA, 2005. IEEE Computer Society.

[8] Y. Kim, J. Lee, A. Shrivastava, J. Yoon, and Y. Paek. Memory-aware application mapping on coarse-grained reconfigurable arrays. In *HiPEAC 2010*, LNCS 5952, pages 171–185, 2010. Springer-Verlag.

[9] J. Lee, K. Choi, and N. D. Dutt. An algorithm for mapping loops onto coarse-grained reconfigurable architectures. *ACM SIGPLAN Notices*, 38(7):183–188, 2003.

[10] J. Lee, K. Choi, and N. Dutt. Compilation approach for coarse-grained reconfigurable architectures. *IEEE D&T*, 20:26–33, Jan./Feb. 2003.

[11] J. Lee, K. Choi, and N. Dutt. Evaluating memory architectures for media applications on coarse-grained reconfigurable architectures. In *ASAP '03: Proceedings of the conference on application-specific systems, architectures, and processors*, pages 172–182, 2003. IEEE Computer Society.

[12] B. Mei, S. Vernalde, D. Verkest, H. De Man, and R. Lauwereins. Dresc: a retargetable compiler for coarse-grained reconfigurable architectures. pages 166–173, Dec. 2002.

[13] B. Mei, S. Vernalde, D. Verkest, H. De Man, and R. Lauwereins. Adres: An architecture with tightly coupled vliw processor and coarse-grained reconfigurable matrix. pages 61–70. 2003.

[14] T. Oh, B. Egger, H. Park, and S. Mahlke. Recurrence cycle aware modulo scheduling for coarse-grained reconfigurable architectures. *SIGPLAN Not.*, 44(7):21–30, 2009.

[15] H. Park, K. Fan, M. Kudlur, and S. Mahlke. Modulo graph embedding: mapping applications onto coarse-grained reconfigurable architectures. In *CASES '06: Proceedings of the 2006 international conference on Compilers, architecture and synthesis for embedded systems*, pages 136–146, New York, NY, USA, 2006. ACM.

[16] H. Park, K. Fan, S. A. Mahlke, T. Oh, H. Kim, and H.-s. Kim. Edge-centric modulo scheduling for coarse-grained reconfigurable architectures. In *PACT '08: Proceedings of the 17th international conference on Parallel architectures and compilation techniques*, pages 166–176, New York, NY, USA, 2008. ACM.

[17] C. O. Shields, Jr. *Area efficient layouts of binary trees in grids*. PhD thesis, 2001. Supervisor-Ivan Hal Sudborough.

[18] H. Singh, G. Lu, E. Filho, R. Maestre, M.-H. Lee, F. Kurdahi, and N. Bagherzadeh. Morphosys: case study of a reconfigurable computing system targeting multimedia applications. In *DAC '00: Proceedings of the 37th Annual Design Automation Conference*, pages 573–578, New York, NY, USA, 2000. ACM.

[19] Y. Tamir and G. L. Frazier. Dynamically-allocated multi-queue buffers for vlsi communication switches. *IEEE Trans. Comput.*, 41(6):725–737, 1992.

[20] G. Venkataramani, W. Najjar, F. Kurdahi, N. Bagherzadeh, and W. Bohm. A compiler framework for mapping applications to a coarse-grained reconfigurable computer architecture. In *CASES '01: Proceedings of the 2001 international conference on Compilers, architecture, and synthesis for embedded systems*, pages 116–125, New York, NY, USA, 2001. ACM Press.

[21] J. W. Yoon, A. Shrivastava, S. Park, M. Ahn, R. Jeyapaul, and Y. Paek. Spkm: a novel graph drawing based algorithm for application mapping onto coarse-grained reconfigurable architectures. In *ASP-DAC '08*, pages 776–782, 2008.

Look Into Details: The Benefits of Fine-Grain Streaming Buffer Analysis

Mohammad H. Foroozannejad   Matin Hashemi   Trevor L. Hodges   Soheil Ghiasi

Department of Electrical and Computer Engineering
University of California, Davis, CA, USA
{mhforoozan,hashemi,tlhodges,ghiasi}@ucdavis.edu

Abstract

Many embedded applications demand processing of a seemingly endless stream of input data in realtime. Productive development of such applications is typically carried out by synthesizing software from high-level specifications, such as dataflow graphs. In this context, we study the problem of inter-actor buffer allocation, which is a critical step during compilation of streaming applications. We argue that fine-grain analysis of buffers' spatio-temporal characteristics , as opposed to conventional live range analysis, enables dramatic improvements in buffer sharing. Improved sharing translates to reduction of the compiled binary memory footprint, which is of prime concern in many embedded systems. We transform the buffer allocation problem to two-dimensional packing using complex polygons. We develop an evolutionary packing algorithm, which readily yields buffer allocations. Experimental results show an average of over 7X and 2X improvement in total buffer size, compared to baseline and conventional live range analysis schemes, respectively.

Categories and Subject Descriptors   D.3.4 [*Processors*]: Compilers

General Terms   Algorithms, Performance

Keywords   Streaming applications, Software synthesis, Synchronous Data Flow, Buffer management, Optimization

1. Introduction

Streaming applications are characterized by the need for processing a seemingly endless steady stream of input data as they are presented to the system. Typically, the processing demands access to a small window of input data and hence, the output can be generated and streamed out, as the input flows into the system. Streaming applications are abundant in the embedded and portable systems space. Examples include various encoding, decoding, transformation and inspection protocols in signal processing, multi-media, security and networking domains.

Most streaming application either exhibit fixed-rate behavior, or have fixed-rate kernels at the heart of the application [4]. Synchronous data flow graphs (SDF) [10] and its variations such as

cyclo-SDFs [14], are widely used to model fixed-rate streaming applications. In these models, the functionality is specified as a number of independent tasks that communicate using channels with in-order data delivery. Among other purposes, the models are utilized to synthesize software implementation of the application.

Synthesizing embedded software from the models involves a number of challenges one of which, deals with implementation of inter-task communication channels [13]. The channels are often implemented as first-in-first-out (FIFO) buffers that are allocated as contiguous regions in the memory. Since streaming applications are data intensive, inter-task buffers tend to be large. As a result, buffers account for a substantial portion of the memory footprint of the synthesized programs.

In this paper, we study the problem of buffer management during synthesis of embedded software from SDF models. We argue that fine-grain perturbations to spatio-temporal behavior of individual buffers would enable aggressive sharing among buffers. That is, the time-dependent *details* of variations in buffered data should not be ignored. This is in contrast with conventional live range analysis techniques that do not allow overlap between two buffers if both of them happen to be *alive* at even one point in time.

Following the *look into details* principle, we transform the buffer allocation problem into packing of complex polygons in the two dimensional time-space plane. We develop an evolutionary algorithm for the packing problem, which readily allocates buffers in the memory during compilation. The technique is implemented within the MIT StreamIt compiler, which compiles a specific variation of SDF. Experimental results on a number of applications show significant improvement in buffer size over existing competitors. The improvements are as high as 95.8% and 62.5%, and on average 85.9% and 52%, compared to the baseline and live range analysis-based approaches, respectively. This work complements our previous results on code generation for embedded multi-processors with limited memory [6].

2. Background

2.1 Application Model

Synchronous Data Flow (SDF) graphs are widely used to model streaming applications. Let V_G and E_G denote the set of vertices and directed edges of the SDF graph G, respectively. Vertices of the SDF graph, also known as actors, model application tasks, and directed edges represent inter-task communication channels. Edge e starts from the actor $src(e)$ (source), and ends at the actor $snk(e)$ (sink). Figure 1 depicts an example.

Upon execution, each task consumes a fixed number of data items, also known as tokens, from each of its input channels. The consumed tokens are processed to generate output data, which is subsequently written to output channels of the task after completion

LCTES'10,   April 13–15, 2010, Stockholm, Sweden.
Copyright © 2010 ACM 978-1-60558-953-4/10/04. . . $10.00

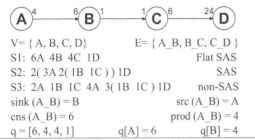

$V = \{ A, B, C, D \}$ $E = \{ A\_B, B\_C, C\_D \}$

S1: 6A 4B 4C 1D   Flat SAS

S2: 2(3A 2(1B 1C)) 1D   SAS

S3: 2A 1B 1C 4A 3(1B 1C) 1D   non-SAS

sink (A_B) = B   src (A_B) = A

cns (A_B) = 6   prod (A_B) = 4

$q = [6, 4, 4, 1]$ q[A] = 6   q[B] = 4

Figure 1. An example SDF graph, several valid schedules and some definitions are illustrated. SDF edges are annotated with corresponding production and consumption rates.

of the execution. The generated output also has fixed rate. Equivalently, each edge e is annotated with two $prod(e)$ and $cns(e)$ numbers, which refer to the number of tokens produced by $src(e)$ and consumed by $snk(e)$ upon execution, respectively.

Application tasks can be executed only after there are enough tokens to consume on their incoming edges. The produced tokens after execution of a task might enable execution of other tasks. Execution of a task is also referred to as firing of the corresponding actor in the model. Note that execution of a task implies that enough tokens already existed at its inputs. The streaming assumption implies that there are sufficiently-large number of tokens at the primary input, input from outside the model, to be processed.

2.2 Static Task Scheduling

Task can be executed in different orders, also known as task schedules. Due to production and consumption rates, task execution changes the storage requirement of the inter-actor channels. If repetitive execution of a fixed task schedule maintains the channels storage requirement bounded, the schedule can be utilized to synthesize an implementation at compile time. Such a schedule identifies one period of execution of the application, which is iteratively invoked to process the input stream.

It follows that a periodic task execution schedule has to meet two conditions: 1) actors can be fired only after there is enough tokens to consume on their incoming edges, 2) all of the generated tokens have to be consumed by the end of the period, to enable infinite repetition of the schedule using finite channel storage. It is well-known that realistic application SDF can be scheduled statically [9].

Let vector q denote the number of repetition of actors in the periodic schedule. Without loss of generality, we assume q refers to the simplest such vectors, i.e., not all of its elements can be divided by an integer larger than 1. To guarantee that all produced tokens are consumed by the end of the period, any static schedule has to guarantee the following for all edges of the SDF:

$$q[src(e)] \times prod(e) = q[sink(e)] \times cns(e)$$

The vector q is unique for real-life streaming applications [9]. Thus, the number of firings of actors in any static schedule is constant, although their ordering might differ in the period. In particular, "Single Appearance" (SA) schedule refers to the ordering, in which each actor appears exactly once. Figure 1 depicts an example SDF graph, along with several example schedules and notations.

2.3 Software Synthesis from SDF

To synthesize software from a given SDF model, one needs to determine a periodic ordering for execution of the tasks, which can be infinitely repeated. In the baseline synthesis scheme, task v appears in a loop whose iteration count is $q[v]$. Subsequently, the loops are "stitched" together in the given order, with appropriate

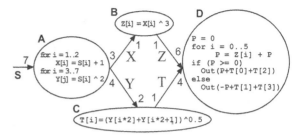

Schedule: 2A 6B 4C D

```
while(1)
    for i = 0..1
        for j = 0..2
            X[i*3+j] = S[j] + 1
        for j = 3..6
            Y[i*4+j] = S[j] ^ 2
    for i = 0..5
        Z[i] = X[i] ^ 3
    for i = 0..3
        T[i]=(Y[i*2]+Y[i*2+1])^0.5

    P = 0
    for i = 0..5
        P = Z[i] + P
    if (P >= 0)
        Out(P+T[0]+T[2])
    else
        Out(-P+T[1]+T[3])
end While
```

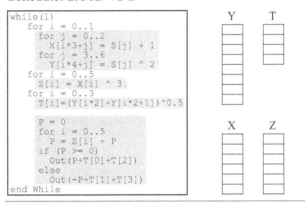

Figure 2. An example SDF, and the corresponding baseline implementation. Channels are implemented as distinct buffers.

fixtures to implement inter-task communication. Figure 2 illustrates the synthesized code for the depicted SDF.

SA task scheduling enables the synthesizer to save in application code size by instantiating tasks' internal computations exactly once, possibly within nested loops. The code size overhead of looping constructs is negligible with respect to typical size of task internal computations. Therefore, SA schedules are widely used in embedded systems, since they lead to small size synthesized software. In this work, we assume the given schedule to be SA, unless otherwise noted.

Recall that edge e in a SDF graph represents a FIFO communication channel between $src(e)$ and $sink(e)$. The channel stores the produced data after firings of $src(e)$, and its data is consumed during firings of $sink(e)$. Let $MT(e, S)$ denote the maximum number of tokens stored in channel e during firing of tasks according to schedule S. Clearly, $MT(e, S)$ indicates the minimum memory space required on this channel to implement the communication functionality.

The channels are typically implemented as buffer arrays to realize *in-order* communication with little cost. In the synthesized software, $src(e)$ writes into the buffer that implements channel e by maintaining a write index, referred to as the *Head*. The Head is reset at the beginning of the period, and is incremented after writing every token. The initial resetting enables reusing the same buffer memory in subsequent iterations. Similarly, $snk(e)$ maintains its own *Tail* index for reading from the buffer of channel e (buffer e for short), which is also reset at the beginning of the period, and is incremented after reading a token. Figure 2 illustrates the buffers in the synthesized code for the example SDF.

3. Buffer Memory Management

Streaming applications tend to require fairly large channel buffers, which is primarily due to the data intensive nature of their processing. As a result, total size of the buffer arrays usually accounts for a substantial portion of the application binary memory footprint. Enhanced management of the buffer memory can potentially lead to considerable reduction in memory requirement, which would be of great value in the resource constrained embedded space.

3.1 Baseline Buffer Allocation

For a given schedule S, the minimum size of the buffer e would be $MT(e, S)$. Smaller buffers would lead to incorrect or infeasible execution under S, because at least at one point during execution $MT(e, S)$ tokens need to be stored in the buffer e. In our discussions, therefore, we assume that the size of buffer e is exactly $MT(e, S)$.

The baseline synthesis scheme would be to allocate the buffers as independent regions in the data memory. In the "baseline buffer allocation" scheme, the buffers do not share any physical memory location at any point during execution. It follows that the overall buffer size would be the sum total of individual buffers, i.e., $\sum_{e \in E_G} MT(e, S)$. Figure 2 depicts a simple example.

3.2 The Impact of Scheduling

Changes to task scheduling can impact individual buffer sizes, which in turn, would influence total buffer memory requirement. In case of Figure 1, for example, $MT(A\_B, S_1) = 24$ and $MT(A\_B, S_2) = 12$. Note that under S_2, following production of 12 tokens by the actor A the consumer B gets fired, which consumes all of the tokens in the channel. Thus, the maximum number of tokens in the channel does not exceed 12. Unlike MT, the number of exchanged tokens over an edge does not depend on the schedule, and is only a function of the SDF structure and rates.

It is known that finding the optimal task schedule to minimize total buffer size is a NP-hard problem. Bhattacharyya et al. present two effective algorithms for constructing a single appearance schedule with emphasis on reducing the memory requirement [2]. Furthermore, phased scheduling has been proposed as a method for scheduling a SDF graph to minimize the memory size considering both code and data memory [8].

In addition to scheduling, the data memory requirement is impacted by the scheme used to allocate individual buffers in the memory. In this work, we direct our attention to this problem, i.e., minimizing overall buffer size through improved buffer analysis and allocation techniques. That is, we seek to improve buffer management without perturbing the given schedule.

3.3 Buffer Sharing

In the baseline allocation scheme, separate portions of the memory are allocated to implement the channels of the SDF graph. During most of the execution time, however, the channel buffers are completely or partially empty. For example in figure 1, buffer A_B is completely empty during the firings of C and D in the first schedule. Therefore, the memory allocated to this buffer can be reused to implement buffer C_D. That is, the two buffers can *share* at least one physical memory location during execution, without compromising the functionality of the streaming application.

Figure 3 illustrates the synthesized code, under the buffer sharing assumption, for the example depicted in Figure 2. Note that buffers X, Y, Z and T are allocated at different offsets of the same array.

Extending the idea, any two channel buffers can be allocated to allow sharing of physical memory locations (space) as long as the two buffers do not conflict in time. In other words, the two buffers must not need to maintain a token at the same memory location at the same time.

The program synthesis framework, including its code generation protocol, impacts the possibility of sharing between two buffers. In this work, we assume that code generation follows the following rules:

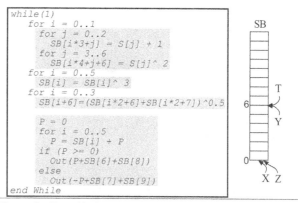

Figure 3. Shared buffer implementation of the SDF in Figure 2

1. None of the tokens of any buffer must be over-written or read by another buffer at anytime during the execution of the program.

2. Buffers must be statically allocated as contiguous regions in the application memory space.

3. The data should not be moved around within the buffer, i.e., data production and consumption operations are the only primitives to access FIFO channels. Token production and consumption increment Head and Tail indexes, respectively.

The rules collectively guarantee that the generated code conforms to SDF semantics, and the generated code safely implements the functionality. They eliminate the need for implementation of a complex inter-actor communication mechanism, which would incur large performance and code size penalty. Outstanding examples of academic and commercial SDF synthesis frameworks follow the same basic principles [1, 3].

4. Granularity in Buffer Analysis

The storage requirement (capacity) of any channel buffer changes with progress in the execution. The changes to the capacity of a buffer occur on execution of producer and consumer tasks of the corresponding channel. Such temporal change, however, can be captured at different levels of granularity [12].

The highest resolution temporal view of a buffer's storage requirement would need to follow the execution at the granularity of firing individual actors. In this scheme, execution of a task forms the unit of time for temporal analysis. We use the term *fine-grain* buffer analysis to refer to this level of abstraction.

At the other end of the spectrum, temporal changes to required capacity can be largely abstracted away. Specifically, buffers can be viewed to require storage of the maximum number of tokens during their lifetime. This leads to a *coarse-grain* temporal view of the buffer storage requirement, in which the buffer has the capacity $MT(e, S)$ during its live range, and zero otherwise.

A middle ground between the two ends of the granularity spectrum would be to consider consecutive execution of the same task as the time unit. In this level of abstraction, the storage requirement of the buffer is viewed to change only when a different actor is fired next. Among the consecutive firings of the same actor, the storage requirement of the buffer is viewed to be its maximum value in the range. Figure 4 illustrates a simple SDF, and the impact of granularity in temporal analysis of the buffer capacity.

4.1 Visualizing Buffer Analysis and Allocation

Figure 5 illustrates an example SDF, a given flat SAS, and three different buffer allocations. The allocations are visualized in a two-dimensional plane, in which the X-axis shows actor firings in the

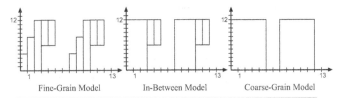

Fine-Grain Model   In-Between Model   Coarse-Grain Model

Figure 4. The impact of analysis granularity on the estimated temporal behavior of buffer A_B (Figure 1 under S_2). X and Y axis represent actor firings and buffer size, respectively.

schedule (time), and the Y-axis represents the buffer location in the memory (space). The unit of time is firing of a single actor.

The gray area of each buffer illustrates the range between Head and Tail indices that contain valid data. The temporal update in the gray area is due to the production and consumption operations, which increment the Head and Tail indices, respectively. The buffers are indexed relative to an *offset*. The offset indicates the start of the buffer, which is determined after the allocation process.

For a given analysis granularity, the capacity requirement of a buffer at any point in time is fixed. Thus, the X coordinate of any buffer in the two dimensional time-memory plane cannot be modified, i.e., the buffers can not be moved horizontally. The Y coordinate, however, represents the physical location of the allocated memory to implement the buffers.

The memory allocation problem can be viewed as a geometric layout instance, in which a solution is valid of the *laid out* buffers do not conflict in the time-memory plane. The only operation for perturbing the layout is vertical movement of the buffers. The geometric placement of a buffer in the plane readily gives its offset in the memory space. The objective is to minimize the vertical dimension of the layout, which represents the total size of the buffers.

4.2 Granularity and Buffer Allocation

The granularity in buffer analysis compromises accuracy in temporal behavior of buffers with analysis complexity. Our conviction is that fine-grain analysis, though more expensive in terms of analysis complexity, provides temporal details that enable *substantial* improvements in buffer sharing. The three layouts in the Figure 5 illustrate the idea.

Figure 5.A shows the baseline buffer allocation scheme, in which every buffer is assumed to have maximum capacity throughout the execution. Therefore, buffers have to be allocated in dedicated locations in the memory. The figure shows that the total size of channel buffers is 45.

Figure 5.B depicts the optimal buffer allocations under coarse-grain analysis of their temporal behavior. In this scheme, buffers are assumed to have maximum capacity throughout their live range in the schedule. Therefore, two buffers would conflict if they are alive in at least one point in time in which case, they cannot share any physical memory location and have to be allocated in distinct memory spaces [12].

For example $MT(A\_B, S) = 6$, and under the coarse-grain analysis model six memory cells have to be allocated during its entire life time (three time steps) to implement this buffer. The gray areas in the picture illustrate the actual storage requirement, and the border lines represent the memory assignments for each buffer. The white space inside the borders represent memory space that is left unused at the corresponding point during execution. In the example of figure 5.B, the total size of channel buffers is 24.

Finally, figure 5.C shows the optimal allocation of buffers under fine-grain analysis scheme, in which, buffers' temporal behavior is updated at the granularity of actor firings. Intuitively, fine-grain view of the buffers' spatiotemporal patterns enables more

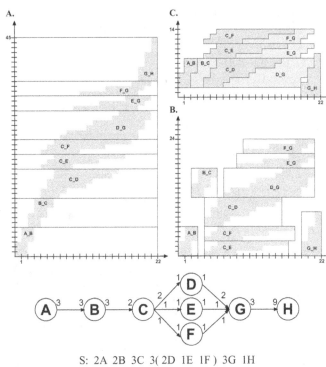

S: 2A 2B 3C 3(2D 1E 1F) 3G 1H

Figure 5. A. Baseline, **B.** Coarse-grain, and **C.** Fine-grain allocation schemes for the illustrated example. X and Y axis show actor firings in the schedule, and the offset within the memory space, respectively.

condensed packing of the buffers in the memory, which translates into smaller code size. In this example, the total size of channel buffers is 14.

5. Fine-Grain Buffer Allocation

The temporal behavior of FIFO buffers can be characterized as a pair of two <u>H</u>ead and tai<u>L</u> vectors. H keeps the head index $H_e[t]$ and L keeps the tail index $L_e[t]$ at the time step t of the program. The concept of time here is the same as that we described in 3, therefore the length of H and L is the maximum time steps in one iteration of the program which is the summation of the elements in q_G.

$$\forall e \in E \ : \ B_e = (H_e, L_e)$$

B_e : The Buffer on edge e which we call it buffer e in short

$H_e[t]$: Head index at time $0 \le t \le T$ for the buffer on e

$L_e[t]$: Tail index at time $0 \le t \le T$ for the buffer on e

$$T = \sum_{v \in q_G} q[v]$$

In this definition of buffers head and tail indices start from zero and go up to their maximum level and go back to zero again after getting to the end. In the notion of buffer sharing, each buffer is allocated within the shared buffer which means an offset will be assigned to each buffer and will be added to the head and tail of the buffer in a way that no conflict would occur. Note that H and L keep the value of head and tail for each individual buffer without considering the sharing scheme. The offset which will be assigned to each buffer indicates the true location of them within shared buffer. Assume tuple O keeps the offsets for all the buffers on all the edges of the graph:

$$O = \{(o_{e_1}, o_{e_2}, o_{e_3}, \ldots, o_{e_N}) \mid e_1 : e_N \in E, \ N = |E|\}$$

o_e is the offset for the buffer on edge e

The following is the definition of SBS as "Shared-Buffer Size" and the objective of the problem is to minimize SBS:

$$SBS = \max_{\forall e \in E}\{o_e + H_e^{max} \mid H_e^{max} = \max_{0 \leq t \leq T}(H_e[t])\}$$

The following lemma gives us one of the advantages of using SA scheduling and will help us to specify the constraints of the problem:

LEMMA 5.1. *In SA schedules the head index at the time t is always greater than equal the tail index at the same time:*

$$\forall t \leq T \ : \ H_e[t] \geq L_e[t]$$

Proof: The opposite situation might occur when there have been already some tokens written in and read from the buffer, thus both head and tail are pointing to a place in the middle of the buffer. If there are more tokens to be written in the buffer and head has already hit the end, it will start from the beginning of the queue to fill up the empty spots (head never surpasses tail because we assume the size of the buffer is big enough to keep all the required tokens). In this situation, head will be pointing to a location in the vicinity of zero while tail is still somewhere around the maximum size of the buffer.

The claim is obvious for a flat SA schedule. The producer gets the chance to fill up the buffer and it is when head starts going up to its maximum position and stays there. Later on the consumer comes in and empties the buffer and now this is the turn for the tail index to go up. Eventually tail meets head at the end point of the buffer and they both go to zero. Since both the producer and the consumer appear only once in the schedule without being repeated in nesting loops, head and tail never change again in the current iteration of the program. The next iteration will start with an empty buffer exactly the same as the first iteration. However when we have nesting loops, both producer and consumer might be repeatedly fired one after each other.

Let the <u>Round</u> of the edge e and schedule S which we denote $R(e, S)$ be a sequence of actors in schedule s from when $src(e)$ starts being fired to when $sink(e)$ is fired and we are back to $src(e)$ again. This sequence includes the direct repetitions of the both source and sink actors. Because S is a SA schedule, every time $src(e)$ is fired, the same path will be taken to $sink(e)$. In fact if we replace this sequence of actors with the notation $R(e, S)$ in our schedule, none of the $src(e)$ nor $sink(e)$ will appear alone out of $R(e, S)$ in the schedule.

Figure 6 depict an example of this replacement for the given edge and schedule. Therefore all the tokens produced on the edge e during $R(e, S)$ should be consumed by the end of each round, otherwise they will be accumulated at the end of the schedule which is against the definition of a valid schedule. Therefore we only need to prove the claim within a round, which is true because based on the definition of a round, $src(e)$ appears only in the first portion of the round and does not appear again after $sink(e)$ is fired.∎

In the problem of buffer sharing, the vectors H and L are known and given. We also have a consistent SDF graph and a valid SA schedule which means at any given time we know the number of tokens exist on each edge of the graph and the relative value of head and tail. Therefore lemma 5.1 does not impose any constraint

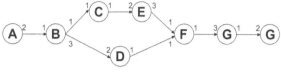

S: 6A 2 (3 (2 (B C) 1E 3 (D F)) 3G) 3H
R(B_D, S) = B C B C E D F D F D F
New Sequence with R: 6A 3R 3G 3R 3G 3H

Figure 6. SA schedule with nested loops and the notion of "Round". The example is for buffer B_D

to the problem. However by using this lemma we can specify the constraint and the objective of the problem as the following:
Constraint:

$$\forall e, b \in E \quad \forall 0 \leq t \leq T \ :$$
$$H_e[t] + o_e \leq L_b[t] + o_b \quad OR \quad H_b[t] + o_b \leq L_e[t] + o_e$$

Objective:

$$minimize \ SBS$$

The constraint suggest that no buffer can write in or read from the significant data of another buffer. Therefore for buffer e at any given time the meaningful data of other buffers have to be assigned after or before this buffer. The real location of head and tail within the shared buffer is relative to the assigned offsets (o_e and o_b). Since these offsets will not change in time, thus a place in shared-buffer is assigned to the buffer only once, and the data will be written in and read from this location in the entire program without conflicting with any other buffer nor requiring any data to be relocated.

6. ILP Formulation

Integer Linear Programming (ILP) provides a mechanism to obtain the optimal solution of a problem as long as its constraints and objective can be described as linear constraints of integer variables. Since there are many commercial ILP solvers available, one only has to cast the problem in ILP formulation to solve a specific instance. In case of the buffer sharing problem, linear constraints have to ensure that all buffers are allocated without any conflict.

The subtle difficulty in such formulation is to avoid buffer conflicts using linear constraints, because two conflicting buffers can be allocated in either order in the shared buffer. In other words, formulation of the "OR" logic is non-trivial, since a buffer can be allocated either before or after another conflicting buffer as long as there is no violations of the stated guidelines.

Because linear constraints cannot be easily used to articulate the "OR" logic, we had to reformulate the problem. For each buffer and each location in the shared memory space, specifically, we define a binary variables, whose '1' value would indicate allocation of the corresponding buffer in the corresponding memory location. Subsequently, buffer conflict constraints can be formulated as a large number of linear constraints. Note that the constraints have to be generated for all time steps. We do not include the details of the formulation for brevity.

The complexity of buffer sharing instance, and ILP runtime grows exponentially. Therefore, it does not provide a scalable approach to solving the buffer sharing problem. Nevertheless, we utilize ILP to obtain the optimal solution to problem instances, although at the cost of unreasonably long solver runtime, primarily for measurement of the optimality gap using other techniques (Section 10).

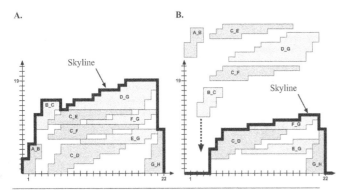

Figure 7. For the SDF graph of Figure 5: **A.** A non-optimal permutation: (G_H, C_D, A_B, E_G, C_F, F_G, C_E, D_G, B_C). The line in bold is the final skyline. **B.** MDA is moving down the buffers in following order: (G_H, E_G, C_D, F_G, B_C, C_F, D_G, A_B, C_E). Each step forms a skyline with the placed buffers.

7. Strip Packing Problem and Buffer-Sharing

In several industries there is a need for packing a set of 2-dimensional objects on a larger rectangular unit of material by minimizing the waste. This larger unit can be a standardized sheet of material, from which the set of objects have to be cut. The objective is to pack all the items into the minimum number of units. This problem is a variation of the well-known bin-packing (BP) problem, and is used in some industrial applications such as wood or glass industries.

In other contexts the standardized unit is a roll of material such as a roll of paper or cloth and the objective is to use the minimum roll length. This problem is called strip-packing (SP) problem and we will be using it in this paper to realize the buffer-sharing problem. These two problems are known as NP-complete and there has been various attempts to solve them in the algorithms community. [11] provides a survey on some of the two-dimensional packing problems and solutions.

In the context of buffer sharing one can realize a large array of memory (which we call shared-buffer) analogous to the roll of material in the SP problems, and the different buffers on different edges of the graph could be the set of objects. Figure 5 shows the geometrical aspect of buffers where we have time on one axis and the indices of shared-buffer on the other axis. In this model the objects are being constructed from the number of tokens that exist in the buffer during the run time of the program. Subsequently, we adopt a SP packing algorithm proposed in [7] with some adjustments specific to the buffer-sharing problem.

8. Move-Down Algorithm

Move Down Algorithm (MDA) is the main piece of our method and will be most repeated during the run time of the main algorithm. It also gives us the ability to make sequences among our input which is essential for Genetic Algorithms. The idea is very simple. we push each buffer toward the beginning of the shared-buffer array as much as possible so that they will take less space after all being allocated. As we can see in figure 5 the order of moving down the buffers matters and some of the sequences take less space than others. Figure 7A. shows another sequence of buffers from the SDF graph of figure 5 which is not optimal.

To understand how far a buffer can go down we introduce another vector which is called skyline and denoted $Vsk[t]$. In this section we consider buffers as solid geometrical shapes which can stand on the top of each other to construct a wall. Looking this way, skyline is the highest level of the constructed wall in each time step.

Figure 7 shows two different skylines for different situations while running MDA.

To construct the skyline vector we introduce skyline function which takes a Vsk and buffer B_e and also an offset o to place the buffer, and it will calculate the skyline vector $\acute{V}sk$ constructed from adding the new buffer at the point o to the existing skyline.

$$\forall e \in E \quad \forall 0 \le o \le BBS \quad \forall 0 \le t < T :$$
$$\acute{V}sk = skyline(Vsk, e, o) = \begin{cases} Vsk & \text{if } S_e[t] = 0 \\ h_e[t] + o & \text{otherwise} \end{cases}$$

MDA takes a skyline vector and a buffer, and returns the lowest offset it can get from pushing down this buffer before hitting the skyline.

$$o_e = MDA(Vsk, B_e)$$

The algorithm first places the buffer on the first level of the skyline by setting the offset to $Vsk[0]$. Then moving to the right, it compares the skyline to the seated buffer to see if there is any conflict and if there is one, it will adjust the offset to remove the conflict. Move Down Algorithm:

$$o_e := Vsk[0]$$
$$for \ i := 0 \rightarrow T :$$
$$\quad if(S_e[t] \ne 0) \ and \ (H_e[t] - S_e[t] + o_e < Vsk[t]) :$$
$$\quad\quad o_e := Vsk[t] - H_e[t] + S_e[t]$$
$$return \ o_e$$

If we run MDA on all the buffers in a pre-defined order, and also calculate the skyline on each step and use it for the next step, we have done the buffer allocation. If we call the pre-defined order a permutation of buffers and denote it with π, then we have:

$$O = PlaceAll(\pi)$$
$$\pi = (B_1, B_2, B_3, \dots, B_N)(\text{any order of buffres})$$
$$O = (o_{e1}, o_{e2}, o_{e3}, \dots, o_{eN})$$

The function *PlaceAll* will place each buffer in the same order they have in π as follows:

$$o_{e1} = MDA(Vsk_1, B_1) = 0$$
$$o_{e2} = MDA(Vsk_2, B_2)$$
$$\dots$$
$$o_{eN} = MDA(Vsk_N, B_N)$$

The first buffer always gets zero for the offset, and it is because we are pushing down the buffers as much as possible and there is nothing in the shared-buffer yet so it goes all the way down. For the skyline vectors we have:

$$Vsk_1 = V_{zero}(\text{the vector zero})$$
$$Vsk_2 = skyline(V_{zero}, B_1, 0) = H_{e1}$$
$$Vsk_3 = skyline(Vsk_2, B_2, o_{e2})$$
$$\dots$$
$$Vsk_N = skyline(Vsk_{N-1}, B_{N-1}, o_{en-1})$$
$$Vsk_{N+1} = skyline(Vsk_N, B_N, o_{eN})$$

The very first skyline vector is $V_{zero} = [0, 0, \dots, 0]$ which we can consider the ground. The second skyline forms when we push the first buffer down to the ground. Therefore skyline forms exactly on the top of this buffer which is the vector H.

The final skyline is Vsk_{N+1} and determines the height of the wall which is actually the size of shared-buffer:

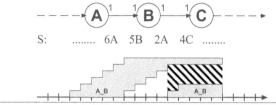

Figure 8. Part of a SDF graph with a non-SA schedule. The figure shows that for the buffer A_B the striped space is not reachable by MDA.

$$SBS = \max_{0 \le t \le T} (Vsk_{N+1}[t])$$

The size of shared-buffer depends on the sequence of buffers we are using, and *PlaceAll* itself does not guarantee that it will give us the optimal solution. However because it uses the notion of sequence in placing the buffers, it reduces the search space from $(BBS)^N$ (all the possible places for buffers to be in an array with the size of BBS) to $N!$ (the number of different sequence of buffers that we can have). Moreover having a sequence of data as the input, is one of the fundamentals of a genetic algorithm and enables us to use them to find the optimal or near optimal solution.

Lastly in this section, the following lemma shows weather MDA is capable of giving us the optimal solution or not. In fact this is another advantage of using SAS:

LEMMA 8.1. *The optimal solution can be found by using MDA in SA schedules. It is only the matter of finding the right sequence of buffers.*

Proof: Figure 8 depicts a buffer in a non-SA Schedule and as we can see there is an area inside buffer A_B which MDA can not reach. However because of lemma 5.1, in a SA schedule the head index is always greater than the tail index, thus any empty space inside a buffer is open from the top or the bottom of the buffer and can be reached by MDA.■

9. Evolutionary Optimization using MDA

In this section, we utilize the move-down algorithm to construct an evolutionary genetic optimization technique. Genetic optimization is composed of several key components, including chromosome, inheritance and fitness function. Chromosome provides an abstract representation of solutions in the search space, and is normally represented as a sequence of numbers. Inheritance models the basic operations through which, chromosomes are perturbed to improve the solution quality. Typically, there are two crossover and mutation inheritance operations in a genetic optimization framework. Finally, the fitness function quantifies the "quality" of candidate solutions, and determines survival of selected candidates. Our objective is to define the notions of chromosome, inheritance and fitness, in the context of buffer sharing, and subsequently, utilize genetic optimization to solve our problem at hand.

MDA provides the ability to work on a sequence of buffers as the input and to allocate all of them inside the shared buffer according to their order in the sequence (Section 8). The size of the shared-buffer is the height of the final structure, in the corresponding packing instance. We propose to use different permutations of buffers as chromosomes, or individuals of a population, and the height of the final skyline as the fitness function, in the genetic optimization framework. Consequently, the algorithm will work in the following steps:

To initialize the algorithm with a sample population, we randomly select a set of permutations. The size of the sample population is a pre-defined parameter. We used the number of buffers ($N = |E|$) to be the size of the population in our algorithm.

$$\text{Sample set} = \{\pi_1, \pi_2, \pi_3, \ldots, \pi_N\}$$

Since genetic algorithm keeps track of different lines of breeding patterns, having a larger sample population gives us the ability to keep track of more candidate solutions. On the other hand, having a very large population slows down the algorithm, and reduces the chance of finding the optimal solution in a reasonable time.

Now we can run *PlaceAll* algorithm and calculate the height of the final solution in every individual permutation in the set. We choose the height of each permutation (denoted as $height(\pi)$) to be the fitness function (denoted as $f(\pi)$) as follows:

$$f(\pi) = \frac{1}{height(\pi)}$$

For any permutation there is a chance that part of its sequence matches the sequence in the optimal solution. Basically, we would like to find these parts from different members and concatenate them, so that we can get closer to the optimum. The mechanism to recognize if we are getting closer to this goal is the fitness function. To generate new members first we need to select two of the existing members, which we refer to as parents. We select the parents depending on their fitness. The fitter individuals (shorter in height), have a higher chance of being selected. The probability of selection of an individual permutation (denoted as $p(\pi)$ is likely to change in each iteration of the algorithm due to changes to the fitness of the other members of the group.

$$p(\pi_i) = \frac{f(\pi_i)}{\sum_{j=1}^{N} f(\pi_j)}$$

In practice we can divide the interval $[0, 1)$ into N sub-intervals as follows:

$$[0, p(\pi_1)) \,,\, [p(\pi_1), p(\pi_2)) \,,\, \ldots \,,\, [p(\pi_{N-1}), p(\pi_N))$$

Two random numbers from the interval $[0, 1)$ will determine the selected permutations.

Subsequently, the parent chromosomes are used to create the children using the crossover operation. Our crossover function generates two random numbers $1 \le p \le q \le N$. Then it copies the sub-sequence of the first parent from position p to q, and place it at the beginning of the child's chromosome. The sequence from p to q is the part that we would like to preserve, hoping that the same sequence exists in the optimal solution. Finally, we fill the rest of the offspring with the remaining genes (buffers) in the second parent in the same order that they appear in the second parent. The following example shows how crossover function works:

$$p = 2 \quad q = 4$$
$$\pi_{parent1} = (B_{e1}, \underbrace{\mathbf{B}_{e2}, \mathbf{B}_{e3}, \mathbf{B}_{e4}}, B_{e5}, B_{e6})$$
$$\pi_{parent2} = (\mathbf{B}_{e6}, \mathbf{B}_{e5}, B_{e4}, B_{e3}, B_{e2}, \mathbf{B}_{e1})$$
$$\pi_{child} = (B_{e2}, B_{e3}, B_{e4}, B_{e6}, B_{e5}, B_{e1})$$

Copying and matching different sequences from existing permutation may lead the process to stay in a local minimum region. To avoid this situation we can mutate the child based on the probability $p_{mutation}$, which is another parameter of the algorithm. If the child is to be mutated, then the function generates two random numbers $1 \le i, j \le N$, and swaps the buffers in those positions within the sequence.

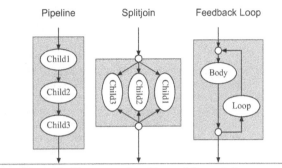

Figure 9. The composite objects of StreamIt language

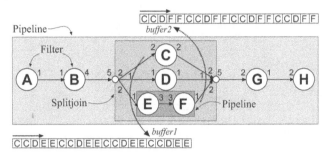

S: 1(5A 5B 4(1C 1D 2(1E 1F)) 10G 5H)

Figure 10. The split-joins share a buffer at their start and end terminals. The split-join in this picture works in round robin fashion. The letters inside *buffer1* and *buffer2* illustrate the mapping of array elements to the actors.

$p_{mutation} = 0.4$: the probability of being mutated

$i = 2$ $j = 4$

π_{child} Before $= (B_{e2}, \mathbf{B}_{e3}, B_{e4}, \mathbf{B}_{e6}, B_{e5}, B_{e1})$

π_{child} After $= (B_{e2}, B_{e6}, B_{e4}, B_{e3}, B_{e5}, B_{e1})$

The *PlaceAll* algorithm is run on the newly generated child to calculate the height of the offspring. The child is then added to the population set. To maintain the pre-defined population of the sample set we kill (remove) the weakest (highest) member of the sample set. Therefore the offspring will be compared against the weakest member of the population, and may or may not remain in the sample set.

Iteratively, we generate new children and compare them to the existing members until the termination point where we can return the best solution found. Termination can be an acceptable size of the shared buffer (the height of the best permutation). Alternatively, the optimization can be terminated at a time limit. We selected the number of iterations as the termination criterion. We set the value to be the product of N and an iteration parameter.

10. Experimental Evaluation

10.1 Setup

We have integrated our algorithm into the MIT StreamIt compiler [5]. StreamIt refers to both a programming language developed for specifying the streaming applications, and a java-based compiler. The StreamIt language conforms to the SDF semantics, by modeling an application as a graph of interconnected but independent "filters" with statically-defined input and output rates that communicate via FIFO channels.

StreamIt utilizes four stream objects to hierarchically build the application graph: *filters* form the basic data processing unit, while the other three objects, *pipeline*, *split-join*, and *feedback loop* (Figure 9), are composite objects that contain children stream objects. The children are recursively constructed out of the four different object types. In other words, the three composite stream objects (*pipeline*, *split-join*, and *feedback loop*) act as containers to build different graph structures, and the *filter* specifies data processing. The design ensures that the graph is highly structured while providing the programmers with a simple, yet flexible, set of objects to construct the stream graph for their streaming application.

We used the built-in single appearance scheduler to construct task execution order. The StreamIt scheduler is designed based on the hierarchical nature of the language. Specifically, the composite objects form virtual tasks, under which its children are scheduled. If any of the children happens to be a composite object itself, its firing in the schedule will be replaced by its own children. Consequently, only filters appear in the schedule as data processing actors. Figure 10 depicts a simple example.

	Number of Buffers	Number of Actores	Number of Time Steps	Base-line	Coarse-Grain	Fine-Grain (Best Case)	Fine-Grain (Worst Case)	Compile Time with GA in Sec.	Optimal Solution by ILP
Bitonic Sort	119	214	340	1152	96	48	64	91	32
Insertion Sort	8	9	263	1024	256	128	128	6	128
FFT2	22	24	446	3072	640	384	384	10	~
FFT3	38	64	175	960	192	72	96	11	64
TDE	48	51	17204	77120	23168	11776	23040	510	~
Matrix Mult.	10	21	2712	5000	4000	2000	2000	13	~

Figure 11. Benchmark characteristics and experimental results

The StreamIt compiler translates stream programs to C, which can be passed to any standard C compiler to generate executable binaries. The compiler defaults to the baseline buffer allocation scheme, in which channels in the stream graph are implemented with distinct arrays. We instrumented the compiler to allocate all the buffers within the same array, though at different indices. The baseline and instrumented synthesized codes were compiled and executed on a Unix machine to ensure that functional correctness is preserved after our transformation.

10.1.1 Benchmark Applications

We selected six different streaming kernels as our benchmarks to evaluate the proposed technique. They include two sorting algorithms, two different implementation of the fast Fourier transform (FFT), time delay estimation (TDE) and matrix multiplication kernels. These kernels frequently appear in many higher-level application that are used in portable and handheld embedded systems.

The table in Figure 11 shows the benchmarks. The benchmarks are implemented in the StreamIt language. The second and third column of the table list the complexity of each application in terms of number of channel buffers and actors (tasks), respectively. The fourth column of the table shows the number of time steps, i.e. sum total of task executions in the periodic schedule, for each benchmark.

Note that unlike generic SDF tasks, StreamIt filters have only one input and one output buffer. More complex inter-actor communications are modeled using split-join objects. In synthesizing split-joins, one large buffer is used to implement multiple channels that either split to or join from several actors. The sinks of a split (or sources of a join) read from (write to) the corresponding locations in the large buffer (Figure 10). The size of the large buffer is the sum total of the individual channel buffers, i.e., no sharing between channels is performed when allocating them in the same

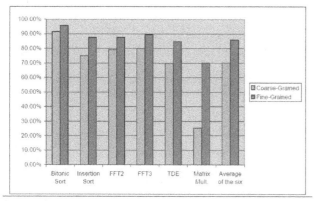

Figure 12. The Improvement of coarse-grain and fine-grain methods compared to the baseline.

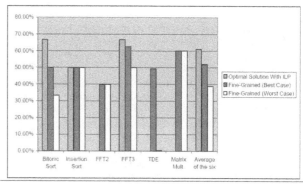

Figure 13. The Improvement in all fine-grain cases: GA worst case, GA best case, and ILP, compared to the coarse-grain method.

buffer. Consequently, the number of buffers in the StreamIt program tends to be less than the number of actors. Figure 10 depicts a split-join and the buffers in its terminals.

In general, stream programs might have two different initialization and steady state execution phases. The initialization phase might be needed if a non-trivial buffer content configuration has to be created to enter the steady state phase. In this work, we have focused on the steady state buffer analysis of the stream programs.

10.1.2 System and Algorithm Configuration

Our proposed genetic algorithm for buffer optimization uses a number of configurable parameters. In our experiments, we have set the iteration number of the algorithm to $1000\times$ number of buffers in the application. In addition, the sample population in the genetic algorithm is configured to be equal to the number of buffers in the application, and the probably of mutation operation is 0.4. The parameters are configured with very small effort to create a reasonable balance between optimization runtime and solution quality. The experiments are performed on a Unix PC with Intel Pentium 4 CPU running at 2.80GHz, 1024KB of cache, and 3GB of main memory.

10.2 Results

Figure 11 shows the result of baseline, coarse-grain and our genetic-algorithm based fine-grain buffer allocation on the benchmark applications. The genetic algorithm is intrinsically non-deterministic. We report the worst and the best buffer size that we observed in 10 runs.

The coarse-grain analysis is done according to the buffer lifetime analysis principle, developed by Murthy and Bhattacharyya [12]. The *first fit* heuristic is used to allocate the buffers in the shared buffer, under the same SA schedule. Note that first fit algorithm is concluded to perform well under coarse-grain buffer analysis model [12].

We also generated ILP instances for the benchmark application, according to the formulation developed in Section 6. Due to the exponential growth of the ILP complexity with respect to time steps for the problem, our system was unable to load the enormous-sized ILP instances of *FFT2*, *TDE*, and *Matrix Mult*. The ILP approach is clearly not scalable, nevertheless, it is helpful in establishing an optimality gap for the selected benchmarks.

Figure 12 visualizes the performance of coarse grain and fine grain buffer allocation, in terms of savings in total buffer size over the baseline scheme. Our evolutionary allocation method reduces the buffer size by 86% on average. The improvements are as dramatic as 24X in case of *Bitonic Sort*.

Figure 13 compares the performance of fine-grain analysis, either via using ILP or our proposed algorithm, versus the conven-

tional live range analysis coarse-grain method. The data shows that both the best and worst case results of our scheme outperform the coarse-grain results. Considering the best case, our allocator improves the result of coarse-grain allocation by about 52%, and is only marginally inferior to the theoretically optimal ILP solution. Note that the best and worst case results are collected over only 10 different runs. Thus, it is reasonable to consider best case performance for comparison purposes, given our algorithms' decent latency and the small number of required repetitions.

The complete compile time in our experiments varied from a few seconds to a few minutes depending on the complexity of the program. We believe that the compilation latencies are quite reasonable, considering their absolute value, our old experimentation platform, and the fact that compile-time analysis latency is justified given the gains in application memory footprint.

Varying the analysis granularity involves a natural tradeoff between buffer size and optimization latency (compiler runtime). It is important to strike a balance between the two competing elements. Our study has showed that not only fine-grain analysis is not to be dismissed due to its complexity [12], but it can be the method of choice in a large number of application scenarios.

11. Conclusions

Streaming kernels and applications are abundant in the embedded systems domain, where underlying hardware platforms have to deal with strict resource constraints. It is critical to optimize the streaming applications for resource requirement, such as their memory footprint. We contribute to this important goal by developing a novel buffer allocation technique during synthesis of streaming applications from synchronous dataflow specifications.

We argue that fine-grain analysis of buffers' temporal behavior, as opposed to conventional coarse-grain live range analysis, enables dramatic improvements in buffer sharing. We transform the buffer allocation problem into packing of complex polygons in the two-dimensional space, and present an evolutionary algorithm to solve the problem. Experimental results demonstrate the superiority of our approach compared to existing competitors in terms of the memory footprint of the synthesized applications. We conclude that the benefits of considering buffers' fine-grain temporal behavior outweighs the reasonable increase in static analysis latency for a large class of resource-constrained embedded systems.

Acknowledgments

The support of National Science Foundation, under grant CCF-0903549, and Semiconductor Research Corporation, under contract 2009-HJ-1971, is gratefully acknowledged.

References

[1] Mathworks simulink - simulation and model-based design. available online at http://www.mathworks.com/products/simulink/.

[2] S. S. Bhattacharyya, P. K. Murthy, and E. A. Lee. *Software Synthesis from Dataflow Graphs*. Kluwer, 1996.

[3] J. Eker, J. W. Janneck, E. A. Lee, J. Liu, X. Liu, J. Ludvig, S. Neuendorffer, S. Sachs, and Y. Xiong. Taming heterogeneity - the ptolemy approach. *Proceedings of the IEEE*, 91(1):127–144, 2003.

[4] M. Geilen and T. Basten. Reactive process networks. In *International Conference on Embedded Software*, pages 137–146, 2004.

[5] M. I. Gordon, W. Thies, M. Karczmarek, J. Lin, A. S. Meli, A. A. Lamb, C. Leger, J. Wong, H. Hoffmann, D. Maze, and S. P. Amarasinghe. A stream compiler for communication-exposed architectures. In *International Conference on Architectural Support for Programming Languages and Operating Systems*, pages 291–303, 2002.

[6] M. Hashemi and S. Ghiasi. Versatile task assignment for heterogeneous soft dual-processor platforms. *IEEE Transactions on Computer-Aided Design of Integrated Circuits and Systems (TCAD)*, 2010.

[7] S. Jakobs. On the genetic algorithms for the packing of polygons. *European Journal of Operational Research*, 88:165–181, 1996.

[8] M. Karczmarek, W. Thies, and S. Amarasinghe. Phased scheduling of stream programs. In *Conference on Languages, Compilers and Tools for Embedded Systems*, pages 103–112, 2003.

[9] E. A. Lee and D. G. Messerschmitt. Static scheduling of synchronous data flow programs for digital signal processing. *IEEE Transactions on Computers*, 36(1), 1987.

[10] E. A. Lee and D. G. Messerschmitt. Synchronous data flow. *Proceedings of the IEEE*, 75(9):1235–1245, September 1987.

[11] A. Lodi, S. Martello, and M. Monaci. Two-dimensional packing problems: a survey. *European Journal of Operational Research*, 141 (2):241–252, 2003.

[12] P. K. Murthy and S. S. Bhattacharyya. Shared buffer implementations of signal processing systems using lifetime analysis techniques. *IEEE Transactions on Computer-Aided Design of Integrated Circuits and Systems*, 20(2), 2001.

[13] S. Stuijk, M. Geilen, and T. Basten. Throughput-buffering trade-off exploration for cyclo-static and synchronous dataflow graphs. *IEEE Transactions on Computers*, 57(10):1331–1345, 2008.

[14] M. Wiggers, M. Bekooij, and G. J. M. Smit. Efficient computation of buffer capacities for cyclo-static dataflow graphs. In *Design Automation Conference*, pages 658–663, 2007.

Modeling Structured Event Streams in System Level Performance Analysis *

Simon Perathoner   Tobias Rein
Lothar Thiele   Kai Lampka

Computer Engineering and Networks Laboratory
ETH Zurich, Switzerland
{perathoner, thiele, lampka}@tik.ee.ethz.ch

Jonas Rox

Institute of Computer and Network Engineering
TU Braunschweig, Germany
rox@ida.ing.tu-bs.de

Abstract

This paper extends the methodology of analytic real-time analysis of distributed embedded systems towards merging and extracting sub-streams based on event type information. For example, one may first merge a set of given event streams, then process them jointly and finally decompose them into separate streams again. In other words, data streams can be hierarchically composed into higher level event streams and decomposed later on again. The proposed technique is strictly compositional, hence highly suited for being embedded into well known performance evaluation frameworks such as Symta/S and MPA (Modular Performance Analysis). It is based on a novel characterization of structured event streams which we denote as Event Count Curves. They characterize the structure of event streams in which the individual events belong to a finite number of classes. This new concept avoids the explicit maintenance of stream-individual information when routing a composed stream through a network of system components. Nevertheless it allows an arbitrary composition and decomposition of sub-streams at any stage of the distributed event processing. For evaluating our approach we analyze a realistic case-study and compare the obtained results with other existing techniques.

Categories and Subject Descriptors   C.3 [*Computer Systems Organization*]: Special-Purpose and Application-Based Systems—Real-time and Embedded Systems;   C.4 [*Computer Systems Organization*]: Performance of Systems—Modeling techniques

General Terms   Design, Verification, Theory

1. Introduction

1.1 Motivation

The design of stream-based distributed embedded systems poses tremendous difficulties in terms of efficiency and predictability. In particular, the various event streams that provide communication between the system components interact and interfere on joint re-sources such as buses, bridges, routers and communication networks. In a similar way, components of the application that are responsible for processing the data packets interfere in terms of their timing behavior on shared computing resources such as microprocessors, digital signal processors or dedicated computing components.

Accurate performance analysis is a central step in the design of distributed and parallel embedded systems. This fact is based on its role during design space exploration for early performance analysis as well as on its instrumental role for final system validation after the design is finished. It is widely acknowledged that models and methods for system-wide performance analysis need to satisfy a few requirements such as (a) coverage of possible system behaviors, (b) accuracy of the obtained results and (c) computational efficiency of the deployed evaluation tools.

Previous research developed a rich methodology for carrying out analytic performance analysis. Furthermore, the employed methods such as the Modular Performance Analysis (MPA) [3, 14], SymTA/S [6], MAST [9], and holistic methods [10] resulted in a range of mature software tools for carrying out the analysis of system designs. As main feature, the developed workbenches allow to compute key characteristics like buffer sizes, event delays and resource utilization rates. In contrast to an empirical approach as provided by system simulation, the analytic methodologies are exhaustive, i.e., they cover all possible system behaviors such that one obtains hard bounds on the above characteristics. Furthermore, some of the above mentioned approaches are compositional, hence they are computationally efficient, scale with system sizes and allow to analyze distributed heterogeneous embedded systems with a wide range of resource arbitration and scheduling principles.

However, one of the major drawbacks of the above mentioned analytic methods for performance analysis is their restricted modeling scope. Each of the methods has an associated model of computation which covers computation, resource sharing, and communication among others. A loss in analysis accuracy can be expected if the system under analysis does not closely fit the class of models that is directly supported. As a result, there is a great interest in extending the underlying model of computation for each of the compositional methods.

In distributed embedded systems that involve complex communication systems such as networks or buses, one can very often find a highly relevant design pattern which (a) merges different event streams into a single one and (b) extracts different types of event streams from a single stream based on event type information. For example, data from different streams could be combined in packets and transmitted jointly over a communication channel. In [11], the combined data stream is denoted as hierarchical event stream (HES). Once a packet has been successfully delivered and arrives at the end-point of the communication channel, the data have to be de-packaged, i. e. the hierarchical event stream has to be decomposed

---

* This work is funded by the European Union project COMBEST under grant number 215543 and by the Swiss National Science Foundation under grant number 200020-116594.

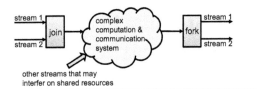

stream 1
stream 2
join
complex computation & communication system
fork
stream 1
stream 2

other streams that may interfer on shared resources

Figure 1. Joining and forking of streams.

into the individual data streams. Another related scenario is the simple merging of event or data streams from different sources without packaging, the joint processing or communication of the corresponding individual events or data packets and finally, the splitting of the joined data stream in its individual streams, see Fig. 1.1.

In this paper, we introduce a major extension to the aforementioned methods that allows to join and fork event streams with high accuracy. Furthermore, we keep the compositionality of the analysis methodology in contrast to all other known methods: The proposed extension based on Event Count Curves is completely transparent to all other analysis components, i.e. they can be used without any change and can ignore the fact that the modeled subsystem computes or communicates joined event streams. As a result, one of the main prerequisites for a compositional performance analysis is met.

1.2 Contributions and outline of the work

The paper contains the following new results:

- We propose two new approaches to analyze the processing and communication of joined event streams in modular system performance analysis. The first approach uses the principle of FIFO scheduling (first-in-first-out) to manage event hierarchies whereas the second approach uses Event Count Curves.
- The concept of Event Count Curves is shown to be orthogonal to previously used stream models such as PJD (periodic with jitter) and arrival curves. Therefore, compositionality of previous analysis methods is not affected as the new representation is transparent to all other analysis components.
- We extend the analysis method based on Event Count Curves in order to support *arbitrary* decompositions of streams.
- Experiments compare the different available methods (hierarchical event streams [11], FIFO scheduling, ECC) and a realistic application scenario (heterogeneous communication system) is analyzed in detail.

Organization of the paper: Section 2 discusses related work. In Section 3 we give details about the Modular Performance Analysis (MPA) framework [3, 13] adopted in this paper. We introduce a small application scenario in Section 4 which will be used to illustrate the proposed methods. In Sections 5 and 6 we present two different approaches to deal with structured event streams. The first approach is considering FIFO scheduling while the second uses a new concept denoted as Event Count Curves. Finally, in Section 7, we evaluate the proposed methods by means of a realistic case study and conclude our work in Section 8.

2. Related Work

Recently, Rox et al. [11] introduced the concept of Hierarchical Event Streams (HES) that allow to embed different types of streams in a higher level structure and proposed a Hierarchical Event Model (HEM) to represent such hierarchical streams. The key of the approach are the so-called inner event streams that are embedded in the HES bounding the event occurrences of events related to an individual input stream. When an operation is applied to the HES, i.e. the stream is processed in a task, an inner update function keeps track of the status of the inner event streams. Therefore, the HES can be decomposed into the individual streams whenever needed. The authors demonstrated significant improvements in terms of tightness of the

worst case response time by using HEM instead of flat event stream models. However, the method is not transparent to the component models: The components need to explicitly handle the HES and their analysis requires a deep processing of HEM.

Albers [1] uses a hierarchical data structure to describe repetitively occurring patterns within event streams. Since such scenarios refer to the combination of streams, the authors also refer to their approach as hierarchical event stream. Nevertheless, the topic faced in the present work is not related to the work of [1], since it does not assume any pattern of event occurrence.

In this paper, we use the Modular Performance Analysis (MPA) based on Real-Time Calculus, as described in [3, 13, 14], as the basis for our analysis. With this compositional approach, a system is modeled as a set of components interconnected by streams representing the flow of events or resource units. However, contrary to other techniques, the streams are not defined on a straight time-line, but on the time-interval domain.

In the context of modular performance analysis methods, tasks activated by multiple inputs have been considered. In particular OR- and AND-activated tasks have been modeled, see [5, 8]. The OR-activation of tasks is closely related to the joining of event streams discussed in this work. But the results in [5, 8] do not allow to separate a joined stream again into its individual sub-streams. Timing correlations in the presence of simple split-join scenarios of event streams have been studied in [7, 12]. However, the present work is different, as we consider join and fork operations based on event types and focus on the structure of the joined streams.

FIFO scheduling has been considered in Network Calculus, see [2]. The results are related to the service that is given to individual streams that are processed in a FIFO order by some resource. These results closely relate to one of our approaches to model hierarchical event streams.

3. Analytic Real-time Performance Analysis

The authors of [3, 13] extend the classical Network Calculus [4] towards the analysis of embedded real-time systems. The obtained compositional methodology is denoted as Modular Performance Analysis (MPA) and allows the computation of upper and lower bounds on key performance metrics, such as delays, buffer sizes and resource utilizations. In the following, we will briefly summarize some basic concepts of MPA that are necessary for the paper.

Event stream model: Event streams are abstracted by a pair $\alpha(\Delta) = [\alpha^u(\Delta), \alpha^l(\Delta)]$ of upper and lower arrival curves which provide an upper and a lower bound on the number of events in *any* time interval of length Δ. Let $R(s, t)$ denote the number of events that arrive in the time interval $[s, t)$. Then the following inequality holds

$$\alpha^l(t - s) \le R(s, t) \le \alpha^u(t - s), \qquad (1)$$

with $s < t$ and $\alpha^l(0) = \alpha^u(0) = 0$. Arrival curves generalize classical event stream models such as sporadic, periodic or periodic with jitter.

Resource model: The availability of processing or communication resources is abstracted by a pair $\beta(\Delta) = [\beta^u(\Delta), \beta^l(\Delta)]$ of upper and lower service curves which provide an upper and a lower bound on the available service in *any* time interval of length Δ. The service is expressed in an appropriate unit such as number of cycles for a processing resource or number of bytes for a communication resource. Let $C(s, t)$ denote the number of service units available from a resource in the time interval $[s, t)$. Then the following inequality holds

$$\beta^l(t - s) \le C(s, t) \le \beta^u(t - s), \qquad (2)$$

with $s < t$ and $\beta^l(0) = \beta^u(0) = 0$.

Component model ana analysis: In distributed embedded systems event streams are typically processed by several HW/SW components. In the framework of MPA such processing or communication components are represented by abstract performance components that act as curve transformers in the domain of arrival and service curves. The particular transfer function depends on the modeled processing semantics. A typical example for an abstract performance component in MPA is a Greedy Processing Component (GPC), shown in Fig. 2(a). It models a task that is triggered by the events of an input event stream α and produces a stream of output events α'. The input events queue up in a FIFO buffer. The task greedily processes the events in the buffer, while being restricted by the availability of processing resources β. The amount of remaining processing resources is characterized by β'. On the basis of min- and max-plus algebra, the MPA framework permits to compute the outputs α' and β' of a GPC as function of the inputs α and β, see, e.g., [14]:

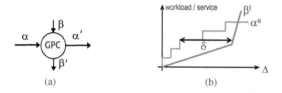

Figure 2. (a) Abstract Greedy Processing Component (b) Graphical interpretation of delay

$$\begin{aligned}
\alpha^{u\prime} &= \min\{(\alpha^u \otimes \beta^u) \oslash \beta^l, \beta^u\} \\
\alpha^{l\prime} &= \min\{(\alpha^l \oslash \beta^u) \otimes \beta^l, \beta^l\} \\
\beta^{u\prime} &= (\beta^u - \alpha^l)\overline{\oslash}\, 0 \\
\beta^{l\prime} &= (\beta^l - \alpha^u)\overline{\otimes}\, 0
\end{aligned} \quad (3)$$

Here we use the abbreviations

$$\begin{aligned}
(a \otimes b)(\Delta) &= \inf_{0 \le \lambda \le \Delta}\{a(\Delta - \lambda) + b(\lambda)\} \\
(a \oslash b)(\Delta) &= \sup_{\lambda \ge 0}\{a(\Delta + \lambda) - b(\lambda)\} \\
(a \overline{\otimes} b)(\Delta) &= \sup_{0 \le \lambda \le \Delta}\{a(\Delta - \lambda) + b(\lambda)\} \\
(a \overline{\oslash} b)(\Delta) &= \inf_{\lambda \ge 0}\{a(\Delta + \lambda) - b(\lambda)\}
\end{aligned} \quad (4)$$

which are denoted as min-plus and max-plus convolution and deconvolution operators, respectively. The response time experienced by an event at a GPC satisfies the following upper bound:

$$\delta = \sup_{\lambda \ge 0}\left\{\inf\{\tau \ge 0 \,:\, \alpha^u(\lambda) \le \beta^l(\lambda + \tau)\}\right\} \quad (5)$$

Graphically, δ is given as the largest horizontal distance between the upper arrival curve (maximally requested service) and the lower service curve (minimally offered service), see Fig. 2(b). Note that the above equations assume that the arrival and service curves are expressed in the same unit. In particular, we use workload-based arrival curves which are derived from event-based arrival curves as defined above by scaling with the best-case/worst-case resource demand of events. The workload-based interpretation of arrival curves applies also to Sec. 5, where we introduce a new abstract performance component for the MPA framework.

Based on the above concepts, one can describe a complex embedded real-time system as a network of GPCs interacting via abstract bounding functions α and β. The sharing of resources is modeled by connecting the respective GPCs via outgoing and ingoing service curves, where the order of the GPCs reflects the fixed priorities of the modeled processing tasks. Other scheduling schemes like TDMA can be modeled by adapting the ingoing service curves accordingly.

4. Motivational Example

In this section we introduce a simple application scenario of a multi-processor system in which different data flows are merged, processed, and separated again. The system will serve as example throughout the paper and will be used to illustrate the presented

methods. In Section 6.5 we provide the analysis of the system and discuss the obtained results.

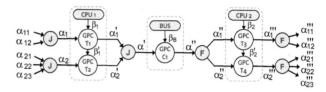

Figure 3. MPA model of example system

The MPA model of the considered system is shown in Figure 3. It contains various event streams abstracted by arrival curves α that model the flow of data through the system. The system consists of several computation and communication tasks, which are represented as GPC components in the MPA model. The service curves β represent the amount of computation or communication resources available to the single tasks.

The system processes five input event streams α_{ij} that are joined (J) and forked (F) several times between the various processing components. For the joining of streams we assume 'OR' semantics. This means that the join operator produces one output event for each input event arriving on any of the inputs. We assume that the events of the joined stream are still distinguishable with respect to their provenance. In particular, we will talk about events 'of type e_x' to say that they origin from stream α_x and we will adopt this notation also in the reminder of the paper. Note that in the case of successive joins, the single events of the joined stream belong to several types. For instance, in the model shown in Figure 3, an event in the stream α' originating from stream α_{12} is of type e_1 but at the same time of type e_{12}. For the forking of streams we assume that every input event is forwarded to only one output stream, depending on its type. In the figure, the indices of the event streams denote the paths of the different event types. For instance, the streams represented by α_{21} and α_{21}''' contain events of the same type.

We assume that both CPU1 and CPU2 implement a preemptive fixed-priority scheduling policy, where task T1 has higher priority than task T2, and task T3 has higher priority than task T4. Note that this scheduling policy is modeled by properly connecting the service inputs/outputs of the GPC components. For instance, the output service curve of GPC_{T1} is used as input service curve for GPC_{T2}, which represents the fact that T2 gets only the resources left over by T1.

For simplicity, we assume that all input event streams are periodic streams with jitter and that the tasks are characterized by best-case and worst-case execution times (BCET, WCET). The corresponding parameters can be found in Table 1. The goal of the analysis is to characterize the output event streams as precisely as possible.

Stream	Period	Jitter		Task	BCET	WCET
α_{11}	100	30		T1	2	3
α_{12}	90	15		T2	3	4
α_{21}	30	0		C1	9	12
α_{22}	80	20		T3	2	3
α_{23}	75	5		T4	4	5

Table 1. Parameters for the example system

Terminology: Note that in this paper we distinguish *simple* and *structured* event streams. The former term refers to an event stream in which all events have the same type. The latter is used for a stream in which the events have different types, i.e., belong to different substreams. In particular, a structured event stream results if we merge several simple (or structured) event streams. Note further, that in this paper we use the terms 'structured stream' and 'joined stream' interchangeably.

5. FIFO Scheduling

A first way to model the processing of joined event streams in system level performance analysis is to keep the individual substreams separated in the representation of the system and to adapt the existing models of the processing and communication components such that they can explicitly handle multiple input streams. To this end, we introduce a new abstract component for the MPA framework that is based on FIFO scheduling. The use of such a component to represent the processing of a joined event stream is justified by the observation that the combination of two or more event streams preserves the arrival order of the individual events. A simple example of this modeling principle is shown in Figure 4. The left side of the figure shows the processing of a joined event stream by a task T. After the processing the stream is forked into its composing substreams. The right side of the figure shows the equivalent model making use of a FIFO component. The component represents the processing of two equivalent tasks T that are scheduled in FIFO order of their activations. The suggested modeling approach represents

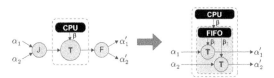

Figure 4. Processing of structured stream modeled by FIFO component

structured streams as bundles of distinct streams. Hence, each time a system processes a structured stream, in the MPA model this has to be considered by abstracting the corresponding task by means of a FIFO component processing a bundle of streams. In the following, we describe how such an abstract FIFO component can be realized in the context of MPA.

5.1 The FIFO component

An abstract FIFO component as depicted in Figure 5(a) models a set of tasks that share an available resource in a FIFO manner. The activation patterns of the individual tasks are bounded by n arrival curves $\alpha_1, \cdots, \alpha_n$. The service curve β bounds the availability of processing resources for the component. The FIFO component computes n arrival curves $\alpha'_1, \cdots, \alpha'_n$ that characterize the outgoing event streams and a service curve β' that captures the amount of remaining processing resources.

For the computation of β' we adapt the corresponding formulas of the GPC component reported in (3). In particular, as input event stream α we use the sum of all the input streams $\alpha_1, \cdots, \alpha_n$:

$$\beta'^u = (\beta^u - \sum_i \alpha_i^l)\overline{\oslash}0 \quad ; \quad \beta'^l = (\beta^l - \sum_i \alpha_i^u)\overline{\otimes}0 \quad (6)$$

To determine valid upper and lower bounds for the outgoing event streams, we first look at the maximum and minimum possible amount of resources available for the processing of the corresponding input stream, respectively. In particular, for the task associated with input stream α_i we consider the best case and the worst case in a fixed assignment of priorities, as shown in Figure 5(b). The corresponding service curves are given by:

$$\beta_i^u = \beta^u \quad ; \quad \beta_i^l = (\beta^l - \sum_{j \neq i} \alpha_j^u)\overline{\otimes}0 \quad (7)$$

Under FIFO scheduling, the amount of resources available for the processing of α_i can clearly only be less or equal than β_i^u and larger or equal than β_i^l and hence the two bounds are a valid abstraction. Given β_i^u and β_i^l, we can compute bounds for the corresponding outgoing event stream α'_i using the formulas for the GPC component

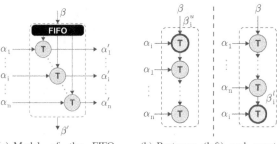

(a) Model of the FIFO Component in MPA

(b) Best-case (left) and worst-case (right) scenario for an event stream α_i under fixed priorities

Figure 5. Model of the FIFO Component

as given in (3):

$$\alpha_i'^u = \min\{(\alpha_i^u \otimes \beta_i^u) \oslash \beta_i^l, \beta_i^u\}$$
$$\alpha_i'^l = \min\{(\alpha_i^l \oslash \beta_i^u) \otimes \beta_i^l, \beta_i^l\} \quad (8)$$

6. Event count curves

The approach presented in the previous section allows to model arbitrary compositions and decompositions of event streams. However, it has a major drawback. It is not transparent to the existing modeling components of the MPA framework. In particular, it requires to explicitly adapt all the components of a system model that process a structured event stream. In this section we present a second approach to handle structured event streams. The method is based on Event Count Curves (ECC) and is totally orthogonal to the modeling of the processing semantics of components.

The method applies join and fork operations on event streams to compose and decompose structured streams. It relies on the fact that the order of the events in a stream is preserved no matter how many and what kind of components process the stream. Hence, when joining different event streams into one, we can store some information about the structure of the resulting stream and then use this information later, after arbitrary processing operations on the joined stream, to split it again into the corresponding sub-streams.

Obviously, we cannot store the exact pattern of the composition whenever we join different event streams in a model. This would not only lead to an unbearable overhead for the composition and decomposition of event streams, but is also not feasible in the abstraction of MPA which operates in the time-interval domain. However, for any sequence of events in a joined stream, we can still bound the number of events belonging to a given sub-stream, which is the main idea behind ECCs.

Note that the concept of ECCs is orthogonal to any event stream model such as PJD or arrival curves; event stream models describe the timing of event occurrences in a stream, whereas ECCs describe the occurrence of event types in a sequence of heterogeneous events. Note further, that ECCs are involved in join/fork operations of event streams only. They are completely transparent to the abstract performance components of an MPA model. This means that the components ignore whether or not they are processing a structured event stream and hence the ECCs are not affected by the processing. For this reason the computation of ECCs depends only on the arrival curves of the event streams involved in join/fork operations, but does not need to consider any service curves.

6.1 Definitions

Definition 1 (Structured Event Stream). *A structured event stream with event types e_i, $i \in I$ is described by a set of positive monotonically increasing arrival functions $R_i(s,t)$, $i \in I$, $s < t$. Given some* times s and t, then $R_i(s,t)$ denotes the number of events of type e_i that arrived in the time interval $[s,t]$.

In the context of MPA, we can characterize a structured event stream by a tuple of arrival curves bounding the total number of events in the stream, and by a tuple of ECCs for each of the composing sub-streams. Intuitively, an ECC bounds the number of events belonging to a particular sub-stream for a given number of consecutive events in the structured stream.

Definition 2 (Characterization of structured event streams). *A structured event stream can be characterized by a tuple of upper and lower arrival curves $\alpha(\Delta) = [\alpha^l(\Delta), \alpha^u(\Delta)]$, $\Delta \geq 0$ and a set of upper and lower ECCs $\gamma_i(n) = [\gamma_i^l(n), \gamma_i^u(n)]$, $n \geq 0$, one for each event type e_i, $i \in I$. In particular, the upper and lower arrival curves bound the number of events in any time interval, i.e. for all $s < t$, $i \in I$ we have*

$$\alpha^l(t-s) \leq \sum_{i \in I} R_i(s,t) \leq \alpha^u(t-s) \qquad (9)$$

The upper and lower ECCs bound the number of events of type e_i within a certain number of events, i.e. for all $s < t$, $i \in I$ we have

$$\gamma_i^l\left(\sum_{j \in I} R_j(s,t)\right) \leq R_i(s,t) \leq \gamma_i^u\left(\sum_{j \in I} R_j(s,t)\right) \qquad (10)$$

For the single sub-streams we can again define arrival curves that bound the number of events in any time interval:

Definition 3 (Arrival curves for sub-streams). *For each event type e_i, $i \in I$, of a structured event stream the arrival curves $\alpha_i(\Delta) = [\alpha_i^l(\Delta), \alpha_i^u(\Delta)]$, $\Delta \geq 0$, satisfy*

$$\alpha_i^l(t-s) \leq R_i(s,t) \leq \alpha_i^u(t-s) \qquad (11)$$

for all $s < t$.

Let us now illustrate the concept of ECCs by means of a simple example.

Example 1. *Consider two strict periodical event streams α_1 and α_2 with periods $p1 = 10$ and $p2 = 20$, respectively. Two example traces for the two streams are shown on the left side of Figure 6(a). Consider now the structured stream α obtained by joining α_1 and α_2. A representative trace for α is shown on the right side of Figure 6(a). The ECCs γ_1 and γ_2 describing the structure of the joined stream α are depicted in Figure 6(b). For any number of consecutive events in α, γ_1 and γ_2 give upper and lower bounds on the number of possible occurrences of events of type 1 and 2, respectively. For instance, for 4 consecutive events in the structured stream α, at least 2 and at most 3 events are of type 1, or in short, $\gamma_1^l(4) = 2$ and $\gamma_1^u(4) = 3$.*

Note that ECCs are defined for integer values only. In the representation of Figure 6(b) the interconnecting lines are shown for illustration purposes only.

In the following we will also need the concept of pseudo-inverses of arrival curves and ECCs.

Definition 4 (Pseudo-inverse of arrival curve). *The pseudo-inverses of upper and lower arrival curves $\alpha(\Delta) = [\alpha^l(\Delta), \alpha^u(\Delta)]$ are defined as*

$$\begin{aligned} \alpha^{-l}(n) &= \sup\{\Delta \geq 0 : \alpha^l(\Delta) \leq n\} \\ \alpha^{-u}(n) &= \inf\{\Delta \geq 0 : \alpha^u(\Delta) \geq n\} \end{aligned} \qquad (12)$$

Lower and upper arrival curves $\alpha^l(\Delta)$ and $\alpha^u(\Delta)$ denote the minimum and maximum number of events that may arrive in a stream in any time interval of length $\Delta \in \mathbb{R}^+$, respectively. Their pseudo-inverses have the following meaning: $\alpha^{-l}(n)$ denotes the length of the longest time interval in which there can be n event arrivals in the stream; $\alpha^{-u}(n)$ denotes the length of the shortest time interval with n event arrivals.

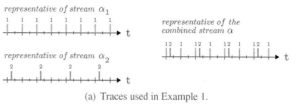

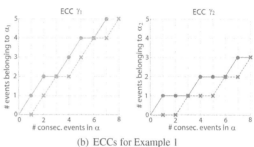

(a) Traces used in Example 1.

(b) ECCs for Example 1

Figure 6. Example traces and ECCs of Ex. 1

Definition 5 (Pseudo-inverse of ECC). *The pseudo-inverses of upper and lower ECCs $\gamma_i(n) = [\gamma_i^l(n), \gamma_i^u(n)]$ are defined as*

$$\begin{aligned} \gamma^{-l}(n_i) &= \sup\{n \geq 0 : \gamma_i^l(n) \leq n_i\} \\ \gamma^{-u}(n_i) &= \inf\{n \geq 0 : \gamma_i^u(n) \geq n_i\} \end{aligned} \qquad (13)$$

Lower and upper ECCs $\gamma_i^l(n)$ and $\gamma_i^u(n)$ denote the minimum and maximum number of events of type e_i in any sequence of $n \in \mathbb{N}$ events of the structured stream, respectively. Their pseudo-inverses are interpreted as follows: $\gamma_i^{-l}(n_i)$ denotes the maximum length of an event sequence that contains n_i events of type e_i; $\gamma_i^{-u}(n_i)$ denotes the minimum length of a sequence with n_i events of type e_i.

6.2 Join and Fork of Simple Event Streams

In the following, we show how ECCs can be computed when joining streams, and how they can be applied to split structured streams into sub-streams.

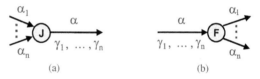

Figure 7. (a) Join operator for merging n simple event streams into one structured stream. (b) Fork operator for decomposing a structured event stream into n sub-streams.

Consider first the fork operator shown in Figure 7(b). Given the structured event stream and the various ECCs, we can derive the individual sub-streams as follows.

Theorem 1. *Given is a structured event stream with arrival curve α and ECCs γ_i, $i \in I$. Then we have*

$$\alpha_i^l(\Delta) = \gamma_i^l(\alpha^l(\Delta)) \quad ; \quad \alpha_i^u(\Delta) = \gamma_i^u(\alpha^u(\Delta)) \qquad (14)$$

Proof (Sketch): The evaluation of $\alpha^l(\Delta)$ gives the minimum number n of events in the structured stream for a given interval Δ. This number can be translated using γ_i^l which by definition determines the minimum number of events of type e_i in a sequence of n events in the structured stream. The proof for $\alpha^u(\Delta)$ is analogous. $\square$

Consider now the join operator shown in Figure 7(a). Given the individual streams $\alpha_1, \cdots, \alpha_n$ we can compute the resulting structured event stream and the individual ECCs as follows.

Theorem 2. *Given are n event streams with arrival curves $\alpha_1, \cdots, \alpha_n$ that are joined to a single event stream. Then the resulting structured event stream is characterized by the arrival curve*

$$\alpha(\Delta) = [\alpha^l(\Delta), \alpha^u(\Delta)] = \left[\sum_i \alpha_i^l, \sum_i \alpha_i^u \right]. \quad (15)$$

The ECCs of the structured event stream are determined by

$$\gamma_i(n) = [\gamma_i^l(n), \gamma_i^u(n)] = [\epsilon_i^{-u}(n), \epsilon_i^{-l}(n)] \quad (16)$$

with

$$\epsilon_i^u(n_i) = n_i + \sum_{j \neq i} \alpha_j^u(\alpha_i^{-l}(n_i))$$
$$\epsilon_i^l(n_i) = n_i + \sum_{j \neq i} \alpha_j^l(\alpha_i^{-u}(n_i)) \quad (17)$$

Proof (Sketch): The join operator forwards the events of all input streams without delay. Hence, for any time interval we have that the number of event arrivals in the structured stream is equal to the sum of the event arrivals in the individual sub-streams, which justifies (15). Formally, we can prove (15) by combining the inequalities (9) and (11).

For the computation of the ECCs, let us focus on $\gamma_i^l(n)$. The curve $\gamma_i^l(n)$ represents the minimum number n_i of events of type e_i in a sequence of n events of the structured stream. Consider now the pseudo-inverse of $\gamma_i^l(n)$ which we denote as $\epsilon_i^u(n_i)$. The curve $\epsilon_i^u(n_i)$ represents the maximum length n of an event sequence that contains n_i events of type e_i. Intuitively, we can determine $\epsilon_i^u(n_i)$ by constructing a scenario in which during a time interval there are n_i event arrivals in sub-stream α_i and as many event arrivals as possible in all the other sub-streams α_j with $j \neq i$. This is done by first considering the largest time interval Δ for which in sub-stream α_i there can be exactly n_i event arrivals, given by $\Delta = \alpha_i^{-l}(n_i)$. Successively, we determine the maximum number of event arrivals in all the other sub-streams in a time interval of length Δ. This is done by evaluating the sum of the corresponding upper arrival curves α_j^u. At this point we can easily determine $\epsilon_i^u(n_i)$, and hence, $\gamma_i^l(n)$. The derivation of $\gamma_i^u(n)$ is analogous. □

Note that in terms of $\alpha(\Delta)$, the above described join operator is equivalent to the OR-composition of the input streams $\alpha_1, \cdots, \alpha_n$, as introduced in [5].

6.3 Hierarchical application of ECCs

In the presence of multiple successive join and fork operators, we can organize and apply ECCs in an hierarchical manner. Consider for instance the example system of Figure 3. We can model the joins and forks of streams in the system by the operators introduced in Section 6.2. In particular, by joining the streams α_{11} and α_{12} we will obtain the structured stream α_1 and two ECCs γ_{11} and γ_{12}. Similarly, the join of α_{21}, α_{22} and α_{23} will result in the structured stream α_2 and the ECCs γ_{21}, γ_{22} and γ_{23}. The processed event streams α_1' and α_2' are then joined again which yields the structured stream α' and two ECCs γ_1 and γ_2. Following the various stream compositions, we can organize the ECCs that describe the structure of the stream α' with respect to the different event types hierarchically. In particular, we can represent the hierarchy of event types by means of a tree, as shown in Figure 8. The edges of the tree represent ECCs that are applied to extract sub-streams from a structured stream

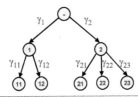

Figure 8. ECC hierarchy for the system of Figure 3

In the model of Figure 3, we can apply the described hierarchy of ECCs to fork the stream α'' into its composing sub-streams. In particular, we first apply γ_1 and γ_2 to fork α'' into α_{21}'' and α_{22}''. Successively, we fork α_{21}'' and α_{22}'' again by applying γ_{11}, γ_{12}, γ_{21}, γ_{22}, and γ_{23}.

6.4 Arbitrary Join and Fork of Structured Event Streams

The hierarchical organization of ECCs described above has a major disadvantage: The resulting structured stream can be decomposed only in the inverse order in which it has been composed. However, in order to enable the modeling of realistic systems, it is highly desirable to provide join/fork operators that allow an *arbitrary* decomposition of a structured stream into sub-streams, no matter how the structured stream was constructed. Consider again the motivational example introduced in Section 4. Assume that in the system the division of the event stream α'' is different from the one depicted in Figure 3. For instance, require that stream α_{21} needs to be processed by T3 instead of T4, that is, the composition and decomposition of the streams are not symmetrical. In such a case, with the ECC model described so far, we have no means to correctly abstract the system behavior.

In this section we tackle the above described problem and introduce more general join and fork operators that operate on *structured* event streams. The new operators allow to arbitrarily join and fork structured event streams by keeping the ECC hierarchy flat. That is to say that a structured stream is characterized only by ECCs referring to its *simple* sub-streams. ECCs referring to *structured* sub-streams will not be computed and forwarded any longer.

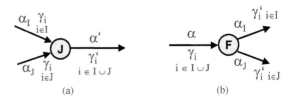

Figure 9. (a) Join operator for merging a two structured event streams. (b) Fork operator for decomposing a structured event stream into two structured sub-streams.

Consider the join operator shown in Figure 9(a). It merges two *structured* event streams α_I and α_J. In contrast to the case of a hierarchical organization of ECCs, this join operator computes a new ECC for all *simple* sub-streams composing the outgoing structured event stream. Hence, at any further point in the model it will be possible to isolate arbitrary subsets of the joined event streams. The outgoing structured event stream of the described join operator can be characterized as follows.

Theorem 3. *Assume that we join two structured event streams with arrival curves α_I and α_J and ECCs γ_i, $i \in I$ and γ_i, $i \in J$, respectively. Then the resulting structured event stream is characterized by the arrival curve*

$$\alpha'(\Delta) = [\alpha'^l(\Delta), \alpha'^u(\Delta)] = [\alpha_I^l(\Delta) + \alpha_J^l(\Delta), \alpha_I^u(\Delta) + \alpha_J^u(\Delta)] \quad (18)$$

The ECCs of the structured stream are determined by

$$\gamma_i'(n) = [\gamma_i'^l(n), \gamma_i'^u(n)] = [\gamma_i^l(\gamma_I^l(n)), \gamma_i^u(\gamma_I^u(n))] \quad (19)$$

for $i \in I$. Here, we use the partial ECCs for stream I

$$\gamma_I^l(n) = \epsilon_I^{-u}(n) \quad \gamma_I^u(n) = \epsilon_I^{-l}(n) \quad (20)$$

with

$$\epsilon_I^u(n_I) = n_I + \alpha_J^u(\alpha_I^{-l}(n_I)) \; ; \; \epsilon_I^l(n_I) = n_I + \alpha_J^l(\alpha_I^{-u}(n_I)) \quad (21)$$

The ECCs $\gamma_i'(n)$ for $i \in J$ are determined similarly.

42

Proof (Sketch): We have again that for any time interval the number of event arrivals in the joined output stream is equal to the sum of the event arrivals in the two input streams, which justifies (18).

For the outgoing ECCs, let us focus on $\gamma'^{l}_{i}(n)$ with $i \in I$. We first ignore that α_I and α_J are structured streams, and apply the join operator described in Theorem 2. This yields the ECC $\gamma^{l}_{I}(n)$ that defines the minimum number of events that belong to stream α_I in a sequence of n events of the structured stream α'. At this point we consider that α_I is a structured stream itself. Hence, given a sequence of events of α_I, by applying the ECC γ^{l}_{i} we can determine the minimum number of events of type e_i in the sequence. This leads to $\gamma'^{l}_{i}(n) = \gamma^{l}_{i}(\gamma^{l}_{I}(n))$. The derivation of $\gamma'^{u}_{i}(n)$ is analogous. $\square$

The above theorem can easily be extended to more than two inputs.

Finally, consider the fork operator shown in Figure 9(b), which splits a structured event stream into two *structured* event streams α_I and α_J. The outgoing structured event streams can be characterized as follows.

Theorem 4. *Given is a structured event stream with arrival curve $\alpha(\Delta)$ and ECCs $\gamma_i(n)$, $i \in I \cup J$. Then the arrival curve $\alpha_I(\Delta) = [\alpha^{l}_{I}(\Delta), \alpha^{u}_{I}(\Delta)]$ of a sub-stream I with event types e_i, $i \in I$, is characterized by by the bounds*

$$\alpha^{l}_{I}(\Delta) \geq \sum_{i \in I} \gamma^{l}_{i}(\alpha^{l}(\Delta)) \qquad (22)$$

$$\alpha^{l}_{I}(\Delta) \geq \max\left\{ \inf_{\lambda \geq \Delta}\left\{ \alpha^{l}(\lambda) - \sum_{i \in J}\gamma^{u}_{i}(\alpha^{u}(\lambda)) \right\}, 0 \right\} \qquad (23)$$

and

$$\alpha^{u}_{I}(\Delta) \leq \sum_{i \in I}\gamma^{u}_{i}(\alpha^{u}(\Delta)) \qquad (24)$$

$$\alpha^{u}_{I}(\Delta) \leq \sup_{0 \leq \lambda \leq \Delta}\left\{ \alpha^{u}(\lambda) - \sum_{i \in J}\gamma^{l}_{i}(\alpha^{l}(\lambda)) \right\} \qquad (25)$$

The arrival curve $\alpha_J(\Delta)$ is derived in analogous manner. The ECCs $\gamma'_i(n) = [\gamma'^{l}_{i}(n), \gamma'^{u}_{i}(n)]$ with $i \in I$ are characterized by the bounds

$$\gamma'^{l}_{i}(n) \geq g^{-u}_{i}(n) \qquad \gamma'^{l}_{i}(n) \geq f^{-u}_{i}(n) \qquad (26)$$

$$\gamma'^{u}_{i}(n) \leq g^{-l}_{i}(n) \qquad \gamma'^{u}_{i}(n) \leq f^{-l}_{i}(n) \qquad (27)$$

with

$$g^{u}_{i}(n_i) = n_i + \sum_{k \in I\setminus\{i\}}\gamma^{u}_{k}(\gamma^{-l}_{i}(n_i)) \qquad (28)$$

$$f^{u}_{i}(n_i) = \sup_{0 \leq \lambda \leq n_i}\left\{ \gamma^{-l}_{i}(\lambda) - \sum_{k \in J}\gamma^{l}_{k}(\gamma^{-u}_{i}(\lambda)) \right\} \qquad (29)$$

$$g^{l}_{i}(n_i) = n_i + \sum_{k \in I\setminus\{i\}}\gamma^{l}_{k}(\gamma^{-u}_{i}(n_i)) \qquad (30)$$

$$f^{l}_{i}(n_i) = \max\left\{ \inf_{\lambda \geq n_i}\left\{ \gamma^{-u}_{i}(\lambda) - \sum_{k \in J}\gamma^{u}_{k}(\gamma^{-l}_{i}(\lambda)) \right\}, 0 \right\} \qquad (31)$$

The ECCs $\gamma'_i(n)$ with $i \in J$ are characterized in analogous manner.

Due to space constraints, we do not prove the above theorem. We will, however, illustrate the idea behind the above formulae. Let us start with the bounds for $\alpha^{l}_{I}(\Delta)$. The curve $\alpha^{l}_{I}(\Delta)$ represents the minimum number of events that are seen on the upper output stream in any interval of length Δ. In order to compute $\alpha^{l}_{I}(\Delta)$, we consider $\alpha^{l}(\Delta)$, the minimum number of events on the input stream, and determine how many of those events do certainly belong to α_I. This can be done in two ways. We can either use the ECCs γ^{l}_{i}, $i \in I$, to determine how many events do certainly belong to the individual sub-streams of α_I and then compute their sum, as shown in (22). Alternatively, we can subtract from $\alpha^{l}(\Delta)$ the maximum

number of events that can possibly belong to α_J, as shown in (23). For $\alpha^{u}_{I}(\Delta)$ the reasoning is analogous. Note that when we compute the difference of arrival curves, we have to use appropriate sup or inf operators to guarantee the monotonicity of the resulting curve.

Let us now consider the bounds for the outgoing ECCs. The approach for the computation of $\gamma'^{l}_{i}(n)$ relies on the same idea as adopted in Theorem 2, namely by deriving a bound for the pseudo-inverse of the unknown curve. In this case, the pseudo-inverse of $\gamma'^{l}_{i}(n)$ represents the maximum length n of an event sequence in α_I that contains n_i events of type e_i. In order to bound it, we first consider $\gamma^{-l}_{i}(n_i)$, the maximum length of a sequence on the input stream α that contains n_i events of type e_i, and then determine how many of those events can at most belong to α_I. This can again be done in two ways: Using the ECCs γ^{u}_{k}, $k \in I \setminus \{i\}$, as shown in (28), or using the ECCs γ^{l}_{k}, $k \in J$, as shown in (29). The ECCs $\gamma'^{u}_{i}(n)$ are determined similarly.

6.5 Analysis of Motivational Example

In this section we compare the analysis results of the different proposed approaches for the example system introduced in Section 4. We first build three new MPA models for the system of Figure 3. In the first one we apply the method described in Section 5, that is, we use FIFO components with multiple inputs instead of the depicted GPCs. In the second model, we adopt hierarchies of ECCs as described in Section 6.3. In particular, the tree of Figure 8 is used to model the structure of the streams α' and α''. The third model is based on a flat organization of ECCs as described in Section 6.4. Thus, it contains two ECCs for α_1 and α'_1, five ECCs for α' and α'', etc. Note that in the two latter models we can employ standard GPCs, as shown in Figure 3, that are not affected by the structure of their input event stream.

We use the three models to bound the five output streams of the system. The Figures 10 and 11 depict the results achieved for the output curves α'''_{12} and α'''_{21}. The figures show that the two approaches based on FIFO scheduling and on hierarchically organized ECCs provide similar results. For the output stream α'''_{12} the FIFO approach determines tighter (i.e., less conservative) bounds. For the output stream α'''_{21} the approach based on hierarchical ECCs is tighter. The method based on the flat organization of ECCs provides the worst bounds for both output streams, with local exceptions as α'''^{u}_{21} shows. However, as pointed out earlier, it is the only method applicable in scenarios with unsymmetrical join and fork operations (which is not the case in the described example) and hence it is still highly useful in general.

We also compare the results of the proposed approaches with the bounds obtained when applying the method described in [11]. The figures show that the HEM of [11] provide slightly better bounds than the proposed approaches. However, it has to be noted that, in contrast to the HEM of [11], the approaches based on ECCs do not affect the compositionality of previous analysis methods and are totally transparent to the modeling of processing components.

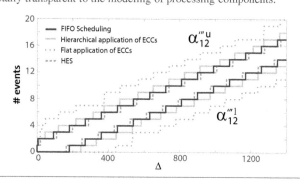

Figure 10. Results for the characterization of stream α'''_{12}

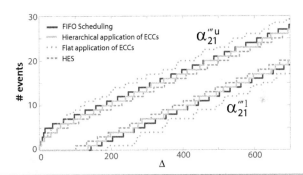

Figure 11. Results for the characterization of stream α'''_{21}

7. Case Study

In this section we show how the proposed theory can be applied to the analysis of a realistic distributed embedded system. We consider a heterogeneous communication system which we denote shortly as HCS. The HCS implements a distributed information/audio streaming application deployed in the waiting lounge of a large railway station.

General System Description

The system consists of various devices connected by a communication network. In particular, the HCS comprises a central server (SERV), an Ethernet backbone network, and a large number of end-devices (DEV). We assume that there are n network controllers (NC) connected in a chain along the backbone network and that m distinct end-devices are connected to each NC. Figure 12 shows the architecture of the HCS for the case $n = 3$, $m = 3$.

We assume that there is an end-device for each seat of the lounge. The main function of the end-devices is the playback of audio streams transmitted over the backbone network from the server. We consider an on-demand audio system where each traveler can choose its individual audio content from a large database stored on the server. Hence we assume that the audio streams are transmitted in unicast mode, meaning that for each end-device there is a dedicated data stream from the server to the device. Besides on-demand audio streaming, the server executes a second application, namely the periodic broadcast of live train arrival/departure information (shortly denoted as status data) over the backbone network. We assume that in the lounge there are a number of LCDs connected to some of the NCs in the system, displaying the transmitted live status data.

In this case study we focus on the *communication* between the components of the HCS. In particular, we are going to analyze the timing of the data transmissions over the links of the described network. We will neglect the *computations* carried out by the components themselves, i.e., we will not consider the execution times of the various processes on the server and the end-devices.

We consider a scenario in which the HCS provides different QoS for the two different kinds of network traffic (audio streams and status data). In particular, we assume that for the transmission of frames over the outgoing links both, the server and the NCs, implement a preemptive fixed-priority arbitration policy where audio traffic has higher priority than status traffic. This means that an ongoing transmission of status data over a link will be interrupted whenever there is an audio frame to be transmitted over the same link. The interrupted transmission will be resumed as soon as the link is free again. For the sake of simplicity, we assume that the transmission of frames can be interrupted and resumed at any time without need of retransmitting previously send data.

The goal of the analysis is to determine whether the frames with status data will reach their destination within a given deadline under the described arbitration policy. To keep the illustration of the proposed methods simple, we will restrict ourselves to the analysis

of the small system architecture shown in Figure 12. In order to still show meaningful effects, we choose an accordingly small bandwidth for the Ethernet backbone network.

Detailed specification

We consider a full duplex Ethernet backbone network with a bandwidth of 5 Mbit/s. We are interested in the traffic from the server to the end-devices only. We assume that the server sends an individual audio stream to each of the nine devices shown in Figure 12. Without loss of generality we index the audio streams with the number of the corresponding destination device. We consider audio streams with a net data rate of 384 kbit/s. The server partitions the data of each audio stream in frames of constant size. The audio frames are send to the network periodically with a small jitter. The complete specification of the audio traffic in the network is given in the upper part of Table 2.

	Size	Period	Jitter	Deadline
Audio Frames	1'518 Bytes	30 ms	5 ms	100 ms
Status Frames	106'500 Bytes	5 s	0 s	1.5 s

Table 2. Characteristics of the network traffic

The server also periodically sends status data to the LCD. We assume that all the needed data is transmitted in a single frame of constant size. The details for the transmission of status frames are specified in Table 2. The aim of the analysis is to clarify whether each status frame is guaranteed to reach its destination within the specified deadline.

Models and Analysis

In the following we are going to describe how the specified system can be modeled using the different methods proposed in this paper to handle join/fork scenarios of event streams. In order to obtain a baseline for the comparison of the new methods, we also build a rough model of the system behavior using the classic MPA abstraction, where join/fork scenarios cannot be faithfully represented.

The common basic abstraction of the models is to represent the frame traffic in the network by means of timed event streams. This allows to model communication components of the network such as data links by means of abstract components that process event streams. Figure 17 illustrates the basic modeling principle. The abstract processing components are triggered by incoming events which represent frames that need to be transmitted over the corresponding link. The processing time of an event in the abstract component corresponds to the transmission time of the frame in the concrete network component. The completion of a frame transmission is represented by the generation of an event on the output of the abstract component.

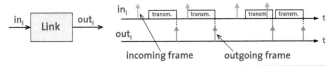

Figure 17. Frame transmission modeled as processing of timed event streams

In the MPA modeling framework event streams on the conventional time-line are abstracted by arrival curves in the time-interval domain. Hence, in the MPA models of the HCS we have to capture the timing behavior of all streams by means of appropriate arrival curves. In particular, exploiting the periodic nature of the streams, we can use the equations $\alpha^u(\Delta) = \left\lceil \frac{\Delta + \text{jitter}}{\text{period}} \right\rceil$, $\alpha^l(\Delta) = \left\lfloor \frac{\Delta - \text{jitter}}{\text{period}} \right\rfloor$ to the determine nine arrival curves $\alpha_1, \cdots, \alpha_9$ which

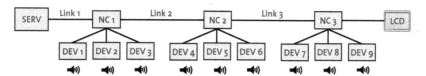

Figure 12. Application scenario

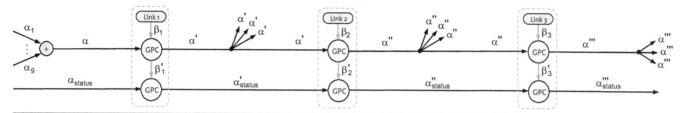

Figure 13. Model of communication system in classic MPA

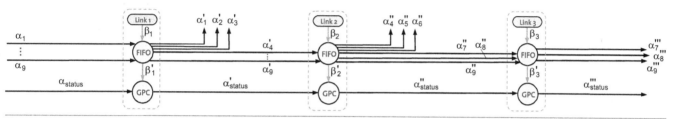

Figure 14. Model of communication system in MPA with FIFO components

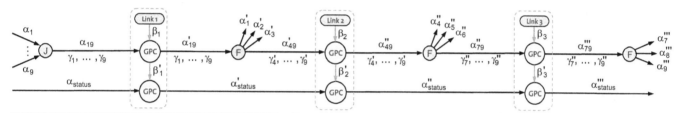

Figure 15. Model of communication system in MPA with ECCs (flat organization)

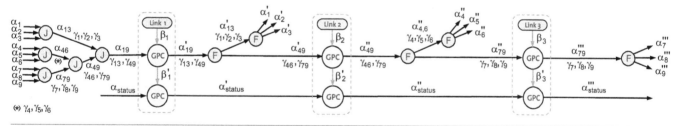

Figure 16. Model of communication system in MPA with ECCs (hierarchical organization)

represent the audio streams produced by the server. Similarly, we model the status stream by an arrival curve α_{status}. We use three service curves $\beta_1, \beta_2, \beta_3$ to represent the full availability of the three network links for the two considered traffic classes (audio streams and status stream). The fixed-priority arbitration policy described above is modeled by appropriately connecting the service curve inputs and outputs (β, β') of the abstract event processing components, as shown in Figure 13. The transmission times for the corresponding frames on the network links are derived from the frame sizes and the network bandwidth. They amount to 2.429 ms for audio frames and 170.4 ms for status frames.

Figure 13 shows a model of the HCS in the classic MPA framework, that is, without the methods introduced in this paper. The joining of the nine audio streams into a single stream is modeled by a simple sum of the corresponding arrival curves, which is a correct representation for the traffic sent over link 1. However, in contrast to the newly proposed methods, there is no means to decompose the resulting stream again into sub-streams. We can only forward the joined event stream to other components. Since in this model on the links 2 and 3 we represent more audio traffic than actually present in the real system, we expect overly conservative results for the worst-case end-to-end delay of status frames.

In Figure 14 we report the MPA model that makes use of the FIFO scheduling component as introduced in section 5. The models of the HCS that employ ECCs are shown in Figures 15 and 16. In the model of Figure 15 we consider a flat organization of the ECCs. Hence, whenever we have to branch off sub-streams from a structured stream, this can be done with one single fork operator as shown in the figure. In contrast, in the model of Figure 16 we join and fork sub-streams in an hierarchical manner.

Results

Table 3 summarizes the results of the performance analysis. It reports the worst-case end-to-end delay for status frames predicted by the different models. For the sake of simplicity, we compute the end-to-end delay as sum of the response times of the individual links. Tighter bounds for the end-to-end delay could potentially be obtained by considering that a status frame cannot experience the worst-case interference of audio frames consecutively on all three links. However, such a holistic analysis is more involved and out of the scope of this paper.

	Classic	FIFO	ECC (flat)	ECC (hierar.)
Max. delay	1.954 s	1.255 s	1.316 s	1.248 s

Table 3. Worst-case end-to-end delay for status frames derived with the different models

The table shows that the methods proposed in this paper to model join and fork scenarios of streams lead to considerably better results for the analysis of the HCS compared to the naive modeling approach of Figure 13. In particular, based on the classic MPA analysis, we would have to reject the designed system, as we could not guarantee that all status frames meet their deadline. On the other hand, the MPA models based on the abstract FIFO component or on ECCs show that the deadline for the transmission of status frames is never violated and hence the designed system fulfills the requirement. The reason for the better results is that the newly proposed methods permit to capture the amount of audio traffic on Links 2 and 3 more precisely than the naive MPA model. This is confirmed by the better worst-case bounds on the availability of Links 2 and 3 for the transmission of status frames. Figure 18 shows the improvement for the lower service bound β'^l_2 for Link 2. These improved bounds yield to the the tighter worst-case delay predictions.

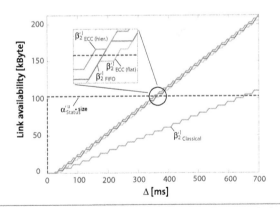

Figure 18. Minimum availability of Link 2 for the transmission of status frames (β'^l_2) determined by the different models. The dashed line (α'^u_{status}) represents the maximum demand of link capacity.

Table 3 and Figure 18 show that for the particular system under analysis, the model based on the hierarchical organization of ECCs turns out to be best. Nevertheless, the results achieved with a flat organization of ECCs are comparable and also the method based on abstract FIFO components provides similar results. However, as pointed out before, the FIFO technique requires the designer to stick to a particular model for the processing semantics of components and hence it is less general.

8. Conclusion

We introduced two new methods for the modeling and the analysis of joined event streams in modular system performance analysis. The methods allow to precisely capture the structure of joined event streams that are processed by the computation and communication components of distributed embedded systems. The first approach, based on FIFO scheduling, keeps individual sub-streams separated and extends the Modular Performance Analysis framework by a new abstract processing component. The second approach, based on Event Count Curves, explicitly handles the joining and forking of event streams and is totally transparent to existing modeling components. Hence, it is highly suited for being embedded into present modular performance analysis frameworks. We further extended the approach based on Event Count Curves such that arbitrary decompositions of event streams can be represented, which considerably extends the modeling scope of the method. By means of experiments we evaluated and compared the presented methodologies, and highlighted the utility of all proposed approaches. Finally, we demonstrated the applicability of the described methods by a analyzing a realistic application scenario.

References

[1] K. Albers, F. Bodmann, and F. Slomka. Hierarchical event streams and event dependency graphs: a new computational model for embedded real-time systems. *18th Euromicro Conference on Real-Time Systems*, pages 97–106, 2006.

[2] J.-Y. L. Boudec and P. Thiran. *Network Calculus: A Theory of Deterministic Queuing Systems for the Internet*, volume 2050 of *LNCS*. Springer, 2001.

[3] S. Chakraborty, S. Künzli, and L. Thiele. A general framework for analysing system properties in platform-based embedded system designs. In *Design Automation and Test in Europe (DATE)*, pages 190–195, Munich, Germany, Mar. 2003. IEEE Press.

[4] R. Cruz. A calculus for network delay, Parts 1 & 2. *IEEE Transactions on Information Theory*, 37(1), 1991.

[5] W. Haid and L. Thiele. Complex task activation schemes in system level performance analysis. In *Proc. 5th Intl Conf. on Hardware/Software Codesign and System Synthesis (CODES+ISSS 2007)*, pages 173–178, Salzburg, Austria, Oct. 2007. ACM Press.

[6] R. Henia, A. Hamann, M. Jersak, R. Racu, K. Richter, and R. Ernst. System level performance analysis-the SymTA/S approach. *IEE Proceedings-Computers and Digital Techniques*, 152(2):148–166, 2005.

[7] K. Huang, L. Thiele, T. Stefanov, and E. Deprettere. Performance analysis of multimedia applications using correlated streams. In *Design, Automation and Test in Europe (DATE 07)*, pages 912–917, Nice, France, Apr. 2007.

[8] M. Jersak and R. Ernst. Enabling scheduling analysis of heterogeneous systems with multi-rate data dependencies and rate intervals. In *Design Automation Conference, 2003. Proceedings*, pages 454–459, 2003.

[9] J. Pasaje, M. Harbour, and J. Drake. MAST real-time view: A graphic UML tool for modeling object-oriented real-time systems. In *22nd IEEE Real-Time Systems Symposium, 2001.(RTSS 2001). Proceedings*, pages 245–256, 2001.

[10] T. Pop, P. Eles, and Z. Peng. Holistic scheduling and analysis of mixed time/event-triggered distributed embedded systems. In *Proceedings of the 10th International Symposium on Hardware/Software Codesign*, pages 187–192. ACM New York, NY, USA, 2002.

[11] J. Rox and R. Ernst. Modeling event stream hierarchies with hierarchical event models. In *Design, Automation and Test in Europe (DATE 2008)*, pages 492–497, March 2008.

[12] S. Schliecker and R. Ernst. A recursive approach to end-to-end path latency computation in heterogeneous multiprocessor systems. In *Proceedings of the International Conference on Hardware-Software Codesign and System Synthesis 2009*, pages 433–442, 2009.

[13] L. Thiele, S. Chakraborty, and M. Naedele. Real-time calculus for scheduling hard real-time systems. In *IEEE International Symposium on Circuits and Systems (ISCAS 2000)*, volume 4, pages 101–104, Geneva, Switzerland, Mar. 2000.

[14] E. Wandeler, L. Thiele, M. Verhoef, and P. Lieverse. System architecture evaluation using modular performance analysis: a case study. *International Journal on Software Tools for Technology Transfer (STTT)*, 8(6):649–667, 2006.

Translating Concurrent Action Oriented Specifications to Synchronous Guarded Actions

Jens Brandt and Klaus Schneider

Embedded Systems Group
Department of Computer Science
University of Kaiserslautern, Germany
http://es.cs.uni-kl.de/

Sandeep K. Shukla

FERMAT Lab
Electrical and Computer Engineering
Virginia Tech, Blacksburg, VA, USA
http://www.fermat.ece.vt.edu/

Abstract

Concurrent Action-Oriented Specifications (CAOS) model the behavior of a synchronous hardware circuit as asynchronous guarded actions at an abstraction level higher than the Register Transfer Level (RTL). Previous approaches always considered the compilation of CAOS, which includes a transformation of the underlying model of computation and the scheduling of guarded actions per clock cycle, as a tightly integrated step. In this paper, we present a new compilation procedure, which separates these two tasks and translates CAOS models to synchronous guarded actions with an explicit interface to a scheduler. This separation of concerns has many advantages, including better analyses and integration of custom schedulers. Our method also generates assertions that each scheduler must obey that can be fulfilled by algorithms for scheduler synthesis like those developed in supervisory control. We present our translation procedure in detail and illustrate it by various examples. We also show that our method simplifies formal verification of hardware synthesized from CAOS specifications over previously known formal verification approaches.

Categories and Subject Descriptors   B.5.2 [*Hardware*]: Register-Transfer-Level Implementation—design aids; B.6.3 [*Hardware*]: Logic Design—design aids; D.3.4 [*Programming Languages*]: Processors—compilers and code generation; D.3.2 [*Programming Languages*]: Language Classifications—concurrent, distributed, and parallel languages

General Terms   Algorithms, Languages

Keywords   Concurrent Action-Oriented Specifications, Guarded Commands, Synchronous Languages, Code Generation

1. Introduction

Guarded actions are a well-established concept for the description of concurrent systems. With their original theoretical background in term rewriting systems, they have been used in many specification and verification formalisms, e. g. Dijkstra's guarded commands [7], Unity [5], Murφ [8], DisCo [12], or the Temporal Logic of Actions [13].

In recent years, guarded actions have also found their way into hardware synthesis. Concurrent Action-Oriented Specifications [10] model the behavior of a hardware circuit as guarded actions at an abstraction level higher than the RTL. Thus, they aim at describing the data-flow of a hardware circuit without fixing its timing but only its causalities. Thereby, developers can defer the difficult task of global scheduling and coordination to the compiler. The Bluespec language and compilation[1] is based on these considerations, and it has proven to be very efficient for synthesizing hardware from CAOS models. It transforms the set of asynchronous guarded actions into a synchronous model by merging so-called conflict-tree transitions, which are executed (a. k. a. fired) in the same clock cycle.

Guarded actions are also very useful for the compilation of imperative synchronous languages like the Quartz language [4, 17, 19]. They are used as an intermediate code format, which abstracts from the various control-flow features and their complicated semantics, so that synthesis tools only have to read code with a simple semantics. While synchronous guarded actions have the same structure as guarded actions in all the other formalisms, they have a different underlying model of computation.

In general, a guarded action (which is often referred to as a *rule* in CAOS) has the form $\langle \gamma \Rightarrow \mathcal{C} \rangle$. The Boolean condition γ is called the guard and $\mathcal{C}$ is called the body of the guarded action, which usually modifies the variables over which the guards are defined. The intuition behind guarded actions is that the body is executed if the whole action is activated, i. e. if and only if its guard evaluates to true in the current state.

Usually, and in particular in CAOS, guarded actions are seen as an asynchronous model. In the current state, the guards of all actions are checked and subsequently, any one among the activated actions is selected and subsequently its body is executed. Inside the body, there are multiple statements which are considered to execute in parallel. We consider this model as an asynchronous one because there is no notion of synchronous execution of multiple rules in this reference semantics of CAOS. Rules execute one by one as their guards become true, and in the order the reference scheduler picks them. Note that the execution of behavior under this model of computation is also nondeterministic. As a result, a CAOS model under reference semantics is considered as a specification, and any possible execution behavior has to be implemented by a deterministic implementation. Hence, a deterministic implementation is one where a scheduler deterministically chooses the rules with certain predefined properties.

Synchronous guarded actions differ from that behavior: their model of computation does not only fire all activated actions, but

LCTES'10,   April 13–15, 2010, Stockholm, Sweden.

---

[1] http://www.bluespec.com/

the execution of the actions is postulated to happen simultaneously to the evaluation of the guards so that there may be interdependencies. In practice, this means that the execution follows the data dependencies between the actions. While this seems to be an unnatural model at first, this represents exactly the way a synchronous hardware circuit works: all computation and communication within a clock cycle happens more or less simultaneously according to the data dependencies. No synchrony assumption regarding execution time is required either in this execution model. Note that synchronous guarded actions provide a deterministic model, in the sense that all nondeterminism is pushed to the inputs. For a given input sequence, the execution sequence is determined, which is not the case for a CAOS model. This shows the distinction between the underlying models of computation. Therefore, the transformation of a CAOS model to a synchronous guarded action model requires to control the nondeterminism by some additional inputs. The stimuli to these inputs are then generated by schedulers. Since different schedulers may provide different stimuli that may not be compatible with the original CAOS model, the properties of acceptable schedulers must be provided by the transformation algorithm. Temporal assertions are one way to achieve this goal.

The contribution of this paper is the provision of a compilation procedure from CAOS to synchronous guarded actions. In contrast to previous work, which always considered the translation of the model of computation and the scheduling simultaneously, our approach separates these two tasks. From the original CAOS model, we do not construct one particular synchronous implementation, but we create synchronous guarded actions that cover all possible implementations. Since this model is deterministic, we encode the choice between all the possible schedules as additional inputs to the system which are constrained by generated assertions. Thus, linking a scheduler to the system which complies with the assertions results in one of the possible deterministic synchronous implementations that implement the original CAOS model.

In order to construct the scheduler constraints, we formally define the correctness preservation criterion, i. e. we fix the properties of the system which have to be obeyed by an implementation so that it is considered to be valid with respect to the original CAOS model. In principle, all previous definitions of conflict-free transitions had the same goal, but they were always made with consequences for a specific implementation in mind. Since we do not want to make any restrictions in advance, we aim at providing very general constraints, which are only implied by the CAOS semantics.

The separation of concerns does not only provide a better theoretical understanding of existing CAOS languages and synthesis tools such as Bluespec, but it also has many practical advantages: The representation as synchronous guarded actions allows us to carry out many analyses and optimizations known from the synchronous domain. In particular, specification and verification based on temporal logics becomes possible. Moreover, we can reuse synthesis tools for synchronous guarded actions (as provided by the Averest system[2]), which support hardware and software as targets.

Since the scheduler is not compiled into the system, it is possible to verify an unscheduled CAOS model within this context, i. e. it is possible to prove system properties which do not depend on a concrete scheduler. From the theoretical side, it is even possible to create a scheduler according to a specified property using supervisory control [14, 27]. One can contrast this against [26] where verification always considers models that integrate data-flow and scheduling, even for properties that only depend on one part. In our approach, this can be separated, and substantially simplified. In addition, the framework makes it possible to create custom schedulers according to some requirements (e. g. latency, peak-power require-

ments [25]) and link them to the translated model. With the help of the previously created assertions, the resulting system can be checked for correctness before synthesis. Thereby, custom schedulers can be generated by any tool and their correctness can be formally verified. Currently, developers cannot describe schedulers separately, they only have the possibility to encode them by compiler options or explicitly in the system model. Especially the last alternative is infeasible if several variants of a system are generated, which only differ in nonfunctional requirements reflected in the scheduler.

As far as we know, the closest paper to this is [6], which presented scheduling as rule composition. It gives a formal semantics of the execution of individual guarded actions and defines how the set of guarded actions can be composed to new derived ones. Scheduling is then defined to be the process of combining all guarded actions to a single one, which can be trivially translated into the synchronous domain. Our approach is different: We immediately switch to the synchronous domain, which also requires that we give a correctness preservation criterion which relates the model and its implementations. In addition, the scheduler is not mixed up with the data-path. It is kept separate until the final synthesis step which gives us all the advantages mentioned above.

This paper is structured as follows: Section 2 gives an overview of our starting point (Concurrent Action-Oriented Specifications). Section 3 subsequently highlights synchronous guarded actions (our target) and their underlying model of computation. In Section 4, we show our translation procedure in detail. In Section 5, we highlight how our approach can be advantageous for the formal verification of custom schedulers over the approach in [26]. In Section 6, we illustrate our approach by an example, before we conclude with a short summary in Section 7.

2. Concurrent Action-Oriented Specifications

2.1 Syntax

In this paper, Concurrent Action-Oriented Specifications (CAOS) are the starting point of our translation process. Instead of their full syntax and semantics, we focus on simple asynchronous guarded actions in the form of rules and methods, which are the language core and sufficient to define other statements as simple syntactic sugar. We first give an overview of the syntax before we describe their semantics in the next subsection.

Each CAOS model is defined over a set of explicitly declared variables $\mathcal{V}$, which represent the state of the modeled component. The behavior is described by a set of *rules*, which are guarded atomic actions of the form $r_i : \texttt{when}(\gamma_i)\ S_i$, where γ_i is called the guard and S_i is called the body of rule r_i.

$$\texttt{rule}\ r_1\ \texttt{when}(\gamma_1)\ S_1$$
$$\vdots$$
$$\texttt{rule}\ r_n\ \texttt{when}(\gamma_n)\ S_n$$

Provided that σ is a Boolean expression, τ an expression of appropriate type over the readable variables, and x a writeable variable, the body S is one of the following statements:

$\texttt{nothing};$	(no operation)
$x = \tau;$	(wire assignment)
$\texttt{next}(x) = \tau;$	(register assignment)
$S_1\ S_2$	(parallel composition)
$\texttt{if}(\sigma)\ S_1\ \texttt{else}\ S_2$	(alternative)

CAOS provides two kinds of assignments: while wire assignments are immediately visible, register assignments are committed with the current state update. Other CAOS formalisms (like Bluespec) often distinguish these two variants by variable declarations,

[2] http://www.averest.org

i. e. variables are declared either as wires or as registers. We use the more general approach in which appropriate assignment types distinguish between a state variable and a wire type variable. Several assignments can be combined in the body by parallel composition, which is simply written as the concatenation. Finally, alternatives in rules can be given by the if operator.

For the interaction with the environment, CAOS uses so-called methods, which are parameterized rules. In addition to the local variables, the action of a method has access to the variables specified in its parameter list. Traditionally, CAOS distinguishes so-called *action methods*, *value methods* and *action-value methods*: as the name suggests, an action method executes an action, which only transports data given by the parameters into the system, while a value method does not change the system state and simply returns a value — thus, they only transport data from the system to the outside. Action-value methods are just combinations of them. Frequently, it is required that the outputs of these methods do not depend on the inputs, since this can lead to cyclic dependencies. We do not make this assumption here, since our translation target (synchronous guarded actions) can deal with cyclic dependencies, and well-established analysis tools will spot problematic situations.

$$\texttt{method } m_1(p_{11}, p_{12}, \ldots) \texttt{ when}(\gamma_1)\, S_1$$
$$\vdots$$
$$\texttt{method } m_n(p_{n1}, p_{n2}, \ldots) \texttt{ when}(\gamma_n)\, S_n$$

In the following, we do not use the names *action methods*, *value methods* and *action-value methods*, but we take simple parameter lists for our methods, which may contain inputs and outputs and thereby encode the appropriate variants of the method. In the concrete syntax, we use the prefix ? to mark a parameter as an input and ! to mark a parameter as an output.

2.2 Semantics

The CAOS semantics is very simple. After the initialization of all the variables, the following two steps are repeated forever: first, the guards of all actions are evaluated with respect to the current state. Among the actions whose guards evaluate to true, an arbitrary one is chosen and its body is executed. The execution generally modifies the system state so that other actions will be possibly activated in the following iteration. If no action is activated, the loop may be also aborted, since no state change will occur from there on.

Let q_0 be the initial state of the system, and $q \xrightarrow{S} q'$ denote that action S transforms the system in state q to state q'. Then, a run of a CAOS model is a sequence of system states $\langle q_0, q_1 \ldots \rangle$ where $q_i \xrightarrow{S_x} q_{i+1}$ and $\texttt{when}(\gamma_x)\, S_x$ is an arbitrary action which is activated in state q_i, i. e. $q_i(\gamma_x) = \texttt{true}$. Obviously, the system description is nondeterministic: even in the presence of the same inputs, which lead to the same activation of guards, the system can produce different outputs by choosing different activated actions. Hence, CAOS models are intended to be specifications, which describe a set of acceptable implementations.

Usually, one considers sequential hardware circuits as the implementation target for CAOS models. Thus, the compilation of a CAOS model involves a translation from one model of computation to another one, since the specification is asynchronous while the implementation is synchronous. Since the underlying model of computation has been changed, including the interface of the system, the communication has to be modified also: Input signals may change in each state without being considered by the system, because the rules that interact with them are not activated. Output signals must be also encoded in some way so that it is clear, what a single value is. In CAOS, methods are triggered by the environment of a module. They are commonly implemented by handshakes. The external module waits until the module can accept the request, then acknowledges it. Asynchronous behavior is thus implemented in synchronous one. Hence, the obvious question is: what properties have to preserved by the translation?

The correctness issue is addressed by the so-called *reference implementation* of a CAOS model. It maps all variables to hardware registers and each element (step) of the sequence to a clock cycle: i. e. in each step, it chooses exactly one action. Due to its inefficiency, the reference implementation is not considered as a real implementation. Instead, its main purpose is to define the correctness of real implementations. Since CAOS models are considered to be asynchronous, any implementation that respects the data dependencies given by the firing rules is by definition correct. Thus, schedulers usually try to fire as many activated actions as possible in a single clock cycle in order to produce an implementation with *minimal* latency.

Thereby, a real implementation only has to guarantee that it still complies with the CAOS semantics. This is guaranteed if the sequence of observed states is a subsequence of a run. Formally, to be considered correct, an implementation must always produce $\langle q_0, q_{i_1}, q_{i_2} \ldots \rangle$ as its state sequence, such that there exist a run $\langle q_0, q_1 \ldots \rangle$ of the original CAOS model, where $i_1, i_2, \ldots \in \mathbb{N}$ is an ascending subsequence of indices ($0 < 1 < \ldots$). Hence, if two actions are fired in the same step, the result must be the same as some sequence of them. Otherwise, this would not be a correct implementation.

In addition to this semantic constraint, there are more restrictions for merging actions: Executing the same CAOS methods (which are responsible for the interaction with the environment) more than once in a step, is not possible since simultaneous write accesses to the same interface signal would only preserve the last event (and simultaneous read accesses to the interface signal would replicate events). Similarly, a practical constraints is often given by available resources: Actions that share the same resource cannot be executed in the same clock cycle either. Thus, to save additional resources and to preserve traces, an implementation cannot arbitrarily merge a sequence of iterations into a single one, but only a sequence of iterations that is caused by different non-conflicting actions. Therefore, an implementation is assumed to fire a subset of actions of the CAOS model in each step, such that the choice of the subset guarantees the desired property by construction.

The CAOS compiler creates an implementation from a CAOS model by eliminating the nondeterminism from the original CAOS model according to the constraints presented above. It selects the action that is actually fired among the activated ones in dependence of the current inputs, and it merges a sequence of iterations into a clock cycle. These two tasks are handled by a scheduler, which is statically generated by the CAOS compiler. In each step, it dynamically selects among the activated actions the ones which are actually executed. To this end, it has access to the original guards γ_1 of the actions and triggers their execution (see Figure 1). For the reference implementation, this scheduler consists of a simple priority encoder or a round-robin scheduler (if weak fairness is desired). A real implementation would try to select a somehow maximal set of activated actions according to the constraints explained above.

The overall synthesis approach is depicted in Figure 1. For all actions, hardware circuits to compute the next state is generated according to the corresponding right-hand sides τ_i (lower cloud). Similarly, all guards γ_i are synthesized (upper cloud). They are used as input for the scheduler, which outputs the triggers for the actions ξ_i. The actual execution of actions is implemented by a selector component, which chooses the values computed from the next state logic according to the trigger signals ξ_i. These are finally used to update the system state for the following step.

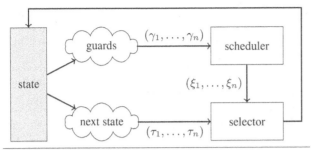

Figure 1. General CAOS Synthesis [16]

$$
\begin{array}{rcl}
a & \Rightarrow & y = x + 1 \\
\neg a & \Rightarrow & x = y + 2 \\
\text{true} & \Rightarrow & z = x + y
\end{array}
\qquad
\begin{array}{rcl}
a & \Rightarrow & x = \neg y \\
a & \Rightarrow & y = x
\end{array}
$$

Figure 2. Synchronous Guarded Actions

3. Synchronous Guarded Actions

Synchronous guarded actions have the same syntactic appearance as the guarded actions of CAOS models. However, their execution is governed by the synchronous model of computation [1, 9] which is explained as follows: In general, the execution of a synchronous program is divided into macro steps that correspond with the inter-action steps of a reactive system and its environment. Hence, for each macro step, new inputs are read from the environment, and new outputs and internal state changes are computed by the reactive system before the next interaction step takes place. To this end, macro steps are further divided into micro steps. Since the execution of micro steps is based on the same values of the input variables, their execution is viewed to be done in zero time, while the execution of a macro step requires one logical unit of time. In the programmer's view, variables are therefore constant during the execution of micro steps and synchronously change at macro steps. Moreover, in the programmer's view, all macro steps take the same amount of logical time, which has the consequence that concurrent threads run in lockstep and automatically synchronize at macro steps.

The introduction of this logical time is not only the key for a straightforward translation of synchronous programs to hardware circuits [2, 15, 19]; it also provides a very convenient programming model, which allows compilers to generate *deterministic* single-threaded code from multi-threaded synchronous programs [3]. Thus, synchronous programs can be directly executed on simple micro-controllers without using complex operating systems. Furthermore, the concise formal semantics of synchronous languages makes them particularly attractive for reasoning about program properties and equivalences [18, 23].

The *semantics of synchronous guarded actions* implements the synchronous model of computation in the following way: In each macro step, all guards are simultaneously evaluated within the current variable environment. If a guard is true, its action is immediately executed. To this end, we have to distinguish between delayed ($\text{next}(x) = \tau$) and immediate assignments ($x = \tau$), which transfer the computed value to the left-hand side of the assignment in the next and current step, respectively. In the case of immediate assignments, the program may suffer from causality problems due to the immediate feedback.

To illustrate the effect of immediate feedback, consider the examples shown in Figure 2. The guarded actions in the first column have the following behavior: Depending on a, one of the first two actions is executed, which is immediately seen by the last action.

Hence, if x has been 1 in the preceding step and a is currently true, the actions compute $y = 2$ and $z = 3$ in the same macro step. While these actions have no causality problem, the actions of the second column in Figure 2 represent a so-called causally incorrect program, which has no consistent behavior.

To avoid problems caused by causality cycles, compilers may check in the simplest case for absence of such cycles, or they can analyze the cycles by means of a causality analysis that guarantees that there exists an equivalent cycle-free system. This is a well-studied problem for synchronous systems and many analysis procedures have been developed to spot and eliminate these problems [20–22, 24].

Synchronous guarded actions without causality problems are always deterministic, because there is no choice among enabled guarded actions, since all of them must be fired. Hence, any system is guaranteed to produce the same outputs for the same inputs. However, forcing conflicting actions to fire simultaneously leads to semantical problems.

To conclude this section, we claim that synchronous guarded actions are a very useful intermediate format for the compilation of synchronous languages, since they address a suitable level of abstraction: in particular, they provide a good balance between (1) removal of complex statements available at the source code level and (2) the independence of a specific synthesis target: On the one hand, complex control-flow statements like preemption statements have been eliminated during the translation to guarded actions. Hence, synthesis tools do not have to deal with the complex semantics of the statements and can focus on much simpler guarded actions. Despite their very simple structure, translation to both software and hardware is efficiently possible from guarded actions.

4. Translation

Translating CAOS to synchronous guarded actions gives rise to a fundamental problem: as CAOS is nondeterministic and our synchronous guarded actions are deterministic, we have to model the nondeterminism explicitly. To this end, we add additional inputs to the system, which are used to choose among the different alternative behaviors of the system. Intuitively, these additional inputs determine which activated actions are actually fired and when they are fired. In our translation, these new inputs will be provided by an explicit scheduler. Note that this scheduler is not part of the system itself, since we do not want to fix a concrete schedule. Instead, we enrich the system description by assertions, which are checked in all steps to preserve of the CAOS semantics.

Thus, our design flow is as follows (see Figure 3): a CAOS model is translated to synchronous guarded actions with additional assertions. Then, a scheduler is written by hand or generated by some external tool according to the desired constraints and metrics (number of available resources, low latency, peak-power performance etc). After verifying that the assertions hold for the concrete scheduler, the guarded actions of the system and the scheduler are linked, constants are propagated and subexpressions are shared, and finally the synthesis procedures for synchronous guarded actions are invoked.

We implemented the translation presented in this section within the Averest system. This framework provides the basis for our approach by its various tools for synchronous systems. All its tools are built upon the common intermediate format AIF (Averest Intermediate Format), which is based on synchronous guarded actions and which can thus serve as the concrete synthesis target of our translation. Hence, the framework provides us with the tool support to implement and verify custom schedulers, to link all parts together and to finally synthesize hardware as well as software from synchronous guarded actions. For the implementation, we translate the CAOS primitives like rules and methods as presented in the rest of

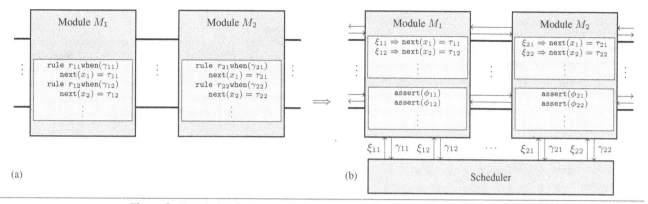

Figure 3. Translation Overview: (a) CAOS and (b) Synchronous Guarded Actions

---

```
function CompileRule(φ, S)
   case S of
      nothing :
         return { };
      x = τ :
         return {⟨φ ⇒ x = τ⟩};
      next(x) = τ :
         return {⟨φ ⇒ next(x) = τ⟩};
      S₁ S₂ :
         R₁ = CompileRule(φ, S₁);
         R₂ = CompileRule(φ, S₂);
         return (R₁ ∪ R₂);
      if(σ) S₁ else S₂ :
         R₁ = CompileRule(φ ∧ σ, S₁);
         R₂ = CompileRule(φ ∧ ¬σ, S₂);
         return (R₁ ∪ R₂);
```

Figure 4. Preliminary Translation of Rules

---

this section into synchronous guarded actions. Then, the computation of the assertions is accomplished as described above, and both parts are finally assembled in an AIF file.

In this section, we provide more details about this translation: first, we show how the rules of the system are translated into the synchronous domain, before presenting the transformation of the methods in Section 4.2. In Section 4.3, we explain the construction of the assertions for the scheduling constraints, and finally Section 4.4 highlights confluence, an important property of CAOS models.

4.1 Rules

The rules of the CAOS model are defined over a set of variables. These are translated to so-called `memorized` variables in the synchronous model. These variables store their values from one step to another, and they are mapped to registers in the final hardware synthesis step. In contrast, wires of the CAOS model become `event` variables in the synchronous model. These variables are reset to their default value if no action assigns them in the current step. Thereby, no registers to store the contained values are generated during the final synthesis for `event` variables.

The translation of the rules itself is given in Figure 4: for each rule [`rule` r `when`(γ_r) S_r], we declare an additional Boolean variable ξ_r, which represents the trigger of r by the scheduler. Then, the guarded actions are simply translated into synchronous guarded actions by a call to CompileRule(ξ_r, S_r), which decomposes the body and creates for each assignment a synchronous guarded action. The new signal ξ_r as well as the original guard γ_r are exposed

at the interface (see Figure 3) so that a scheduler can be connected, which drives the activation conditions depending on the activated guards. For example, the following rule R

```
rule R when(x > 0) {
   if(x = 42) {
      next(y) = y + 1;
      next(z) = true;
   } else
      next(y) = y - 1;
}
```

is translated to the following four guarded actions:

$$\begin{bmatrix} & \text{true} & \Rightarrow & \gamma_R = (x > 0) \\ \xi_R \wedge (x = 42) & \Rightarrow & \text{next}(y) = y + 1 \\ \xi_R \wedge (x = 42) & \Rightarrow & \text{next}(z) = true \\ \xi_R \wedge \neg(x = 42) & \Rightarrow & \text{next}(y) = y - 1 \end{bmatrix}$$

As already described above, the variable γ_R is declared as an additional output and ξ_R as an additional input, both connected to the scheduler of the system (see Figure 3).

4.2 Methods

CAOS uses methods to communicate with the environment. Unfortunately, they cannot be translated like all the other rules, because the interface of the system has changed from an asynchronous one to a synchronous one. This has some important consequences: the asynchronous CAOS interface implicitly guarantees that inputs are actually read by the system, since it assumes that methods are controlled by the environment. Thereby, the environment can be sure that its data has actually entered the system.

In contrast, the interface of module based on synchronous guarded actions just takes new input values in each step, no matter whether the system actually reads them or not. Thus, if a rule which is responsible for reading a value does not get activated in a step, the value at the interface is lost. The sender has no chance to detect this situation and to retransmit it, since there are no feedback signals in the opposite direction.

As a consequence, our translation has to generate the feedback explicitly, like any other CAOS compiler for synchronous target architectures. This can be accomplished by introducing a handshaking protocol for each method of the CAOS model, which ensures a correct interaction with the environment. In order to be compatible with previously synthesized circuits, we use the same interface as the Bluespec compiler, which implements this handshake by additional signals rdy_m (method can be safely called) and en_m (invoke method call).

```
function CompileRule(φ, S)
    case S of
        nothing :
            return ({}, true) ;
        x = τ :
            return ({⟨φ ⇒ x = τ⟩}, true) ;
        next(x) = τ :
            return ({⟨φ ⇒ next(x) = τ⟩}, true) ;
        m(x₁,...xₙ) :
            //m has the signature method m (p₀,...,pₙ)
            R = {φ ⇒ pᵢ = mᵢ | 1 ≤ i ≤ n}
            return ({φ ⇒ enₘ = true} ∪ R, true) ;
        S₁ S₂ :
            (R₁, ψ₁) = CompileRule(φ, S₁);
            (R₂, ψ₂) = CompileRule(φ, S₂);
            R'₁ = {ψ₂ ∧ γ ⇒ C | γ ⇒ C ∈ R₁};
            R'₂ = {ψ₁ ∧ γ ⇒ C | γ ⇒ C ∈ R₂};
            return (R'₁ ∪ R'₂, ψ₁ ∧ ψ₂);
        if(σ) S₁ else S₂ :
            (R₁, ψ₁) = CompileRule(φ ∧ σ, S₁);
            (R₂, ψ₂) = CompileRule(φ ∧ ¬σ, S₂);
            return (R₁ ∪ R₂, ψ₁ ∧ σ ∨ ψ₂ ∧ ¬σ);
```

Figure 5. Translation of Rules and Methods

Basically, the synchronous interface of a CAOS model is the collection of all its methods. Hence, we concatenate all parameter lists of the module to get the data interface of the synchronous module. Before this, we prefix all method parameters by the method names to avoid potential name clashes. In addition to this, the interface also contains control signals: for each method m, we introduce two Boolean signals of storage type event (i.e. they do not store values between clock cycles), an input en_m and an output rdy_m. (In Figure 3 they are depicted by additional small arrows between the modules.) en_m triggers method m and tells the module that its input parameters are valid. rdy_m tells the environment that method m is ready to be called and that the provided output parameters are valid. The feedback via rdy_m is necessary, since there may be situations, where methods cannot be called (e. g. due to the lack of required resources or in the course of an uncompleted computation). Otherwise, the module would have no chance to refuse a method call.

With the help of this extended interface, we can translate a method [method m $(p_0, \ldots, p_n)$ when(γ_r) S_r] as follows: on the callee's side, we generate synchronous guarded actions for the method almost like for ordinary rules (see Figure 4). The only difference is that we take the method trigger en_m as guard for the actions, thus we call CompileRule(en_m, S_m). In addition, we create the guarded action $\langle \gamma_m \Rightarrow rdy_m = \text{true} \rangle$, which drives the *ready* signal if the guard of the method holds. In contrast to ordinary rules, we do not expose the methods to the scheduler interface, since they are assumed to be controlled by the environment of the module.

On the caller's side, we replace the method call by actions that set the trigger signal and the parameters of the corresponding method. Hence, we extend the function CompileRule(φ, S) for method calls, i.e. the case $S = m(x_1, \ldots x_n)$ as follows: For method m, we return the guarded actions $\langle \varphi \Rightarrow p_1 = x_1 \rangle, \ldots,$ $\langle \varphi \Rightarrow p_n = x_n \rangle$ and $\langle \varphi \Rightarrow en_m = \text{true} \rangle$. Additionally, we must handle the enabling conditions of the methods on the caller's side by adding en_m to the guards of all actions in the same alternative.

The revised version of the CompileRule functions (see Figure 5) implements the translation of the methods as described above. To handle the backward propagation of the method en-abling conditions, it has two return values: the generated actions R and an additional enabling condition ψ for parallel actions (in the same rule). When CompileRule is applied to a parallel composition S_1 S_2, the enabling conditions of one part is applied to the guards retrieved from the other part. When applied to an alternative if(σ) S_1 else S_2, both enabling conditions are combined with the help of the guard of the alternative σ.

The following code fragment illustrates the generation of synchronous guarded actions for methods. Assume that we have a rule R, which uses methods M_1, M_2 and M_3:

```
rule R when(x > 0) {
    M₁();
    if(x = 42) M₂(); else M₃();
}

method M₁() when(b){
    next(x) = 0; }
```

Then, our translation extracts the following guarded actions for R and M_1. While the guarded actions for the bodies are similar to the preliminary code generation for rules, the result for γ_R is due to the backward propagation of the activation conditions of methods.

$$
\begin{bmatrix}
\text{true} & \Rightarrow & \gamma_R = (x > 0) \wedge rdy_{M_1} \wedge \\
 & & ((rdy_{M_2} \wedge (x = 42)) \vee \\
 & & (rdy_{M_3} \wedge \neg(x = 42))) \\
\xi_R & \Rightarrow & en_{M_1} = \text{true} \\
\xi_R \wedge (x = 42) & \Rightarrow & en_{M_2} = \text{true} \\
\xi_R \wedge \neg(x = 42) & \Rightarrow & en_{M_3} = \text{true} \\
\text{true} & \Rightarrow & rdy_{M_1} = b \\
en_{M_1} & \Rightarrow & next(x) = 0
\end{bmatrix}
$$

4.3 Scheduling Constraints

The synchronous guarded actions which have been constructed for a rule r in the sections before, have been endowed by a completely new trigger ξ_r, which is not bound to the original guards γ_r in the system description. This is accomplished by the external scheduler, which must ensure two basic properties: First, the scheduler must be safe, i. e. it should only fire actions that are activated. Thus, we add for each rule r the assertion $\xi_r \rightarrow \gamma_r$. Second, the scheduler should preserve liveness, which is expressed by the LTL formula $\text{GF} \bigvee_r \xi_r$ (where $\text{G}\Phi$ means that Φ must hold in all cycles, and $\text{F}\Phi$ means that Φ must hold eventually). Hence, for the rules $\mathcal{R}$ we generate the following assertions:

$$
\begin{aligned}
\text{safety} & : \quad \text{assert} \left(\text{G} \bigwedge_{r \in \mathcal{R}} \xi_r \rightarrow \gamma_r \right) \\
\text{liveness} & : \quad \text{assert} \left(\text{GF} \bigvee_{r \in \mathcal{R}} \xi_r \right)
\end{aligned}
$$

As already pointed out in Section 2, the CAOS semantics additionally requires that an implementation only executes a set of guarded actions simultaneously if they could have also been fired in a sequential order with the same result. So far, our synchronous system does not necessarily obey this rule and it can fire any set of actions depending on the original guards of the system. Since we do not want to fix any specific solution, we use synchronous assertions again to constrain the system behavior

Obviously, all CAOS compilers have to solve a related problem. However, there is an important difference. We are not interested in an optimal schedule with respect to some property, but we want to give the set of all correct schedules. Nevertheless, we need to analyze the dependencies between the actions in the same manner. Thus, we first look at already existing definitions, e. g. the ones given be Hoe and Arvind in [10].

In essence, two rules can be fired simultaneously if the first rule does not have an impact on the activation of the second one in any state q of the system. This is the underlying consideration of the following definition $r_1 \rightharpoonup r_2$ of *sequentially composable* rules:

$$r_1 \rightharpoonup r_2 \Leftrightarrow \quad \forall q.(r_1 \neq r_2) \wedge [\![\gamma_1]\!]_q \wedge [\![\gamma_2]\!]_q \rightarrow$$
$$[\![\gamma_2]\!]_{\delta_1(q)} \wedge \delta_2(\delta_1(q)) = \delta_{1\|2}(q)$$

Two rules r_1 and r_2 are considered to be sequentially composable $(r_1 \rightharpoonup r_n)$ if the following property holds in all states: provided that the guards γ_1 and γ_2 hold in a state q, i.e. $[\![\gamma_1]\!]_q \wedge [\![\gamma_2]\!]_q$, then the guard of the second one still evaluates to true after firing the first one, i.e. $[\![\gamma_2]\!]_{\delta_1(q)}$, and the parallel firing of the bodies results to the same state as the sequential firing, i.e. $\delta_2(\delta_1(q)) = \delta_{1\|2}(q)$.

Obviously, a list of such rules $\langle r_1, \ldots, r_n \rangle$ such that two subsequent ones are *sequentially composable*, i.e. $r_1 \rightharpoonup \ldots \rightharpoonup r_n$, can be combined in a single step. In the synthesized circuit, this operation chains the next-state logic of all involved actions in exactly the same order. This is automatically accomplished by the synchronous synthesis tools, which considers the dependencies between all actions. As already shown in [10], the *sequentially composable* definition can be visualized by a directed graph whose edges represent dependencies between rules. In this so-called *conflict graph*, there are nodes for all rules and edges (r_i, r_j) if the rules r_i and r_j do not satisfy $r_i \rightharpoonup r_j$.

The conflict graph is also important for our approach, since we can extract our assertions from it. Remember the goal is to find for any selected set of simultaneously fired actions a sequence of firing that has the same effect. Since the edges represent potential causal dependencies between actions, the sought order is just any one that does not contain any edge of the graph. If the actions are executed like this, no action can see the effect of any of its predecessors. Obviously, such an order can be always constructed if the selected set of actions does not contain a cycle of dependencies. All we need to extract the assertions is to find the cycles in the conflict graph: if a set of actions is fired which form a cycle in the graph, then none of them could have been fired first without making its effect visible to the others.

Hence, we add an assertion for each cycle in the graph, which is the conjunction of all rule triggers in the cycle. Thereby, our assertions guarantee that the scheduler never selects a set of mutually dependent rules. Formally, let $\mathcal{C} = \text{cycles}^{\rightharpoonup}$ be the sets of nodes that form a cycle in the conflict graph for relation $\rightharpoonup$. Then we add for each cycle $C \in \mathcal{C}$ in the graph an assertion of the following form:

$$\text{seqCompose}_C \quad : \quad \text{assert}\left(\mathsf{G}\neg\bigwedge_{r \in C} \xi_r\right)$$

In principle, cycles in the graph can be formed by mutually exclusive rules, which can be never activated simultaneously. Although we do not consider them separately, these assertions are quickly found by the verification tool with the help of the *safety* conditions given above.

Finally, the developer can add resource constraints given by his target architecture. All rules that use a shared resource can be set in conflict by additional assertions, which just forbid simultaneously executing the actions by setting corresponding ξ_i trigger conditions.

From the theoretical side, this concludes the generation of assertions. However, large systems often make an extensive analysis of the conditions presented above very hard. While the safety property can be usually checked very efficiently, the liveness property and the conflict analysis can become very difficult. In particular, statically determining the *sequentially composable* relation is not

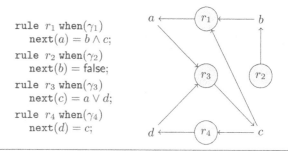

Figure 6. Conflict Graph Example

simple[3], conservative approximations can be used instead. By forbidding idle cycles, we can reformulate the liveness property as follows: in all steps, at least one trigger ξ_r of the set of rules $\mathcal{R}$ must hold, formally:

$$\text{liveness'} \quad : \quad \text{assert}\left(\mathsf{G}\bigvee_{r \in \mathcal{R}} \xi_r\right)$$

Similarly, we use a syntactical heuristic for the composition analysis, which just considers the read and write sets of the corresponding actions. This is given by the following definition of *syntactically sequentially composable* rules $r_1 \overset{\rightharpoonup}{\Rightarrow} r_2$:

$$r_1 \overset{\rightharpoonup}{\Rightarrow} r_2 \Leftrightarrow \quad (r_1 = r_2) \vee$$
$$(\text{grdVars}(r_2) \cup \text{rdVars}(r_2)) \cap \text{wrVars}(r_1) = \{\}$$

Thereby, $\text{grdVars}(a)$ is the set of variables occurring in the guard of a, $\text{rdVars}(a)$ is the set of variables read in the body, and $\text{wrVars}(a)$ is the set of variables written in the body. Again, the conflicts can be illustrated by a graph. A better alternative in this case is a bipartite graph, which contains a set of nodes for the variables and another set of nodes for the actions. However, the overall approach stays the same: we use $r_1 \overset{\rightharpoonup}{\Rightarrow} r_2$ as a replacement for $r_1 \rightharpoonup r_2$, build its graph instead, determine all cycles and then add assertions accordingly:

$$\text{seqCompose'}_C \quad : \quad \text{assert}\left(\neg\bigwedge_{r \in C} \xi_r\right)$$

Since these definitions are not as accurate as the original ones, some correct schedulers may be rejected by the verification tool. However, the approximations scale better and therefore, they are the first choice for practical implementations.

Figure 6 shows a simple example. For the rules r_1, r_2, r_3, r_4, which are shown on the left-hand side, the conflict graph on the right-hand side can be retrieved. It has been constructed with the *syntactically sequentially composable* relation $\overset{\rightharpoonup}{\Rightarrow}$, which only analyses the read and write sets of the rules. Two cycles can be identified: one containing the node set $\{r_1, r_3\}$ and another one containing the node set $\{r_3, r_4\}$. Thus, we add the following two assertions to constrain the synchronous guarded actions by the trigger signals ξ_i:

$$\begin{bmatrix} \texttt{assert}(\neg(\xi_1 \wedge \xi_3)); \\ \texttt{assert}(\neg(\xi_3 \wedge \xi_4)); \end{bmatrix}$$

4.4 Confluence

In addition to pure correctness, which is described by the assertions of the previous section, developers are often interested in *conflu-*

---

[3] The problem becomes even more difficult if one does not use the set of *all* states but set of actually *reachable* states, which even depends on the concrete scheduler (which again depends on the *sequentially composable* relation).

ence. Since CAOS models are intended to be a specification and not a complete description of the system, they are nondeterministic. From the developers point of view, this nondeterminism is acceptable even if they have a single input-output behavior in mind, because the nondeterministic part may only affect the order in which actions fire and not the final observable result. In this case, the compiler can exploit the additional freedom and choose the optimal order (according to some criterion) among the possible ones. Formally, developers aiming to describe deterministic systems want confluence as known from term-rewriting systems.

Unfortunately, checking confluence is generally undecidable so that developers are responsible for guaranteeing this property. In particular, the CAOS semantics (and therefore the assertions presented in the previous section) do *not* require that a given model is confluent, and its compilers will not check for it.

What confluence basically says is that any permutation of a given set of rules applied sequentially leads to the same state as their concurrent execution. This is more restricted than *sequentially composable*, which only requires that the first rule does not have an impact on the activation of the second one (therefore, we could omit the assertions derived from the *sequentially composable* relation if we check for confluence). The *conflict free* relation given in [10] can be used for this task: it defines a bounded version of confluence, where the confluence point must be reached after executing each rule at most once. Obviously, two rules can be fired in any order if there are no dependencies between each other. This is the underlying consideration of the *conflict free* relation $r_1 \rightleftharpoons r_2$:

$$
\begin{aligned}
r_1 \rightleftharpoons r_2 \Leftrightarrow \quad & \forall q. (r_1 \neq r_2) \wedge [\![\gamma_1]\!]_q \wedge [\![\gamma_2]\!]_q \rightarrow \\
& [\![\gamma_2]\!]_{\delta_1(q)} \wedge [\![\gamma_1]\!]_{\delta_2(q)} \wedge \\
& \delta_2(\delta_1(q)) = \delta_1(\delta_2(q)) = \delta_{1\|2}(q)
\end{aligned}
$$

Given a set of guarded rules such that they are pairwise conflict-free ($r_i \rightleftharpoons r_j$ for all i and j), the rules can be executed independently from each other in the same step – in any order. In the generated hardware circuits, this has the effect that the next-state logic for all rules can be run in parallel and is not chained as in the case for sequentially composable rules so that its maximum latency is just the *maximum* of all fired rules and not the *sum* of them.

The *conflict free* definition can be visualized by a directed graph again: there, one adds for each pair of rules that does not satisfy $r_1 \rightleftharpoons r_2$, the edges (r_1, r_2) and (r_2, r_1) to the graph. Extracting assertions from the graph follows exactly the same approach as described above for the *sequentially-composable* relation. Thus, we end up with the assertions of the following form (provided that $C \in \mathcal{C}$ is a cycle in the graph of $\rightleftharpoons$):

$$\text{locConfluent}_C \quad : \quad \text{assert}\left(G\neg \bigwedge_{r \in C} \xi_r\right)$$

Again, statically determining the *conflict free* relation is a hard problem, so that there is an alternative syntactic check, which conservatively approximates the relation:

$$
\begin{aligned}
r_1 \overset{\cdots}{\rightleftharpoons} r_2 \Leftrightarrow \ & (r_1 = r_2) \vee \\
& (\text{grdVars}(r_1) \cup \text{rdVars}(r_1)) \cap \text{wrVars}(r_2) = \{\} \wedge \\
& (\text{grdVars}(r_2) \cup \text{rdVars}(r_2)) \cap \text{wrVars}(r_1) = \{\}
\end{aligned}
$$

Unfortunately, this definition has shown to be very coarse and overly conservative. In many cases, schedulers are very restricted and cannot find a large enough set of rules that can be executed together in a cycle. Therefore, rules are only checked to be sequentially composable in CAOS designs.

5. Verification

The previous section presented the translation of CAOS models to synchronous guarded actions and assertions for the scheduler. As already mentioned in the introduction, separating the guarded actions and the scheduler is the basis for integration of custom schedulers. In this section, we illustrate how this makes the formal verification task substantially easier and simpler compared to previously presented techniques [26].

For instance, the synthesis of low-power hardware from CAOS models is considered in [25]. Its authors aim to reduce the peak power of a circuit generated from a CAOS model. Obviously, this nonfunctional requirement is mainly due to the scheduler of the system: the maximal set of rules that a scheduler selects in a given clock cycle directly influences the peak power of the overall circuit. Hence, they replace the scheduler that they have retrieved by their CAOS compiler by a custom one that is generated by an external tool according to the power requirements. One important problem then is to check whether the new scheduler complies with the original semantics of the CAOS model.

The authors try to answer this question in [26] in that they reduce the verification problem to a restricted form of automata language containment. Thus, each CAOS model is related to an automaton $\mathcal{A}$, and its behavior is represented by the language of the automaton $\mathcal{L}(\mathcal{A})$. Thereby, an implementation R is considered to be correct if the language of its corresponding automaton is contained in the one of the original specification S: $\mathcal{L}(\mathcal{A}_R) \subseteq \mathcal{L}(\mathcal{A}_S)$. The whole process is implemented with the help of SPIN [11], where the automata are described as instances of PROMELA, the input language of SPIN. Since the current Bluespec compiler does not separate the scheduling and datapath during synthesis, the formal model built from the synthesized implementation contains all the complexities of the integrated datapath and the scheduler.

Hence, to verify that a given implementation complies to the original model, developers first synthesize the scheduled CAOS implementation model and generate a reference SPIN model for the whole system. Similarly, a SPIN model is created for the alternatively scheduled system. To this end, developers have to formalize the scheduler within the CAOS model, since there is no easy way for them to separate the datapath from the scheduler (the additional scheduler that the CAOS compiler creates for this is trivial). Finally, both SPIN models are used for the language containment check.

The advantages for carrying out formal verification using our approach over [26] can be summarized as follows:

- In the approach presented above, the alternative scheduler is intricately integrated into the CAOS model, which leads to a large description of the SPIN system, since it integrates the scheduler with the data path. In our approach, this data path is abstracted by the generated assertions. The actual computation of the data flow is not required in many cases.

- Since each scheduler integrated with the CAOS model represents a completely new hardware, the synthesis of the whole system needs to be repeated each time a scheduler is modified. In our case, we can use the separate compilation of synchronous components [4] in order to only repeat the linking.

- To check containment of the real implementation behavior in the reference implementation behavior set, intermediate steps from the reference model generally need to be hidden. This has shown to produce a considerable amount of additional variables in the models [26].

- Furthermore, we can use any temporal logic property checker for verifying the scheduler, since we do not depend on specific features of PROMELA or any other specification language. The assertions generated by our translation are simple LTL

```
module TokenRing {
    struct { int data; int addr; }
        buf12, buf23, buf34, buf41 = { 0, 0 };
    Bell b1 = Bell();

    rule node1
    when( (buf41.addr!=1) & (buf12.data==0) ) {
        next(buf12.addr) = buf41.addr;
        next(buf12.data) = buf41.data;
    }

    rule node2
    when( (buf12.addr!=2) & (buf23.data==0) ) {
        next(buf23.addr) = buf12.addr;
        next(buf23.data) = buf12.data;
    }

    rule node3
    when( (buf23.addr!=3) & (buf34.data==0) ) {
        next(buf34.addr) = buf23.addr;
        next(buf34.data) = buf23.data;
    }

    rule node4
    when( (buf34.addr!=4) & (buf41.data==0) ) {
        next(buf41.addr) = buf34.addr;
        next(buf41.data) = buf34.data;
    }

    method send1(int ?a, int ?d)
    when (buf12.data == 0) {
        next(buf12.addr) = a;
        next(buf12.data) = d;
    }

    method receive1(int !d)
    when ((buf41.data != 0) & (buf41.addr == 1)) {
        next(buf41.data) = 0;
        d = buf41.data;
        b1.ring();
    }
}
```

```
interface :
    bool ?xi_node1, bool !gamma_node1,
    bool ?xi_node2, bool !gamma_node2,
    bool ?xi_node3, bool !gamma_node3,
    bool ?xi_node4, bool !gamma_node4,
    bool ?en_send1, bool !rdy_send1,
        int !send1_a, int !send1_d,
    bool ?en_receive1, bool !rdy_receive1,
        int !receive1_d
init :
    struct { int data; int addr; }
        buf12, buf23, buf34, buf41 = { 0, 0 };
main:
    // --- rule node1 ---
    gamma_node1 = (buf41.addr!=1) & (buf12.data==0);
    if xi_node1 : next(buf12.addr) = buf41.addr;
    if xi_node1 : next(buf12.data) = buf41.data;
    // --- rule node2 ---
    gamma_node2 = (buf12.addr!=2) & (buf23.data==0);
    if xi_node2 : next(buf23.addr) = buf12.addr;
    if xi_node2 : next(buf23.data) = buf12.data;
    // --- rule node3 ---
    gamma_node3 = (buf23.addr!=3) & (buf34.data==0);
    if xi_node3 : next(buf34.addr) = buf23.addr;
    if xi_node3 : next(buf34.data) = buf23.data;
    // --- rule node4 ---
    gamma_node4 = (buf34.addr!=4) & (buf41.data==0);
    if xi_node4 : next(buf41.addr) = buf34.addr;
    if xi_node4 : next(buf41.data) = buf34.data;
    // -- methods ---
    rdy_send1 = (buf12.data==0);
    if en_send1: next(buf12.addr) = send1_a;
    if en_send1: next(buf12.data) = send1_d;
    rdy_receive1 =
        (buf41.data != 0) & (buf41.addr == 1) & b1.rdy_ring;
    if en_receive1: d = buf41.data;
    if en_receive1: next(buf41.data) = 0;
    if en_receive1: d = b1.en_ring = true;
    // -- assertions ---
    assert !(xi_node1&en_send1);
    assert !(xi_node1&xi_node2&xi_node3&xi_node4);
```

Figure 7. CAOS Example and its Translation: Token Ring

---

formulas. To be precise, with the exception of the assertion *liveness* (see Section 4.3), all properties are even simple safety conditions, which can be verified by most model-checkers. In particular, language containment checks are not needed any more.

- Finally, our approach makes it possible to verify properties of the data path without supplying a scheduler at all. In this case, one uses the generated assertions as assumptions for the verification of the given properties.

6. Example

In this section, we illustrate our approach by a complete example. The CAOS model is given on the left-hand side of Figure 7, and the synchronous guarded actions derived from our translation on the right-hand side. The system describes a token ring, where messages can be only exchanged between neighbors by a common single-place buffer. Communication is directed and its direction is static,

i.e. each buffer is always the input of the following node and the output of the preceding node.

In this example, we have four nodes connected to the ring, which all have the same behavior: if the output buffer is empty and the message in the input buffer is not for the node itself, the packet is forwarded. This part of the behavior is described by the rules *node1*, *node2*, *node3* and *node4*. Packets are inserted and removed from the ring by *send* and *receive* methods. For the sake of simplicity, this example contains these methods only for the first node. By firing a *send1*, a new packet is inserted into the ring, which can be only done if the current output buffer of the first node is empty. Packets can be received by a call to *receive1*, which requires that there is a packet waiting in the input buffer of the node. If the packet is received, an external bell is rung by calling its *ring* method.

Obviously, all rules write to different buffers. The only resource conflict is between the forwarding of the first node and the introduction of a new packet, which both write to *buf12*. Hence, the scheduler cannot fire them both, which would result to a write conflict. In the synchronous guarded actions, this is represented by the first assertion $\neg(\xi_{node1} \wedge en_{send1})$.

Another constraint is more interesting, which is due to the CAOS semantics. It forbids that all four nodes fire in parallel, since this cannot be represented by any sequential firing. This always requires that at least one buffer in the ring is empty in order to transmit a packet. Hence, one assertion is retrieved from the conflict graph, which describes exactly the apparent cycle: $\neg(\xi_{node1} \wedge \xi_{node2} \wedge \xi_{node3} \wedge \xi_{node4})$. Thereby, the scheduler can fire up to three arbitrary nodes if its aim is to produce maximum throughput. Another scheduler, which is optimized for low power, may only fire a single node in each step.

It is interesting to see that the case which has been identified by the analysis is not a critical one for the synchronous model. Due to its lockstep semantics, it allows the ring to forward all packets simultaneously, without the need for a bubble in the ring.

In the guarded actions given on the right-hand side of Figure 7, one may notice that many guards have a similar structure. This is a consequence of the translation, which prepends the activation condition of rule to all its actions. This could result to a quadratic blowup of the code size, which could quickly become a bottleneck for any practical translation. However, the actual intermediate code is more efficient: tables to store common terms are used to keep the size of the guarded actions linear to the CAOS model. This storage also eases a subsequent synthesis of the system.

7. Conclusions

In this paper, we presented a translation of CAOS models to synchronous guarded actions. While both descriptions are very similar to each other from the syntactical side, the main difference is the underlying model of computation. Hence, the main task of the translation is to bridge the gap between an untimed asynchronous description and a synchronous one. Thereby, scheduling constraints imposed by the CAOS semantics play a significant role. In contrast to previous approaches, we do not immediately include a scheduler in the synchronous model, but encode the constraints by additional synchronous assertions. This is not only a separation of concerns but it also pays off if custom schedulers should be connected to the system. They can be developed separately and integrated after the code generation of the main system. Additional assertions allow the developers to check whether the integrated scheduler complies to the CAOS semantics of the original module.

References

[1] A. Benveniste, P. Caspi, S. Edwards, N. Halbwachs, P. Le Guernic, and R. de Simone. The synchronous languages twelve years later. *Proceedings of the IEEE*, 91(1):64–83, 2003.

[2] G. Berry. A hardware implementation of pure Esterel. In *Workshop on Formal Methods in VLSI Design*, Miami, Florida, 1991.

[3] G. Berry. Synchronous languages for hardware and software reactive systems. In C. Delgado Kloos and E. Cerny, editors, *Conference on Computer Hardware Description Languages and Their Applications (CHDL)*, Toledo, Spain, 1997. Chapman & Hall.

[4] J. Brandt and K. Schneider. Separate compilation of synchronous programs. In *Software and Compilers for Embedded Systems (SCOPES)*, volume 320 of *ACM International Conference Proceeding Series*, pages 1–10, Nice, France, 2009. ACM.

[5] K. Chandy and J. Misra. *Parallel Program Design*. Addison Wesley, Austin, Texas, May 1989.

[6] N. Dave, Arvind, and M. Pellauer. Scheduling as rule composition. In *International Conference on Formal Methods and Models for Co-Design (MEMOCODE)*, pages 51–60, Nice, France, 2007. IEEE Computer Society.

[7] E. Dijkstra. Guarded commands, nondeterminacy and formal derivation of programs. *Communications of the ACM*, 18(8):453–457, 1975.

[8] D. Dill. The Murphi verification system. In R. Alur and T. Henzinger, editors, *Computer Aided Verification (CAV)*, volume 1102 of *LNCS*, pages 390–393, New Brunswick, NJ, USA, 1996. Springer.

[9] N. Halbwachs. *Synchronous programming of reactive systems*. Kluwer, 1993.

[10] J. Hoe and Arvind. Operation-centric hardware description and synthesis. *IEEE Transactions on Computer-Aided Design of Integrated Circuits and Systems*, 23(9):1277–1288, September 2004.

[11] G. Holzmann. *The Spin Model Checker: Primer and Reference Manual*. Addison-Wesley, 2004.

[12] H. Järvinen and R. Kurki-Suonio. The DisCo language and temporal logic of actions. Technical Report 11, Tampere University of Technology, Software Systems Laboratory, 1990.

[13] L. Lamport. The temporal logic of actions. Technical Report 79, Digital Equipment Cooperation, 1991.

[14] P. Ramadge and W. Wonham. Supervisory control of a class of discrete event processes. *SIAM Journal of Control and Optimization*, 25(1): 206–230, 1987.

[15] F. Rocheteau and N. Halbwachs. Pollux, a Lustre-based hardware design environment. In P. Quinton and Y. Robert, editors, *Conference on Algorithms and Parallel VLSI Architectures II*, Chateau de Bonas, 1991.

[16] D. Rosenband and Arvind. Modular scheduling of guarded atomic actions. In *Design Automation Conference (DAC)*, pages 55–60, San Diego, CA, USA, 2004. ACM.

[17] K. Schneider. Embedding imperative synchronous languages in interactive theorem provers. In *Conference on Application of Concurrency to System Design (ACSD)*, pages 143–154, Newcastle upon Tyne, UK, 2001. IEEE Computer Society.

[18] K. Schneider. Proving the equivalence of microstep and macrostep semantics. In V. Carreño, C. Muñoz, and S. Tahar, editors, *Theorem Proving in Higher Order Logics (TPHOL)*, volume 2410 of *LNCS*, pages 314–331, Hampton, VA, USA, 2002. Springer.

[19] K. Schneider. The synchronous programming language Quartz. Internal Report 375, Department of Computer Science, University of Kaiserslautern, Kaiserslautern, Germany, 2009.

[20] K. Schneider and J. Brandt. Performing causality analysis by bounded model checking. In *Conference on Application of Concurrency to System Design (ACSD)*, pages 78–87, Xi'an, China, 2008. IEEE Computer Society.

[21] K. Schneider, J. Brandt, and T. Schuele. Causality analysis of synchronous programs with delayed actions. In *Compilers, Architecture, and Synthesis for Embedded Systems (CASES)*, pages 179–189, Washington, DC, USA, 2004. ACM.

[22] K. Schneider, J. Brandt, T. Schuele, and T. Tuerk. Maximal causality analysis. In J. Desel and Y. Watanabe, editors, *Application of Concurrency to System Design (ACSD)*, pages 106–115, St. Malo, France, 2005. IEEE Computer Society.

[23] K. Schneider, J. Brandt, and T. Schuele. A verified compiler for synchronous programs with local declarations. *Electronic Notes in Theoretical Computer Science (ENTCS)*, 153(4):71–97, 2006.

[24] T. Shiple. *Formal Analysis of Synchronous Circuits*. PhD thesis, University of California at Berkeley, Berkeley, CA, USA, 1996.

[25] G. Singh and S. Shukla. Algorithms for low power hardware synthesis from concurrent action oriented specifications CAOS. *International Journal of Embedded Systems (IJES)*, 3(1/2):83–92, 2007.

[26] G. Singh and S. Shukla. Verifying compiler based refinement of Bluespec specifications using the SPIN model checker. In K. Havelund, R. Majumdar, and J. Palsberg, editors, *Model Checking Software (SPIN)*, volume 5156 of *LNCS*, pages 250–269, Los Angeles, CA, USA, 2008. Springer.

[27] R. Ziller and K. Schneider. Combining supervisor synthesis and model checking. *Transactions on Embedded Computing Systems (TECS)*, 4 (2):331–362, May 2005.

Contracts for Modular Discrete Controller Synthesis *

Gwenaël Delaval

INRIA, Grenoble, France
gwenael.delaval@inria.fr

Hervé Marchand

INRIA, Rennes, France
herve.marchand@inria.fr

Eric Rutten

INRIA, Grenoble, France
eric.rutten@inria.fr

Abstract

We describe the extension of a reactive programming language with a behavioral contract construct. It is dedicated to the programming of reactive control of applications in embedded systems, and involves principles of the supervisory control of discrete event systems. Our contribution is in a language approach where modular discrete controller synthesis (DCS) is integrated, and it is concretized in the encapsulation of DCS into a compilation process. From transition system specifications of possible behaviors, DCS automatically produces controllers that make the controlled system satisfy the property given as objective. Our language features and compiling technique provide correctness-by-construction in that sense, and enhance reliability and verifiability. Our application domain is adaptive and reconfigurable systems: closed-loop adaptation mechanisms enable flexible execution of functionalities w.r.t. changing resource and environment conditions. Our language can serve programming such adaption controllers. This paper particularly describes the compilation of the language. We present a method for the modular application of discrete controller synthesis on synchronous programs, and its integration in the BZR language. We consider structured programs, as a composition of nodes, and first apply DCS on particular nodes of the program, in order to reduce the complexity of the controller computation; then, we allow the abstraction of parts of the program for this computation; and finally, we show how to recompose the different controllers computed from different abstractions for their correct co-execution with the initial program. Our work is illustrated with examples, and we present quantitative results about its implementation.

Categories and Subject Descriptors D.3.3 [*Programming Languages*]: Language Constructs and Features—Control structures; C.3 [*Special-purpose and Application-based Systems*]: Real-time and embedded systems; D.2.2 [*Software Engineering*]: Design Tools and Techniques—Computer-aided software engineering, State diagrams; D.2.4 [*Software Engineering*]: Software / Program Verification—Formal methods, Programming by contract

General Terms Design, Languages, Reliability, Verification

Keywords Discrete controller synthesis, modularity, components, contracts, reactive systems, synchronous programming, adaptive and reconfigurable systems

* This work was partially supported by the Minalogic project MIND.

1. Motivations

We integrate discrete controller synthesis (DCS) into a modular compilation process for a synchronous language: BZR, with motivations concerning the design of programming languages, the use of DCS, and the control of adaptive and reconfigurable systems.

Programming languages. We propose a compilation concretely exploiting a representation of the dynamical behavior of the program. Classically, compilation considers properties holding for all states (i.e., static); but we propose to consider state and path-dependent aspects (i.e., dynamical) [21].

DCS is a constructive operation, as it computes not a diagnostic about correctness, but a correct solution. A few works exist about its integration into a programming language framework [4]. We associate it to a contract mechanism, making it easier to use by programmers and favoring scalability (see further). Symmetrically, we propose a new point of view on the design by contracts principle: our programming language allows contracts to be enforced in non-deterministic programs, instead of being checked or proved correct.

Discrete controller synthesis. The modular application of DCS, which we are addressing in this paper, is based on contract enforcement and abstraction of components, with the aim of improving the scalability of the techniques devoted to DCS. Furthermore, the integration of these techniques in a high-level programming language also contributes to make it more widely usable in computer systems, and to study implementations of the controllers at a higher level than programmable logic controllers used in automation.

Control of adaptive and reconfigurable systems. Embedded systems have to be predictable, for safety-criticality issues. They also have to be able of dynamical adaptivity and reconfiguration, in reaction to environment changes, related to resources or dependability. This requires abilities for sensing the state of a system, deciding, based on a representation of the system, upon reconfiguration actions, and performing and executing them. These functionalities are assembled into a decision loop as illustrated in Figure 1(a).

Approach followed in our work. We want to combine these two different requirements, i.e., to be *adaptive and predictable.* Our

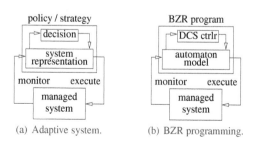

(a) Adaptive system.   (b) BZR programming.

Figure 1. BZR programming of adaptation control.

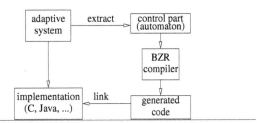

Figure 2. Development process using BZR.

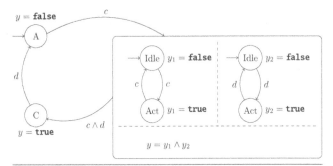

Figure 3. Mixed state / dataflow example

programming language is specially suited for user-friendly design of safe control loops of adaptive systems, relying on discrete control theory techniques. It separates concerns, as illustrated in Figure 1(b), by supporting separate specification of, on one hand, the possible behaviors of the components, and on the other hand, the control objectives for the components assembly. From these two specifications, DCS can automatically generate, if a solution exists, a correct control decision component.

Contribution of the paper. Our precise contribution is the definition of a new construct, added to the HEPTAGON language, for defining behavioural contracts to be enforced on a node. The semantics of this new construct is defined in terms of a DCS problem, where resulting behaviours of the node are controlled in order to enforce the contract. We present the implementation of this language extension, involving a DCS tool encapsulated in the compilation.

The position of our contribution in the development process of an adaptive or reconfigurable system is illustrated in Figure 2. Our language is used for specifying the discrete control part of the system with automata. If explicitly defined in the host language, this part can be automatically extracted from the global specification by compilation; then the programmer does not need to know technicities of BZR or of DCS. Other, more data-related parts of the adaptive system are best developed in appropriate host languages. It is compiled with an encapsulated phase of DCS, relying upon its formal semantics. Executable code is generated towards target languages, e.g., C or Java. This code is then linked back into the concrete implementation of the system, with appropriate interfacing of the monitoring and adaptation execution functionalities provided by the platform. This way, the discrete feedback control loop of the computing system is in place as in Figure 1(b). We are currently working on instantiations of this development process at different levels, ranging from architecture-level reconfigurable FPGAs, through operating systems administration loops, through component-based middleware, to application-level aspects.

Outline of the paper. Section 2 briefly recalls notions upon which we base our contribution (synchronous mode automata, DCS). Section 3 describes the BZR programming language, extending the previous ones with a notion of contract. Section 4 then formally describes the compilation of this language, where DCS operations are applied upon nodes with contracts. Section 5 outlines implementation and Section 6 discusses performances and scalability.

2. Context

2.1 Synchronous mode automata

We place our work in the framework of reactive systems and synchronous programming [7], and adopt its classical basic notions. More particularly, we will adopt notations inspired from the Lucid Synchrone language, mixing dataflow and automata [10].

2.1.1 Behavior

For our examples, we consider programs expressed as synchronous Moore machines, with parallel and hierarchical composition.

The states of such machines define data-flow equations, as in Lucid Synchrone or Lustre. At each step, according to inputs and current state values, equations associated to the current state produce outputs, and conditions on transitions are evaluated in order to determine the state for next step. Figure 3 gives an example. At the highest level, a three-state automaton is initially in state A, associated with equation $y = \texttt{false}$. Upon condition c, it takes the transition to state B, itself associated with the parallel composition of three sub-nodes: two sub-automata and one simple equation, defining y in terms of y_1 and y_2 defined in each of the sub-automata, by equations associated with the states, following the same principle as previously for state A. Upon $c \wedge d$, a transition is taken to state C, from where, upon d, another is taken to A.

2.1.2 Structure

For scalability and abstraction purpose, synchronous programs are structured in *nodes*, with a name f, inputs $x_1, \ldots, x_n$, outputs $y_1, \ldots, y_p$ and declarations D. y_i variables are to be defined in D, using operations between values of x_j and y_j. Figure 4 gives the graphical syntax of node definitions. The nodes are the abstraction level we will use in BZR to perform modular application of DCS.

The program of Figure 3 can then be structured as in Figure 5. The high-level automaton is specified in node defining f, with inputs c and d, and output y, and with state B is associated a an equation calling g. The latter is defined as a node with a body with three equations in parallel, two of which calling the node h. Finally, node f is defined with a body containing a two-state automaton, with associated equations in the states.

$$\boxed{\begin{array}{|c|}\hline f(x_1, \ldots, x_n) = y_1, \ldots, y_p \\ \hline D \\ \hline \end{array}}$$

Figure 4. Node definition graphical syntax

2.1.3 Corresponding transition system

Behavior of such programs can be represented by a transition system, as illustrated in Figure 6, in its equational form. Synchronous compilers essentially compute this transition system from source programs, particularly handling the synchronous parallel composition of nodes. For a node f as in Figure 4, a transition function $Trans$ takes as inputs X as well as the current state value, and produces the next state value. The latter is memorized by $State$ for the next step. The output function Out takes the same inputs as T, and produces the outputs Y. We will use this representation to explain the notion of DCS, and to illustrate the behavior of our language.

2.2 Discrete Controller Synthesis

Discrete controller synthesis (DCS), emerged in the 80's [8, 20] allows to use constructive methods, that ensure, off-line, required

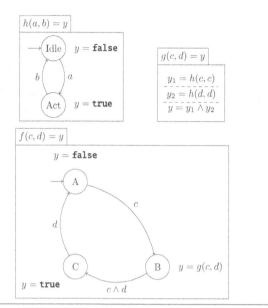

Figure 5. Structured program example

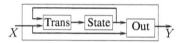

Figure 6. Transition system for a program

properties on the system behavior. DCS is an operation that applies on a transition system (originally uncontrolled), where inputs X are partitioned into uncontrollable (X^u) and controllable variables (X^c). It is applied with a given control objective: a property that has to be enforced by control. In this work, we consider essentially invariance of a subset of the state space.

The purpose of DCS is to obtain a controller, which is a constraint on values of controllable variables X^c, function of the current state and the values of uncontrollable inputs X^u, such that all remaining behaviors satisfy the property given as objective. The synthesized controller is maximally permissive, it is therefore *a priori* a relation; it can be transformed into a control function. This is illustrated in Figure 7, where the transition system of Figure 6, as yet uncontrolled, is composed with the synthesized controller $Ctrlr$, which is fed with uncontrollable inputs X^u and the current state value from $State$, in order to produce the values of controllables X_c which are enforcing the control objective. The transition system then takes $X = X^u \cup X^c$ as input and performs a step.

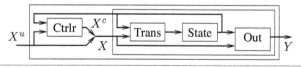

Figure 7. Controlled transition system

Modular DCS. In our approach, transitions systems are the starting point to model fragments of a large scale system, which usually consists of several composed and nested subsystems. To avoid state space explosion induced by the concurrent nature of the systems, there has been a growing interest in designing algorithms that perform the controller synthesis phase by taking advantage of the structure of the system without expanding the system. For the compositional aspect one can consider the works of [3, 11, 22]. More re-

lated to our framework are the methods of [1, 15, 14, 18]. However, their models is different from ours (asynchronous vs synchronous) as well as the way the low-level controlled system is abstracted in order to compute the controller of a higher level.

2.3 Their combinations

Previous work on the integration of DCS in a synchronous programming environment existed related to the Polychrony environment: SIGALI [17] is a tool that offers functionalities for verification of synchronous reactive systems and discrete controller synthesis. It manipulates Symbolic Transitions Systems (See Section 4.1), an equational and symbolic representation of automata. A wide variety of properties, such as invariance, reachability and attractivity, optimality w.r.t. to some quantitative criteria can be ensured by control. In the Polychrony environment, DCS is available as a formal tool amongst others, but not integrated at the programming language-level. A methodology for property-enforcing layers was proposed, [4] related to Mode Automata, but did not propose the language-level integration of objectives and DCS operations, as we do here. A deeper integration was proposed in a domain-specific language called NEMO [12], but it remained at the front-end of synchronous compilation, whereas this paper proposes full integration.

2.4 Contracts, validation and DCS

The notion of "design by contracts" have been introduced first in the Eiffel language [19]; contracts are require/ensure pairs on Eiffel functions which are then used at compilation time to add defensive code to these functions. The same design principle have been extended for reactive systems in [16], where reactive programs are given logical-time contracts, validated automatically by model-checking. We use here the same principle of logical-time contract, the difference with this latter work is essentially that our contracts are enforced by controller synthesis, instead of being validated. A more generic model of contracts has been proposed in [6], defining an algebra of contracts, which allows to consider the relation between sets of contracts defining one system, whereas our language only allows one contract to be associated to one node.

On the use of contracts for controller synthesis, [5] proposes a synthesis method based on the game theory, where contracts are used as assumptions to help the synthesis process. The modular aspect of the "design by contract" approach is not exploited.

Another related approach is interface synthesis [9]: the difference is that it is about constraining the environment of a component so that the component is used correctly, whereas in this work we constrain the component so that it works correctly whatever the environment does (within the assumptions) : the latter way is a more usual application of DCS. In particular, at the uppermost level, the assumption is taken as a hypothesis, to be checked by the programmer, in a way similar to the synchrony hypothesis, which has to be checked by the programmer on his system; on this basis the controller enforces the "guarantee" part. However, one can think of enforcing a guaranty condition at the top level but without any assumptions on the environment variables.

3. The BZR language

This section describes the original language construct which we add to the mode automata language introduced previously, and illustrates how to use it to design controllers in a modular way.

3.1 Nodes with contracts

We define basic contract nodes, and then composite contract nodes, and give the corresponding DCS problem solved at compilation.

3.1.1 Basic BZR node, with a contract

Definition As illustrated in Figure 8, we associate to each node f a *contract*, which is a program associated with two outputs : an output e_A representing the environment model of the node and an invariance predicate e_G that should be satisfied by the node. Its inputs are the inputs x_i and outputs y_i of the node f. At the node level, we assume the existence of a set $C = \{c_1, \dots, c_n\}$ of controllable variables, that will be further used for ensuring this objective. This contract means that the node will be controlled, i.e., that values will be given to $c_1, \dots, c_n$ such that, given any input trace yielding e_A *at each instant*, the output trace will yield the true value for e_G *at each instant*. This will be done by DCS. One can remark that the contract can itself feature a program, e.g., automata, observing traces, and defining states (for example an error state where e_G is false, to be kept outside an invariant subspace). Also, one can define several such nodes with instances of the same body, that differ in assumptions and enforcements.

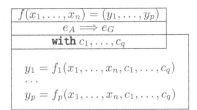

Figure 8. BZR node graphical syntax

Corresponding DCS problem For the compilation of such a BZR node, we will encode it into a DCS problem where, assuming e_A (produced by the contract program, which will be part of the transition system), we will obtain a controller for the objective of enforcing e_G (i.e., making invariant the sub-set of states where $e_A \Rightarrow e_G$ is true), with controllable variables C.

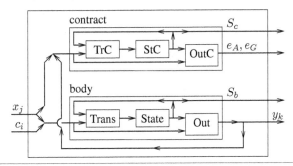

Figure 9. BZR node transition system

This is illustrated in Figure 9, re-using instances of the transition system of Figure 6: one for the contract (with transition function TrC, state memory StC and output function $OutC$) and one for the body of the node. The contract program has access to the node inputs $x_1, \dots, x_n$ and outputs $y_1, \dots, y_p$ of the body. Its outputs are e_A and e_G, and the variables $c_1, \dots, c_q$ are inputs of the body. We show explicitly the states S_c and S_b for clarity.

Figure 10 shows how the controller is synthesized and integrated to obtain the contract-enforcing node, similarly to Figure 7. The global state comprises both body and contract program state, and is taken as input by the controller, as well as the (uncontrollable) inputs $x_1, \dots, x_n$ and contract Boolean outputs e_A and e_G.

3.1.2 BZR composite node

Definition A composite BZR node has a contract of itself, and sub-nodes which are also BZR nodes, with their own contracts,

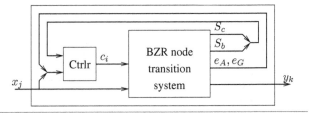

Figure 10. BZR node as DCS problem

as illustrated in Figure 11. Sub-nodes may communicate. This is where modularity gets involved, and the information about contracts of the sub-nodes, which is visible at the level of the composite, will be re-used for the compilation of the composite node.

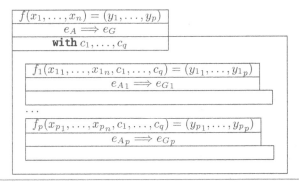

Figure 11. BZR composite node

The objective is still to control the body, using controllable variables $c_1, \dots, c_q$, so that e_G is true, assuming that e_A is true. Here, we have information on sub-nodes, so that we can assume not only e_A, but also, in the case of two sub-nodes, $(e_{A1} \Rightarrow e_{G1})$ and $(e_{A2} \Rightarrow e_{G2})$. Accordingly, the problem becomes that: assuming e_A, $(e_{A1} \Rightarrow e_{G1})$ and $(e_{A2} \Rightarrow e_{G2})$, we want to enforce e_{A1}, e_{A2} and e_G. In particular, control at composite level takes care of enforcing assumptions of the sub-nodes.

Corresponding DCS problem The control objective is to make invariant the subset of states where $e_A \Rightarrow e_G \wedge e_{A1} \wedge e_{A2}$ is true. This objective is applied on the global transition system composing the contract and the body of the node, as well as the contracts for each of the sub-nodes. Note that the bodies of the sub-nodes are not used for the controller computation. Instead, we use the contracts as an abstraction of these sub-nodes. This is to partially avoid the classical state space explosion occurring when computing the whole system.

Figure 12 illustrates this; only the state variables of contracts of sub-nodes are used by the controller of the upper-level node.

3.2 Example: Multi-task System

We now illustrate the previous section through a simple example of a multi-task system. This example is shown for readability purpose with an ad-hoc graphical syntax; the whole final example in concrete textual syntax can be seen in appendix A.

We first specify the controller for one task, and then build a n-tasks server. We then illustrate how the composition of two n-tasks servers in order to build a $2n$-tasks server involves introducing controllability, without which solutions cannot be found by DCS. For this, we voluntarily show pedagogic examples where the control cannot be found, before fixing them into a fully working program.

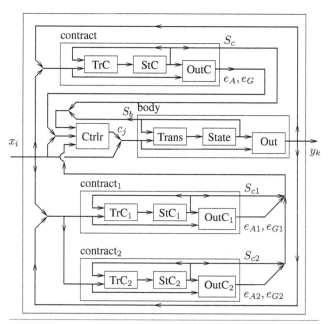

Figure 12. BZR composite DCS problem

3.2.1 Delayable Tasks

Figure 13 shows the control of a delayable task specified in mode automata. A delayable task takes three inputs r, c and e: r is the task launch request from the environment, e is the end request, and c is meant to be a controllable input controlling whether, on request, the task is actually launched (and therefore goes in the active state), or delayed (and then forced by the controller to go in the waiting state by stating the false value to c). This node outputs a Boolean act which is true when the task is active.

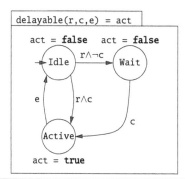

Figure 13. Delayable task (graphical syntax)

The Figure 14 shows a node $\mathtt{ntasks}$ where n delayable tasks have been put in parallel. The tasks are inlined i.e., their code is expanded at the location of the call, so as to be able to perform DCS on this node, taking into account the tasks' states. Until now, the only interest of modularity is, from the programmer's point of view, to be able to give once the delayable task code.

This $\mathtt{ntasks}$ node is provided with a contract, stating that its composing tasks are exclusive, i.e., that there are no two tasks in the active state at the same instant. This is encoded in the equations defining conflicts: ca_i is true if task i is active and some other task $j, i < j \leq n$ is active too. This contract is enforced with the help of the controllable inputs c_i. Typically, the expected behavior of the obtained controller is to force to the false value the c_i variables, when the task i is requested while another task is in the active state.

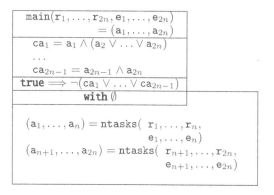

Figure 14. $\mathtt{ntasks}$ node: n delayable tasks in parallel

3.2.2 Contract composition

We now reuse the $\mathtt{ntasks}$ node, to build modularly a system composed of $2n$ tasks. Figure 15 shows the parallel composition of two $\mathtt{ntasks}$ nodes. We associate to this composition a new contract, which role is to enforce the exclusivity of the $2n$ tasks.

$$
\begin{array}{|l|}
\hline
\mathtt{main}(\mathtt{r}_1,\ldots,\mathtt{r}_{2n},\mathtt{e}_1,\ldots,\mathtt{e}_{2n}) \\
\quad = (\mathtt{a}_1,\ldots,\mathtt{a}_{2n}) \\
\hline
ca_1 = a_1 \wedge (a_2 \vee \ldots \vee a_{2n}) \\
\ldots \\
ca_{2n-1} = a_{2n-1} \wedge a_{2n} \\
\hline
\mathbf{true} \implies \neg(ca_1 \vee \ldots \vee ca_{2n-1}) \\
\hline
\mathbf{with}\ \emptyset \\
\hline
(a_1,\ldots,a_n) = \mathtt{ntasks}(\ r_1,\ldots,r_n, \\
\qquad\qquad\qquad\qquad e_1,\ldots,e_n) \\
(a_{n+1},\ldots,a_{2n}) = \mathtt{ntasks}(\ r_{n+1},\ldots,r_{2n}, \\
\qquad\qquad\qquad\qquad e_{n+1},\ldots,e_{2n}) \\
\hline
\end{array}
$$

Figure 15. Composition of two $\mathtt{ntasks}$ nodes

It is easy to see that the contract of $\mathtt{ntasks}$ is not precise enough to be able to compose several of these nodes, because there is no way to control them to avoid that one task is active in each of the two subsystems. Therefore, we need to refine this contract by adding some way to externally control the activity of the tasks.

3.2.3 Contract refinement

We first add an input c, meant to be controllable at an upper level. The refined contract will enforce that:

1. the tasks are exclusive, i.e., that there are no two tasks in the active state at the same instant;

2. one task is active only at instants when the input c is true. This property, appearing in the contract, allows a node instantiating $\mathtt{ntasks}$ to forbid any activity of the n tasks instantiated.

The Figure 16 contains this new $\mathtt{ntasks}$ node.

However, the controllability introduced here is now too strong. The synthesis will succeed, but the computed controller, without knowing how c will be instantiated, will actually block all tasks in their idle state. Indeed, if the controller allows one task to go in its active state, the input c (uncontrollable at the $\mathtt{ntasks}$ level) can become false at the next instant, violating the property to enforce.

$$
\begin{array}{|c|}
\hline
\texttt{ntasks}(c, r_1, \ldots, r_n, e_1, \ldots, e_n) \\
= (a_1, \ldots, a_n) \\
\hline
ca_1 = a_1 \wedge (a_2 \vee \ldots \vee a_n) \\
\ldots \\
ca_{n-1} = a_{n-1} \wedge a_n \\
one = a_1 \vee \ldots \vee a_n \\
\hline
\textbf{true} \\
\implies \neg(ca_1 \vee \ldots \vee ca_{n-1}) \wedge (c \vee \neg one) \\
\hline
\textbf{with}\; c_1, \ldots, c_n \\
\hline
a_1 = \textbf{inlined}\; \texttt{delayable}(r_1, c_1, e_1) \\
\vdots \\
a_n = \textbf{inlined}\; \texttt{delayable}(r_n, c_n, e_n) \\
\hline
\end{array}
$$

Figure 16. First contract refinement for the `ntasks` node

Thus, we propose to add an assumption to this contract: the input `c` will not become false if a task was active an instant before. This assumption will be enforced correct by the controller of the upper level. This new contract is visible in Figure 17.

$$
\begin{array}{|c|}
\hline
\texttt{ntasks}(c, r_1, \ldots, r_n, e_1, \ldots, e_n) \\
= (a_1, \ldots, a_n) \\
\hline
ca_1 = a_1 \wedge (a_2 \vee \ldots \vee a_n) \\
\ldots \\
ca_{n-1} = a_{n-1} \wedge a_n \\
one = a_1 \vee \ldots \vee a_n \\
pone = \textbf{false fby}\; one \\
\hline
(\neg pone \vee c) \\
\implies \neg(ca_1 \vee \ldots \vee ca_{n-1}) \wedge (c \vee \neg one) \\
\hline
\textbf{with}\; c_1, \ldots, c_n \\
\hline
a_1 = \textbf{inlined}\; \texttt{delayable}(r_1, c_1, e_1) \\
\ldots \\
a_n = \textbf{inlined}\; \texttt{delayable}(r_n, c_n, e_n) \\
\hline
\end{array}
$$

Figure 17. Second contract refinement for the `ntasks` node

We can then use this new `ntasks` version for the parallel composition, by instantiating the `c` input by two controllable variables. This composition can be found in Figure 18.

$$
\begin{array}{|c|}
\hline
\texttt{main}(r_1, \ldots, r_{2n}, e_1, \ldots, e_{2n}) \\
= (a_1, \ldots, a_{2n}) \\
\hline
ca_1 = a_1 \wedge (a_2 \vee \ldots \vee a_{2n}) \\
\ldots \\
ca_{2n-1} = a_{2n-1} \wedge a_{2n} \\
\hline
\textbf{true} \implies \neg(ca_1 \vee \ldots \vee ca_{2n-1}) \\
\hline
\textbf{with}\; c_1, c_2 \\
\hline
(a_1, \ldots, a_n) = \texttt{ntasks}(c_1,\; r_1, \ldots, r_n, \\
e_1, \ldots, e_n) \\
(a_{n+1}, \ldots, a_{2n}) = \texttt{ntasks}(c_2,\; r_{n+1}, \ldots, r_{2n}, \\
e_{n+1}, \ldots, e_{2n}) \\
\hline
\end{array}
$$

Figure 18. Two refined `ntasks` parallel composition

4. BZR compilation

This section describes in a formal way the compilation process of our language. This compilation process is modular, meaning that each node will be compiled in an independent way; and it comprises a discrete controller synthesis stage for each of these nodes. We first recall the notations used, then present the controller synthesis for one contract, and last show how the synthesized controllers are recombined to obtain the whole controlled system.

4.1 Control of Symbolic Transition Systems (STS)

4.1.1 Definitions

Notations. Given a set of Boolean variables $Z = Z_1, \cdots, Z_k$, we define a valuation of Z as a function $val : Z \rightarrow \mathbb{B}^k$ that assigns to each variables in Z a value either true or false. In the sequel, we shall use X, Y, Z as vectors of Boolean variables and x, y, z for a possible valuation of these vectors. Given a predicate $B \in \mathbb{B}[Z]$ a polynomial over Z and $z \in val(Z)$, we denote by $B(z) \in \mathbb{B}$ the predicate B valuated by z. We further denote $\bar{z} = z_0.z_1.z_2 \cdots$ an infinite sequence of valuations of Z. Given a sequence $\bar{z}$ and a predicate $G \in \mathbb{B}[Z]$, we denote $\bar{z} \models \Box G$ the fact that G hold for the sequence $\bar{z}$ at every instant.

$$\bar{z} \models \Box G \text{ iff } \bar{z} = z_0.z_1.z_2 \cdots \text{ and } \forall i, G(z_i).$$

Symbolic Transition Systems. We represent synchronous programs by Synchronous Symbolic Transition Systems (STS). A STS $S(X, Y, Z)$, defining a synchronous program of state variables $X \in \mathbb{B}^m$, input event variables $Y \in \mathbb{B}^n$, output event variables $Z \in \mathbb{B}^p$, is a tuple (P, O, Q, Q_0):

$$
S = \left\{
\begin{array}{l}
X' = P(X, Y) \\
Z = O(X, Y) \\
Q(X, Y) \\
Q_0(X)
\end{array}
\right.
$$

where:

- the vectors X and X' respectively encode the current and next states of the system and are called *state variables* (they contain the memory necessary for describing the system behavior).

- $P \in \mathbb{B}[X, Y]$ represent the transition function. It is a vector-valued function $[P_1, \ldots, P_n]$ from $\mathbb{B}^{n+m}$ to $\mathbb{B}^n$. Each polynomial component P_i represents the evolution of the state variable X_i. It characterizes the dynamic of the system. between the current state X and events Y and next state X'.

- $O \in \mathbb{B}[X, Y]$ represents the output function.

- $Q_0 \in \mathbb{B}[X]$ defines the set initial states, and $Q \in \mathbb{B}[X, Y, Z]$ the constraints between current states and events and encodes the *static* part of the system (invariant for all instants t).

The semantics of a STS S is that it defines a set of sequences $\overline{(x, y, z)}$ such that : $Q_0(x_0)$ and $\forall i$,

$$Q(x_i, x_i) \wedge \Big(x_{i+1} = P(x_i, x_i) \Big) \wedge \Big(z_i = O(x_i, y_i) \Big).$$

We denote by $\text{Traces}(S)$ this set of sequences.

STS transformations. Given two STS S_1 and S_2, we note by $S_1 \| S_2$, the synchronous parallel composition of S_1 and S_2 which consists in performing the conjunction of the composing predicate of S_1 and S_2, and is defined iff state and output variables are exclusive. Communications between the two systems are expressed via common inputs and outputs variables, which are considered as outputs of the composition. Formally, $S_1 \| S_2$ is a STS $S_1 \| S_2 (X_1 \cup$

$X_2, (Y_1 \cup Y_2) \setminus (Z_1 \cup Z_2), Z_1 \cup Z_2$:

$$S_1 \| S_2 = \left\{ \begin{array}{l} X_1', X_2' = P_1(X_1, Y_1) \wedge P_2(X_2, Y_2) \\ Z_1, Z_2 = (O_1(X_1, Y_1), O_2(X_2, Y_2)) \\ Q_1(X_1, Y_1) \wedge Q_2(X_2, Y_2) \\ Q_{01}(X_1) \wedge Q_{02}(X_2) \end{array} \right.$$

Finally, we denote by $S \triangleright A$ the extension of constraints of S with the predicate $A \in \mathbb{B}[X, Y, Z]$:

$$S \triangleright A = \left\{ \begin{array}{l} X' = P(X, Y) \\ Z = O(X, Y) \\ Q(X, Y, Z) \wedge A(X, Y, Z) \\ Q_0(X) \end{array} \right.$$

Contracts satisfaction. In the sequel, we shall consider properties expressed by means of contracts that are defined as follows:

Definition 1 (Contract). *A contract is a tuple* $C = (S^c, A, G)$ *where* $S^c(X^c, (Y \cup Z), \emptyset)$ *is a STS,* $A \in \mathbb{B}[X^c]$ *and* $G \in \mathbb{B}[X^c]$ *are predicates.*

Intuitively, S^c can be seen as an abstraction of a component program, G is the property to be satisfied by the traces of the component on which this contract is placed providing the fact that the model of the environment A is satisfied. For clarity, we define the contract predicates A and G on only state variables of the contract. We remark though that this does not restrict the expressiveness of these properties, as one can add dummy state variables constrained with inputs or outputs values, so as to be able to express properties upon inputs and outputs variables.

Definition 2 (Contract fulfilment). *A STS* $S(X, Y)$ *fulfills a contract* $C = (S^c, A, G)$, *noted* $S \models C$, *if* $\forall (x, x^c, y, z) \in$ Traces$(S\|S^c)$, $\overline{(x^c)} \models \Box A \Rightarrow \overline{(x^c)} \models \Box G$.

Hence, a contract is satisfied whenever the traces of S, composed with S^c and satisfying $\Box A$, satisfy $\Box G$. This constitutes one of the main difference with the work of [6], as in their framework, A and G are assertions of any kind on traces. Our restriction is due to the technique used: only safety properties (vs liveness or equity) can be ensured by abstracted state space exploration, and preserved by synchronous composition.

As the above definition does not allow to be easily applied on STS, we give below a property on contracts: the environment model can be viewed as additional constraints of the STS composed of S and the contract program S^c.

Proposition 1. $(S\|S^c) \triangleright A \models G \Rightarrow S \models (S^c, A, G)$.

4.1.2 Contracts enforcement

Assume given a system S and a contract C on S. Our aim is to restrict the behavior of S in order to fulfil the contract.

The control of a STS relies on a distinction between events. We distinguish between the *uncontrollable* event variables Y^{uc} which are defined by the environment, and the *controllable* event Y^c which are defined by the controller of the system (they are considered as internal variables). Now, in order to enforce $C = (S^c, A, G)$ with $S^c(X^c, Y^{uc} \cup Z, \emptyset)$, $A \in \mathbb{B}[X^c]$ and $G \in \mathbb{B}[X^c]$ on S we consider the STS $(S\|S^c) \triangleright A$:

$$(S\|S^c) \triangleright A = \left\{ \begin{array}{l} X', X'^c = P(X, X^c, Y^c, Y^{uc}) \\ Z = O(X, X^c, Y^c, Y^{uc}) \\ Q(X, X^c, Y^c, Y^{uc}) \\ Q_0(X, X^c) \end{array} \right.$$

The property we wish to enforce by control on this system is given by the invariant G. In our framework, a controller is a predicate $K \in \mathbb{B}[X, X^c, Y^c, Y^{uc}]$ that constraints the set of admissible event so that the traces of the controlled system always satisfy the predicate G. We do not detail here how such a controller

can be computed. It relies on a fix-point computation w.r.t. the function $Pre_{uc}(E) = \{(x, x^c) \mid \forall y^{uc}, \exists y^c, Q(x, y^{uc}, y^c) \Rightarrow P(x, y^{uc}, y^c) \in E\}$. We will present a more generic algorithm in the next section. The controller describes how to choose the static controls; when the controlled system is in state (x, x^c), and when an event y^{uc} occurs, any value y^c such that $Q(x, x^c, y^{uc}, y^c)$ and $K(x, x^c, y^{uc}, y^c)$ can be chosen. The behavior of the system supervised by the controller is then modeled by $(S\|S^c) \triangleright K$.

Determination of the controller. Assume now that we have computed a controller $K \in \mathbb{B}[X, X^c, Y^c, Y^{uc}]$. K is non-deterministic w.r.t. the controllable variables, in the sense that for each state of the system and for each valuation of the uncontrollable variables, there might exists several valuations for the controllable ones that respects K. Obviously, this non-determinism has to be solved in some ways. One possibility is to encapsulate in the system, a predicate solver, that either asks an external user to make a choice amongst the possible solutions or that itself performed a random choices amongst them. Following a method similar to the one described in [13], another possibility is to derive from the controller a set of functions F_i^c that depends on X, X^c, Y^{uc} and some fresh *phantom* variables ϕ_i, one for each controllable variables, namely:

$$K(X, X^c, Y^c, Y^{uc}) \Leftrightarrow$$
$$\exists (\phi_i)_{i \leq \ell} \left\{ \begin{array}{l} Y_1^c = F_1^c(X, X^c, Y^{uc}, \phi_1) \\ \cdots \\ Y_i^c = F_i^c(X, X^c, Y^{uc}, Y_1^c, \cdots, Y_{i-1}^c, \phi_i) \\ \cdots \\ Y_\ell^c = F_n^c(X, X^c, Y^{uc}, Y_1^c, \cdots, Y_{\ell-1}^c, \phi_\ell) \\ K'(X, X^c, Y^{uc}) \end{array} \right.$$

In other words, whatever the valuation of a tuple (x, x^c, y^{uc}, y^c), there exists a valuation $(v_{\phi_i})_{i \leq \ell}$ of $(\phi_i)_{i \leq \ell}$ such that $y_i^c = F_i^c(x, x^c, y^{uc}, v_{\phi_i})$.

At this point, either the variables (ϕ_i) can be seen as new inputs of the system or can be eliminated by choosing for each of them a value. Note that in this case, we loose the equivalence (only $\Rightarrow$ implication is kept). For clarity reasons, this is the second choice we have made in this paper.

Remark 1. *With the determination of the controller, part of the solutions can be actually lost, when the synthesized controller is not deterministic (but the safety property is kept); and in this sense the modular control is sub-optimal. It is an interesting perspective indeed to replace local random selections with a heuristic taking into account some of the interactions between components. Note however, that it is possible to keep the maximal behavior by keeping the new phantom variables.*

4.2 Modular control of STS

4.2.1 Contracts composition

Let consider now a hierarchically designed program, i.e., a STS $S(X, Y, Z)$ composed of subcomponents $S_1, \ldots, S_n$, together with additional local code S' (as in Figure 19). We have then :

$$S(X, Y, Z) = (S'\|S_1\| \ldots \|S_n)$$

Note that $Y_i^{uc} \subseteq X \cup Y^{uc} \cup Y^c \cup Z$, namely the uncontrollable variables of the lower level can be defined either by state, uncontrollable or controllable inputs, or outputs variables of the upper system. Thus to proceed to the encapsulation we need to rename the variables Y_i^{uc} according to their new name in the new system.

We assume that each sub-component $S_i(X_i, Y_i, Z_i)$ comes with a contract $C_i = (S_i^c, A_i, G_i)$, with $S_i^c(X_i^c, Y_i \cup Z_i, \emptyset)$, $A_i \in \mathbb{B}[X_i^c]$, $G_i \in \mathbb{B}[X_i^c]$, and that a controller K_i has been computed such as, for all i, $(S_i\|S_i^c) \triangleright K_i \models C_i$.

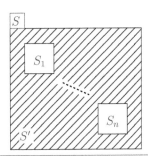

Figure 19. STS composed of several subcomponents

We want now to obtain a controller K for the system S to fulfill a contract $C = (S^c, A, G)$, with $S^c(X^c, Y \cup Z, \emptyset)$, $A \in \mathbb{B}[X^c]$ and $G \in \mathbb{B}[X^c]$. One way to do this is to compute the whole dynamic of S and to control it using the previous method, but this would lead to a state space explosion. Instead, we will use the contracts of the sub-components as an abstraction of them. Thus, we use an abstracted STS $\hat{S}$, defined as the composition of S' with the system part of the subcontracts, constrained with the properties enforced by K_i on each of the sub-components. In other words, we take the assume and enforced parts of the subcontracts as environment model of the abstracted system. Moreover, the Z_i variables were outputs of the lower level. As we abstract away the body of this system, these variables have now to be considered as uncontrollable variables of the upper system (indeed, there is no way to know their value). Besides, the value of these variables is normally computed according to the value of Y_1^{uc} and internal variables. Hence there exists causality problems between these variables and the variables of the upper level. This causality constraint will be resolved by the design of a more general controller synthesis algorithm (see Section 4.2.2). We define the new system to be controlled as follows:

$$\hat{S}(X, Y^{uc} \cup Z_1 \cup \ldots \cup Z_n, Y^c, Z) =$$
$$\left(S' \| \left(S_1^c \rhd (A_1 \Rightarrow G_1) \right) \| \ldots \| \left(S_n^c \rhd (A_n \Rightarrow G_n) \right) \right)$$

We should notice that, in order to the STSs S_i, controlled by their controller, to be evaluated in a correct environment, the predicates A_i must be satisfied. Therefore, we define a new contract $\hat{C}$, which will be used to compute a controller on $\hat{S}$:

$$\hat{C} = (S^c, \hat{A}, \hat{G}) \text{ where } \begin{cases} \hat{A} = A \\ \hat{G} = G \wedge A_1 \wedge \ldots \wedge A_n \end{cases}$$

We then compute controller K, enforcing contract C on STS $\hat{S}$:

$$\hat{S} \rhd K \models \hat{C}$$

The correction of this method is given by the following result, stating that the controller K, computed for the abstracted system $\hat{S}$, is a correct controller for the concrete system, i.e., S controlled by K fulfils the contract C.

Theorem 1.
If $\hat{S} \rhd K \models \hat{C}$ and for all i, $(S_i \| S_i^c) \rhd K_i \models C_i$, then:

$$\left(S' \| (S_1 \| S_1^c) \rhd K_1 \| \ldots \| (S_n \| S_n^c) \rhd K_n \right) \rhd K \models C$$

4.2.2 Control of an STS with sub-contracts

As mentioned in the previous section, there exists causality dependencies between the Z_i variables and the Y_i^c variables, in the sense that the computation of the value of the variables Z_i depends on the value of Y_i^c, which must then be computed before. Moreover, the Y_i^c can be computed according to the value of some other variables of the upper-level system. In the following, we denote by $X_1 \prec X_2$

the fact that X_2 depends on X_1. This relation is straightforwardly extended to variable sets:

$$\tilde{X} \prec \tilde{Y} \overset{def}{=} \forall(X, Y) \in \tilde{X} \times \tilde{Y}, X \prec Y$$

In the sequel, we shall consider the following subsets of Z_i : $(\tilde{Z}_i)_{i \leq n}$, where $\forall i \leq n, \tilde{Z}_i \subseteq \tilde{Z}_{i-1}$, and such that $Y_i^c \prec \tilde{Z}_i$. Furthermore, we note $\tilde{Z}_i' = \tilde{Z}_i \setminus \tilde{Z}_{i-1}$.

$$Y \prec \tilde{Z}_0 \prec \{Y_1^c\} \prec \tilde{Z}_1 \prec \cdots \prec \{Y_n^c\} \prec \tilde{Z}_n \tag{1}$$

Control synthesis algorithm overview. Computing the controller K as in Section 4.1.2 is not suitable as it does not take into account the dependencies between the variables. Intuitively, in order to be able to compute the value of Y_i^c we need to know the value of the variables $\tilde{Z}_i$. Thus, if we want to be sure that there exists a solution to the determination, the controller should take into account that the value of the variable Y_i^c is correct whatever the value of $\tilde{Z}_i$. This is what we capture by computing the Pre_{uc} operator as follows:

$$Pre_{uc}(E) = \Big\{ (x, x^c) \,|\, \forall y^{uc}, \tilde{z}_0, \exists y_1^c, \forall \tilde{z}_1', \ldots, \exists y_n^c, \forall \tilde{z}_n',$$
$$Q(x, y^{uc}, y^c, z) \Rightarrow P(x, y^{uc}, y^c, z) \in E \Big\}$$

Further the computation of K is similar to the one of Section 4.1.2.

Deterministic controller. For the determination of K, we also need to take into account the dependencies between the variables: the order relation (1) implies that the deterministic controller, as defined in Section 4.1.2, will be a set of functions $\tilde{F}_i^c$ that depends on X, X^c, Y^{uc}, ϕ_i and the additional uncontrollable inputs $\tilde{Z}_{i-1}$:

$$K(X, X^c, Y^c, Y^{uc})$$
$$\Leftrightarrow$$
$$\exists(\phi_1, \cdots, \phi_l),$$
$$\begin{cases} Y_1^c = \tilde{F}_1^c(X, X^c, Y^{uc}, \tilde{Z}_0, \phi_1) \\ \cdots \\ Y_i^c = \tilde{F}_i^c(X, X^c, Y^{uc}, Y_1^c, \cdots, Y_{i-1}^c, \tilde{Z}_{i-1}, \phi_i) \\ \cdots \\ Y_n^c = \tilde{F}_n^c(X, X^c, Y^{uc}, Y_1^c, \cdots, Y_{n-1}^c, \tilde{Z}_{n-1}, \phi_l) \end{cases}$$

These $\tilde{F}_i^c$ functions are related with F_i^c, defined in Section 4.1.2, by $\tilde{F}_i^c = \forall \tilde{Z}_i, F_i^c$. The existence of $\tilde{F}_i^c$ is then ensured by the modified version of the control synthesis algorithm we give further. Once again, we can further eliminate the variables (ϕ_i) by choosing a particular value for each of them.

5. Implementation

Figure 20 illustrates the compilation process for BZR implementing our method. Boxes with round corners indicate data (source code, target code, intermediate formats); rectangular boxes indicate tools and operations. It is built around synchronous compilation and DCS technology, and borrows essentially two pre-existing tools (indicated in stripped boxes). One is a synchronous compiler: HEPTAGON, used in order to (i): compile the nodes into a format accepted by the DCS tool, and (ii): compile the composition of the triangularized controller with the originally uncontrolled automaton, hence building the controlled automaton, and generating executable code for it. The other is the DCS tool: SIGALI. BZR has been used for a case study of a video display on a mobile phone [2].

Our approach is target independent, in the sense that the compilation process from automata to code generation concerns the transition function of the controller. The target is taken into account, as shown in the development process of Figure 2, when the control part is extracted from the target, and when the resulting step function is linked back into the executive, with the proper interface. The general structure of the generated code consists of two functions:

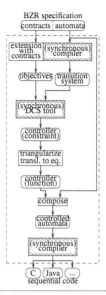

Figure 20. BZR compilation process.

a *step* function, performing one transition, with input events as parameters, producing output values, and updating the internal state of the automaton; and a *reset* function, for initialization purposes. These functions (signature and body) are simple enough to allow to target any general-purpose language. The compiler currently generates C or Java code. It would not be difficult to consider also more domain-specific languages like VHDL.

6. Performances

The bottleneck of our approach is clearly the synthesis time, as the algorithm is based on the exploration of the state space of each node. This section thus shows some typical synthesis time on multitasks systems, with and without use of modularity.

The system considered here is composed of $3n$ tasks, to be enforced exclusive, as showed in Section 3.2. These $3n$ tasks are composed of n delayable tasks (Figure 13) and $2n$ rejectable tasks (Figure 21: tasks requests can be rejected but are not memorized). Three experiments are made:

1. the $3n$ tasks are inlined into the same node: the state space to explore corresponds then to the entire state space of the 3n automata composition;

2. the $3n$ tasks are decomposed into three nodes instantiation of n inlined tasks, as in Section 3.2: three separate synthesis are then performed (one for n delayable tasks, one for n rejectable tasks and one for the main node);

3. likewise, the $3n$ tasks are decomposed into three nodes, but we also use the modularity to perform the three synthesis in parallel, as they do not depend on each other's results.

Figure 22 shows the compared synthesis time for each of these experiments. They have been fulfilled on a standard PC with two 2.33 GHz cores, and 4 Gb of RAM. The non-monotony of the two curves are explained by the sensitivity of the underlying algorithms, which makes the synthesis time hard to predict. Nevertheless, these measurements shows that modularity can improve the usability of discrete controller synthesis. We can see, e.g., that while synthesis fail (for lack of memory) in "inlined" mode for $n = 14, 15$ and $n > 16$, such systems when adequately structured can be handled in few seconds. Moreover, modularity allows to gain some synthesis time by parallelizing the synthesis computations.

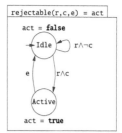

Figure 21. Rejectable task

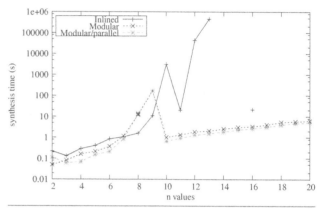

Figure 22. Compared synthesis time for $3n$ automata in inlined, modular and modular+parallel modes

Concerning other performance aspects, the final controller size is, for the same reasons as the synthesis time, exponential in the size of the initial program (typically, number of states and inputs). This controller consists of sequences of conditionals (translation of binary decision diagrams), and also its online evaluation is polynomial in the size of the initial program.

7. Conclusion

We have proposed a programming-level method, based on the "design by contracts" principle, to apply modular discrete controller synthesis, integrated into a compilation process. This method allows to apply DCS on subcomponents of a system, in order to compute one single controller for each of these subcomponents. These controllers can then be composed with their associated components, before their composition in an upper-level component. The contracts can then be used to compute a controller for this upper-level component, abstracting the bodies of its subcomponents; and so on. On the other hand, in the comparison between modular and monolithic synthesis, we have the advantage of breaking down the cost of synthesis computations (as we only keep the guaranty at the upper level and not the current node that can be itself a composition of several nodes), for which real-size evaluations are in our projects. More precisely, our contribution is a new nondeterministic synchronous language with contracts, named BZR. We have shown how this language can be compiled towards symbolic transition systems, and how modular controllers are computed and recomposed.

Further work can be fulfilled toward several directions. This method could be applied in different component framework, so as to explore its interaction with actual industrial design flow. Some work is in progress within the Fractal framework. Such integration in actual design flow entails a greater interactivity with the programmer: thus, efforts on diagnosis should be made. Some methods should be proposed to get intelligible informations to the programmer when the synthesis fail, which is not currently possible. Another interesting prospect would also be, when synthesis fail, to use the synthesis algorithm to infer some additional constraints on the contracts of the program to allow the synthesis to succeed.

In a more technical concern, some other controller synthesis methods or algorithms could replace the SIGALI tool. This work only addresses invariance objectives: other kinds of synthesis objective (accessibility, attractivity) would jeopardize the modularity properties, but are an interesting prospect to deal with.

References

[1] S. Abdelwahed and W. Wonham. Supervisory control of interacting discrete event systems. In *41th IEEE Conference on Decision and Control*, pages 1175–1180, Las Vegas, USA, December 2002.

[2] S. Aboubekr, G. Delaval, and E. Rutten. A programming language for adaptation control: Case study. In *2nd Workshop on Adaptive and Reconfigurable Embedded Systems (APRES 2009). ACM SIGBED Review*, volume 6, Grenoble, France, Oct. 2009.

[3] K. Akesson, H. Flordal, and M. Fabian. Exploiting modularity for synthesis and verification of supervisors. In *Proc. of the IFAC*, 2002.

[4] K. Altisen, A. Clodic, F. Maraninchi, and E. Rutten. Using controller synthesis to build property-enforcing layers. In *Proceedings of the European Symposium on Programming (ESOP'03)*, number 2618 in LNCS, Warsaw, Poland, Apr. 2003.

[5] R.-J. Back and C. C. Seceleanu. Contracts and games in controller synthesis for discrete systems. In *IEEE Int. Conf. on Engineering of Computer-Based Systems*, page 307, 2004.

[6] A. Benveniste, B. Caillaud, and R. Passerone. A generic model of contracts for embedded systems. Res. Rep. RR-6214, INRIA, 2007.

[7] A. Benveniste, P. Caspi, S. Edwards, N. Halbwachs, P. L. Guernic, and R. de Simone. The synchronous languages twelve years later. *Proc. of the IEEE*, 91(1):64–83, Jan. 2003.

[8] C. Cassandras and S. Lafortune. *Introduction to Discrete Event Systems*. Kluwer Academic Publishers, 1999.

[9] A. Chakrabarti, L. de Alfaro, T. Henzinger, and F. Mang. Synchronous and bidirectional component interfaces. In *CAV 2002: 14th Int. Conf. on Computer Aided Verification, LNCS*, 2002.

[10] J.-L. Colaço, B. Pagano, and M. Pouzet. A Conservative Extension of Synchronous Data-flow with State Machines. In *ACM Int. Conf. on Embedded Software (EMSOFT'05)*, Jersey city, New Jersey, USA, September 2005.

[11] M. De Queiroz and J. Cury. Modular control of composed systems. In *Proceedings of the American Control Conference*, pages 4051–4055, Chicago, Illinois, June 2000.

[12] G. Delaval and E. Rutten. A domain-specific language for multi-task systems, applying discrete controller synthesis. *J. on Embedded Systems*, 2007(84192):17, Jan. 2007. www.hindawi.com/journals/es.

[13] Y. Hietter, J.-M. Roussel, and J.-J. Lesage. Algebraic Synthesis of Transition Conditions of a State Model. In *Proc. of 9th Int. Workshop On Discrete Event Systems (WODES'08)*, Göteborg, June 2008.

[14] R. Leduc, W. Wonham, and M. Lawford. Hierarchical interface-based supervisory control: Parallel case. In *Proc. of the 39th Allerton Conf. on Comm., Contr., and Comp.*, pages 386–395, October 2001.

[15] C. Ma and W. Wonham. A symbolic approach to the supervision of state tree structures. In *13th Mediterranean Conference on Control and Automation*, Limassol, Cyprus, June 2005.

[16] F. Maraninchi and L. Morel. Logical-time contracts for the development of reactive embedded software. In *30th Euromicro Conference, Component-Based Software Engineering Track (ECBSE)*, Rennes, France, Sept. 2004.

[17] H. Marchand, P. Bournai, M. L. Borgne, and P. L. Guernic. Synthesis of discrete-event controllers based on the Signal environment. *Discrete Event Dynamic System: Theory and Applications*, 10(4), Oct. 2000.

[18] H. Marchand and B. Gaudin. Supervisory control problems of hierarchical finite state machines. In *41th IEEE Conference on Decision and Control*, Las Vegas, USA, December 2002.

[19] B. Meyer. Applying "design by contract". *Computer*, 25(10):40–51, Oct 1992.

[20] P. J. Ramadge and W. M. Wonham. The control of discrete event systems. *Proceedings of the IEEE; Special issue on Dynamics of Discrete Event Systems*, 77(1):81–98, 1989.

[21] Y. Wang, S. Lafortune, T. kelly, M. Kudlur, and S. Mahlke. The Theory of Deadlock Avoidance via Discrete Control. In *ACM Symposium on Principles of Programming Languages (POPL '09)*, Savannah, Georgia, USA, January 2009.

[22] Y. Willner and M. Heymann. Supervisory control of concurrent discrete-event systems. *Int. J. of Control*, 54(5):1143–1169, 1991.

A. BZR Example in Concrete Textual Syntax

The following is the concrete BZR code (apart from indices of identifiers) for the example.

```
node delayable(r,c,e:bool) returns (act:bool)
let
  automaton
    state Idle
      do act = false
      until r & c then Active
        | r & not c then Wait
    state Wait
      do act = false
      until c then Active
    state Active
      do act = true
      until e then Idle
  end
tel
```

```
node ntasks(c,r₁,...,rₙ,e₁,...,eₙ) returns (a₁,...,aₙ:bool)
  contract
  let
    ca₁ = a₁ & (a₂ or ... or aₙ);
      ⋮
    caₙ₋₁ = aₙ₋₁ & aₙ;
    one = a₁ or ... or aₙ;
    pone = false fby one;
  tel
  assume (not pone or c)
  enforce not (ca₁ or ... or caₙ₋₁) & (c or not one)
    with (c₁,...,cₙ:bool)
let
  a₁ = inlined  delayable(r₁,c₁,e₁);
    ⋮
  aₙ = inlined  delayable(rₙ,cₙ,eₙ);
tel
```

```
node main(r₁,...,r₂ₙ,e₁,...,e₂ₙ) returns (a₁,...,a₂ₙ:bool)
  contract
  let
    ca₁ = a₁ & (a₂ or ... or a₂ₙ);
      ⋮
    ca₂ₙ₋₁ = a₂ₙ₋₁ & a₂ₙ;
  tel
  assume true
  enforce not (ca₁ or ... or ca₂ₙ₋₁)
  with (c₁,c₂:bool)
let
  (a₁,...,aₙ) = ntasks(c₁,r₁,...,rₙ,e₁,...,eₙ);
  (aₙ₊₁,...,a₂ₙ) = ntasks(c₂,rₙ₊₁,...,r₂ₙ,eₙ₊₁,...,e₂ₙ);
tel
```

Semi-Automatic Derivation of Timing Models for WCET Analysis

Marc Schlickling   Markus Pister

Universität des Saarlandes, Postfach 15 11 50, D-66041 Saarbrücken, Germany and
AbsInt Angewandte Informatik GmbH, Science Park 1, D-66123 Saarbrücken, Germany
{schlickling,pister}@cs.uni-saarland.de

Abstract

Embedded systems are widely used for supporting our every day life. In the area of safety-critical systems human life often depends on the system's correct behavior. Many of such systems are hard real-time systems, so that the notion of correctness not only means functional correctness. They additionally have to obey stringent timing constraints, i.e., timely task completion under all circumstances is essential. An example for such a safety-critical system is the flight control computer in an airplane, which is responsible for stability, attitude and path control.

In order to derive guarantees on the timing behavior of hard real-time systems, the worst-case execution time (WCET) of each task in the system has to be determined. Saarland University and AbsInt GmbH have successfully developed the *aiT* WCET analyzer for computing safe upper bounds on the WCET of a task. The computation is mainly based on abstract interpretation of timing models of the processor and its periphery. Such timing models are currently hand-crafted by human experts. Therefore their implementation is a time-consuming and error-prone process.

Modern processors or system controllers are automatically synthesized out of formal hardware specifications like VHDL or VERILOG. Besides the system' functional behavior, such specifications provide all information needed for the creation of a timing model. But due to their size and complexity, manually examining the sources is even more complex than only looking at the processor manuals. Moreover, this would not reduce the effort nor the probability of implementation errors.

To face this problem, this paper proposes a method for semi-automatically deriving suitable timing models out of formal hardware specifications in VHDL that fit to the tool chain of the *aiT* WCET analyzer. By this, we reduce the creation time of timing models from months to weeks.

Categories and Subject Descriptors   J.7 [*Computers in other systems*]: Real time; C.3 [*Special-purpose and application-based systems*]: Real-time and embedded systems

General Terms   Performance, Verification

Keywords   Hard real-time, worst-case execution time, VHDL

1. Introduction

Embedded systems are the most used computer systems in our lives. They can be found in mobile phones, portable multimedia players, cars, etc. Most of them are subject to stringent timing constraints which are dictated by the surrounding physical environment. We are concerned with the problem of guaranteeing that the timing constraints of tasks when executed on a given processor architecture will be met ("timing validation").

Consequences of improper timing behavior are severe: often lives depend on correct working systems (like the flight control system in airplanes). So, it must be guaranteed that each real-time task in the system meets its given time frame to complete its execution even in the worst-case scenario. To ensure this, we need to perform a *timing analysis* that computes the *worst-case execution time (WCET)* of each real-time task in the system.

Systems show a variability of execution times depending on

- *the input data:* this has always been so and will remain so as it is a property of the algorithm,

- *the initial execution state:* this is caused by modern architectural features such as caches, pipelines, and speculation, and

- *interference from the environment:* preemptions and interrupts.

The unit-time (executing an instruction always takes exactly one time unit) or constant-time abstraction used in many approaches to timing validation is thus rendered obsolete by the advent of modern processors (with features like branch prediction, out-of-order execution or speculation, etc.).

In general, the state space of input data and initial states is too large to exhaustively explore all possible executions and so determine the exact worst-case execution time. Some abstraction of the execution platform is necessary to make a timing analysis of the system feasible. These abstractions inevitably lose information, and yet must guarantee upper bounds for the worst-case execution time. Nevertheless, the theory of *abstract interpretation* [6, 7, 8] enables the application of static program analysis [27] for determining the timing behavior of embedded applications.

The computation of worst-case timing bounds for a program is realized by first employing an abstract processor model ("*timing model*") to compute a cycle-level abstract semantics of the program and, in a second phase, mapping resulting time bounds for program portions to an Integer Linear Program (ILP) whose maximal solution yields the final bound. This tool architecture has been successfully used to determine precise upper bounds on the execution times of real-time programs running on processors used in embedded systems [10]. A commercially available tool, *aiT* by *AbsInt GmbH*, cf. http://www.absint.de/wcet.htm, was implemented and is used in the aeronautics [31] and automotive industries [19].

The more compute-intensive first phase is a micro-architectural analysis and has the following three constituents:

1. Value analysis [30] attempts to compute information about data accesses and control flow, in particular it tries to identify infeasible paths, syntactically possible paths that will never be taken because of contradictory conditions.

2. Cache-behavior prediction [13] determines a safe and concise approximation of the contents of caches in order to classify memory accesses as definite cache hits or misses.

3. Pipeline-behavior prediction [33] analyzes how instructions pass through the pipeline taking cache-hit or miss information into account. At the end of simulating one instruction, a certain set of final states has been reached. The pipeline analysis starts the analysis of the next instruction in all those states. Here, the timing model introduces non-determinism that leads to multiple possible execution paths in the analyzed task. The pipeline analysis need to examine all of these paths.

Currently, these timing models are *hand-crafted* by human experts [33, 34, 12]. Therefore the model creation as well as the implementation of the corresponding pipeline analysis is a very time-consuming and error-prone process.

As modern processors are synthesized out of formal hardware description languages, like VHDL [3, 18, 17], in which their behavior (including the timing) is exactly specified, the timing model could be semi-automatically derived from them. This would avoid errors introduced by manual implementations due to human involvement, and it would speed up the process, too.

VHDL models of real-world processors are usually very big and complex making WCET determination a very difficult task [37]. Just generating a pipeline analysis that covers the whole micro-architectural behavior[1] would additionally increase the state space. This would render the resulting timing analysis infeasible in terms of space and time consumption.

This paper describes how to derive timing models out of formal VHDL specifications in a semi-automatic way.

In a first step, we reduce the size of the model by pruning out all parts that do not contribute to the timing behavior. For example, we do not need information about each step within a multiplier unit. Instead, it suffices to know for many clock cycles an instruction occupies each stage of the multiplier pipeline.

The pruned model still contains a lot of detailed information about the processor state. But for practical reasons it is impossible to represent all state information in full detail. If we were to exactly record e.g., the contents of all memory cells or registers, the space required for the analysis would be prohibitive. Luckily, in many cases the exact knowledge about these things is not important as far as timing is concerned: an addition always takes the same amount of time, no matter what the arguments are. In other cases, the timing does depend on such information, but we may choose to lose the exact timing knowledge in order to make the analysis more efficient, or even to make it possible at all. One example for this are multiplications on some architectures, which are faster if one argument has many leading zero bits. By not keeping track of the arguments exactly, we have to assume an entire range of execution times for multiplication. The loss in precision is acceptable in this case, as the difference is usually only a few processor cycles and multiplications are rare.

Therefore, the second part of the timing model derivation is the abstraction of the processor state. Abstractions mean that we either leave out some details of the processor state or we approximate them. An example for an approximation is the replacement of

concrete addresses by address intervals. For memory accesses, we do not need to know the exact address. We only need to know the type of memory that is accessed in order to simulate its timing behavior.

Using the methodology of abstract interpretation, one can trade precision of the analysis against efficiency by choosing different processor abstractions and concretization relations between the concrete processor state and the abstract one.

In theory, this was done in [34] by manually examining the VHDL sources of a memory controller. This shows the theoretical feasibility of our approach. The contribution of this paper is twofold. Firstly we provide a method that automates the manual process as much as possible. Secondly we apply our method to whole system's specifications (the processor core including the peripheral components as e.g., the memory controller).

The implementation of the outlined sequence of model analyses and transformations is currently under development, so we cannot give any reasonable experimental results so far. The same holds for a comparison to a manually derived timing model.

The paper is structured as follows: Section 3 gives details about the hardware description language VHDL and its formal semantics. In Section 4, we give an overview about the problem of computing safe and precise upper bounds on the worst-case execution time of safety-critical applications. Section 5 and Section 6 then introduce transformations and abstractions on VHDL that are used to derive a timing model out of the original VHDL specification. Section 7 illustrates our automation process and its seamless integration into the *aiT* tool chain. Section 8 concludes.

2. Related Work

There are a variety of tools for computing worst-case execution time bounds for embedded system applications. According to [36], these tools can be categorized into two classes: static methods and measurement-based methods.

The first category employs static analyses to determine the timing bounds. Most of the tools in this category examine the fully linked executable. The hybrid prototype of TU Vienna [20] performs static analyses on source code level. There, it must be assured that the compiler does not significantly change the structure of the program code. Most of the static methods do not model complex processor pipeline features like out-of-order or speculative execution, static/dynamic branch prediction or caches in general. Examples are Bound-T [15], SWEET [9], Chalmers research prototype [24] or Chronos [22]. The most powerful and industrially usable tool in this context is *aiT* [11]. It can cope with highly complex processor architectures, computes precise WCET bounds and is user-friendly (e.g., warns about unrealistic code annotations).

The second category are the measurement-based WCET tools. Their methodology is not based on static analyses but on determining timing bounds by measuring the WCET path. The most prominent and successful tools are RapiTime [4] and a research prototype from TU Vienna [28]. In contrast to the static analyses based tools, one needs to generate input vectors that trigger the worst-case execution path to be executed during measurement. This cannot be computed in general. Solutions are to generate test cases that provide a full execution coverage or to measure basic blocks separately and combine the basic block execution times to the time bound. In the latter case, the user needs to find the correct combination of execution paths of consecutive basic blocks.

In addition to the different WCET tools described above, there are many VHDL simulators like GHDL [32] or ModelSim [5]. Such simulators cannot be used to compute timing bounds by program execution simulation because:

---

[1] in this case, the timing model would be equivalent to the full VHDL model

```
entity counter is
    port (clk, rst : in std_logic ;
          val : out std_logic_vector (2 downto 0));
end entity ;

architecture rtl of counter is
    signal cnt : std_logic_vector (2 downto 0);
begin
 P1: process (clk, rst ) is
        if ( rst = '1') then
            cnt <= "000" ;
        elsif ( rising_edge (clk)) then
            cnt <= cnt + '1';
            val <= cnt ;
        end if ;
    end;
end;
```

Figure 1. 3-bit counter in VHDL.

- Modern real world processors (like Motorola PowerPC755 [16]) used in embedded systems are far too complex. The computational complexity of the simulation would render the method infeasible for industrial usage.

- Due to the complexity of the problem, we introduce non-determinism into the computation model. No traditional VHDL simulator can cope with that.

To the best of our knowledge, nobody has tried before to automate (at least partly) the development process of a timing model for processors with the goal of WCET determination.

3. VHSIC Hardware Description Language (VHDL)

VHDL is an IEEE Standard defined in IEEE 1076 [3, 18]. The focus of the language ranges from specifying circuits at wavefront level to describing large system behaviors with high-level constructs. As a result, the standard is huge, thus, this paper only considers the *synthesizable subset* of VHDL, defined in [17].

Figure 1 shows the specification of a simple 3-bit counter. The VHDL description of a circuit consists of an interface declaration defining the in- and output signals of the circuit and of one or more implementations. In VHDL, the interface declaration is called an *entity*, the implementation an *architecture*.

The entity declaration defines the input ports of the circuit (clk and rst). The counter is designed as a synchronous circuit, i.e., all computations are synchronized on the transitions of a global signal. This signal is referred to as the *global clock* (clk in the sample circuit). The current value of the counter is provided by the output port val which is a 3-bit binary number.

The implementation is given in form of a *process* (P1). A process executes its code, whenever one of the *signals* contained in the processes *sensitivity list* (clk and rst) changes its value. Thus, the sensitivity list of a process is an implicit wait-statement at its end.[2] After execution of all statements, execution suspends until another change of at least one signal's value.

VHDL also supports component-based circuit specifications. Figure 2 gives an example for hierarchical circuit composition. Here, a circuit for the logical implication $a \rightarrow b$ for two inputs a and b and the output c is built from a logical-or gate or2bit and a negation gate invert, implementing the implication by the

```
entity implies is
    port (a, b: in std_logic ;
          c: out std_logic );
end entity ;
```

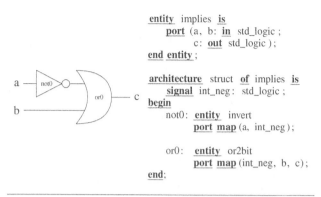

```
architecture struct of implies is
    signal int_neg: std_logic ;
begin
    not0: entity invert
          port map (a, int_neg );

    or0:  entity or2bit
          port map (int_neg, b, c);
end;
```

Figure 2. Composition of VHDL components.

formula $c = \neg a \lor b$. Note that or0 is an instance of the generic entity or2bit, as not0 is one of the entity invert.

Having a hierarchically composed specification of a circuit, *elaboration* has to be performed in order to get a flat definition of it. Elaboration does all the required renaming for unifying names, wires all structural descriptions, etc. The result is one large entity consisting of a number of processes and some locally defined signals.

A VHDL process consists of a set of local *variables* that are only accessible from inside the process. By contrast, local *signals* can be accessed by more than one process, but only one process is allowed to drive the value of a signal.[3] Within a process, execution of statements is done sequentially.

VHDL makes a distinction between assignments to a variable and to a signal. Assigning a value to a variable takes effect immediately (i.e., the next reference of this variable returns the newly assigned value), whereas the assignment of a value to a signal is only *scheduled* to be the future value (i.e., the next reference returns the old value). E.g., in Figure 1, the signal assignment cnt <= cnt + '1'; schedules the next value of cnt to be cnt plus one, but the next reference val <= cnt; schedules the next value of val to be the *current* value of cnt. These future values take effect as soon as all processes *suspend* their execution.

The semantics of a VHDL program, i.e., a set of processes, can be described as follows:

1. Execute processes until they suspend.

2. If all processes are suspended, make all scheduled signal assignments visible at once.

3. If there is a process being sensitive on a signal having changed its value, resume this process and go to step 1.

4. Otherwise, an external signal must change its value (e.g., the clock signal). If this happens, resume all processes waiting for this signal and go to step 1.

Thus, the semantics of VHDL can be seen as a two-level semantics: sequential process execution at its first, signal update and process revocation at its second level. A formal definition of the semantics of VHDL can be found in [25].

4. WCET Computation

Current state-of-the-art processors in embedded systems make use of instruction pipelines, i.e., the execution of consecutive instructions is overlapped. They pass simultaneously through different

---

[2] In VHDL, the use of explicit wait-statements and sensitivity lists is exclusive. We assume, that the only place within a process, where wait-statements may occur, is at the end of the body of a process.

[3] In full VHDL, *resolution functions* can be used for value computation of signals being driven by two or more processes.

pipeline stages: An instruction has to be first loaded from the memory. The residence time of the instruction in the *fetch stage* thereby is determined by the content of the instruction cache. After being loaded, the instruction can be decoded and dispatched to its corresponding execution unit (*decode stage*). While in the *execution stage*, instructions compete for resources, such as execution units and buses.[4] After finishing its execution, the instruction waits for completion (*writeback stage*). Having passed this stage, all changes made to operands, etc., are part of the architectural state, thus, after this point, the instruction does not longer affect the behavior of the processor. This is called instruction retirement. Please note, that in modern processors, there can be several locations in the pipeline, where retirement ("leaving the pipeline") can happen.

The number of cycles an instruction spends within one stage (and therewith its overall execution time) varies and depends on several criteria, namely

- the current state of the processors pipeline,
- the current environmental state, i.e., the content of the cache(s), etc. and
- the input program.

As stated before, pipeline-behavior prediction is based on the abstract interpretation of a timing model. The execution of a program is simulated by feeding instruction sequences from a control-flow graph to the timing model which computes the processor state changes at cycle granularity and keeps track of the elapsing clock cycles. Therefore the timing model is at a very detailed level.

Figure 4 (dashed box "Timing Analyzer") shows the structure of the *aiT* timing analyzer that implements this theory. The starting point is the fully linked binary that contains the task(s) for which the WCET should be computed. After control-flow reconstruction, the above mentioned *Micro-architectural Analyses* are performed. *Path Analysis* computes the worst-case execution path based on the basic block execution times computed by the micro-architectural analyses. For further details on the *aiT* WCET analyzer, please refer to [10].

Abstract interpretation of the timing model is guaranteed to give upper WCET bounds for the execution of an instruction sequence [33]. The guarantee, however, is relative to the timing model itself. If the model fails to correctly describe the system's behavior, the computed WCET bound may be incorrect.

As nowadays the system hardware is automatically synthesized from formal specifications (e.g., in VHDL or VERILOG), they determine the complete system's behavior – including timing information. So, it is highly desirable to extract the information needed for the timing model creation from such specifications. This would ensure that the timing model is correct by construction and would speed up the creation time massively.

Unfortunately, VHDL specifications contain many details on processor state changes during program execution. If we would derive a timing model from a processor specification without any model preprocessing, the resource consumption of the resulting pipeline analysis would be prohibitive. Therefore, we need to reduce the size of the model.

Section 5 introduces some needed simplifications and transformations that compress a VHDL specification without loosing information about the timing behavior. Based on this, Section 6 describes the process of how to derive a computationally handable timing model from a VHDL specification.

5. Transformations of VHDL

A VHDL specification of a complete processor is quite large, e.g., about 70000 lines of VHDL for the Leon 2 processor [14]. Simply transforming the specification into a timing model would render the resulting timing analysis infeasible, especially in terms of space consumption. The design of a hard real-time system in hardware and software defines, which scenarios have to be modeled for timing analysis. E.g., if a CPU offers support for floating point instructions, but the software does not use them, the floating point unit does not have to be modeled for timing analysis. In the following, we describe some techniques to reduce the complexity of a VHDL specification in order to make timing analysis feasible.

5.1 Environmental Constraints

Modern embedded architectures offer a huge variability concerning their configuration (e.g., dynamic or static branch prediction, bus pipelining enabled or disabled, write-through or write-back cache behavior, etc.) but also with respect to connected devices. Many of them allow to use a huge variety of memory types and therewith memory controllers, connected buses, etc. Those hardware settings are fixed during run time which renders some parts of the hardware specification obsolete for a timing analysis. The removal of those parts contributes to the reduction of the complexity of the created timing analysis.

Some events in modern architectures are either asynchronous to program execution (e.g., interrupts, DMA) or not predictable (e.g., ECC errors in RAM, exceptions) in the model. Timing analysis cannot deal with those events.

In order to make static timing analysis still applicable, it is necessary to make assumptions about the environment. An exception or interrupt brings the whole system to a state where no timing bound for the current task is needed. So for timing analysis, we can safely assume that those events do not happen.

Based on this assumption, some signals in the VHDL description never change their value, so we can "hardwire" these signals to their default value (i.e., the value during system reset). As a result, parts of the VHDL become unreachable (i.e., control never reaches these statements), so we can use dead-code elimination to remove those parts from the VHDL specification.

The same has to be done for asynchronous events that occur frequently (e.g., SDRAM refreshes). Their effect on the execution time has to be incorporated, e.g., by adding penalties based on the computed WCET and the worst-case occurrence of the events or by statistical means.

5.2 Domain Abstraction

Registers in hardware are used for storing data processed by the CPU. For timing analysis, the concrete value stored in a register is often not important, e.g., we are not interested in the result of an addition but in the time it takes to add two registers. Thus register content can be abstracted from the VHDL model to make it smaller.

For other parts in the model, an approximated value of a register might suffice to model the correct timing behavior, e.g., when accessing the memory composed of a slow and a fast region, it suffices to abstract a concrete address by the information, which memory region will be accessed.

Same argumentation also holds for queues in the VHDL model, where not the content of a queue entry is interesting, but the size of the queue to determine if it is full or not.

This type of transformation of VHDL we call *domain abstraction*. It is more or less a change of types of signals and variables in the VHDL model. Changing a domain type also necessitates the adaptions of functors working on the abstracted domain.

Domain abstraction might introduce non-determinism into the VHDL model (e.g., abstracting a concrete address to an address

---

[4] Note that in modern architectures, the different execution units may also be designed as pipelines.

interval and checking it for a concrete value might result in three values: equal, not equal, and perhaps). It is the task of the timing analysis framework to cope with and handle all possibilities.

5.3 Process Substitution

As stated in Section 3, the active parts of a VHDL specification are processes. Normally, a process drives at least one signal containing the result of its computational task, e.g., the next address to be fetched from memory.

For timing analysis, the details on how a process derives its result might be uninteresting or modeling all its details might result in a model being too large to be used for timing analysis. *Process substitution* allows for replacing a concrete VHDL process implementation by a custom implementation modeling less details or using a powerful abstraction. E.g., this has been successfully done for caches and is known as the cache abstraction [13]. Thereby, the concrete cache is replaced by an abstracted cache storing the maximal ages of all lines that are definitely in the cache.

Process substitution might introduce non-determinism into the model. Whenever a decision depends on abstracted data and the abstraction is not able to precisely determine the result, the timing model has to follow all possibilities (cf. [25] for the semantics of abstracted VHDL).

5.4 Memory Abstraction

Processors execute programs that are kept in memory. For execution, instructions have to be fetched from main memory, decoded, executed and the results are written back to memory.

Especially large memory arrays like main memory blow up the timing model. Content of registers, addresses of memory cells being accessed by a program, and content of memory cells can be computed using the value analysis and do not require a cycle-wise simulation of the processor's behavior [30].

To make timing analysis applicable, large memory arrays must be abstracted. Otherwise, the resulting timing models cannot be used for WCET computation due to space limitations. As stated in Section 4, our timing analysis is based on a reconstructed control-flow graph of the executable program. Thus, instructions have to be inserted into the timing model using the information from the control-flow graph, so a pseudo VHDL process has to be added to the model acting as interface to this graph.

Due to domain abstraction and process substitution (cf. Section 5.2 and Section 5.3), and also due to static analysis, data access addresses of instructions might only be known as safe intervals, not as single addresses. Thus, the VHDL design must be adapted to utilize the information from the value analysis instead of the real computation of addresses. For this, all places where data access addresses are generated by instructions have to be identified. At these places pseudo VHDL processes have to be added that interfaces with the value analysis to retrieve the previously computed intervals. Consequently, addresses must be abstracted to address intervals (cf. Section 5.2).

6. Deriving the Timing Model

This section describes the derivation process starting from the VHDL model and ending in the corresponding timing model that can be used within the pipeline analysis of the WCET computation framework (cf. Section 4).

Figure 3 illustrates the process flow. At the top, there is the incoming VHDL model. As mentioned in the introduction and Section 4, the size of the model needs to be reduced. Most of this is done by the *Model preprocessing* step which is described below. Then the preprocessed model is the starting point for the search and application of *Processor State Abstractions* (cf. Section 6.2).

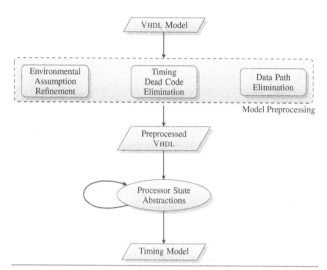

Figure 3. Timing Model Derivation Process – Overview.

This iterative step results in the *Timing Model* used for the pipeline behavior prediction within the WCET computation framework presented in Section 4.

As the derived timing model is the basis for the determination of WCET guarantees for safety-critical systems, we need to prove that the resulting model after the application of our size-reducing transformations and state abstractions correctly approximates the timing behavior of the examined system. This is ongoing work in cooperation with researchers from the *Electronic Design Automation Group* of TU Kaiserslautern, Germany.

The next sections detail about the preprocessing step as well as the processor state abstractions.

6.1 Model Preprocessing

The task of the model preprocessing step mainly is to reduce the overall size of the VHDL model by eliminating parts that are not relevant for the timing behavior of the system.

Embedded systems are very specific, both in terms of the hardware and software components. Section 5.1 details about so-called environmental constraints that results from the fact that there are hardware features that are unused at all in the analyzed application or only in a limited way.

In the VHDL code, such *configurable parts* of the hardware are guarded by control signals that indicate whether the particular hardware feature is enabled or disabled. These control signals usually are constant, i.e., they are read but never written. If we analyze the model with an activated `reset` signal, we get some initial/default values for these control signals. Performing a constant propagation afterwards effectively "marks" parts of the model which process disabled hardware components/features as dead code. These can be pruned out by a dead code elimination. We call this model transformation **Environmental Assumption Refinement** (cf. Figure 3).

A similar optimization that reduces the size of the original VHDL model is the **Timing Dead Code Elimination**. This also means the removal of model parts that does not contribute to the timing behavior of the system. In contrast to the Environmental Assumption Refinement, we can remove code pieces of hardware components that are enabled in the processor configuration. For example, the VHDL code of a multiplier unit describes the way this unit works in all details. This includes the algorithmic implementation of the execution units or the control logic that influence the result of the computation of a unit. We do not need to know, how exactly the functional units are designed. We only need detailed information about the timing of the instruction flow through the pipeline. This means that it suffices to know how long each instruction stays in each stage of the processor pipeline.

In order to restrict the model to "*timing-alive*" code, we need to identify all locations where instructions can leave the pipeline, i.e., where instruction retirement happens. Please note that there can be several locations for instruction retirement due to early-out-conditions for some instruction classes. Having identified the instruction retirements, we compute backward slices from these locations. This yields all VHDL statements that influence the instruction retirement and therefore contribute to the instruction flow through the pipeline. All VHDL code that is not contained in the union over all computed backward slices is simply "*timing-dead*" and can be safely removed.

The third size reduction transformation is the **Data Path Elimination**. As already mentioned in the introduction, incorporating the data paths in the timing model would prohibitively increase the resource consumption during analysis. Fortunately, the latency of instructions is normally not affected by the content of registers and/or memory cells they use.[5] Therefore, we can factor out (i.e., remove completely) all data paths from the model. The information about contents of registers and memory cells is then computed by an external value analysis. In contrast to the real address computation, this value analysis operates on a different domain, i.e., address intervals. On the one hand, this is a consequence of the lack of precise information when analyzing at the assembly level [33]. On the other hand, it is implied by the methodology of abstract interpretation [7]. This factorization of address/value information of course introduces the need of a domain abstraction from addresses to address intervals (cf. Section 5.4) which is used in the next section.

6.2 Processor State Abstractions

The model preprocessing described above reduces the size of the original VHDL model significantly so that the resulting pipeline analysis becomes computationally feasible. Depending on the complexity of the hardware model, this size reduction might not suffice.

So far, we removed parts of the model that do not contribute to the timing behavior. Further size reduction can only be achieved by approximating state information rather than precisely modelling it. In principle, such a lack of information about the system state might result in a loss of precision (i.e., safe upper bounds) in the computed WCET bound because we do not model the timing behavior exactly anymore. Fortunately, the timing often is not affected by this as for example an addition always takes the same amount of time independent of the argument values. In contrast to that multiplications can be finished faster if one argument has many leading zero bits. The lack of precise information about that forces us to assume an entire range of execution times for multiplication. But this might be acceptable as multiplications are rare.

In general, we can perform three different abstractions (from Section 5) to the processor state:

- Process Substitution,
- Domain Abstractions, and
- Memory Abstraction.

As shown in Figure 3, the first two of these three abstractions are employed iteratively until the resource consumption of the resulting pipeline analysis is acceptable. Certainly, the memory abstraction can only be applied once. The exact usage of process substitution and domain abstraction then is an engineering problem. It mainly depends on the actual complexity of the architecture to be modeled. For more simple architectures (like ARM7 [23]), we

---

[5] There are some exceptions, e.g., early out conditions in the multiply unit.

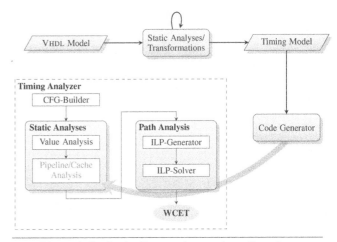

Figure 4. Derivation Process Automation – Overview.

can model nearly everything precisely without getting trouble with computational resources. More complex systems however require more abstractions. However, there are common abstractions to be done for all processors. These are:

- *Cache abstraction:* This is an example for a process substitution where the update of the caches is replaced by a custom C++ implementation. Details can be found in [13].

- *Address intervals:* This is an example for a domain abstraction as we replace concrete addresses by address intervals. This replacement is implied by the removal of the data paths as mentioned above.

All of these abstractions [7] of the original VHDL model certainly must not semantically change the timing behavior. Moreover, they are very architecture specific in terms of applicability and necessity. As described in Section 5, imprecise values lead to several possibilities in the execution of a program/task. If the number of alternatives is large, the computational complexity might be higher as without the particular abstraction. So the introduced transformations must be chosen carefully.

The processor state abstractions can lead to the loss of precise information about the processor state. During the successor state computation of an input state, this possibly results in multiple successor states if precise information is needed but not available. In that case, the micro-architectural analysis computes multiple execution paths through the program and annotates each path with the execution times. In other words, the timing model might become non-deterministic by the introduction of processor state abstractions. As described in Section 7.3, our code generator needs to cope with that non-determinism when generating the pipeline analysis based on the computed abstracted timing model.

7. Automation of the Derivation Process

The previous section has given an overview of the steps needed to derive a timing model from a formal hardware description. Performing these steps by hand is very time-consuming on the one hand [34], and error-prone on the other hand. To eliminate these harms, automation of the derivation process is mandatory.

All parts of model preprocessing described in Section 6.1 are based on static analysis methods known from compiler construction. Since variables in VHDL are local w.r.t. a process and signal changes are delayed to the synchronization point, choosing a fixed order for the process execution is possible. Thus, a VHDL model

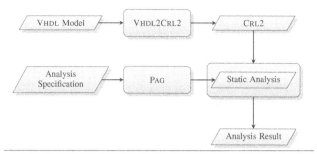

Figure 5. VHDL Analysis Framework – Structure.

can be transformed into a sequential program [29] allowing the application of these static analysis methods.

Our proposed framework for the derivation process automation is shown in Figure 4. Starting from an initial VHDL processor specification, a set of static analyses and transformations can be performed to derive an abstracted timing model. A code generator then creates simulation code fitting into the timing analysis framework as part of the micro-architectural analysis.

7.1 VHDL Analysis Framework

In order to ease the process of analyzing a VHDL specification of a processor, [29] describes a framework for static analysis of VHDL. A general overview of this analysis framework is shown in Figure 5. Given a rtl processor specification, VHDL2CRL2 transforms it into an intermediate representation language called CRL2 [21]. Sequentialization as well as elaboration are performed during this translation phase. Thereby, CRL2 is hierarchically organized in instructions, basic blocks and routines, i.e., basic blocks are completely enclosed within routines and analogously instructions are completely enclosed within basic blocks.

The CRL2 representation is the input for each static analyzer. To ease the implementation of the different analyzers, the *Program Analyzer Generator* (PAG) [26] is used. PAG is based on abstract interpretation. The tool can generate fast and efficient static analyzers out of concise analysis specifications of a data flow problem in PAG specific languages, called OPTLA and DATLA [1].

In order to transform a VHDL description into a sequential program, a fixed ordering of all processes is automatically chosen by VHDL2CRL2. This order is embedded into a special simulation routine that is required by the analysis framework. The sensitivity lists of processes are represented by newly created guards within the simulation routine. Furthermore, a special wait node is inserted in the simulation routine representing the VHDL synchronization point (cf. Section 3).

Using this analysis framework enables the easy implementation and use of static analyses in order to perform environmental assumption refinement and timing dead code elimination as described in Section 6.1, but also eases the process of implementing domain abstractions. This is described in following.

7.1.1 Obtaining Initial Values

When simplifying a VHDL design, we want to remove assignments to signals (or variables). Remaining read-references to these then read a constant value. This value is the *initial value* of the signal/variable being assigned during system reset.

Identifying the default values of signals or variables can be achieved by evaluating the code segments that are active during system reset. The contents of all signals and variables after the code segments have finished are the initial values. Note that the computation of the initial values may not happen in just one clock cycle after the reset signal is asserted. Several parts of a system may

have a longer initialization sequence, e.g., memory controllers going through a sequence of activation steps for the attached memory chips.

Determining the set of instructions that are executed to compute the initial values can be automated by computing a forward slice [35]. A *forward slice* on VHDL determines the set of instructions that *may* be executed, depending on the values of a set of signals (or variables). This set of instructions is referred to as the *slicing criterion*. All instructions not in the slice are guaranteed to not depend on any of those signals. Certainly, the computation of a slice has to take into account transitive dependencies and dependencies introduced by the sensitivity lists.

Computing the forward slice for the criterion "*reset is activated*" yields a slice containing all instructions that may be executed during system reset. To obtain the default values for all signals/variables, a constant propagation analysis can be performed on this slice.

A *constant propagation analysis* determines for each program point, i.e., each statement, if a signal or variable has a constant value when execution reaches that point.

To show the effectiveness and simplicity of the VHDL analysis framework, the following example describes, how a constant propagation analysis on VHDL can be modeled. We introduce a mapping from signal/variable names to their corresponding value and extend it by a bottom and a top element to denote not yet considered program points and unknown values respectively.

$$F \equiv (identifier \rightarrow (value \cup \top)) \cup \bot \qquad (1)$$

As stated in Section 3, VHDL differentiates between signal and variable assignments. Thus, the domain of the data flow problem (see [27] for details on data flow analysis) for constant propagation has to cover *current* and *future* values of the identifiers used. Furthermore, to evaluate the condition of process guards (cf. Section 7.1), it is necessary to decide whether a signal has changed its value or not. Therefore, the domain has to be extended by the *old* values of signals. Thus, the domain dfi for the constant propagation analysis is:

$$dfi \equiv F \times F \times F \qquad (2)$$

The transition functions for updating an incoming data flow value

$$dfi_{pre} = (cur_{pre}, fut_{pre}, old_{pre}) \qquad (3)$$

to the output value dfi_{post} for the different nodes can be directly defined as follows:

- assignment node
  The data flow value for an assignment can be computed from the incoming value in case of a variable assignment by updating the current and the future value of dfi_{pre} with the newly assigned value or $\top$, if this value is statically not computable. In case of a signal assignment, only the future value has to be updated.

- guard node
  The guard encapsulates the sensitivity list of a process and is responsible for process revocation. A process is only re-executed, if one of the signals in its sensitivity list changes its value. This can be checked by comparing cur_{pre} with old_{pre}. Based on this result, the data flow value is propagated into the process or not.

- wait node
  At this node, all scheduled signal assignments take effect and are made visible at once. The new data flow value is computed by copying the future values to the current one and the current ones to the old ones.

$$dfi_{post} = (fut_{pre}, fut_{pre}, cur_{pre}) \qquad (4)$$

Using PAG and the rules above yields in a constant propagation analysis on VHDL. Running the analysis on the example code from Figure 1 results in the initial value of "000" for the signals cnt and val.

7.1.2 Identifying Timing-Dead Code

As stated in Section 6.1, eliminating timing dead code in a VHDL specification can be achieved by backward slicing as defined in [35].

A *backward slice* contains all instructions that *may* influence the value of a signal (or variable) at the end of process execution (i.e., at suspension time). Any instruction not in the slice is guaranteed to not influence the value of the signal (variable).

Computing backward slices with the criterion defined in Section 6.1, i.e., the set of points where instructions are retired in the VHDL model, results in a set of slices. All instructions not contained in the union over these slices do not have any influence on the timing of the processor. Thus, all of these statements can be safely removed from the model.

[12] describes how to compute backward slices by combining several data flow problems, namely reaching definitions, dominator and post-dominator analyses. Thus, the VHDL analysis framework can be easily used also for timing dead code elimination.

7.1.3 Domain Abstraction Analysis

One of the most common abstractions used for simplifying a VHDL processor specification is the domain abstraction as described in Section 5.2. Thereby, the type of a signal (variable) or even a whole type shall be changed to a different type. Naturally, changing the domain of a signal (variable) induces a change of all functors used by the signal (variable).

Due to procedure and function calls within the VHDL code, identifying all places that might have to be changed is not done on a syntactical level. Since VHDL is fully typed, and due to the fact, that this type information is still present in the intermediate representation created by VHDL2CRL2, it is easy to use the analysis framework to construct an analysis finding all points of interest. We call this analysis *domain abstraction analysis*.

Given a mapping from old to new types, the automatically created analyzer reports all places, where functors need to be adjusted. If a functor for the new type already exists (e.g., during a sequence of abstractions, we first abstract the type of a signal, and in a second step, we want to change another signal to be of the same abstract type), this is also detected by the analyzer and the functor is suggested for usage. The result of the analysis forms the input for the *domain transformation tool* described in the next section.

7.2 Transformation Tools

As the idea for domain abstractions remains an engineering problem, human involvement in this step will never be eliminated completely. Nevertheless, the analyses and abstractions described in the previous section form the basis to develop support tools that automate as much as possible of the model transformations.

As illustrated in Figure 3, the way from the unmodified VHDL model to the timing model is an iterative process concerning the processor state abstractions. Each iteration consist of the following sub tasks:

1. Exploration and visualization of the model,
2. Abstraction specific analyses,
3. Model transformation, and
4. Timing dead code elimination.

In the exploration phase, the model can be visualized with the AbsInt graph viewer *aiSee* [2]. For this, we are able to emit the model in GDL format. These visualization and exploration techniques can assist a human expert in developing ideas for space saving abstractions (e.g., a domain abstraction or a process substitution).

The abstraction specific analyses are the ones mentioned in Section 7. They are used to find all points where the concrete abstraction implies transformations.

To automate the application of a *domain abstraction*, one can use the tool domain-abstract. Its input is the model itself as well as a specification for the domain abstraction. The latter specifies a type conversion of either the type of a single variable or all variables of a given type into a new type. domain-abstract then transforms the model accordingly and informs about newly needed operators on the new domain. These operators have to be provided manually. For the *process substitution* support, there is the tool process-replace. Its input is the model, the name of the process to be removed and the name of an update function that contains the custom simulation implementation for this process. process-replace then removes the specified process and adjusts all parts of the model that potentially trigger a reactivation of this process (e.g., writes to signals that are in the sensitivity list of the removed process).

Each abstraction results in one or several transformations of the model. After having applied the transformation, we need to recheck for newly timing dead code as the transformation itself made parts of the model timing dead. For example, removing statements due to abstractions can lead to constant signals if all signal writes were removed by that. Then, the only possible values for those signals are their defaults which marks some parts of the model as dead code.

After the model ran through all needed transformations, the code generator presented in the next section can then be used for generating the pipeline analysis out of it.

7.3 Code Generator

Having applied the several transformations and abstractions described before, we get a timing model from which C++ simulation code can be generated [25]. The generated code provides functionality to simulate the processor state update that results by exactly one core clock cycle (*clock cycle updater*). Remembering the two-level semantics of VHDL (cf. Section 3), this includes the process execution as well as the reevaluation level as both steps together form the clock cycle update. In addition to the clock cycle update functionality, framework code is generated that supports the seamless integration into the *aiT* tool chain (cf. Figure 4). Concretely, we need to generate code that simulates the process revocation level of the VHDL semantic (cf. Section 3).

The transformations and abstractions of the original VHDL model introduce non-determinism into the timing model, which then is called *abstract timing model* (cf. Section 6). In contrast to a traditional hardware simulation, where the simulated execution yields a trace of processor states, our simulation of the abstract timing model yields a tree of processor states (*execution tree*). A processor state can have multiple successor states due to the impreciseness of parts of the processor state. In that case, all possible execution paths in the execution tree are simulated, so that the worst-case path can be selected by the path analysis (cf. Figure 4).

Please note that due to the abstractions, a possible execution path through the execution tree does not necessarily need to correspond to a real execution trace on the hardware. For example, if there are some exclusive conditional paths in the binary and due to some unknown memory accesses, all paths are combined although some of them are mutually exclusive. Such situations can lead to over-estimations of the real WCET if such a combined path is selected as the worst-case execution path.

One of the main advantages of our code generator is that it can cope with this non-determinism. In order to correctly generate simulation code for the abstracted timing model, we need a clear transition from the VHDL semantics to an abstract simulation semantics that define the state transitions from one abstract processor state to its successor states. This can be found in [25].

8. Conclusions

There are many safety-critical applications within the area of embedded systems, e.g., flight control computers in avionics or airbag control systems in cars. Certainly, failures within such systems can lead to severe damage or even loss of human life. Therefore, safety-critical applications need a validation of their timing behavior beside proving their functional correctness.

For a timing validation of an embedded system, we need to know the WCET of each systems task. Saarland University and AbsInt GmbH developed the *aiT* tool that can compute safe and precise upper bounds on the worst-case execution time of a task/program by performing an abstract simulation of the tasks execution within the so called pipeline analysis. This pipeline analysis is based on timing models (of the processor) that are currently hand-crafted by human experts. The implementation of the pipeline analysis out of the timing model is as well very time-consuming as error-prone.

In order to get rid of these disadvantages, this paper shows how to semi-automatically derive such timing models out of formal hardware specifications in VHDL. The derivation process starting from the VHDL model up to the generated combined cache/pipeline analysis consists of the following steps:

- Fully automatic transformation of the VHDL model into the intermediate representation CRL2.

- Automatic transformation tools for generally needed model compactions.

- Semi-automatic transformation and analysis tools for supporting the introduction of processor state abstractions.

- Fully automatic simulation-code generation that seamlessly integrates into the existing *aiT* tool chain.

By this, we removed human involvement as far as possible. The remaining engineering task is the introduction of the processor state abstractions which are dependent on the particular processor and its complexity. This means that our method eliminates the possibility of implementation/modeling errors as well as dramatically decreasing the development time of a timing analyzer for a given processor architecture. The first is of utmost importance in the context of safety-critical applications and their certification while the lower development time faces the industrial time-to-market speedup of new embedded applications.

Future work besides the implementation of the presented approach is the comparison between a hand-crafted timing model and its correspondent semi-automatically derived one. This should confirm our claims about the advantages of the described timing model derivation.

Acknowledgments

The authors would like to thank Reinhard Wilhelm and Stephan Thesing for their help, support and advice in making this work possible.

Work reported here was partly supported by the German Research Council (DFG) as part of the Transregional Collaborative Research Center "Automatic Verification and Analysis of Complex Systems" (SFB/TR 14 AVACS), by the European Community's 7th Framework Programme in the Network of Excellence "ArtistDesign" under grant agreement number 214373, by the BMBF as part of the "Verisoft^{XT}" project and by ITEA 2 as part of the "ES_PASS" project under grant agreement number 06042.

References

[1] AbsInt Angewandte Informatik GmbH, *The Program Analyzer Generator User's Manual*, 2002.

[2] AbsInt Angewandte Informatik GmbH, *aiSee. Graph Visualization User's Documentation*, 2005.

[3] P. J. Ashenden, *The Designer's Guide to VHDL*, Morgan Kaufmann Publishers Inc., San Francisco, CA, USA, 2001.

[4] G. Bernat, A. Burns, and M. Newby, *Probabilistic timing analysis: An approach using copulas*, Journal of Embedded Computing 1 (2005), no. 2, 179–194.

[5] Mentor Graphics Corporation, *ModelSim User's Manual*, May 2008.

[6] P. Cousot, *Abstract Interpretation Based Formal Methods and Future Challenges, invited paper*, Informatics — 10 Years Back, 10 Years Ahead (R. Wilhelm, ed.), Lecture Notes in Computer Science, vol. 2000, Springer, 2001, pp. 138–156.

[7] P. Cousot and R. Cousot, *Abstract Interpretation: a Unified Lattice Model for Static Analysis of Programs by Construction or Approximation of Fixpoints*, Conference Record of the Fourth Annual ACM SIGPLAN-SIGACT Symposium on Principles of Programming Languages (Los Angeles, California), ACM Press, New York, NY, 1977, pp. 238–252.

[8] _____, *Abstract Interpretation and Application to Logic Programs*, Journal of Logic Programming 13 (1992), no. 2&3, 103–179.

[9] A. Ermedahl, *A Modular Tool Architecture for Worst-Case Execution Time Analysis*, Ph.D. thesis, Uppsala University, 2003.

[10] C. Ferdinand and R. Heckmann, *aiT: Worst-Case Execution Time Prediction by Static Programm Analysis*, Building the Information Society. IFIP 18th World Computer Congress (R. Jacquart, ed.), Kluwer, 2004, pp. 377–384.

[11] C. Ferdinand, R. Heckmann, M. Langenbach, F. Martin, M. Schmidt, H. Theiling, S. Thesing, and R. Wilhelm, *Reliable and Precise WCET Determination for a Real-Life Processor*, Proceedings of the First International Workshop on Embedded Software (EMSOFT 2001) (Berlin) (Thomas A. Henzinger and Christoph M. Kirsch, eds.), Lecture Notes in Computer Science, vol. 2211, Springer, 2001, pp. 469–485.

[12] C. Ferdinand, F. Martin, C. Cullmann, M. Schlickling, I. Stein, S. Thesing, and R. Heckmann, *New Developments in WCET Analysis*, Program Analysis and Compilation. Theory and Practice. Essays Dedicated to Reinhard Wilhelm on the Occasion of His 60th Birthday (T. Reps, M. Sagiv, and J. Bauer, eds.), Lecture Notes in Computer Science, vol. 4444, Springer, 2007, pp. 12–52.

[13] C. Ferdinand, F. Martin, R. Wilhelm, and M. Alt, *Cache Behavior Prediction by Abstract Interpretation*, Science of Computer Programming 35 (1999), no. 2, 163–189.

[14] J. Gaisler, *Leon2 Processor User's Manual - version 1.0.30*, July 2005.

[15] N. Holsti, T. Långbacka, and S. Saarinen, *Worst-Case Execution Time Analysis*, Proceedings of the European Conference on Signal Processing (EUSIPCO 2000), 2000.

[16] Freescale Semiconductor Inc., *MPC750 RISC Microprocessor Family User's Manual*, December 2001.

[17] Institute of Electrical and Electronics Engineers, New York, *IEEE Standard P1076.6 1999 VHDL Register Transfer Level Synthesis*, 1999.

[18] Institute of Electrical and Electronics Engineers, New York, *IEEE Standard P1076 2000 VHDL Language Reference Manual*, 2000.

[19] D. Kästner, R. Wilhelm, R. Heckmann, M. Schlickling, M. Pister, M. Jersak, K. Richter, and C. Ferdinand, *Timing Validation of Automotive Software*, 3rd International Symposium on Leveraging Applications of Formal Methods, Verification and Validation (ISOLA) 2008 (T. Margaria and B. Steffen, eds.), Communications in Computer and Information Science, vol. 17, Springer, 2008, pp. 93–107.

[20] R. Kirner, R. Lang, G. Freiberger, and P. Puschner, *Fully Automatic Worst-Case Execution Time Analysis for Matlab/Simulink Models*, Proceedings of the 14th Euromicro Conference on Real-Time Systems (ECRTS 2002), IEEE Computer Society, 2002, pp. 31–40.

[21] M. Langenbach, *CRL – A Uniform Representation for Control Flow*, Tech. report, Saarland University, 1998.

[22] X. Li, Y. Liang, T. Mitra, and A. Roychoudhury, *Chronos: A timing analyzer for embedded software*, Science of Computer Programming **69** (2007), no. 1-3, 56 – 67, Special issue on Experimental Software and Toolkits.

[23] ARM Limited, *ARM Architecture Reference Manual*, June 2000.

[24] T. Lundqvist and P. Stenström, *An Integrated Path and Timing Analysis Method based on Cycle-Level Symbolic Execution*, Real-Time Syst. **17** (1999), no. 2-3, 183–207.

[25] M. A. Maksoud, M. Pister, and M. Schlickling, *An Abstraction-Aware Compiler for VHDL Models*, Proceedings of the International Conference on Computer Engineering and Systems (ICCES '09), IEEE Computer Society, December 2009, pp. 3–9.

[26] F. Martin, *Generating Program Analyzers*, Ph.D. thesis, Saarland University, 1999.

[27] F. Nielson, H. R. Nielson, and C. Hankin, *Principles of Program Analysis*, Springer, 1999.

[28] P. Puschner and R. Nossal, *Testing the Results of Static Worst-Case Execution-Time Analysis*, IEEE Real-Time Systems Symposium, 1998, pp. 134–143.

[29] M. Schlickling and M. Pister, *A Framework for Static Analysis of VHDL Code*, Proceedings of 7th International Workshop on Worst-Case Execution Time Analysis (WCET 2007) (C. Rochange, ed.), Internationales Begegnungs- und Forschungszentrum für Informatik (IBFI), Schloss Dagstuhl, Germany, 2007.

[30] M. Sicks, *Adreßbestimmung zur Vorhersage des Verhaltens von Daten-Caches*, Master's thesis, Saarland University, 1997.

[31] J. Souyris, E. Le Pavec, G. Himbert, V. Jégu, G. Borios, and R. Heckmann, *Computing the Worst Case Execution Time of an Avionics Program by Abstract Interpretation*, Proceedings of the 5th International Workshop on Worst-case Execution Time (WCET 2005), 2005, pp. 21–24.

[32] T. Gingold, *GHDL. A VHDL compiler*, 2007.

[33] S. Thesing, *Safe and Precise WCET Determination by Abstract Interpretation of Pipeline Models*, Ph.D. thesis, Saarland University, 2004.

[34] ———, *Modeling a System Controller for Timing Analysis*, Proceedings of the 6th ACM & IEEE International conference on Embedded software (EMSOFT 2006) (S. L. Min and W. Yi, eds.), ACM, 2006, pp. 292–300.

[35] M. Weiser, *Program Slicing*, IEEE Transaction in Software Engineering **10** (1984), no. 4, 352–357.

[36] R. Wilhelm, J. Engblom, A. Ermedahl, N. Holsti, S. Thesing, D. Whalley, G. Bernat, C. Ferdinand, R. Heckmann, F. Mueller, I. Puaut, P. Puschner, J. Staschulat, and P. Stenström, *The Worst-Case Execution Time Problem—Overview of Methods and Survey of Tools*, **7** (2008), no. 3.

[37] R. Wilhelm, D. Grund, J. Reineke, M. Schlickling, M. Pister, and C. Ferdinand, *Memory Hierarchies, Pipelines, and Buses for Future Architectures in Time-critical Embedded Systems*, IEEE Transactions on CAD of Integrated Circuits and Systems **28** (2009), no. 7, 966–978.

Design Exploration and Automatic Generation of MPSoC Platform TLMs from Kahn Process Network Applications

Ines Viskic

Center for Embedded Computer Systems
University of California, Irvine
USA
iviskic@uci.edu

Lochi Yu

Center for Embedded Computer Systems
University of California, Irvine
USA
yulol@uci.edu

Daniel Gajski

Center for Embedded Computer Systems
University of California, Irvine
USA
gajski@uci.edu

Abstract

With increasingly more complex Multi-Processor Systems on Chip (MPSoC) and shortening time-to- market projections, Transaction Level Modeling and Platform Aware Design are seen as promising approaches to efficient MPSoC design.

In this paper, we present an automatized 3-phase process of Platform Aware Design and apply it to Kahn Process Networks (KPN) applications, a widely used model of computation for data-flow applications. We start with the KPN application and an abstract platform template and automatically generate an executable TLM with estimated timing that accurately reflects the system platform. We support homogeneous and heterogeneous multi-master platform models with shared memory or direct communication paradigm. The communication in heterogeneous platform modules is enabled with the transducer unit (TX) for protocol translation. TX units also act as message routers to support Network on Chip (NoC) communication.

We evaluate our approach with the case study of the H.264 Encoder design process, in which the specification compliant design was reached from the KPN application in less than 2 hours. The example demonstrates that automatic generation of platform aware TLMs enables a fast, efficient and error resilient design process.

Categories and Subject Descriptors C.4 Computer Systems Organization [*Performance of Systems*]: Modeling Techniques

General Terms Design, Performance

Keywords Kahn process, automatic generation, process mapping, process network, transaction level model

1. Introduction

The traditional top-down and bottom-up approaches to System Level Design are getting to be time consuming and error prone as the MPSoCs grow bigger and more complex. Transaction Level Modeling tackles this issue by abstracting away the cycle-accurate details of the communication protocol and instead models the overall transaction as a unit to achieve fast simulation. In addition, Platform Aware Design begins the design process with an abstract

platform template [15], [5] and considers the effects of platform-imposed restrictions on system performance early in design process. However, these approaches require application recoding to accommodate the platform structure. Also, the design space exploration with various platforms introduces repetitive changes to the Transaction Level Model (TLM). Therefore, automation of design process has become an essential requirement of MPSoC design methodologies.

This paper presents an automatized 3-phase process of Platform Aware Design and applies it to Kahn Process Networks (KPN) applications. Kahn Process Network (KPN) [11], [12] models computation with concurrent Kahn Processes that communicate with uni-directional FIFO channels or Kahn Channels. Kahn Processes execute independently from any centralized scheduler, which makes them particularly suitable for modeling parallel execution of components in large MPSoCs. However, KPNs have no notion of the system platform or process hierarchy.

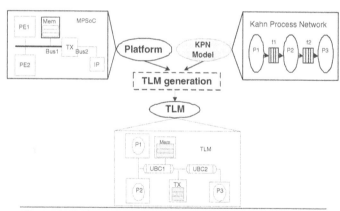

Figure 1. Problem definition: KPN to MPSoC platform mapping.

Therefore, we propose a Platform Aware Design approach, in which the application (Kahn Processes and Channels) is mapped to the general MPSoC platform template [7] based on the reconfigurable properties of platform modules. Note that the mapping options are limited to selecting the best fit from the pre-existing template. Model simulation then guides the designer to modify the template to reach a better design. Our approach is outlined in Figure 1.

For this approach to be efficient, we must address the following problems: (1) how to map point-to-point channels to a bus centric MPSoC plaform and (2), how to quickly produce an executable system model to validate the mapping choices. The second problem touches on several issues: how to capture the platform and application information in a structured way to allow its automatic generation.

Proposed Solutions:

We tackle the first issue with an interactive, graphical user interface (GUI) to decompose each Kahn Channel to a memory fragment modeling a circular FIFO accessed by two Spec Channels. The GUI interactively performs mapping of Kahn Processes to computing modules (Processor Modules), FIFOs to storage modules (Memory Modules, Transducers) and Spec Channels to the bus models (UBCs) in the MPSoC platform.

Second, we automatically generate an executable platform TLM of the system. By simulating the TLM, the performed mapping choices are quickly evaluated. TLM simulation is fast because each data transfer between modules is modeled as a single transaction instead of a collection of numerous bus signals that switch during communication. Moreover, in TLMs both software and hardware are described using the same language (SystemC) and executed natively on the host machine. In contrast, the SW/HW cosimulation in the traditional design flow interfaces the instruction set simulator (ISS) for SW simulation with a HW design language simulator. Higher abstraction level and uniformity of TL modeling yields the TLM simulation speed several orders of magnitude faster than cycle-accurate simulation speed.

After outlining the related research in Section 2, we define our design flow in Section 3. The 3-phase adaption process is described in Section 4. The automatic generation algorithms are described in Section 4.3. The strengths of our approach is presented with a design case study of an H264 Encoder in Section 6. The conclude the paper with a summary in Section 7

2. Related Work

As MPSoCs become larger and more complex, platform aware modeling is seen as an efficient methodology that improves design productivity. METROPOLIS [8] is a three phase simulation model for platform aware design of heterogeneous MPSoCs.

Kopetz [14], [13] proposes a component model for dependable automotive systems. Both approaches aim to achieve dependability and reliability of heterogeneous MPSoC by modeling systems using predefined platform templates. However, their design flow requires input models that are compatible with the given platform.

The Eclipse architecture [18] offers a platform template for heterogeneous media processing systems. It focuses on bus centric platforms with shared on-chip memory communication, while our work supports both same protocol communication (via memory) and communication of incompatible bus protocols (via transducers).

Several approaches work on implementing application models such as KPN to MPSoC platforms. ESPAM tool [19] inputs KPN application model, an abstract platform description and an application-to-platform mapping to automatically generate communication components and drivers. However, the supported platforms are limited to processors with local memories for local write operation and remote read access to the local memory of every other processor in the platform. Furthermore, all processors need to support the same communication protocol in order to read each others local memories. Our MPSoC communication architecture is less restricted and supports all types of remote/local memory accesses.

There have been several approaches to automatically generate executable SystemC code from abstract descriptions. Modeling languages as UML [4] and behavioral descriptions of systems in SystemC [16] have been proposed. These approaches do not address transaction level platform modeling without the need to use another language.

In [20], [17], the goal is to model the system at transaction level with both purely functional and estimated timing for performace estimation. The inputs are application and platform specifications along with the mapping decisions. The requirement in [20] is that the input application complies with a communication architecture consisting of point-to-point blocking channels with no storage capabilities. We support application models with both blocking channels as well as FIFO channels with bounded storage capacities.

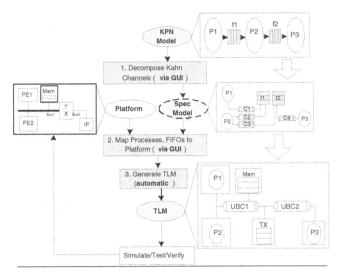

Figure 2. Generating TLM of MPSoC from KPN-to-platform mapping.

3. Platform Aware Design Flow

The Platform Aware Design [6] consists of (a) System Modeling, where the design space is searched for the TLM that best complies with specified requirements and (b) System Synthesis, where the chosen TLM is implemented at the pin and cycle accurate (PCA) level.

The System Modeling consists of 3 phases (as shown on Figure 2), and includes an interactive graphic user interface (GUI) that aids the designer in the first 2 phases.

The first phase includes platform definition, with the user dragging, dropping and connecting the templates of desired modules from the component library. This phase also performs automatic decomposition of Kahn Channels as a preparation to application-to-platform mapping. The application-to-platform mapping is done in the second phase, by binding each application task to the computing modules and each communication primitive to the platform bus models. In third and last phase, an executable SystemC TLM is generated automatically within seconds. The generated TLM enables performance evaluation, since it gives us valuable data on system timing, communication traffic and memory usage. Based on the simulation results, the designer can iteratively modify the platform or the application mapping using our GUI.

Once the TLM satisfies the requirements, the design moves to System Synthesis (outside the scope of this paper).

4. System Modeling with KPNs

This section describes the System Modeling in Platform Aware Design in greater detail.

The first input to System Modeling is the application, represented with the KPN. More specifically, the computation is captured with concurrent Kahn Processes that communicate via FIFO operations on Kahn Channels. A simple example of a KPN consisting of 3

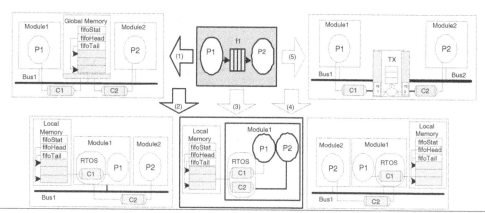

Figure 3. Phase Two: Mapping Kahn Channels to: (1) shared global memory, (2) shared local memory of process P1 in Module1 (3) shared local memory of both processes (4) shared local memory of process P2 in Module2 and (5) TX unit.

Kahn Processes ($P1$, $P2$ and $P3$) and 2 Kahn Channels ($f1$ and $f2$) is shown on Figure 2 (right). Kahn Processes are represented with SystemC [10] objects *sc_module* with a single *sc_thread* executing C code. Kahn Channels are *sc_channel* objects modeling point-to-point process communication.

The second input to Modeling is the general template of an MPSoC platform, shown on Figure 2 (left). It is structured as a top level *sc_module* composed from a set of interconnected components. The platform components include Processor Modules for computation, Memories for storage and Universal Bus Channels (UBC) [3] and transducers (TX) [9] for communication modeling. Processor Modules are *sc_modules* with one or more *sc_threads* that execute C code in parallel. Memories are *sc_modules* with arrays of bytes accessed via channel interfaces and they have no processing capabilities. The UBCs are *sc_channels* modeling a general system bus and its communication protocol. They contain custom generated *communication functions*: send/recv methods for process communication and write/read methods for memory accesses. The *sc_threads* call these functions to indirectly access *sc_channels*. Finally, the TXs are *sc_modules* similar to Processor Modules, but with the specific routing functionality of storing and forwarding the messages to/from channels connected to their interfaces. They model message routing and protocol translation between UBCs with incompatible protocols.

4.1 Phase One: Kahn Channel Decomposition

In our Platform Aware Design, the designer maps the Kahn Processes and Channels to the platform components: Processor Modules and UBCs/transducers (Figure 2, center). However, Kahn Channels are point-to-point primitives and cannot be directly mapped to the bus-centric MPSoC platform. Therefore, the first phase of system modeling automatically decomposes Kahn Channels into memory fragments (FIFOs) accessible with two Spec Channels.

Each FIFO has a bounded capacity equal to the size of the largest message transferred through the corresponding Kahn Channel. The capacity is determined by profiling the KPN application model, but can be changed by the user at any time via GUI.

The Spec Channel implements process communication (*send* and *recv* functions) with a double-handshake point-to-point *sc_channel* that includes FIFO management routines, i.e. preventing reading from an empty or writing into the full FIFO.

4.2 Phase Two: Kahn Process, Kahn Channel Mapping

The second phase of modeling consists of application-to-platform mapping. The Process-to-Module mapping is done by selecting the appropriate identifiers from a mapping menu of the GUI. The Process-to-Module menu contains the identifiers of Kahn Process (name, path to process code) and *sc_thread* object (name).

Kahn Channel mapping is specified with (a) mapping the FIFO to the Memory Module or Transducer and (b) mapping the Spec Channels to UBC(s). The mapping of the Kahn Channel's FIFO depending on the route between the Kahn Process communicating pair, as shown on Figure 3:

FIFO Mapping to a Shared Global Memory: If the Kahn Processes are remote and connected to the same UBC, their Kahn Channel's FIFO is mapped to a global memory fragment (Figure 3(1)) accessed by two Spec Channels modeling bus routines ($C1$ and $C2$). This mapping requires implementing a FIFO routines on top of read/write memory operations. The FIFO is modeled with a circular array of bytes with pointers (*fifoHead*, *fifoTail*) for storage management. Processes test the FIFO status with $readMessageFlag()$ before message transfer and update it ($writeMessageFlag()$) after the transfer. If the sending process attempts to write into a full memory, or if the receiver attempts to read from it, they will block after FIFO status test. The next update of the FIFO status (by another process) will generate the event *MemoryModified_event* that will unblock the waiting process.

FIFO Mapping to a Shared Local Memory: Mapping to a Local Memory fragment is possible when both Kahn Processes are contained in the same Processor Module (shown on Figure 3(3)). The communication is then modeled with service calls to the RTOS (depicted with Spec Channels $C1$ and $C2$). The RTOS is a specialized *sc_thread* invoked on each send/recv call. The RTOS provides the FIFO management and process blocking/unblocking.

FIFO Mapping to a Local Memory of one Kahn Process: A combination of previous two cases is shown in Figure 3 (2) and (4): the Processes are mapped to separate Modules and the FIFO is mapped to the Local Memory of the Module that contains either the Process sending the data, or the Process receiving the data. In either case, the Module hosting the FIFO will also host the RTOS which is managing the FIFO: accessing the FIFO data and signaling the occurance of full or empty FIFO.

FIFO Mapping to TX: Figure 3 (5) shows two Processes supporting different communication protocols and using an intermediary TX for message translation. A TX unit contains a bounded circular FIFO and manages all incoming requests for FIFO access with a TX controller process. The TX will accept the data from the sending Process using one protocol ($C3$) and forward it to the receiving Process with the other protocol ($C4$). If the TX controller cannot process a certain request, the process that called it will block until the TX is available. The request cannot be processed if the TX

Controller is busy servicing another request or if the FIFO segment has insufficient free space to store the incoming message. In case of more than one choice of Memory or TX unit on route between two Kahn Processes, the designer decides which will the memory fragment be mapped to.

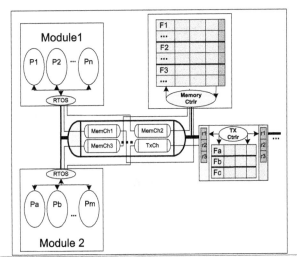

Figure 4. Phase Two: Merging Spec Channels into the UBC object.

Mapping of the Spec Channels to UBC(s) is done automatically, based on the previous mapping decisions for Processes and FIFO. More precisely, the UBC that is on route from a Processor Module containing the Kahn Process to the Memory/TX with the FIFO will contain the Spec Channel used by the Kahn Process to access that FIFO. This is outlined in Figure 4. Processor Modules $Module1$ and $Module2$ contain $P1$, $P2..Pn$ and Pa, $Pb..Pm$, respectively. The UBC will contain Spec Channels that connect to either a Memory (in Figure 4, channels $MemCh1$, $MemCh2$ and $MemCh3$) or a TX ($TxCh$ in Figure 4).

A unique set of communication functions is created per Spec Channel, one for the sending to the FIFO and another for the receiving from the FIFO. These functions are called by the Kahn processes and are the only interface between the Processes and the basic UBC services for synchronization, packetization and data transfer. However, in order to sequentialize the execution of Spec Channels mapped to a single UBC, each Process needs to arbiter for UBC access before calling the Spec Channel's functions. The arbitration is done by acquiring and releasing the UBC's *mutex* lock, with a choice of the UBC arbitration policy ranging from first-come-first-serve (FCFS) to the more complex priority based schemes.

4.3 Phase Three: Generating TLM

The third and final phase, we automatically generate the TLM of the platform-mapped KPN. Our system TLM will be defined by both the MPSoC platform and KPN application. The following section describe TLM generation in greater detail.

5. Automatic TLM generation

Our system definition D contains a set of objects which describe the platform and the application. It can be said that it is a set of Processor Modules, Memory Modules and hardware IPs, UBCs and Transducer Modules for communication. The system is further defined with connectivity and channel information.

5.1 System Definition

Formally, the objects of a D are: $< P, B, T, C, R, Ch_{fifo} >$, where

- P is the set of Processor Modules. Each $p \in P$ describes a Kahn Process and lists its source and header files, which describe the KPN application.

- B is the set of Busses. Each $b \in B$ is a UBC constructed with all mapped Ch_{fifo}s, and contains base addresses of Memories and Transducers, along with synchronization entries of communicating Proccesses, used to construct the synchronization tables.

- T is the set of Transducers. Each $t \in T$ contains data regarding communicating channels and FIFO sizes for each Channel.

- C is the set of Connections. Each $c \in C$ connects a UBC with either a Transducer or a Processor Module.

- R is the set of Routes. Each $r \in R$ describes all the design objects through which the Ch_{fifo} traverses: it lists the source Kahn Process, then all busses and Transducers to the final destination Kahn Process.

- Ch_{fifo} is the set of FIFOs. Each $ch \in Ch_{fifo}$ is mapped to a unique $r \in R$ which describes the data's path from source to destination. It also lists the location and size of the FIFO.

This system definition is preserved in an XML format [1] and the rules which this file must conform to is described in an XML Schema Definition (XSD) [2]. The XML file is created by our GUI from the graphical input of the user. This relieves the user from checking the rules in the XSD file, thus speeding up both the platform creation and the overall system specification.

The alterations to MPSoC platform, performed via GUI with drag-drop or delete operations will automatically update the system information. Furthermore, any platform transformation affects only the platform-specific section of the system definition, making design exploration simple and user-friendly. With this system information detailing the platform specific properties and application specification our automatic TLM generator is able to produce an executable SystemC TLM.

5.2 Communication Functions Generation

The final phase of the generation is the most complex: depending on the type of FIFO mapping selected by the user, the communication function will different. As defined in the previous section, any design will be composed of the objects $< P, B, T, C, R, Ch_{fifo} >$. For a given channel C_x, we will have a corresponding route R_x. Each channel will be composed of $< FIFO, SPR, DPR >$ which defines the location of the FIFO, the Source Kahn Process and the Destination Kahn Process, in that order. For each Route, the objects are $< SPE, DPE, BUS, MEM >$ which defines the Source PE hosting the source process, the Destination PE, the Bus or Busses used by the channel, and the memory hosting the FIFO, if mapped.

Shown in Figure 5 is the main algorithm for the generation of the communication functions. The starting point is a loop around each Kahn Process of the design, since we create unique communication functions for each Process. For each Kahn Process in the platform, all its Channels are evaluated for the location of the FIFO, stated in the $FIFO_x$ property of the Channel.

If the FIFO is mapped into a Global Memory Module ($FIFO_x \in M$), the base address of the Memory is obtained by using the connected bus (BUS_x) and Memory ID (MEM_x). Next, a read() and a write() function are created (GEN_MEM _USED() and GEN_MEM _FREE(), which manages the Memory as a circular buffer, and GEN_READ _BUS and GEN_WRITE_BUS which ac-

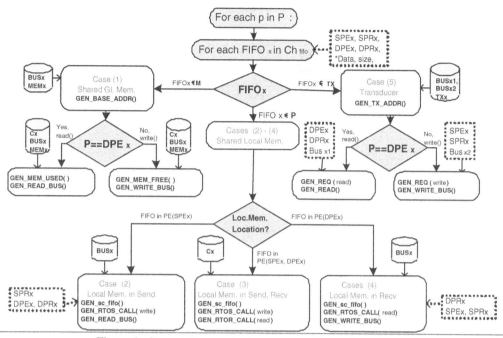

Figure 5. Channel Communication Functions Generation Diagram

cess the UBC), using information from the Channel (C_x), the connected bus and the Memory ID.

If the FIFO is mapped into a Transducer ($FIFO_x \in T$), the base addresses of the Transducer are obtained using both bus IDs (BUS_{x1} and BUS_{x2}) and the Transducer ID (T_x). The following step produces requests for transaction (GEN_REQUEST(read), GEN_REQUEST(WRITE)) followed by the actual bus transaction function (GEN_READ() and GEN_WRITE()). These code sections are generated using the source and destination Processor Module and Process IDs (DPE_x, DPR_x, SPE_x and SPR_x) in the Channel and route.

Finally, if the FIFO is mapped into a Local Memory of a Processor Module, the generator checks if this Processor Module matches either the source (SPE_x) or the destination (DPE_x) Processor Module or both. The first case corresponds to FIFO mapping outlined in Figure 3 (2), the second to Figure 3 (4) and the last is the FIFO mapping to Local Memory (Figure 3 (3)). In all cases, a FIFO is instantiated using a SystemC *sc_fifo*, and RTOS calls for read and write are generated (GEN_RTOS_CALL, GEN_WRITE_BUS and GEN_READ_BUS). These RTOS calls manage the FIFO and the interprocess communication across the UBC.

5.3 UBC Generation

Every UBC contains one unique and one common component. The unique component is the Processes' synchronization table and the common component is composed of UBC services such as *send()*, *receive()*, *memoryService()* and the arbiter module.

The synchronization tables are individually generated for each UBC based on the Spec Channels mapped to it. This information is stored in the XML file describing the system, under the *B(bus)* element. For each Spec Channel mapped, there is a synchronization entry in the XML. The generation algorithm traverses these entries and builds a table to be accessible by a *synchronize()* call by both communicating Kahn Processes.

The UBC services component are constant regardless of the channels that are mapped, and hence, are composed of elements retrieved from a library. The arbiter module is constant as well,

with the Processes' priority list as the only variable, in case the user selects a priority-based arbitration policy.

5.4 TLM Top module generation

The final SystemC TLM is generated by top level parsing of the XML file, instantiating *sc_modules* for Processor Modules, instantiation of all UBCs (declared in the generation phase described in the previous subsection) and Transducers, and port connections between them. This step uses the Connections C set of the XML to instantiate and bind the ports.

5.5 TLM performance

Introducing a platform into the KPN naturally slows down the model execution. For example, all processes in KPN are concurrent, while in TLM, processes mapped to a shared Processor Module are made sequential with an RTOS process scheduler. The timing estimates for Processor Modules. execution are computed during simulation, by adding the delays introduced by RTOS calls for context switching, process blocking and unblocking to the execution time of applications' Kahn Processes. Further, the channels mapped to the same UBC are serialized with arbitration over UBC access. The channel scheduling introduces TLM communication delays that are not present in the application KPN. For example, the Receiver will be delayed in *receive* function if the Sender is blocked by RTOS process scheduling or by arbitration for the UBC access. This is a change from KPN, where all processes are self-scheduled. Depending on the complexity of MPSoC platform and the chosen Kahn Process and Kahn Channel mapping decisions, we have observed between 5 and 10 times slower simulation of system TLM, as compared to the input KPN. However, TLM simulation is invaluable in revealing process scheduling conflicts, bus access contentions and communication bottlenecks that KPN inherently cannot model. We detail our approach with a case study of an industry size application: H.264 Encoder. Our Platform Aware Design process includes our 2-phase KPN mapping to MPSoC Platform and describes platform and mapping modifications enabled by simulations of the output TLM.

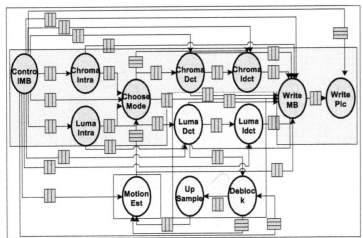

Kahn Process	compEst
ControlMB	70
ChromaIntra	250
LumaIntra	2000
ChooseMode	10
ChromaDct	180
LumaDct	200
WriteMB	50
WritePic	0.5
Deblock	450
ChromaIdct	110
LumaIdct	170
UpSample	1500
MotionEst	10000

Process-to-Module Map:

	Module1
	Module2
	Module3

Figure 6. Application model of H.264 Encoder. (a) Kahn Process Network, (b) Process-to-Module mapping, (c) Table of Kahn Process computation estimates

Name	Code size	Simulated exe. time	Development time	TLM Gen. time	Local mem. comm. delay	Shared mem. comm. delay	TX comm. delay
No Platform	600 KB	39.08 s	n/a	n/a	n/a	n/a	n/a
Platform1	1200 KB	151.49 s	1 h	0.650 s	135.26 s	164.87 s	151.80 s
Platform2	1290 KB	135.01 s	< 10 min	0.877 s	146.86 s	n/a	130.60 s
Platform3	1390 KB	134.85 s	< 5 min	0.890 s	146.36 s	132.96 s	112.12 s

Table 1. Comparison of code sizes and simulation times of TLM models of the H264 Encoder

6. Experimental Setup

The H.264 Encoder application is a ITU-recognized standard for compression of a stream of video data frames. It divides each frame into sub-blocks and performs a series of computationally intensive transformations: discrete cosine transformation (DCT), quantization, inverse DCT and motion estimation. The algorithm optimizes computation by attempting to re-apply already calculated transformations to adjacent sub-blocks, i.e. intra-frame prediction. Further, it predicts similarities in adjacent data frames and re-applies performed calculations to the next frame (inter-frame prediction). The described system is required to encode video frames at the speed of $< 1\ frame/second$.

The simplified KPN of H.264 Encoder is shown on Figure 6, with Kahn Channels abstracted with unidirectional FIFO links connecting 13 Kahn Processes. Some Kahn Channels (there are 43 in total) are omitted for clarity. The table on the Figure 6 (right) shows estimates of computation execution *compEst* for each Kahn Process (in millions of cycles).

We start the Platform Based Design with an input KPN of the H.264 Encoder and an initial plaform template (Figure 7 (a)). The H.264 Encoder application transfers the total of 998 messages (5.99 MB in size) per each encoded data frame. The average message size is 6.625 KB, however, the sizes of messages vary from 4 bytes to 945 KB. To create a system with balanced computation load in each processor and avoid execution delays for Processes with long execution, we map Processes that are computationally most intensive (*LumaIntra, UpSample* and *MotionsEst*, from Figure) to separate Processor Modules. Further process mapping maintains a balance between each Module's computation load (i.e. the sum of *compEst* values of its Processes) while aiming to minimize the number of inter-processor message transfers. The assumption is that intra-processor communication (i.e. message transfer within the same Processor Module) has shorter delay than inter-

processor transfers which use buses and transducers as communication media. Therefore, Figure 6 shows Processor *Module1* (highlighted orange) mapped with *LumaIntra* along with 7 more Processes. Processor *Module2* (green) contains *UpSample* and another 3 Processes. Finally, *Module3* (yellow highlight) executes only *MotionEst*, which is computationally most intensive Process. (*MotionEst* performs both motion estimation and prediction calculation for intra- and inter-frame predictions.)

6.1 Modeling with Platform1:

The initial platform template has three processors (*Module1* to *Module3*), two buses and a 2-port transducer (*TX*). The platform supports both inter-processor communication (via Shared Memory and TX) and intra-processor communication (via processor local memory). Shared Memory (via *UBC1*) communication is implemented between *Module1* and *Module2*, while *MotionEst* in *Module3* uses *TX* to buffer and transfer messages to all other Processes. Modules with multitasking have RTOS for intra-processor communication.

Using the GUI of our modeling tool, we have created the described *Platform1* and mapped the input KPN to it within approximately 1 hour. We have generated the TLM in 0.65 seconds and ran TLM simulations on a Pentium with 4 CPUs, running on 3 GHz and with 1 GB of RAM. We recorded the TLM execution time and the local, shared memory and TX communication delays. Each Processor Module has been attributed with specifications for Xilinx *Microblaze* soft-core, running at 27Mhz, and each bus has transaction delays as specified for the OPB (*On-chip Peripheral Bus*) protocol. In addition, we measured the simulation of a KPN (application model) of H264 Encoder as reference. The results of H.264 Encoder models processing 100 coded frames are shown on Table 1 (rows 1, 2).

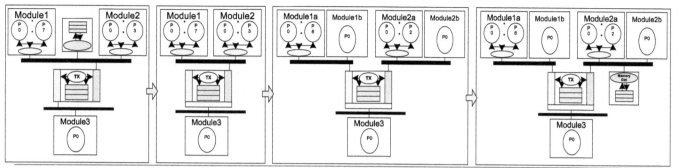

Figure 7. MPSoC Platform development. (a) Platform1, (b) Platform1b (not tested on), (c) Platform2, (d) Platform3

Name	Intra-processor comm.			Inter-processor comm.					
	Local shared mem.			Global shared mem.			TX		
Platform1	24 channels	1.564 MB	(26.11%)	13 ch.	2.772 MB	(46.27%)	6 ch.	1.654 MB	(27.61%)
Platform2	18 channels	3.052 MB	(50.95%)	0 ch.	0 MB		25 ch.	2.938 MB	(49.04%)
Platform3	18 channels	3.052 MB	(50.95%)	1 ch.	0.946 MB	(15.78%)	24 ch.	1.992 MB	(33.25%)

Table 2. Number of Kahn Channels and size of data (in bytes) they transfer per frame, for Platform1 through Platform3

Compared to KPN, the application took 5x more time to execute, exceeding the target decoding speed of 1 frame/s. Columns 4, 5 and 6 present the delays for local/shared memory communication and communication via a TX unit. The communication delay is defined as a time passed between invocation of the send/recv function and its completion. Therefore, high communication delays where processes block waiting for memory/TX access to complete the transaction indicate that memory/TX unit is a communication bottleneck.

6.2 Modeling with Platform 2:

In $Platform1$, both shared memory and TX communication have high delays (even surpasing the total simulation time), because they both sequentially access the same bus. To achieve speed-up with parallel communication, we modified the platform first by merging the Shared Memory with the TX (as shown on Figure 7 (b)) and then by spliting processes of Modules 1 and 2 into four Process Modules. The second MPSoC platform template contains five processors and three buses, as shown in Figure 7 (c). All processors communicate through a single 3-port TX. Processors $Module1a$ and $Module2a$ support multitasking and intra-processor communication: $Module1a$ has 7 processes and $Module2a$ has 3. The addition of the extra bus makes it possible to reduce communication delays by reducing the amount of arbitration requests by bus (fewer masters on each bus).

The transformation from $Platform1$ to $Platform2$ and changes in KPN mapping were perfomed via GUI in less than 10 minutes, with the TLM generated in 0.877 seconds, as shown in Table 1 (row 3). The acquired TLM simulates within the desired speed (1 frame/s). Moreover, the TX communication delay is now impacting the total execution delay less than the delay caused by local memory access.

6.3 Modeling with Platform 3:

Since local memory does not utilize system buses and incurrs excessive execution delay, $Platform2$ could be considered a viable functioning design. However, additional speed-up can be achieved by relieving TX of the traffic between $Module2a$ and $Module2b$ and enabling concurrency of communication via shared memory and via TX. The resulting $Platform3$ is shown on Figure 7 (d), with the final simulation results presented in the forth row of Table

1. It was created from $Platform$ in less than 5 minutes and the corresponding TLM was generated in 0.890 seconds.

Table 2 shows the mapping of 43 Kahn Channels in KPN of an H.264 Encoder to all three platforms. In $Platform1$ (three processors, 1st row of Table 2), 24 pairs of Kahn Processes communicate within processors (via local memory, 2nd column on Table 2.) and 19 are accessing the bus. Further, 13 of pairs using the bus are communicating via global shared memory (3rd column, Table 2) and 6 are using a TX to translate between protocols (4th column, Table 2). In $Platform2$ (five processors, 2nd row of Table 2), 18 Kahn Process pairs are communicating via local shared memory and 25 are requesting the services of the TX. In $Platform3$ (five processors, 2nd row of Table 2), the KPN-to-platform mapping is the same as in $Platform2$. However, in this platform, a pair of Processes in $Module2a$ and $Module2b$ is communicating via shared memory (3rd row, 3rd column) instead of using the TX unit. Note that even though TX unit is releaved from a single Kahn Channel, since the size of data that channel transfers (0.945 MB) constitutes almost 16% of total data transferred per frame, the speed up of $Platform3$ over $Platform2$ is significant (16 ms).

7. Conclusion

We presented a platform aware method of modeling dataflow systems represented with a KPN. Our method of modeling takes into account the MPSoC platform early in the process and automatically generates the corresponding executable TLM.

The contributions of our work lie in defining an interactive method of adapting the components of the KPN to the MPSoC Platform. This process consists of the automatic conversion of Kahn Channel into a memory fragment (FIFO) accessible with to 2 point-to-point Spec Channels and the interactive mapping of Kahn Processes and Channels to the MPSoC components. The presented mapping options for Kahn Channels include: mapping FIFOs to (a) a Global Memory Module, (b) Local Memory of the Processor Module or to (c) a buffer of a Transducer. The Spec Channels that access the FIFOs are automatically assigned to UBC Modules on routes between the sending and receiving Kahn Processes.

In addition, we presented a novel synthesis procedure that automatically generates the executable TLM of the system from the gathered system information. These TLMs provide the user with a fast functional validation of the system that accurately reflects the MPSoC platform. The supported platforms range from homogeneous bus centric systems to heterogeneous multi-processor networks communicating via incompatible protocols.

Simulation results of the TLMs show a tolerable increase in size and simulation time of multi-core platforms, as compared to a reference application KPN with no regard to the underlying platform. Notwithstanding these acceptable increases, the simulation of our automatically generated TLM provides invaluable insight in process scheduling conflicts, bus traffic, bus access contentions and other performance indicators that KPN simulation inherently cannot provide. Finally, the presented platform transformations enable fast and user convenient design space explorations. Our case study of the H.264 Encoder design demonstrates that with our methods, the specification compliant design was reached in less than 2 hours.

In future work, we aim to expand the existing library of processors and communication protocols with timing annotations. We are also working on extending the supported inputs to communication paradigms with mailboxes and semaphores. Finally, we aim to support platform templates of more complex MPSoC and NoC architectures.

A. Appendix Title

This is the text of the appendix, if you need one.

Acknowledgments

Acknowledgments, if needed.

References

[1] Xml. http://www.w3.org/XML.

[2] Xml schema. http://www.w3.org/XML/Schema.

[3] Samar Abdi and Daniel Gajski. Ubc: A universal bus channel for transaction level modeling. Number CECS-TR-06-07, University of California, Irvine, April 2006.

[4] F Bruschi, E Di Nitto, and D Sciuto. Systemc code generation from uml model. In *Proc. Int. Forum on Specification and Design Languages. FDL'04*, Frankfurt, September 2003.

[5] Joseph Buck, Soonhoi Ha, Edward A. Lee, and David G. Messerschmitt. Ptolemy: A framework for simulating and prototyping heterogeneous systems. *International Journal of Computer Simulation*, 4(2):155–182, April 1994.

[6] L. Carloni, F.D. Bernardinis, C. Pinello, and A. Sangiovanni-Vicentelli. *Embedded Systems Handbook*, chapter Platform-based design for embedded systems. CRC Press, 2005.

[7] Wander O. Cesário, Damien Lyonnard, Gabriela Nicolescu, Yanick Paviot, Sungjoo Yoo, Ahmed A. Jerraya, Lovic Gauthier, and Mario Diaz-Nava. Multiprocessor SoC platforms: A component-based design approach. *IEEE Design and Test of Computers*, 19(6), November/December 2002.

[8] Sangiovanni-Vincentelli et al. A next-generation design framework for platform based design. In *In Conference on Using Hardware Design and Verification Languages (DVCon)*, February 2007.

[9] Daniel Gajski, Hansu Cho, and Samar Abdi. General transducer architecture. Number CECS-TR-05-08, University of California, Irvine, August 2005.

[10] Thorsten Grötker, Stan Liao, Grant Martin, and Stuart Swan. *System Design with SystemC*. Kluwer Academic Publishers, 2002.

[11] G. Kahn. The Semantics of Simple Language for Parallel Programming. In *Proceedings of Information Processing*, pages 471–475, Stockholm, Sweden, August 1974.

[12] G. Kahn and D.B. MacQueen. Coroutines and Networks of Parallel Programming. In *Proceedings of Information Processing*, pages 993–998, August 1977.

[13] H. Kopetz, R. Obermaisser, C.E. Salloum, and B. Huber. Automotive software development for a multi-core system-on-a-chip. In *Proceedings of the 4th International Workshop on Software Engineering for Automotive Systems (SEAS'07)*, Washington, DC, USA, 2007.

[14] Hermann Kopetz and Gather Bauer. The Time-Triggered Architecture. *Proceedings of the IEEE*, 91(1):126–113, January 2003.

[15] Achim Österling, Thomas Brenner, Rolf Ernst, Dirk Herrmann, Thomas Scholz, and Wei Ye. The COSYMA system. In Jorgen Staunstrup and Wayne Wolf, editors, *Hardware/Software Co-Design: Principles and Practice*. Kluwer Academic Publishers, 1997.

[16] A Sarmento, W Cesario, and A Jerraya. Automatic building of executable models from abstract soc architectures made of heterogeneous subsystems. In *Proceedings of the 15th IEEE International Workshop on Rapid System Prototyping*, June 2004.

[17] Gunar Schirner, Andreas Gerstlauer, and Rainer Doemer. Abstract Multifaceted Modeling of Embedded Processors for System-Level Design. In *Proceedings of the Asia and South Pacific Design Automation Conference (ASPDAC)*, Yokohama, Japan, January 2007.

[18] M.J. Rutten Stefanov, C. Zissulescu, A. Turjan, B. Kienhuis, and E. Deprettere. Eclipse: Heterogeneous Multiprocessor Architecture for Flexible Media Processing. In *Workshop on Parallel and Distributed Computing in Image Processing, Video Processing and Multimedia (PDVIM'02)*, Fort Lauderdale, Florida, April 2002.

[19] T. Stefanov, C. Zissulescu, A. Turjan, B. Kienhuis, and E. Deprettere. System Design using Kahn Process Networks: The Compaan/Laura Approach. In *Proceedings of the Design, Automation and Test in Europe (DATE) Conference*, pages 340–345, Paris, France, February 2004.

[20] Lochi Yu, Samar Abdi, and Daniel Gajski. Transaction level platform modeling in systemc for multi-processor designs. Number CECS-TR-07-01, University of California, Irvine, July 2007.

Compiler Directed Network-on-Chip Reliability Enhancement for Chip Multiprocessors *

Ozcan Ozturk

Bilkent University, Turkey
ozturk@cs.bilkent.edu.tr

Mahmut Kandemir, Mary J. Irwin

Pennsylvania State University, USA
{kandemir,mji}@cse.psu.edu

Sri H. K. Narayanan [†]

Pennsylvania State University, USA
snarayan@cse.psu.edu

Abstract

Chip multiprocessors (CMPs) are expected to be the building blocks for future computer systems. While architecting these emerging CMPs is a challenging problem on its own, programming them is even more challenging. As the number of cores accommodated in chip multiprocessors increases, network-on-chip (NoC) type communication fabrics are expected to replace traditional point-to-point buses. Most of the prior software related work so far targeting CMPs focus on performance and power aspects. However, as technology scales, components of a CMP are being increasingly exposed to both transient and permanent hardware failures.

This paper presents and evaluates a compiler-directed power-performance aware reliability enhancement scheme for network-on-chip (NoC) based chip multiprocessors (CMPs). The proposed scheme improves on-chip communication reliability by duplicating messages traveling across CMP nodes such that, for each original message, its duplicate uses a different set of communication links as much as possible (to satisfy performance constraint). In addition, our approach tries to reuse communication links across the different phases of the program to maximize link shutdown opportunities for the NoC (to satisfy power constraint). Our results show that the proposed approach is very effective in improving on-chip network reliability, without causing excessive power or performance degradation. In our experiments, we also evaluate the performance oriented and energy oriented versions of our compiler-directed reliability enhancement scheme, and compare it to two pure hardware based fault tolerant routing schemes.

Categories and Subject Descriptors D.3.4 [*Programming Languages*]: Processors—compilers, memory management, optimization

General Terms Experimentation, Management, Design, Performance

Keywords Chip multiprocessors, reliability, NoC, Compiler

1. Introduction

As processor design has become severely power and performance limited, it is now commonly accepted that staying on the current performance trajectory (doubling of chip performance every 24 to 36 months) will come about through the integration of multiple processors (cores) on a chip rather than through increases in the clock rate of single processors. Several chip manufacturers already have dual core chips on the market (e.g., Intel's dual core Montecito [28], the dual core AMD Athlon [2]), with more aggressive configurations being delivered or prototyped (e.g., Sun's eight core Niagara [23], IBM's Cell [20], Intel's quad core Xeon [19], and Intel's 80 core TeraFlop [18]). In the long run, one can expect the number of cores in chip multiprocessors (CMPs) to increase.

It is expected that CMPs will be very successful in data and communication intensive parallel applications such as multimedia data processing, scientific computing, and bioinformatics. However, to achieve the desired performance-power-reliability tradeoffs, suitable software support is critical for CMPs. In fact, it is clear that CMP hardware cannot evolve independently of the proper software infrastructure, and software development tools are really the key to realizing the benefits offered by CMPs. While an overwhelming majority of prior CMP software related efforts focused on performance or power optimizations, there are very few studies that target at improving hardware reliability. This is unfortunate, because as transistor sizes and voltages of electronic circuits continue to scale, one can expect reliability to be even more challenging for future CMPs.

There are several aspects of hardware reliability as far as CMPs are concerned. For example, correct execution of instructions is vital and can be helped with techniques such as dual execution [5]. Similarly, due to their relatively large sizes, memory components of a CMP can be vulnerable to hardware failures. Conventional methods for addressing potential memory related faults include error detection and correction codes. Another emerging problem area is the on-chip communication fabric. Since future technologies offer the promise of being able to integrate billions of transistors on a chip, the prospects of having hundreds of processors on a single chip along with an underlying memory hierarchy and an interconnection system will be entirely feasible. Once the number of cores on one CMP passes some threshold (~16 cores), conventional point-to-point buses will no longer be sufficient. These future CMPs will require an on-chip network (an NoC, Network-on-Chip [11]) in order to be able to handle the required communications between the cores in a scalable, flexible, programmable, and reliable fashion. Consider, as an example, a 2D mesh NoC that can be used to connect the cores in a CMP. There are several advantages of this kind of on-chip network. First, meshes work well with the conventional VLSI technology (which is 2D). Second, meshes scale very well as the number of cores is increased due their high bisection bandwidths and low diameter. Third, communication can be packet based and more regular, and as a result, it can easily be exposed to software for optimization purposes. Fourth, switches in a NoC can be used for strengthening signals flowing through them, helping to reduce data loses.

A NoC can be affected by both permanent failures (e.g., a link is broken) and transient errors such as crosstalks and coupling noises. Technology scaling makes this reliability problem even worse, demanding solutions in both hardware and software. However, since many CMP systems that require fault tolerance also work under severe power-performance constraints, any reliability optimization should be carried out considering the impact on power and performance. A daunting challenge, therefore, involves developing solutions for addressing the NoC reliability problems that are both performance and power aware. This is the problem addressed in this work.

* This research is supported in part by NSF grants CNS #0720645, CCF #0811687, CCF #0702519, CNS #0202007 CNS #0509251, by a grant from Microsoft Corporation, and by a Marie Curie International Reintegration Grant within the 7th European Community Framework Programme.

[†] The author is with the ANL now.

Our belief is that significant power-performance-reliability gains can be achieved by *exposing the NoC-based CMP architecture to the compiler* and letting the compiler optimize a given application code for both thread assignment and inter-thread communications. In this work, we present and evaluate a compiler directed, power-performance aware message reliability enhancement scheme for NoC-based CMPs. The proposed scheme improves on-chip communication reliability by duplicating messages traveling across the CMP nodes such that, for each original message, its duplicate uses a different set of links as much as possible (to satisfy performance constraint). In addition, our approach tries to reuse communication links across the different phases of the program to maximize link shutdown opportunities for the NoC (to satisfy power constraint).

Prior work studied performance-oriented compile techniques for CMPs [10, 25, 31], application/IP block mapping schemes [4, 17], and link power optimizations [8, 9, 21, 26, 27, 34]. Our work is different from these studies in that it is oriented toward improving "reliability" under performance and energy constraints. There also exist several efforts that target modeling/improving network reliability [6, 30, 42, 44, 45]. To our knowledge, *this paper presents the first compiler-based approach to NoC reliability, or even to network reliability in general.*

1.1 Contributions

• We propose a compiler directed NoC reliability enhancement scheme that duplicates communication packets using non-intersecting paths. A unique characteristic of this scheme is that it is both performance and power conscious. In this approach, the compiler identifies program phases and solves the problem for each phase using integer linear programming (ILP). The solution times experienced in our experiments were not very high (between 16.1 seconds and 2.7 minutes on a 2GHz Sun Solaris machine). We also discuss performance oriented and power oriented variants of our baseline implementation.

    • We present an experimental evaluation of the proposed scheme and compare its behavior to a hardware based reliability scheme. The results obtained using the parallelized versions of the SPECFP2000 benchmarks [35] clearly show that our approach is much more effective than alternate approaches to NoC reliability. We also observed that most of the time (more than 90%) our approach was able to send the original message and its replica over non-intersecting paths.

    • To show that our approach can also be used along with profiling to handle a larger set of application codes, we also report results from three applications (mpeg, g.721, and specjbb) where the parallel code structure can be fully captured at compile time. In our experiments, we also compare our approach to two pure hardware based fault tolerant routing schemes. Our results indicate that the proposed scheme is better than these hardware based fault tolerant routing schemes in terms of performance, power, and reliability.

1.2 Roadmap

The rest of this paper is organized as follows. The next section introduces our NoC based CMP architecture. Section 3 introduces the main data structure (Unweighted Memory Access Graph, UMAG) used by our approach, and Section 4 explains how we identify phases in a parallel program using the UMAG. Our approach to reliability enhancement is described in Section 5, and the ILP formulations and an example are presented. Section 6 presents an experimental evaluation of our scheme, and Section 7 concludes the paper.

2. NoC Based CMP Abstraction

We focus on an NoC based CMP architecture where the nodes form a two-dimensional (2D) mesh. In this architecture, each node has a processor core, a memory, and a network interface. The specific NoC we focus on is a 2D mesh but our approach can be adapted to work with other NoC topologies, as long as the topology is exposed to the compiler. The nodes of this mesh are connected to each other using switches and bi-directional links. The on-chip memory in a node is organized as a hierarchy with each node having a private L1 cache and a portion of the shared on-chip memory space (i.e., this is a shared memory CMP). The latency of a data access in this shared on-chip space is a function of the distance between the requester core and the node that holds the data (similar to the NUCA concept [16, 22] except that our on-chip memory space is managed by compiler). We assume static thread and data mappings,

i.e., before our approach is applied, parallel threads are mapped to the CMP nodes and data blocks are mapped to the on-chip memory spaces (we will discuss these mappings later in more detail). When a core requires a data element, it accesses that data from either the on-chip memory space of one of the CMP nodes or the off-chip memory space, depending on the location of the data. While we do not consider data migration/replication within the CMP in our baseline implementation, our approach can also be made to operate under an on-chip memory management scheme that employs data migration and/or replication.

In our discussion we use the terms "message" and "packet" interchangeably, though in reality a message is composed of multiple packets. Each packet in turn is composed of multiple flits. We further assume that all flits of a given message follow the same path on the NoC. Also, while the traditional reliability/fault-tolerance theory distinguishes between the terms "error," "fault," and "failure," in this work we use these terms interchangeably as long as the context/meaning is clear.

In our approach, the selection of the routing paths is done by the compiler. The hardware needed for such "compiler-directed routing" is similar to that used in the Intel Teraflops Processor [15] and [26]. We assume an NoC switch that supports two types of routings: default X-Y routing and compiler-directed routing. The former is used by some of the schemes against which we compare our approach. The header of each packet contains a flag bit indicating which routing mechanism is used for this packet. A packet using the default X-Y routing contains the id of the destination node in its header, as shown in the upper part of Figure 1. When a switch receives such a packet, it uses the X-Y routing algorithm. For a 5 × 5 network, the header of a packet that employs compiler-directed routing contains three fields (see the lower part of Figure 1): the hop counter (4 bits), the orientation (2 bits), and the routing command sequence (13 bits). For each switch on the path from source node to destination node, there is a corresponding bit in the routing command sequence of the packet, which (along with the orientation value) tells the switch which output port to use. Figure 3 gives the meaning of the routing commands for the different values of the orientation field. The hop counter is reduced by one each time the packet is forwarded from one switch to another. It becomes zero, when the packet has arrived at its destination node.

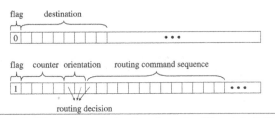

Figure 1. The fields in the header of a packet (Top: default X-Y routing; Bottom: compiler-directed routing).

Orientation	00	00	01	01	10	10	11	11
Routing Command	0	1	0	1	0	1	0	1
Output Port	N	E	N	W	S	E	S	W

Figure 2. Output ports used based on the orientation and routing command bits (N: North; S: South; W: West; E: East).

Future CMPs will contain a number of dynamic power optimizations. For example, each node or a set of nodes may be placed in a voltage island to support dynamic frequency and voltage scaling. The power feature that we are taking advantage of in this paper is NoC link shutdown [34]. When a link has been idle for some period of time, it is shut down to save energy. Shutting some of the links down may result in higher link sharing. This in turn can affect the performance of the application. In addition to this, link state transition (i.e., shutdowns and startups) overheads must be taken into account.

Note that multiple applications can be mapped to and executed on this CMP architecture concurrently. However, we assume that each application is assigned/given a contiguous partition of nodes of the CMP, and no communication links or cores are shared at the same time by the threads that belong to different applications. We assume that the interface between the application and the OS allows the former to request a partition (a sub-mesh) from the latter.

3. Unweighted Memory Access Graph

Our approach has four steps. In the first step, we build a data structure that represents the parallel application and, in the second step, we use this structure to identify different program phases. The third step optimizes each phase in isolation for reliability enhancements using ILP. The last phase modifies the code to insert duplicate messages. Due to space limitation, we only discuss the details of the first three steps.

In the first step, the compiler analyzes the input code and builds a *Unweighted Memory Access Graph* (UMAG) to capture the memory access behavior of the parallel application based on the architecture defined in Section 2. A UMAG[1], which is built using static analysis, is a directed graph where each vertex represents a memory-related activity or a construct in the parallel code and each edge represents the flow. In mathematical terms, we map the given parallel program, T, to its graph representation $G(T)$, where

$$G(T) = V(T) \cup E(T)$$
$$E(T) \subseteq V(T) \times V(T).$$

There are five types of vertices in a UMAG:

$$V(T) = L(T) \cup B(T) \cup A(T) \cup D(T) \cup W(T),$$

where a vertex $l \in L(T)$ represents a loop, more specifically, the entry point of a loop. Similarly, $b \in B(T)$ represents a back-jump of a loop, $ap \in A(T)$ represents an address packet transmission, $dp \in D(T)$ represents a data packet transmission, and $wp \in W(T)$ represents a write packet transmission. The ap and dp vertices capture the memory read activity, while the wp vertices capture the memory write activity.

Data accesses are captured using vertices in $A(T)$, $D(T)$, and $W(T)$. More specifically, a data request is represented by a vertex $ap_i \in A(T)$; the actual data transfer is represented by a vertex $dp_j \in D(T)$. In the case of a write packet, both the address and the data to be updated are sent in one packet by $wp_k \in W(T)$. An edge $e \in E(T)$ is categorized based on the classification of the vertices it connects. We have:

$$E(T) = E_{Control}(T) \cup E_{Data}(T) \cup E_{Comp}(T).$$

There are three types of edges, namely, control edges ($E_{Control}$), memory access edges (E_{Data}), and computation edges (E_{Comp}).

- $E_{Control}(T) \subseteq B(T) \times L(T)$: A back-jump edge that connects a back-jump vertex, $b \in B(T)$, to a loop vertex, $l \in L(T)$.
- $E_{Data}(T) \subseteq D(T) \times A(T)$: A data access edge that connects a data packet vertex, $dp \in D(T)$, to an address packet vertex, $ap \in A(T)$, that belongs to a different loop nest.

Finally, $E_{Comp}(T) = E_L(T) \cup E_B(T) \cup E_A(T) \cup E_D(T) \cup E_W(T)$ gives the computation edges:

- $E_L(T) \subseteq L(T) \times (A(T) \cup D(T) \cup W(T))$: A control edge that connects a loop vertex, $l \in L(T)$, to either an address packet vertex, $ap \in A(T)$, or a data packet vertex, $dp \in D(T)$, or a write packet vertex, $wp \in W(T)$.
- $E_B(T) \subseteq (A(T) \cup D(T) \cup W(T)) \times B(T)$: A control edge that connects an address packet vertex, $ap \in A(T)$, or a data packet vertex, $dp \in D(T)$, or a write packet vertex, $wp \in W(T)$, to a back-jump vertex, $b \in B(T)$.
- $E_A(T) \subseteq A(T) \times (D(T) \cup W(T))$: A computation edge that connects an address packet vertex, $ap \in A(T)$, to a data packet vertex, $dp \in D(T)$, or a write packet vertex, $wp \in W(T)$.
- $E_D(T) \subseteq D(T) \times (A(T) \cup W(T))$: A computation edge that connects a data packet vertex, $dp \in D(T)$, to an address packet vertex, $ap \in A(T)$, or a write packet vertex, $wp \in W(T)$.
- $E_W(T) \subseteq W(T) \times (A(T) \cup D(T))$: A computation edge that connects a write packet vertex, $wp \in W(T)$, to an address packet vertex, $ap \in A(T)$, or a data packet vertex, $dp \in D(T)$.

---

[1] While not used in this paper, one can also envision a weighted version of the memory access graph (WMAG) for implementing link voltage scaling.

```
//Process 1
l₁: for(...) {
        //request to read d₁
        send_ap(1, 2, d₁,...);
        //address packet ap₁ is sent
        recv_dp(1, 2, d₁,...);
        //data packet dp₁ is received
        read(1, 2, d₁,...);
        //reading d₁ is finalized

        //compute d₃ and send
        recv_ap(1, 2, d₃,...);
        //address packet ap₃ is received
        computing d₃;
        //d₃ is ready
        send_dp(1, 2, d₃,...);
        //data packet dp₃ is sent
}

//Process 3
l₄: for(...) {
        //request to read d₄
        send_ap(3, 2, d₄,...);
        //address packet ap₄ is sent
        recv_dp(3, 2, d₄,...);
        //data packet dp₄ is received
        read(3, 2, d₄,...);
        //reading d₄ is finalized

        //compute d₂ and send
        recv_ap(3, 2, d₂,...);
        //address packet ap₂ is received
        computing d₂;
        //d₂ is ready
        send_dp(3, 2, d₂,...);
        //data packet dp₂ is sent
}
```

```
//Process 2
l₂: for(...) {
        //compute d₁ and send
        recv_ap(2, 1, d₁,...);
        //address packet ap₁ is received
        computing d₁;
        //d₁ is ready
        send_dp(2, 1, d₁,...);
        //data packet dp₁ is sent
        l₃: for(...) {
                //compute d₄ and send
                recv_ap(2, 3, d₄,...);
                //address packet ap₄ is received
                computing d₄;
                //d₄ is ready
                send_dp(2, 3, d₄,...);
                //data packet dp₄ is sent

                //request to read d₂
                send_ap(2, 3, d₂,...);
                //address packet ap₂ is sent
                recv_dp(2, 3, d₂,...);
                //data packet dp₂ is received
                read(2, 3, d₂,...);
                //reading d₂ is finalized
                computing;
        }
        //request to read d₃
        send_ap(2, 1, d₃,...);
        //address packet ap₃ is sent
        recv_dp(2, 1, d₃,...);
        //data packet dp₃ is received
        read(2, 1, d₃,...);
        //reading d₃ is finalized
}
```

Figure 3. Program code of a shared memory parallel program.

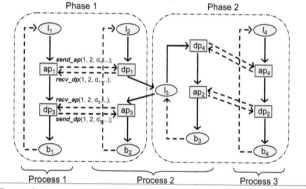

Figure 4. An example UMAG and the corresponding parallel computation phases.

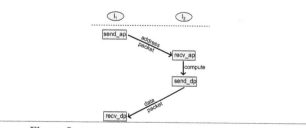

Figure 5. Details of an address/data packet transmission.

87

Figure 3 shows an example parallel code fragment composed of three different processes and four different loop nests (l_1 through l_4). Details of the computation statements as well as local memory accesses are not shown for clarity. However, read and write accesses to non-local memories are shown explicitly. Although there are many parameters involved in a read/write request, we are mostly interested in the source/target process (node) and the data element being accessed. More specifically, a read request is given as **read** ($requester_{id}$, $process_{id}$, $data_{id}$,...), where $requester_{id}$ is the requesting process (i.e., the one executing the read request), $process_{id}$ represents the process that is executing in the node that contains the memory which holds or will hold the requested data, and $data_{id}$ is the requested data item from that memory. Similarly, **write** ($process_{id}$, $data_{id}$,...) writes $data_{id}$ to the memory of the node that is executing $process_{id}$. In case of a write, a single write packet is sufficient since the address and the data to write can be transferred simultaneously in one packet.

Read and write accesses to non-local memories described above are represented with packets in our UMAG representation. Figure 4 shows the UMAG for the example in Figure 3. A read access is denoted by two packets, address and data. First, requesting process sends an address packet containing the address of the data element and the corresponding data packet contains the requested data element. However, as mentioned earlier, in case of a write, a single write packet is sufficient. This packet includes both the address and the value to be written. Note that data dependencies are also expressed using edges in our UMAG representation. Also, we use dashed edges to represent inter-iteration dependencies, whereas solid edges are used to represent intra-iteration dependencies. Lastly, the nodes used for data and address packets (ap_i, dp_i, and wp_i) do *not* mean that the actual packet transmissions occur at these nodes, rather they indicate that specific packets have been sent/received. Figure 5 shows the actual address and data packet transmissions in our UMAG representation. Edges represent the actual packet transmissions which, for clarity, we do not show in this much detail in Figure 4. A read request is an address packet followed by a data packet transmission. For example, as can be seen in Figure 3, process 1 initiates the the read request by sending an address packet, $send\_ap(1, 2, d_1, ...)$. This request is received by process 2 with the $recv\_ap(2, 1, d_1, ...)$ statement and the requested data is sent once the data is available (possibly after a computation step), through a data packet with $send\_dp(2, 1, d_1, ...)$. This data packet is received by the requester with a $recv\_dp(1, 2, d_1, ...)$ call. Although not shown here explicitly, a write request can also be represented similarly.

4. Phase Identification

After obtaining the UMAG representation, we divide it into *parallel computation phases* (PCPs). In this context, a PCP represents a set of loops that will execute in parallel (at runtime) and communicate with each other (through accessing some common data elements). We then apply our reliability enhancement scheme at a PCP granularity.

In order to formally express a PCP, we first define the concept of *loop connectivity*. Two loops are said to be connected if there is a packet transmission between them. For example, in Figure 4, loops l_1 and l_2 are connected due to data and address transmissions, whereas loops l_2 and l_3 do not have any connection. We express loop connectivity using $l_i \Longrightarrow l_j$ and formally define it as:

$$l_i \Longrightarrow l_j \qquad \text{if } \exists e \in (E_A(T) \cup E_D(T) \cup E_W(T))$$
$$\text{s.t. } e.source \in l_i, \ e.dest \in l_j, \ i \neq j.$$

Loop connectivity is a transitive property, that is, if $l_i \Longrightarrow l_j$ and $l_j \Longrightarrow l_k$, then we have $l_i \Longrightarrow l_k$. Similarly, we use $l_i \circ l_j$ to express that loops l_i and l_j are not connected. Using this notion of loop connectivity, collection of PCPs (or simply phases) form the loop nodes given with $L(T)$:

$$L(T) = \bigcup_{i=1}^{n} PCP_i, \text{s.t. } l_j \circ l_k, \ \forall l_j \notin PCP_i \text{ and } \forall l_k \in PCP_i.$$

This definition implies that there cannot be a single $l_j \in PCP_s$ connected to another $l_k \in PCP_t$ directly or indirectly. For example,

the UMAG in Figure 4 can be divided into two PCPs: $PCP_1 = (l_1, l_2)$ and $PCP_2 = (l_3, l_4)$.

Once the parallel program is decomposed into phases, the rest of our approach operates on one phase at a time. Since PCPs do not have any data dependencies between them, we can treat each phase as an independent execution unit and optimize it in isolation. For example, in Figure 4, there is no data dependence indicated by data/address packet transmissions between PCP_1 and PCP_2. This, in turn, allows our scheme to optimize two PCPs in isolation. Note that, the edges between dp_1 and l_3 as well as l_3 and ap_3 are control edges which do not prevent us from optimizing PCPs individually. Since each phase typically has a different inter-node communication pattern, it makes sense to formulate and solve a separate linear problem for each phase. Section 5 explains the ILP formulation we implement for a given phase (PCP).

5. Reliability Enhancement

In this section, we present our ILP formulation for the NoC reliability enhancement scheme that duplicates messages using non-intersecting paths. We implemented our ILP approach such that the number of links traversed between the source and the destination is minimum. Specific constraints that satisfy this property have not been shown explicitly for clarity reasons. We used Xpress-MP [43], a commercial tool, to formulate and solve our ILP problem. Note that, as explained above, the paths selected by the compiler may be different from those that would be adopted by conventional X-Y routing.

5.1 Reliability Centric Formulation

As explained earlier, we focus on a 2D mesh-based CMP, which is represented by a directed graph $G = (V, E)$. Each node in V is assigned an identifier, e.g., i, and each edge in E is denoted using its corresponding nodes, e.g., (i, j). Using static program analysis as explained above, we first identify concurrent messages within each program phase. For example, if phase n has K concurrent messages to be transmitted, each message is represented by (s_k, t_k, b_k) for $k = 1, \ldots, K$, where s_k and t_k are the source node and destination node, respectively, and b_k captures the bandwidth required by this message.

We also employ a binary variable $M_{i,j}^{p,k}$ to describe the routing decision for message k in phase p at link (i, j). Setting the value of this variable to 1 means that message k is transmitted through link (i, j); otherwise, message k does not pass through link (i, j). In order to capture the participation of node n at the transmission of a message k within phase p, we use $A_{p,k,n}$. More specifically, a node participates at the communication if a neighbor is part of the same communication and the link connecting these two nodes is active (not shutdown). We use a different 0-1 variable to capture the activity of a link:

$$E_{p,i,j} = \begin{cases} 1, & \text{if the link between } i \text{ and } j \text{ is active during phase } p. \\ 0, & \text{otherwise.} \end{cases}$$

Recall that, in our NoC-based CMP architecture, there are bi-directional links between neighboring nodes denoted by i, j. A link can be active in one phase of the program and inactive during the next phase. This enables us to control the NoC state, taking into account the communication requirements exhibited by a given phase. As explained earlier, to include a node in a communication activity, we need to ensure that a neighbor is part of the communication and the connecting link is active. This can be expressed as follows:

$$A_{p,k,j} \geq A_{p,k,i} + M_{i,j}^{p,k} - 1, \forall p, i, j. \qquad (1)$$

In order to improve the reliability of the NoC, our approach duplicates the messages in the system. To capture this within our ILP formulation, we use $R_{i,j}^{p,k}$. Similar to $M_{i,j}^{p,k}$, this captures the communication behavior of the duplicate of message k.

$$R_{i,j}^{p,k} = \begin{cases} 1, & \text{if message } k \text{ is transmitted through link } (i, j) \\ & \text{during phase } p. \\ 0, & \text{otherwise.} \end{cases}$$

Like a regular message, a node will be included in the communication activity, if a duplicate message is being transmitted through:

$$A_{p,k,j} \geq A_{p,k,i} + R_{i,j}^{p,k} - 1, \forall p, i, j. \quad (2)$$

The neighbors indicated here correspond to the nodes on the north, south, west and east of the node represented by $A_{p,k,i}$. The nodes that are on the borders of the NoC have a subset of these constraints (depending on their specific locations). Note that, the source and the destination of each message are already known and given by s_k and t_k, respectively. For each node designated as the source or the target, we set these variables to 1. More specifically, we have:

$$A_{p,k,i} = 1, \text{ if } i = s_k \text{ or } i = t_k, \forall p, k, i. \quad (3)$$

We need to ensure that, if a message is sent through a link, that link should be active. We capture this as follows:

$$E_{p,i,j} \geq M_{i,j}^{p,k}, \forall p, k, i, j. \quad (4)$$

Similarly, a link needs to be active during the transmission of a duplicate message over it:

$$E_{p,i,j} \geq R_{i,j}^{p,k}, \forall p, k, i, j. \quad (5)$$

We also need to make sure that both the original and the duplicate messages should follow different routes (paths) to the target. We can express this as follows:

$$M_{i,j}^{p,k} + R_{i,j}^{p,k} \leq 1, \forall p, k, i, j. \quad (6)$$

Next, we introduce $S_{p,i,j}$, the binary variable to indicate whether a link is shared by multiple messages during a phase:

$$S_{p,i,j} = \begin{cases} 1, & \text{if link } (i,j) \text{ is shared during phase } p. \\ 0, & \text{otherwise.} \end{cases}$$

To capture the behavior of this variable correctly, we need to consider all the message pairs including the original messages and duplicates. Consequently, we have:

$$\begin{aligned} S_{p,i,j} &\geq & M_{i,j}^{p,k_1} + M_{i,j}^{p,k_2} - 1, \\ S_{p,i,j} &\geq & M_{i,j}^{p,k_1} + R_{i,j}^{p,k_2} - 1, \\ S_{p,i,j} &\geq & R_{i,j}^{p,k_1} + R_{i,j}^{p,k_2} - 1, \\ & & \forall p, i, j, k_1, k_2 \text{ such that } k_1 \neq k_2. \quad (7) \end{aligned}$$

If any two messages are identified to exercise a link, that link is marked as a shared link, that is, $S_{p,i,j}$ is set to 1.

We also need to capture the link state transitions (i.e., shutdowns and startups). It might be possible to hide the performance overhead due to these activations/deactivations by using a *preactivation* strategy (i.e., by activating a link ahead of the time before it is really needed so that it will be ready when it is needed). However, the energy overheads due to such activities cannot be hidden. To capture this overhead, we use $AE_{p,i,j}$ and $DE_{p,i,j}$ for activation (startup) and deactivation (shutdown), respectively. These constraints can be expressed as follows:

$$\begin{aligned} AE_{p,i,j} &\geq & E_{p,i,j} - E_{p-1,i,j}, \\ DE_{p,i,j} &\geq & E_{p-1,i,j} - E_{p,i,j}, \ \forall p, i, j. \quad (8) \end{aligned}$$

In the above expression, we check each communication link's activity in neighboring phases (PCPs) p and $p-1$. If there is any change in the activity (state) of any link (i.e., any transition), one of the corresponding variables (AE or DE) will be triggered (i.e., the corresponding variable will be set to 1). This overhead is included in our objective function.

Having specified the necessary constraints to be satisfied by our ILP formulation, we next discuss our objective function for reliability enhancement. We define our cost function (to minimize) as the sum of two separate cost factors: one to capture the performance concern and the other to capture the energy concern. Thus, our objective function can be expressed as follows:

$$\min \sum_{p=1}^{P} \sum_{i=1}^{n} \sum_{j=1}^{n} C_1 \times S_{p,i,j} + C_2 \times (AE_{p,i,j} - DE_{p,i,j}). \quad (9)$$

In this expression, C_1 and C_2 capture the weights for the performance concern and energy concern, respectively. Note that, $S_{p,i,j}$ is used for the number of shared links, whereas $(AE_{p,i,j} - DE_{p,i,j})$ represents the number of links activated during this phase. The value of $(AE_{p,i,j} - DE_{p,i,j})$ could be negative meaning that the specific link is deactivated at the given phase. Also, if $C_1 > C_2$ the solution found will be more oriented towards improving performance (by minimizing the number of links shared by the messages in a given phase), whereas $C_1 < C_2$ favors an energy oriented solution (by maximizing the link reuse between neighboring phases).

5.2 Performance Centric Formulation

The formulation presented above duplicates every original message in the phase. This can have performance consequences despite the fact that our approach tries to route original and duplicate messages using non-intersecting paths as much as possible. In this subsection, we present an alternate formulation which favors performance. Specifically, we try to maximize the number of duplicates while not allowing any links to be shared by two or more messages (duplicate or original) in a given phase. We have to make several modifications to the reliability centric formulation presented above to obtain this performance centric formulation. First, Expression (7) above should be modified in order to capture this new constraint. If we consider two different messages, k_1 and k_2, we will have four variables, $M_{i,j}^{p,k_1}$ and $M_{i,j}^{p,k_2}$ for the original messages, and $R_{i,j}^{p,k_1}$ and $R_{i,j}^{p,k_2}$ for their duplicates. All these messages should follow different routes in order satisfy the minimum performance overhead constraint. This can be captured as follows:

$$M_{i,j}^{p,k_1} + M_{i,j}^{p,k_2} + R_{i,j}^{p,k_1} + R_{i,j}^{p,k_2} \leq 1,$$
$$\forall p, i, j, k_1, k_2 \text{ such that } k_1 \neq k_2. \quad (10)$$

We also need to modify the constraints to reflect the fact that a duplicate may not exist. To do this, we introduce another binary variable, $RME_{p,k}$, which indicates whether there exists a duplicate for message k in phase p. All the routing variables related to the duplicates are dependent on this variable. More specifically,

$$R_{i,j}^{p,k} \leq RME_{p,k}, \forall p, k, i, j. \quad (11)$$

Similarly, our objective function given originally by Expression (9) has to be modified to reflect this change:

$$\min \sum_{p=1}^{P} \left(C_2 \times \sum_{i=1}^{n} \sum_{j=1}^{n} (AE_{p,i,j} - DE_{p,i,j}) \right) + \left(C_3 \times \sum_{k=1}^{K} (1 - RME_{p,k}) \right). \quad (12)$$

This objective function tries to minimize the energy consumption and maximize the number of duplicate messages. The portion preceded by a weight of C_2 captures the energy metric, whereas the portion preceded by a weight of C_3 captures the reliability metric. $RME_{p,k}$ indicates whether the duplicate exists and $\sum_{k=1}^{K} (1 - RME_{p,k})$ sums up the non-duplicated messages.

5.3 Energy Centric Formulation

Similar to the performance centric routing, we may formulate an energy centric routing as well. In this case, duplicate messages are not routed through links that were not active in the previous phase, that is, the extra energy consumed due to reliability enhancement is reduced. Expression (5) above ensures that a duplicate message is transmitted through link if that link is already active. In addition to this, our goal is not to keep a link active if only duplicates are transmitted through this link:

$$E_{p,i,j} \leq \sum_{k=1}^{K} M_{i,j}^{p,k}, \forall p, k, i, j. \quad (13)$$

The right-hand side of the above constraint captures the total number of original messages transmitted over the link. If this sum is 0, then the corresponding link will not be active, forcing duplicates to follow different routes. In addition to this, we introduce $RME_{p,k}$ to indicate

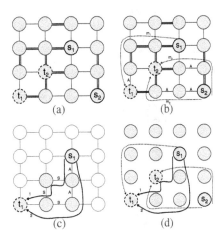

Figure 6. An example showing our ILP-based approach.

whether a duplicate of message k exists during phase p. This is similar to $RME_{p,k}$ that is used in Section 5.2. Hence, we use the corresponding constraint given in Expression (11) to indicate that a duplicate message can be transmitted only if the duplicate exists.

Our new objective function can be written as:

$$\min \sum_{p=1}^{P}(C_1 \times \sum_{i=1}^{n}\sum_{j=1}^{n} S_{p,i,j}) + \qquad (14)$$

$$(C_2 \times \sum_{i=1}^{n}\sum_{j=1}^{n}(AE_{p,i,j} - DE_{p,i,j})) + (C_3 \times \sum_{k=1}^{K}(1 - RME_{p,k})).$$

Coefficients C_1, C_2, and C_3 can be selected based on the relative weights of the performance concern, energy concern, and reliability concern, respectively. We have all three weights (C_1, C_2, and C_3), since we still need to capture the energy concern. This follows from the fact that we still have link activations and deactivations.

5.4 Example

Figure 6 shows an example 4×4 NoC and the corresponding ILP solution based on our baseline formulation discussed in Section 5.1. In this example, we assume that there are two original messages that have to be transmitted in a phase: a message from s_1 to t_1 and a message from s_2 to t_2. Source nodes are represented using solid circles, whereas the destination nodes are represented using dashed circles. Furthermore, we assume that active links from the previous phase are known and denoted using double edges between the NoC nodes. Figure 6(a) shows the messages, their source and destination nodes, and the active links.

With our baseline (reliability centric) formulation (i.e., all messages have their attached duplicates which follow different paths from the original messages as much as possible), three of the four messages (two original and two duplicate) will follow the routes given in Figure 6(b). Note that the shortest paths are used in order not to increase energy consumption. Similarly, for m_1, the ILP solver returns this route as one of the routes for messages from s_1 to t_1 no matter what the C_1 and C_2 parameters are. In order to satisfy these routes, some links that were not active in the previous phase will need to be activated. These links are identified by attaching an A next to the edges in Figure 6(b). In total, there are 4 additional link activations required to transmit the 3 messages in this phase.

So, the question becomes how to route the duplicate message from s_1 to t_1. There are two different routes, marked using 1 and 2 in Figure 6(c). If this message is sent through route 1, there will be an additional activation required on the first link. On top of this link activation, one of the links will be shared with m_2 and another link will be shared with m_3. Instead, if this message is sent through route 2, there will be two link activations followed by a shared link with m_3. Figure 6(d) shows the overall behavior of the system during this phase. Either we will follow route 1 and incur

Table 1. Our simulation parameters and their default values.

Parameter	Value
NoC	5×5 2D mesh
Core	two-issue
CPU Frequency	1GHz
Data/Instr L1 Capacity	8KB (per node)
Local On-Chip Memory	256KB (per node, banked)
Link Speed	1GHz
Link Activation Latency	1 μsec
Link Activation Energy	140 μjoule
Packet Header Size	3 flits
Flit Size	39 bits

$(4A) + (2S + A) = 2S + 5A$, or we will follow route 2 and incur $(4A) + (S + 2A) = S + 6A$. If we consider our objective function in Expression (9), the cost function will be $2 \times C_1 + 5 \times C_2$ for route 1, and $C_1 + 6 \times C_2$ for route 2. At this point, selecting a route from these two depends on the values of C_1 and C_2. If $C_1 = C_2$ either one of the routes could be chosen by the ILP solver. However, if $C_1 > C_2$, the objective function will be minimized when route 2 is selected. This follows from the fact that weight of performance is now increased, i.e., the route with fewer shared links would be preferred (as in the case of route 2) over the alternate route with lower energy consumption. By comparison, if $C_1 < C_2$, route 1 will be chosen since, in this case, link sharing is preferred over link activation.

5.5 Qualitative Comparison Against Existing Schemes

In this section, we discuss how our compiler-directed message duplication approach compares to hardware level approaches for NoC reliability. There are several approaches in the literature that target improving the resilience of NoCs using error detection and correction mechanisms. Most error detection mechanisms target transient link errors and try to cope with them by attaching an error code to each packet to be sent over the network. This error code, typically a parity or cyclic redundancy check, is used to detect at the destination whether the content of the packet has been modified or not. Such schemes typically require retransmission of the packet if an error is detected in it (the error is signaled to the source node using a negative ACK (NACK) signal). An alternate option would be to use a more sophisticated (error protection) code to allow the target node itself to correct the error without requiring any retransmission. As pointed out by prior research [39], as far as power consumption and implementation complexity are concerned, the first option (detection followed by retransmission) is preferred over the second one (self-correction). Therefore, in this paper we consider only the first option, and when we refer to error protection code we mean one that can detect (using a parity bit) an odd-number of errors. In the rest of this paper, we use *PEC* (Parity/retransmission based Error Correction) to refer to this error protection code based approach.

Such protection codes can only be useful in the context of transient link errors. In case of permanent link failures (e.g., broken links), they will not work as the original packet would not have arrived at its destination at the first place. For permanent link failures, our approach is much more effective, as it sends two copies of the same packet over non-intersecting paths as much as possible.[2] From the perspective of transient errors, the comparison between our approach and error protection based schemes is more involved. This is because our scheme can also be used in conjunction with error protection coding, that is, both copies can be augmented with an error protection code. If the copies are not protected with encoding, there are two cases to consider. If both of the copies reach the destination and they are the same, chances of transient error(s) having occurred are very low. Because an error would have had to flip the same bits in both the copies to escape detection. On the other hand, if only one of the copies arrives at the destination (due to permanent errors), there is no way to detect a transient error. If, however, the copies are augmented with protection codes, at the destination we can check both copies and accept the one without errors (based on parity bits), or ask for a retransmit if only one copy arrives.

---

[2] Note that our scheme does not require "the knowledge of which links will fail" at compile time. Instead, it prepares for every scenario, by trying to send any message and its duplicate using non-intersecting paths.

90

To summarize, if permanent link failure occurs, our approach has a clear advantage over conventional error protection based schemes, irrespective of whether transient errors also occur or not. On the other hand, if only transient errors occur and both the copies arrive, our approach can potentially detect more errors than conventional parity or CRC based schemes, since we can perform bit-by-bit comparison of the original message and duplicate message. In our experiments, we evaluate the impact of our approach in mitigating the effects of both permanent and transient errors, and compare it with PEC.

There are also approaches in the literature that can be defined as "hardware based fault tolerant routing" [29, 32, 33, 42, 44]. In many prior studies, researchers propose using virtual channels. Most of these approaches employ algorithms that are based on seminal works such as [13] and [37]. However, if the physical links are broken, such schemes may not be very effective. Another option is to reserve a set of physical links to route a message that could not be routed due to the failure of one or more of the links in its original path. Note that, apart from the implementation complexities involving in detecting the failure and re-routing the message, this approach also reduces the effective network size. To compare our approaches to hardware based fault tolerant routing schemes, we implemented this physical link reservation based approach (referred to as HFT-1 here) and an alternate hardware based fault tolerance scheme based on link state sharing, which is denoted using HFT-2. While there exist several implementations of such link state sharing based schemes, the implementation we adopted is based on the work described in [1]. In this implementation, each router periodically updates its neighboring routers with its health (e.g., which, if any, of its links have failed). In the long run, it is expected that the NoC converges to a stable state where every router has an idea about the global NoC health. Note that the periodic updates can flood the on-chip network and also cause extra power consumption. Therefore, in the implementation of [1] (and in ours as well), instead of using periodic updates, we perform updates only when a link fails. The routers, after receiving the new state information, remove the faulty link from their routing tables and exchange this new information with their own neighbors, and so on. At periodic intervals, each router calculates the shortest paths using Dijkstra's algorithm. Our preliminary experiments showed that both HFT-1 and HFT-2 are more energy efficient than the schemes discussed in [33].

Before moving to our experiments, we want to mention that the paths selected by our scheme do not lead to a deadlock since we have an additional set of constraints in our ILP formulation to prevent potential deadlocks. For the sake of clarity, we do not present our deadlock prevention constraints in detail. A deadlock will happen when there is a circular message dependency between two or more messages. We first identify the deadlock-possible messages and form deadlock sets. We then use these deadlock sets to generate our additional deadlock prevention constraints. If, for example, two messages $M_{i,j}^{p,k_1}$ and $M_{j,i}^{p,k_2}$ can cause a deadlock, then we add an additional constraint, $M_{i,j}^{p,k_1} + M_{j,i}^{p,k_2} \leq 1$, to prevent both of them being enabled. We define these constraints for the replica messages as well.

6. Experiments

6.1 Implementation and Setup

We implemented our compiler directed approach using the SUIF infrastructure [14] and performed experiments with all the applications in the SPECFP2000 benchmark suite [35]. For each of the benchmarks in our suite, we fast-forwarded the first 500 million instructions and simulated the next 2 billion instructions. The default values of our simulation parameters used in our experiments are listed in Table 1.

Our approach is implemented as a separate compilation phase within SUIF. Once the SUIF based analysis is performed, the collected information is passed to our ILP solver (Xpress-MP [43]). The solutions returned by the solver are mapped to SUIF and are used to modify the code to insert duplicate messages and specify the paths (routes) that will be used by the original and duplicate messages. The code modifications required for specifying the routes are similar to those in [8]. The overall compilation times we experienced on a 2GHz Sun Solaris machine varied between 19.8 seconds and 2.9 minutes (dominated by the ILP solution times). These solution times, which correspond to about 30% increase over the original compila-

Table 2. Benchmarks used in our experiments and their important characteristics. Energy values are in mJ, and the latency values are in million cycles.

Benchmark Name	Number of Phases	Number of Messages	Execution Cycles	Energy Consumption
wupwise	72	13.5M	388.1M	781.6mJ (19.3%)
swim	87	22.8M	477.3M	886.1mJ (26.6%)
mgrid	64	11.7M	406.0M	814.2mJ (22.8%)
applu	59	26.9M	461.6M	759.7mJ (15.7%)
mesa	51	14.1M	318.2M	582.8mJ (19.0%)
galgel	89	16.9M	386.7M	609.8mJ (24.8%)
art	37	13.2M	297.3M	424.9mJ (33.2%)
equake	59	9.4M	192.6M	387.2mJ (20.1%)
facerec	73	6.3M	208.9M	390.5mJ (27.4%)
ammp	113	12.7M	241.1M	407.8mJ (24.4%)
lucas	96	5.7M	156.4M	321.4mJ (19.7%)
fma3d	91	9.6M	197.4M	456.3mJ (29.3%)
sixtrack	76	8.2M	148.5M	292.3mJ (28.6%)
apsi	137	12.7M	276.8M	416.7mJ (22.5%)

tion times, are not very large since we formulate a separate linear program for each phase (PCP) in isolation. Also, the maximum increase in code size due to our scheme was less than 3%, and its impact on instruction cache performance was negligible.

Before our approach is applied, two other phases (steps) are executed: *code parallelization* and *thread-to-core mapping*. The code parallelization phase determines loop iteration distribution and data decomposition across the CMP nodes. The specific method used in this phase is very similar to the approach in [3], except that most frequently used data are mapped to the on-chip memory components. The second step applied before our approach is thread-to-core mapping (which we will discuss shortly). After these two steps, our approach is invoked. Note that, while we use specific code parallelization and thread mapping schemes in our experimental evaluation, our approach can work with other parallelization/mapping schemes as well. In our experiments, we also present results with different thread-to-core mappings. Also, in all our experiments, all processor cores are used but the set of links used depend on the communication pattern and message routing strategy.

To conduct our experiments, we implemented a flit-level network-on-chip simulator (built on top of Orion [41]) and connected it with SIMICS [40], a multi-processor simulator. The network is parametrized in a similar fashion to that in [11] except that it is 5×5. The link speed is set to 1Gb/sec. Each input port of switch has a buffer that can hold 64 flits, each of which is 128 bits wide (packet size is 16 flits). The communication links in this network can be shutdown independently, using a time-out based mechanism as described in [34]. We set the time-out counter threshold for the hardware-based power reduction scheme to 1.5μsec based on some preliminary analysis. The time it takes to switch a link from the power-down state to the active state is set as 1μsec, and the energy overhead of this switching is assumed to be 140μJ based on prior research. For modeling the energy consumption of memory components, we used CACTI [38], and for collecting energy data for core-related activities, we enhanced SIMICS with accurate timing models and energy models similar to those employed in [7]. The NoC energy modeling is based on Orion [41]. All the energy numbers presented include both dynamic and leakage energy.

Table 2 presents the important statistics for our benchmarks under the default values of our simulation parameters. The second column lists the number of phases (PCPs) for each benchmark and the next one shows the number of messages sent over the NoC during the entire simulation time. The fourth column gives the execution cycles and the fifth column shows the total energy consumption of the CMP when no reliability optimization is applied. These values include the energy spent in the datapath, on-chip and off-chip memory accesses, and interprocessor communication. The values within parentheses in the last column give the contribution of the NoC to the total energy consumption of the chip.

In our evaluation, for each application code in our experimental suite, we performed experiments with different versions (in addition to the *original version* that does not perform any reliability optimizations but tries to maximize link reuse between neighboring phases to reduce energy consumption); the details of these versions will be explained in Section 6.2. In evaluation of all the versions, including the original one, we assume that a power-saving scheme for NoC is

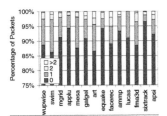
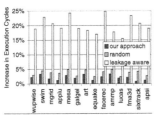
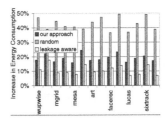
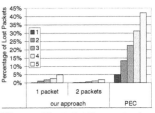

Figure 7. Link sharing statistics for packets.

Figure 8. Performance degradation caused by different versions.

Figure 9. Additional energy consumption caused by different versions.

Figure 10. Reliability evaluation of our approach and PEC regarding permanent link failures.

already in place. Specifically, as stated earlier, we assume the existence of a hardware based link power saving scheme that turns off a link if it has not been used for a while. Note that the original scheme and optimized schemes use the same parallelization and thread mapping steps. Also, we model the overheads incurred by our approach in detail, and the performance and power numbers presented below include *all* overheads (e.g., cost of link shutdowns and startups and additional link contention due to duplicate messages).

6.2 Results

Unless otherwise stated, when we say "our approach" in our discussion below, we mean the reliability centric formulation given in Section 5.1. We start by presenting the increase in message traffic, energy consumption and execution cycles when our reliability centric formulation is used, assuming $C_1 = C_2$ in the objective function. All the numbers presented below are with respect to the corresponding values obtained under the original scheme, i.e., they are given as percentage degradation over the original scheme (see Table 2 for the absolute values with the original scheme). Figure 7 gives, for our scheme, the fraction of packets that share 0, 1, 2 and more than 2 links (denoted > 2), over all the phases of the application. We see that a large fraction of the packets do not share any links, that is, our approach is able to send the original and duplicate packets along the disjoint paths most of the time (90.1% on average). Of the cases when this is not possible (i.e., there is at least one link shared), the most frequent reason is that the source and destination nodes reside along the same row or column.[3] In some other cases, we simply could not find disjoint paths due to large number of packets that have to be routed. To discuss the performance degradation and energy increase caused by our approach, let us consider the first bars, for each application, in Figures 8 and 9.

Our main observation from Figure 8 is that the performance degradation caused by our approach – over the original version – is not high, and varies between 0.7% and 3.3%. Again, this is due to the success of our scheme in finding *non-intersecting* paths, as much as possible, for the duplicate packets. The increases in energy consumption – given in Figure 9 – are higher, mainly due to the increase in dynamic energy consumption as a result of duplicate messages. While our approach keeps the increase in leakage consumption at minimum by maximizing the link reuse between neighboring program phases, it still has to send extra packets (duplicates), which contribute to the dynamic energy consumption. As a result, on average, our approach incurs a 19.1% increase in total energy consumption. We also performed experiments with different C_1 and C_2 values. When we set $C_1 = 2$ and $C_2 = 1$, we observed that the average performance penalty reduced to less than 1%, but the average energy increase jumped to 26.6%. In contrast, when $C_1 = 1$ and $C_2 = 2$, the percentage increase in execution cycles and energy consumption became 3.8% and 9.7% (on average). These results show that by changing the values of C_1 and C_2, one can explore the tradeoffs between performance and energy loses, and select the appropriate reliability-centric solution that satisfies the performance and power constraints at hand. While, for a given power/performance bound, several search algorithms can be developed for determining the best C_1 and C_2 values, studying such algorithms is beyond the scope of this work. We have already implemented in our compiler a simple heuristic that selects the best C_1 and C_2 values for a given power/performance bound. We could not present here the details of this heuristic due to lack of space.

We now compare this baseline implementation of ours against two alternate schemes. The first scheme, called Random, selects the paths for duplicate messages randomly among all paths of minimum links (between the source and destination). Due to its random nature, we can expect this scheme to perform reasonably well as far as performance is concerned. As can be observed from the second bars in Figure 8, the average performance degradation this alternate scheme causes is about 3.7% (compared to 2.1% caused by our scheme). However, since this approach does not care about the link reuse between neighboring phases of the application, it can cause significant increase in leakage energy, as can be observed from Figure 9. It leads to an average increase of 42.6% on total energy consumption. The second alternate scheme we experiment with is fully leakage oriented. Specifically, the duplicate packets in this scheme are always routed along the same path as the corresponding original packets. While this approach is leakage efficient in general, it can also lead to a significant increase in execution latency. We see from Figures 8 and 9 that it increases execution latency (resp. energy consumption) by 20.1% (resp. 1.8%). Therefore, considering both performance and energy consumption, our performance-energy conscious reliability enhancement clearly strikes the right balance. Though not presented here, the average performance and energy degradations caused by the PEC scheme were 3.9% and 4.2%, respectively.

Our next set of experiments study the reliability improvement brought by our approach in more detail. For this purpose, we evaluated the behavior of our approach under both permanent and transient errors. In the case of permanent errors, we simulated the case when a certain number of links are disabled and recorded the fraction of packets that did not arrive at their destination nodes.[4] The results are presented in Figure 10, each bar representing the *average value* across all applications. For each application, we have two versions: 1) our approach without any error encoding and 2) error encoding (PEC) without our approach. We experimented with different numbers of link failures (from 1 to 5), and the y-axis in Figure 10 gives the fraction of packets that could not reach their destinations due to a broken link. In the case of our approach, we also quantified the fraction of packets when both copies failed, and those when only one copy failed. We see that, with our approach, only a small fraction of the packets could not reach their destinations. The reason for such low figures is because our approach is, in general, able to route the two copies using non-intersecting paths. By comparison, the safe delivery rate under the PEC scheme can be very low, indicating that, as far as permanent failures are concerned, our approach is very promising, especially when a large number of links are permanently disabled.

We also quantified the benefits of our approach when transient errors occur. To cover a large set of possibilities, we experimented with different error probabilities. We used the same two schemes above (our approach and PEC). Figure 11 shows the number of errors that could not be detected under each scheme. As before, each bar represents an average value across all benchmarks. Note that in PEC an error may not be detected if it affects an even number of bits. On the other hand, in our scheme, we may fail to detect an error if both copies have the same bit (or set of bits) flipped. Clearly, the likelihood of this is extremely low since the copies usually go over non-intersecting paths. The results in Figure 11 indicate that our approach performs much better than the PEC scheme in the case of transient errors, for all the error injection rates considered.

Let us now quantify the cost of correcting the detected errors in terms of execution cycles. In the case of PEC, to correct the

---

[3] As explained earlier, our baseline approach always uses the minimum number of links between the source and destination.

[4] The fraction of messages lost in transmission is a frequently-used reliability metric in fault-tolerant network research [44].

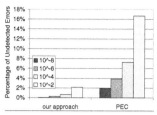

Figure 11. Reliability evaluation of our approach and PEC regarding transient link errors.

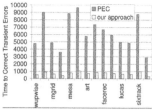

Figure 12. Time (in cycles) to correct the transient errors detected.

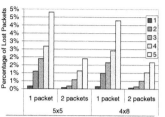

Figure 13. Impact of CMP size regarding permanent link failures.

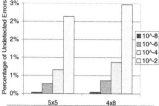

Figure 14. Impact of CMP size regarding transient link errors.

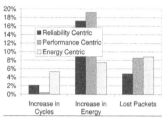

Figure 15. Comparison of reliability centric, performance centric and energy centric formulations.

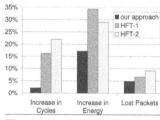

Figure 16. Comparison of our approach against two hardware based fault tolerant routing schemes.

error, the packet is retransmitted. Therefore, the total performance cost of error correction is the time required to retransmit the packet. For our approach, however, the actual cost depends on whether we employ any error protection code. If the copies are not protected with error codes, our approach cannot correct the errors it detects by message comparison (but we can always request a retransmission, if desired, as in the case of the PEC scheme). If, on the other hand, the copies are protected using an error protection code, we can easily select the copy without the error (if there is one, which is highly likely), and therefore, the error correction time is expected to be very short. Figure 12 gives, for the benchmarks in our experimental suite, the average time to correct the detected errors (note that the actual time to correct an error depends on the distance between the source and destination). The results with our approach assume that the packets are augmented with parity. We see that, as expected, the error corrections times with our approach are lower than the corresponding times with the PEC scheme.

As stated earlier, we assume that thread-to-core mapping has already been performed before our approach is applied. While the choice of the thread/data mapping scheme used is orthogonal to the focus of our approach, we may achieve power/performance values of different magnitudes, depending on the thread/data mapping used. In our default mapping scheme, we used an affinity-based approach, wherein the parallel threads are assigned to cores based on the data sharing between them. To do this, the compiler estimates the data sharing between each pair of threads, and the pairs that have high affinity (i.e., share a lot of data between them) are assigned to neighboring nodes of the CMP. This helps reduce the cost of inter-processor communication. Also, each data element is assigned to the on-chip memory of the node that uses that element most. The infrequently-used data elements are assigned to the off-chip memory. We changed our thread mapping scheme and performed a sensitivity analysis. The main difference between our new mapping and our default mapping is that the new one maps the parallel threads to CMP nodes randomly. However, the parallelization step used along with both the schemes is still the same. This allows us to see how our savings change when we do not exploit the affinity among parallel threads. We found that the percentage increases in execution cycles and energy consumption with this alternate thread mapping were very similar to those obtained with the default mapping used so far. Also, while both the percentage of lost packets and the percentage of undetected transient errors increased a little (less than 2.2%) with this alternate mapping (as a result of the increased number of links that have to be traversed by a packet), our approach still generated better reliability results than PEC.

Our next set of experiments study the sensitivity of our approach to network size. Recall that the default network size we have is 5×5. We also performed experiments with a larger network (4×8), and the results are presented in Figure 13 (for permanent link failures)

and Figure 14 (for transient errors). Our approach is more successful with permanent failures with larger networks. This is because a given broken link has less chance of affecting the packets traveling across the network. However, we also observe a reverse trend when we look at the transient errors. More specifically, as the network size is increased, the percentage of undetected errors go up slightly. While not presented here in detail, we also performed experiments with different types of cores (e.g., single issue versus four issue). The results observed were not very different compared to our default core configuration which is two issue. Similarly, when we reduce/increase our default switch buffer capacity (default was 64 flits), the results did not change too much (within 2%).

We now summarize the results of our experiments with performance centric and energy centric formulations discussed in Sections 5.2 and 5.3, respectively. The increase in execution cycles, increase in energy consumption and percentage of lost packets (when 5 links fail) are presented in Figure 15 for the reliability centric, performance centric and energy centric formulations. Each bar represents the average values across all applications we tested and is obtained when C_1, C_2, and C_3 (when used) are set to 1. One can see from these results the tradeoffs between performance, power and reliability. Depending on the constraints at hand, these three different formulations can be explored to reach an acceptable solution. We also want to emphasize that, as mentioned earlier, for each formulation we have also flexibility of changing the values of C_1, C_2, and C_3.

As stated earlier, we also implemented and performed experiments with two hardware based fault tolerant routing schemes: HFT-1 and HFT-2. Figure 16 presents the increase in execution cycles, increase in energy consumption, and fraction of lost packets (again, under the assumption of 5 link failures). In our HFT-1 implementation, we reserved 8 links (that cover an area from the upper left corner to the lower right corner) to be used when any other links fails. The failed links are selected randomly from among the remaining links. Each bar represents the average value when all our applications are considered. The main observation from these results is that our approach generates better results than these two hardware based schemes for all these three metrics. The reason that HFT-1 has high performance overhead is that, under this scheme, part of the network is not available for use as long as there are no failures. While this may not hurt performance much in large chip-to-chip networks, in relatively small NoCs such as ours it may be a big performance bottleneck. The reason that HFT-2 has high performance overhead is because of two factors. First, sending updates of routing tables to neighboring nodes floods the network with messages (this is in fact a general problem with many adaptive routing algorithms). Second, from time to time, the Dijkstra's shortest path algorithm is executed by the switches (in our implementation by the cores) to ensure that the routing tables are up-to-date. These two factors also contribute to the high power consumption. HFT-1 cannot completely eliminate lost packets if one (or more) of the failed links is directly connected to the reserved path and this link is the only connection between a node and the reserved path. Similarly, in the HFT-2 case, since it is not possible to keep all routing tables up-to-date all the time, it is not possible to eliminate all the lost packets. It is reasonable to expect that both HFT-1 and HFT-2 are much more costly to implement – as far as circuit complexities and area demands are considered – than our approach, so, we believe our approach is preferable over the hardware based fault tolerant schemes from the circuit angle as well.

Our approach is a static one meaning that the UMAG is determined at compile time using static analysis. However, in some cases, we may not have the complete information – at compile time – to build the UMAG and identify the phases. In such cases, our approach can be used with *profile information*. More specifically, the application code can be profiled to collect inter-core communication information and this profile data can be used to build the UMAG. Note that, in this case, with a different input, the actual communications can be different from those captured by the UMAG; however, this does not create any correctness issue. In the worst case, we incur extra execution cycles and extra power consumption but the program semantics do not change. To check the feasibility of this approach, we first considered two applications from the MediaBench suite [24], mpeg and g.721, whose UMAGs cannot be completely and accurately captured using static compiler analysis alone. We profiled them, built their UMAGs, and applied our reliability enhancement scheme. Then, we executed the applications with different input sets to measure input sensitivity. We found that the average performance degradation with both the applications varied between 2.4% and 4.1% depending on the input, and the average increase in energy consumption ranged from 16.6% to 21.3%, again depending on the input used. We also observed that, as compared to the PEC scheme, our approach generated much better reliability results.

We also performed experiments with specjbb [36] which is a server application that can really put pressure on the NoC. We ran this benchmark with 12 warehouses, with one client per warehouse, and the UMAG of this application was extracted again using profiling. Due to lack of space, we do not provide the details of how the application code is modified to enable message routings. The experiments with our scheme showed that the increases in execution cycles and energy consumption were around 9.6% and 23.4%, respectively. Clearly, these values are higher than the average values observed with the SPEC benchmarks (and the main reason for this in the high link sharing across different messages). However, when we move to our performance centric formulation, the increases in cycles and energy moved to 3.8% and 26.1%, with only a small (2.1%) increase in the fraction of lost packets. Therefore, we believe that, depending on the target optimization metric, our approach can be used for improving reliability for this application as well, under performance and energy bounds. Further, C_1 and C_2 parameters can be tuned to reach the desired tradeoff points. Overall, the results with g.721, mpeg and specjbb show that our approach can be augmented with profile data to make it applicable to the cases where the compiler cannot completely extract the UMAG from the source code.

7. Conclusion

The main contribution of this paper is a compiler directed NoC reliability enhancement mechanism based on packet duplication. In this approach, the underlying NoC architecture of the CMP is exposed to the compiler, which in turn determines the routes for both original and duplicate messages such that the potential impacts of both transient and permanent link errors could be mitigated. Our approach also tries to satisfy performance and power constraints by, respectively, minimizing the set of common links between an original message and its duplicate and maximizing the link reuse between neighboring program phases. We fully implemented our approach within an optimizing compiler, and the collected results indicate that it is much more effective than an alternate approach to NoC reliability and performs better than two pure hardware based fault tolerance schemes.

References

[1] M. Ali et al. A Fault Tolerant Mechanism for Handling Permanent and Transient Failures in a Network-on-Chip. In Proc. ITNG, 2007.

[2] AMD Athlon 64 X2 Dual-Core Processor for Desktop. http://www.amd.com /us-en/Processors/ProductInformation/0,,30_118_9485_13041,00.html

[3] J. M. Anderson. Automatic Computation and Data Decomposition for Multiprocessors. Ph.D Thesis, Stanford University, 1997.

[4] G. Ascia et al. Multi-objective Mapping for Mesh-based NoC Architectures. In Proc. CODES+ISSS, 2004.

[5] T. Austin. DIVA: A Reliable Substrate for Deep Submicron Microarchitecture Design. In Proc. MICRO, 1999.

[6] D. Bertozzi et al. Low Power Error Resilient Encoding for On-Chip Data Buses. In Proc. DATE, 2002.

[7] D. Brooks et al. Wattch: A Framework for Architectural-level Power Analysis and Optimizations, In Proc. ISCA, 2000.

[8] G. Chen et al. Compiler-directed Channel Allocation for Saving Power in On-chip Networks. In Proc. POPL, 2006.

[9] G. Chen et al. Reducing NoC Energy Consumption Through Compiler-Directed Channel Voltage Scaling. In Proc. PLDI, 2006.

[10] K. Coons et al. A Spatial Path Scheduling Algorithm for EDGE Architectures. In Proc. ASPLOS, 2006.

[11] W. J. Dally and B. Towles. Route Packets, Not Wires: On-chip Interconnection Networks. In Proc. DAC, 2001.

[12] G. De Micheli. Reliable Communication in SoCs. In Proc. DAC, 2004.

[13] J. Duato. A New Theory of Deadlock-Free Adaptive Routing in Wormhole Networks. IEEE TPDS 4(12):1320–1331, 1993.

[14] M. W. Hall et al. Maximizing Multiprocessor Performance With the SUIF Compiler. IEEE Computer, December 1996.

[15] Y. Hoskote et al. A 5-GHz Mesh Interconnect for a Teraflops Processor. In IEEE MICRO, Sept/Oct, 2007.

[16] L. Hsu et al. Exploring the Cache Design Space for Large Scale CMPs. In SIGARCH Comput. Archit. News, 33(4):24–33, 2005.

[17] J. Hu and R. Marculescu. Energy- and Performance-Aware Mapping for Regular NoC Architectures. IEEE TCAD, 24(4):551–562, April, 2005.

[18] http://www.intel.com/idf/.

[19] Intel quad-core Xeon. http://www.intel.com/quad-core/?cid=cim: ggl—xeon_us_clovertown—k7449—s

[20] J. Kahle et al. Introduction to the Cell Multiprocessor. IBM Journal of Research and Development, 49(4-5), 2005.

[21] M. Kandemir and O. Ozturk. Software-Directed Combined CPU/Link Voltage Scaling for NoC-Based CMPs. In Proc. SIGMETRICS, 2008.

[22] C. Kim et al. An Adaptive, Non-Uniform Cache Structure for Wire-Delay Dominated On-Chip Caches. In Proc. ASPLOS, 2002.

[23] P. Kongetira et al. Niagara: A 32-Way Multithreaded SPARC Processor. IEEE MICRO, Apr., 2005.

[24] C. Lee et al. MediaBench: A Tool for Evaluating and Synthesizing Multimedia and Communications Systems. In Proc. MICRO, 1997.

[25] W. Lee et al. Space-Time Scheduling of Instruction-Level Parallelism on a RAW Machine. In *Proc. ASPLOS*, Oct. 1998.

[26] F. Li et al. Profile-Driven Energy Reduction in Network-on-Chips. In Proc. PLDI, San Diego, 2007.

[27] F. Li et al. Compiler-directed Proactive Power Management for Networks. In Proc. CASES, 2005.

[28] R. McGowen. Adaptive Designs for Power and Thermal Optimization. In Proc. ICCAD, 2005.

[29] A. Mejia et al. Segment-Based Routing: An Efficient Fault-Tolerant Routing Algorithm for Meshes and Tori. In Proc. IPDPS, 2006.

[30] S. Murali et al. Analysis of Error Recovery Schemes for Networks on Chips. In IEEE Design and Test, 2005.

[31] R. Nagarajan et al. Static Placement, Dynamic Issue (SPDI) Scheduling for EDGE Architectures. In Proc. PACT, 2004.

[32] E. Oh et al. Fault-Tolerant Routing in Mesh-Connected 2D Tori. In Proc. ICCS, 2003.

[33] M. Pirretti et al. Fault Tolerant Algorithms for Network-on-Chip Interconnect. In Proc. IEEE VLSI, 2004.

[34] V. Soteriou and L.-S. Peh. Design Space Exploration of Power-Aware On/Off Interconnection Networks. In Proc. ICCD, 2004.

[35] SPEC. http://www.spec.org/cpu2000/CINT2000/.

[36] SPEC. http://www.spec.org/jbb2005/

[37] C. C. Su and K. G. Shin. Adaptive Fault-Tolerant Deadlock-Free Routing in Meshes and Hypercubes. IEEE TC, 45(6):666–683, 1996.

[38] D. Tarjan et al. CACTI 4.0. HP Labs, Tech. Rep. HPL-2006-86, 2006.

[39] T. Theocharides et al. Networks on Chip: Interconnects for the Next Generation Systems on Chip. In Advances in Computers, Vol 63, 2005.

[40] Virtutech Simics. http://www.virtutech.com/

[41] H.-S. Wang et al. Orion: A Power-Performance Simulator for Interconnection Networks. In Proc. MICRO, 2002.

[42] J. Wu. Fault-Tolerant Adaptive and Minimal Routing in Mesh-Connected Multicomputers Using Extended Safety Levels. In IEEE TPDS, 11(2):149–159, 2000.

[43] Xpress-MP. http://www.dashoptimization.com/pdf/Mosel1.pdf, 2002.

[44] J. Zhou and F. C. M. Lau. Adaptive Fault-Tolerant Wormhole Routing in 2D Meshes. In Proc. IPDPS, 2001.

[45] X. Zhu and W. Qin. Prototyping a Fault-Tolerant Multiprocessor SoC With Runtime Fault Recovery. In Proc. DAC, 2006.

Improving Both the Performance Benefits and Speed of Optimization Phase Sequence Searches

Prasad A. Kulkarni   Michael R. Jantz

University of Kansas
Department of Electrical Engineering and Computer
Science, Lawrence, KS 66045
{prasadk,mikejant}@ku.edu

David B. Whalley

Florida State University
Computer Science Department
Tallahassee, Florida 32306
whalley@cs.fsu.edu

Abstract

The issues of compiler optimization phase ordering and selection present important challenges to compiler developers in several domains, and in particular to the speed, code size, power, and cost-constrained domain of embedded systems. Different sequences of optimization phases have been observed to provide the best performance for different applications. Compiler writers and embedded systems developers have recently addressed this problem by conducting iterative empirical searches using machine-learning based heuristic algorithms in an attempt to find the phase sequences that are most effective for each application. Such searches are generally performed at the program level, although a few studies have been performed at the function level. The finer granularity of function-level searches has the potential to provide greater overall performance benefits, but only at the cost of slower searches caused by a greater number of performance evaluations that often require expensive program simulations. In this paper, we evaluate the performance benefits and search time increases of function-level approaches as compared to their program-level counterparts. We, then, present a novel search algorithm that conducts distinct function-level searches simultaneously, but requires only a single program simulation for evaluating the performance of potentially unique sequences for each function. Thus, our new *hybrid* search strategy provides the enhanced performance benefits of function-level searches with a search-time cost that is comparable to or less than program-level searches.

Categories and Subject Descriptors D.3.4 [*Programming Languages*]: Processors- compilers, optimization

General Terms Performance, Measurements, Algorithms.

Keywords Phase Ordering, Genetic Algorithms.

1. Introduction

The optimization phase ordering and selection problems have been a long-standing and persistent dilemma for compiler writers [12, 25, 29]. The two problems are related in that phase ordering tries to find the best order in which optimization phases should be applied and phase selection focuses on determining whether or not phases should be applied. Optimization phases depend on machine resources (such as registers) and transformations performed by other phases for their successful application. Consequently, phases depend on and interact with each other, enabling and disabling opportunities for other optimization phases. It is widely recognized, and often reported, that a single sequence of optimization phases is unlikely to achieve the best performance for every application on a given machine [8, 17, 19, 28, 30]. Instead, the ideal phase sequence depends on the characteristics of the application being compiled, the compiler implementation, and the target architecture.

Since it is difficult to predict the optimal phase sequence for each application, compiler writers have recently investigated phase ordering/selection by employing genetic algorithms [8, 19] and other evolutionary techniques [1, 2, 15, 16, 24] during iterative compilation to search for the the most effective sequence. When the fitness criteria for such searches involves dynamic measures (e.g., cycle counts or power consumption), thousands of direct executions of an application may be required. The search time in such cases is significant, often needing hours or days for finding effective sequences for a single application, making it less attractive for developers.

However, there are application areas where long compilation times are acceptable. For example, such iterative search techniques are often suitable for compiling programs targeting embedded systems. Many embedded system developers attempt to construct systems with just *enough* compute power and memory as is necessary for the particular task. Most embedded systems are also constrained for power. Consequently, reducing the speed, memory (code size), and/or power requirements is extremely crucial for such embedded applications, as reducing the processor or memory cost can result in huge savings for products with millions of units shipped.

The search time problem is unfortunately further exacerbated for embedded systems because the software development environment is often different from the target environment. Obtaining performance measures on cross-platform development environments typically requires simulation. The advantages of using simulation include obtaining repeatable and more detailed information about the program's execution. For instance, simulation can easily provide performance information about each function in a program. Furthermore, simulators for embedded processors are in general much more accurate than those for general-purpose processors since embedded processors are inherently simpler. However, simulation can be orders of magnitude slower than native execution. Even when it is possible to use the target machine to gather performance data directly, the embedded processor may be significantly slower (slower clock rate, less memory, etc.) than available general-purpose processors. Searching for an effective optimiza-

LCTES'10,   April 13–15, 2010, Stockholm, Sweden.
Copyright © 2010 ACM 978-1-60558-953-4/10/04...$10.00

tion sequence in such environments can easily require significantly longer periods than even the hours or days reported when using direct execution on a general-purpose processor [2, 4]. Thus, reducing the search time while achieving the intended benefits is critical to make evolutionary searches feasible for embedded systems.

Iterative searches to find the most effective phase sequence can be performed at multiple levels of code granularity: (1) Typically, such searches are performed at the *program-level*, with the same set of optimization flags or phase sequence employed for the entire program [1, 8, 14, 16]. (2) *Function-level* searches attempt to find possibly distinct phase sequences that are most effective over individual functions at a time [19, 28]. Function-level searches are more expensive as they may require several times more program simulations/executions, depending on the number of functions in the program. For example, a simple genetic algorithm based function-level search over a program consisting of *n* functions, will require *n* times more program simulations/executions. However, by potentially achieving enhanced customization, function-level searches may result in more efficient executables.

In this paper, we study and quantify the potential benefits (in terms of execution cycles and code size) and relative costs (in term of search overhead) of function versus program-level evolutionary searches. We suggest a new *hybrid* search strategy that combines the best features of function and program level search techniques. Our approach works by performing multiple function-level searches over all functions in the program simultaneously, but does not simulate the program until each function in the program has a new sequence to evaluate. We show that our hybrid search strategy achieves the performance benefits of a function-level search, but with less cost than is required for even a program-level search. Thus, the main contributions of this paper are:

1. This is the first study of which we are aware to compare the costs and benefits of performing searches for effective optimization phase sequences for individual functions versus an entire program as a single search unit.

2. We also introduce and evaluate a new *file*-level search strategy, which is the finest search granularity that can be achieved by algorithms implemented outside most compilers.

3. We describe and show the results for a hybrid search strategy that produces code with the effectiveness of individual function-level searches and has search costs that match or are more efficient than program-level search costs.

The rest of the paper is organized as follows. In the next section, we discuss previous research related to automatically finding effective phase sequences in optimizing compilers. In Section 3, we describe the three search strategies being compared in this paper, individual function, file, and entire program searches. We then outline our compiler framework and experimental setup in Section 4. In Section 5, we present the configuration of the genetic algorithm based evolutionary search technique used for the searches compared in this paper. We give the results of the comparisons of function, file, and program level searches in Section 6. We present and evaluate our new hybrid search technique in Section 7. Finally, we detail our thoughts regarding future work and conclusions in Sections 8 and 9, respectively.

2. Related Work

Prior work in optimization phase ordering and selection has investigated both analytical and empirical approaches to address the problem. Specifications of code-improving transformations have been automatically analyzed to determine their enabling and disabling interactions [30], as well as other phase properties such as the impact [31] and profitability [32] of optimizations. Such analytical information can provide insight into constructing a single *compromise* phase ordering for a conventional optimizing compiler.

The empirical search community acknowledges that it is unlikely that a single sequence of phases will achieve the best performance for all programs, and instead employs empirical techniques to iteratively search for the most effective phase sequence over programs or individual functions [1, 4, 5, 7, 8, 16, 18–20, 28]. Exhaustive enumeration of the phase application search space, although feasible in some cases [21, 22], has been reported to take many days to several months, depending on the compiler, application programs, and search strategy [2]. Consequently, researchers have primarily focused on heuristic search approaches and aggressive pruning of the search space [1, 20, 28] to address the phase ordering and selection issues.

A number of systems have been developed that use iterative or evolutionary algorithms to find the most effective phase combination. Such searches generally operate on an entire program or a per-function basis. A technique called *Optimization Space Exploration* uses a function-based strategy to search a statically pruned space of 2^{29} optimization parameters for *hot* functions, and uses static performance estimators (instead of program execution) to limit the search time. Kulkarni et al. employed evolutionary algorithms on individual functions to search for effective phase orderings in a search space of up to 15^{44} phase sequences [19, 24]. Cooper et al. were the first to employ genetic algorithms during iterative searches over entire programs to find the best phase ordering to reduce program code size in a solution space size of 10^{12} possible sequences [8]. In addition to finding custom phase orderings for individual programs, they were also able to construct a fixed sequence that generated up to 40% smaller codes than the default sequence used in their compiler. Other approaches used aggressive pruning of the search space to avoid evaluating sequences that are not likely to lead to improved benefits.

Researchers have also investigated the problem of finding the best set of compiler optimization flags (phase selection) for each program. Chow and Wu applied a technique called *fractional factorial design* [5], Haneda et al. used the *Mann-Whitney* test [15], Pan and Eigenmann employed three different feedback-driven orchestration algorithms [27], and Hoste and Eeckhout proposed a multi-objective evolutionary technique called *Compiler Optimization Level Exploration* [16] to effectively select a single setting of compiler optimization flags for the entire application. All such studies attempted to find a single distinct set of optimization flag setting for entire programs, and demonstrated that different programs do achieve their best performance with distinct flag settings.

Researchers have explored various schemes to limit the time of iterative searches. For example, researchers have used static estimation techniques to avoid expensive program simulations for performance evaluation [9, 22, 28]. Agakov et al. characterized programs using static *features* and developed adaptive mechanisms using statistical correlation models to focus their iterative search to those areas of the phase ordering space most likely to provide the greatest performance benefit [1]. A separate study by Kulkarni et al. employed several innovative search space pruning techniques to avoid over 84% of program executions, thereby considerably reducing the search overhead [20, 23]. Fursin et al. devised a novel strategy to evaluate the relative benefit of multiple per-function phase sequences during a single program execution by maintaining different versions of the same function in one executable and switching between them during execution [10]. Thus, this approach can substantially reduce the search overhead when the paths taken within the function are guaranteed to be the same each time. However, to our knowledge, there is no previous work that compares the performance benefit and search time overhead of function-based iterative search approaches over a program-based approach.

3. Entire Program, File, and Individual Function Searches

Empirical searches for finding the most effective optimization phase sequence can be conducted at different levels of code granularity. It is possible to perform these searches at either the function, file, or entire program level. Finer levels of search granularities enable greater flexibility in selecting distinct best sequences for different code segments in a program. This flexibility can potentially produce better-performing code than that achievable by a single phase sequence for the entire program.

At the same time, the search implementation strategy can also affect the levels of code granularities available for conducting the search. Search algorithms can either be implemented inside the compiler, or as a separate external program that invokes the compiler for each new phase sequence. Mechanisms implemented inside the compiler offer the most flexibility in terms of choosing the code granularity for the search. Moreover, such searches can proceed more quickly since the compiler need only be invoked once, and the search technique can have access to many internal compiler data structures for performance evaluation and function instance equivalence matching. However, this approach requires familiarity with the compiler, is more difficult to implement since it involves modifications to the compiler, and may need to be ported to each investigated compiler, which is a substantial development task.

In contrast, a search program to find the best phase sequence may be easier to implement outside the compiler, by invoking the compiler with different phase sequences (as determined by the search technique), and evaluating the performance of the resulting program each time. Moreover, such a search framework will be portable by allowing different compilers to be plugged into the same search program. However, most compilers provide no way to apply different phase sequences to individual functions in a single source file, thus eliminating the option of function-based search approaches. [1] Also, conventional compilers only permit turning optimizations on or off using the provided command-line flags, and do not support reordering optimizations phases, thus preventing investigations into the phase ordering problem.

To allow maximum flexibility in exploring phase order search strategies at different code granularities, we have implemented our search strategy inside the compiler for the techniques evaluated in this paper. This allows us to perform searches for the most effective optimization phase orderings at the function, file, and program levels. These three search algorithms are illustrated using the pseudo code in Figure 1. These algorithms avoid simulating the program when functions are redundant, which will be described later in the paper.

As previously mentioned, empirical search at lower levels of code granularity are desirable since they can potentially produce better performing code for the entire application. However, current implementations of function-based search techniques, [2] conduct their searches for the most effective optimization sequence for each function individually, and in isolation of the searches performed on the remaining functions in the program. For search strategies that employ *wall-time* or *execution cycles* for evaluating the merit of each phase sequence, program execution/simulation time (as compared to compilation time) is typically the dominant factor in the overall search time. For example, Cooper et al. reported execution time comprised 76% of their total search time, in spite of conducting their performance evaluations via native program executions [9]. For evaluation environments that require simulation

---

entire program approach:
```
DO
    determine next compilation settings;
    compile entire program with these settings;
    IF any function is not redundant THEN
        get entire program performance results
            by simulating the program;
UNTIL number of iterations completed;
```

individual file approach:
```
FOR each file in program DO
    DO
        determine next compilation settings;
        compile all functions in file with
            these settings;
        IF any function is not redundant THEN
            get performance of functions in file
                by simulating the program;
    UNTIL number of iterations completed;
END FOR
```

individual function approach:
```
FOR each function in program DO
    DO
        determine next compilation settings;
        compile function with these settings;
        IF function is not redundant THEN
            get function performance
                by simulating the program;
    UNTIL number of iterations completed;
END FOR
```

Figure 1. Pseudo-code for the search algorithms at three different program granularity levels, *entire program* level, *individual file* level, and *individual function* level

(a common scenario for embedded systems), the search overhead will be further dominated by the simulation time. In such cases, *naive* function-based search techniques that require up to n times more program executions/simulations can be up to n times more expensive than the program-based search approach, where n is the number of functions in the program.

Empirical searches at the file-level will typically require more program evaluations than a program-based approach at the cost of potentially losing some performance benefits as compared to the function-based approach. These searches are nonetheless important since they provide the lowest granularity for search algorithms that are implemented outside the compiler. Surprisingly, although several earlier investigations into the phase selection problem designed iterative search algorithms outside the compiler [1, 8, 14, 16], we are not aware of any prior work that suggested or studied the potential of file-based search approaches. Finally, we integrate the best features of function-based (higher performance potential for generated code) and program-based (typically lower search overhead) search approaches into a new *hybrid* search strategy. We provide a detailed description of this new search strategy along with its evaluation in Section 7.

4. Compiler Framework

The research in this paper uses the Very Portable Optimizer (VPO) [3], which is a compiler back end that performs all its optimizations on a single low-level intermediate representation called RTLs (Register Transfer Lists). This strategy allows VPO to apply most analyses and optimization phases repeatedly and in an arbi-

---

[1] Compilation frameworks, such as GCC 4.5 and MILEPOST GCC are notable exceptions [11].

[2] We are unaware of any work in file-based search strategies.

trary order. VPO compiles and optimizes one function at a time, allowing us to perform function-level phase order searches. Different functions may require very different phase orderings to achieve the best results, so a strategy that allows functions in a file to be compiled differently may achieve significant benefits [19].

The usual interface to the VPO compiler allows the user to input a single source file at a time to the compiler. Since the phase order search algorithm is implemented within the compiler, the above interface suffices for searching for the most effective optimization phase sequence at the individual function and file levels. However, to implement the search algorithm at the program level, we modified the VPO interface to accept multiple source files at the same time. While the VPO compilation process keeps track of the individual file boundaries, this distinction is transparent to the search algorithm. At the end of the search, VPO produces a separate assembly file corresponding to each source file to avoid static name conflicts.

For our experiments in this paper, the VPO compiler has been targeted to generate code for the StrongARM SA-100 processor using Linux as its operating system. The ARM is a simple 32-bit RISC instruction set. The relative simplicity of the ARM ISA combined with the low-power consumption of ARM-based processors have made this ISA dominant in the embedded systems domain. We used the SimpleScalar set of functional simulators [6] for the ARM to get dynamic performance measures. However, invoking the *cycle-accurate* simulator for evaluating the performance of every distinct phase sequence produced by the search algorithm is prohibitively expensive during our experimentation process. Therefore, we used a measure of estimated performance based partly on static function properties. [3] Our performance estimate accounts for stalls resulting from pipeline data hazards, but does not consider other penalties encountered during execution, such as branch misprediction and cache miss penalties. This approach has the additional advantage of evaluation of each function or file independent wrt to performance evaluation. Interestingly, we have shown that this measure of dynamic performance has a strong correlation with simulator cycles for an embedded processor [22]. For every unique function instance generated by the search process, our compiler instruments the assembly code and links it to produce an executable. We then use the fast SimpleScalar *functional* simulator on our instrumented executable to produce a count of the number of times each basic block is reached. This information is used by our performance estimator to provide our dynamic performance measures.

Table 1 describes each of the 15 candidate code-improving phases that were used during search algorithms. Unlike the other candidate phases, loop unrolling is applied at most once. Our search algorithm randomly selects one from among three different unroll factors (2, 4, and 8) whenever loop unrolling is present in the search sequence. The default VPO compiler is tuned for generating high-performance code while managing code-size for embedded systems, and hence uses a constant loop unroll factor of 2. In addition, *register assignment*, which is a compulsory phase that assigns pseudo registers to hardware registers, must be performed. VPO implicitly performs register assignment before the first code-improving phase in a sequence that requires it. After applying the last code-improving phase in a sequence, VPO performs another compulsory phase that inserts instructions at the entry and exit of the function to manage the activation record on the run-time stack. Finally, the compiler also performs *predication* and *instruction scheduling* before the final assembly code is produced. These last two optimizations should only be performed late in the compilation

---

[3] Note that reducing this expensive simulation cost without affecting the performance benefits of the generated code is the goal we are attempting to achieve in this research.

process in the VPO compiler, and so are not included in the set of re-orderable optimization phases.

For the experiments described in this paper we used a subset of the benchmarks from the *MiBench* benchmark suite, which are C applications targeting specific areas of the embedded market [13]. We selected two benchmarks from each of the six categories of applications present in MiBench. Table 2 contains descriptions of these programs. VPO compiles and optimizes individual functions at a time. The 12 benchmarks selected contained a total of 251 functions, out of which 90 were executed (at least once) with the standard input data provided with each benchmark.

Category	Program	Files/ Funcs.		Description
auto	bitcount	10	18	test proc. bit manipulation abilities
	qsort	1	2	sort strings using the quicksort algo.
network	dijkstra	1	6	Dijkstra's shortest path algorithm
	patricia	2	9	construct patricia trie for IP traffic
telecomm	fft	3	7	fast fourier transform
	adpcm	2	3	compress 16-bit linear PCM samples to 4-bit samples
consumer	jpeg	7	62	image compression and decomp.
	tiff2bw	1	9	convert color *tiff* image to b&w
security	sha	2	8	secure hash algorithm
	blowfish	6	7	symmetric block cipher with variable length key
office	search	4	10	searches for given words in phrases
	ispell	12	110	fast spelling checker

Table 2. MiBench Benchmarks Used

5. Search Algorithm Configuration

We adopt a variant of a popular genetic algorithm (GA) based search technique for the experiments in this paper [8, 19]. We also employ the latest techniques available in the literature to avoid redundant program compilations and executions during the genetic algorithm search process in order to make the experiments feasible within a reasonable amount of time [20]. At the same time, we also believe that the conclusions of this work are, most likely, independent of the heuristic algorithm that is employed during the empirical search process. In this section, we present the details of our search algorithm, and the techniques employed to avoid redundant program compilations and executions.

5.1 Base Genetic Algorithm

Genetic algorithms are adaptive algorithms based on Darwin's theory of evolution [26]. There are several parameters of a genetic algorithm that can be varied for different search configurations. *Genes* in the genetic algorithm correspond to optimization phases, and *chromosomes* correspond to optimization phase sequences. The set of chromosomes currently under consideration constitutes a *population*. The number of *generations* is how many sets of populations are to be evaluated. Previous studies have indicated that genetic algorithm based searches generally produce better phase sequences faster than a pure random sampling of the search space [8]. Additionally, it has also been revealed that genetic algorithms are competitive with most other *intelligent* phase sequence search techniques, and minor modifications in the configuration of the GA search parameters do not significantly affect their performance [24].

For our current study we have fixed the number of chromosomes in each population at 20. Chromosomes in the first generation are randomly initialized. After evaluating the performance of each chromosome in the population, they are sorted in decreasing order of performance. During crossover, 20% of chromosomes

Optimization Phase	Description
branch chaining	Replaces a branch or jump target with the target of the last jump in the jump chain.
common subexpression elimination	Performs global analysis to eliminate fully redundant calculations, which also includes global constant and copy propagation.
remove unreach. code	Removes basic blocks that cannot be reached from the function entry block.
loop unrolling (unroll factors 2, 4, and 8)	To potentially reduce the number of comparisons and branches at runtime and to aid scheduling at the cost of code size increase.
dead assign. elim.	Uses global analysis to remove assignments when the assigned value is never used.
block reordering	Removes a jump by reordering blocks when the target of the jump has only a single predecessor.
minimize loop jumps	Removes a jump associated with a loop by duplicating a portion of the loop.
register allocation	Uses graph coloring to replace references to a variable within a live range with a register.
loop transformations	Performs loop-invariant code motion, recurrence elimination, loop strength reduction, and induction variable elimination on each loop ordered by loop nesting level.
code abstraction	Performs cross-jumping and code-hoisting to move identical instructions from basic blocks to their common predecessor or successor.
eval. order determ.	Reorders instructions within a single basic block in an attempt to use fewer registers.
strength reduction	Replaces an expensive instruction with one or more cheaper ones. For this version of the compiler, this means changing a multiply by a constant into a series of shift, adds, and subtracts.
reverse branches	Removes an unconditional jump by reversing a cond. branch when it branches over the jump.
instruction selection	Combines pairs or triples of instructions together where the instructions are linked by set/use dependencies. Also performs constant folding and checks if the resulting effect is a legal instruction before committing to the transformation.
remove useless jumps	Removes jumps and branches whose target is the following positional block.

Table 1. Candidate Optimization Phases

from the poorly performing half of the population are replaced by repeatedly selecting two chromosomes from the better half of the population and replacing the lower half of the first chromosome with the upper half of the second and vice-versa to produce two new chromosomes each time. During mutation we replace a phase with another random phase with a small probability of 5% for chromosomes in the upper half of the population and 10% for the chromosomes in the lower half. The chromosomes replaced during crossover are not mutated. During all our experiments, we iterate the genetic algorithm for 200 generations.

The sequence length of each chromosome should be sufficiently long to provide the genetic algorithm maximum opportunity to find the most effective phase sequence. However, too long a sequence can potentially increase the compilation overhead with no benefit to the best generated performance. An *active* phase is one that is able to successfully apply one or more transformations to the program representation. To find the right balance between compilation cost and performance opportunity, we first find the sequence length of active phases applied by our default (*batch*) compiler. Since all phases in a chromosome are not guaranteed to be active, the sequence length is selected to be twice the batch sequence length. For function and file-level searches, all functions in a single file use a sequence length that is twice the maximum batch length over all functions in that file. Similarly, program-level searches choose twice the maximum batch length over all functions in the entire program.

All heuristic-based search algorithms attempt to either maximize or minimize a cost function or *fitness criteria*. In the domains of desktop or high-performance computing, the fitness criteria is typically just the runtime speed of the resulting program. However, in the embedded system domain, memory consumption (measured by the size of the generated code) is often as important as the speed of execution in several cases. Therefore, the fitness criteria employed by our search algorithm attempts to maximize a performance measure that is an equally weighted function of dynamic performance and code size. These weights can be easily modified to meet the constraints of a specific embedded system. Moreover, the fitness criteria of the function and hybrid approaches for each function are relative to the unoptimized performance numbers over

the entire program. Consequently, for a frequently executed function, an intelligent search process would progressively select phase sequences that emphasize reducing execution time at the expense of increasing code size (for example, by selecting more aggressive unroll factors for loop unrolling). In contrast, the search would primarily select optimization phases that reduce code size for an infrequently executed function.

5.2 Techniques to Remove Redundancy During the GA Search

Researchers have observed that several sequences found during a heuristic algorithm search are *similar* to sequences seen earlier in the search. In such cases, if we store the performance results of previous phase sequences, then we can use various redundancy detection schemes to avoid the compilation of several phase sequences and the execution/simulation for similar sequences found later. We have used several techniques derived from our previous studies to detect and eliminate redundancy during our search process [20]. We briefly describe these techniques in this section, and quantify the redundancy found during our experiments.

We employ the following redundancy detection techniques during our experiments:

Identical attempted sequence: If the current phase sequence to be attempted is identical to some chromosome seen earlier, then the algorithm can avoid having the compiler even apply the optimization phases. Performance measures of all distinct attempted phase sequences are maintained in fast access hashtables.

Identical active sequence: After applying the phases in the current chromosome, if the sequence of active phases is identical to some earlier active sequence, then we can avoid program simulation for performance evaluation. All active phase sequences are stored in hashtables.

Identical function instance: Different sequences of active phases can sometimes produce identical code. Our algorithm detects such cases using multi-variable function hash-values, and prevents program simulation in such cases.

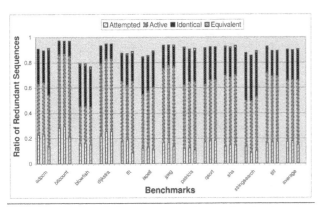

Figure 2. Number of phase sequences that are found to be redundant by various techniques during the GA-based search algorithm. Each benchmark has three bars, one for each of the following configurations: (a) function, (b) entire file, (c) entire program.

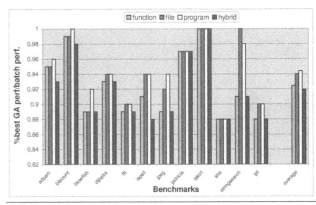

Figure 3. Entire program performance benefit achieved by all four indicated search strategies

Equivalent function instance: Earlier studies reveal that it is also possible for function instances produced by different active phase sequences to not be completely identical, but only differ cosmetically in the register number used or in the labels of basic blocks. Our algorithm avoids program simulation in such cases as well.

The redundancy detection schemes are performed in the order specified above. Figure 2 presents the number of redundant instances detected by each detection technique, and for each of our three search strategies. We can see that close to 90% of the sequences generated by the genetic algorithm are detected to be redundant. Additionally, the redundancy ratio remains about the same for each search strategy. One reason for the large amount of redundancy is the large number of generations (iterations) computed during the genetic algorithm. As the various redundancy detection tables are populated, later generations tend to produce significantly more redundant sequences than earlier generations. However, note that even the evaluation of 10% of the 4000 phase sequences results in 400 program simulations on average for each function, which depending on the search strategy can result in a prohibitively long search time. For example, for our set of benchmarks, the current function-based search strategy requires about (400 ∗ 90 = 36,000) different program simulations, where 90 is the total number of executed functions across all benchmarks.

6. Evaluation of Function, File, and Program Level Search Algorithms

As mentioned earlier, we have implemented our genetic algorithm based search strategy at three different program granularities: function, file, and program. A function-based search approach has the potential of the greatest performance benefit by finding a customized phase sequence for each individual function, but at the cost of more program evaluations via expensive simulations. In contrast, program-based searches lose flexibility by attempting to determine the most effective phase sequence for the entire program, thus overlooking the finer grained program characteristics. However, by conducting a single search (instead of n searches conducted by function-based approaches), program-based searches require less time. A file-based search strategy can provide a compromise between the two alternatives. In this section, we compare the search cost and the performance of the best code generated by each of our three search strategies: (a) function, (b) file, and (c) program level searches. To save space, the graphs in this section also show

results for our hybrid search strategy. The hybrid search strategy and results are described in Section 7.

6.1 Comparing Performance of Generated Code

Figure 3 plots the improvement in performance (50% speed and 50% code size) for each of our three search strategies, as compared to the batch compiler results. The default VPO batch compiler applies the 15 optimization phases in a fixed order, but attempts them repeatedly until the last iteration is unable to make any further changes to the program representation. Thus, the batch compiler provides a very aggressive baseline for the search algorithms. In spite of this aggressive baseline, the function search strategy achieves an average performance improvement of 8%, and up to 12% in the best case. There was also about an 8% improvement in both execution cycles and code size on average for the function-level search strategy.

As expected, the additional flexibility inherent in function-level search strategies enables them to produce code that is optimized by different customized phase sequences for each function. Thus, function-level searches can select a distinct best phase sequence over smaller program units than a file or entire program-level approach. This advantage allows function-based searches to produce the best overall code, surpassing that obtained by the file and program level searches. Correspondingly, file-level searches are also able to leverage the same advantage of optimizing over smaller program units to produce code that performs slightly better than the program-level approach for several benchmarks.

The results in Figure 3 allow us to make several other interesting observations as well. The effectiveness of file-based search in producing efficient code depends on the distribution of functions across the different files in a program. Thus, for benchmarks like *blowfish* that contain only a single function in most files, the performance of the code generated by file-based searches is close to that delivered by function-based searches. In contrast, for single file programs, like *dijkstra*, *qsort*, and *tiff*, a file-based search generates code that is equivalent in performance to that produced by a program-based approach.

6.2 Comparing Search Progress

Another important measure of the effectiveness of a particular iterative search algorithm is the number of iterations required to reach the best or the *steady-state* performance for each benchmark. More adept search algorithms typically reach their steady-state performance during earlier iterations of the search process. For a genetic algorithm based search process, each *generation* of the search is considered to be one iteration.

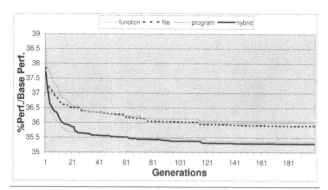

Figure 4. Progress of the GA search during *function, program, file* and *hybrid* mode, averaged over all 12 MiBench benchmarks. *Function* and *hybrid* level searches are using variable sequence lengths per function.

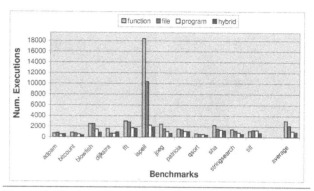

Figure 5. Number of program simulations during genetic algorithm searches at all four indicated search strategies

Figure 4 plots the average performance of the code produced by the best sequence during each generation of the genetic algorithm. The performance number is averaged across all the 12 selected MiBench benchmarks. Since all three search strategies (function, file, program) employ the same genetic algorithm, they all achieve their respective best, or close to best, performances at about the same time, and relatively early, during the search process. However, more importantly, the finer granularity search algorithms start generating better code than their higher granularity counterparts almost immediately after the search starts. Therefore, a function-based search strategy will likely outperform the entire file and program level strategies even if the search is performed for fewer number of generations.

6.3 Comparison of Search Costs

Although finer-granularity search strategies achieve better performing code, current implementations do so at the cost of increased search time. Our experiments were performed on a number of processors and required a period of over a month to complete. We found that the search times varied significantly depending on the processor that was used and the load of the machine when the search was performed. In general, the search times did improve as we expected, but there were a few abberations in specific benchmarks. The search time of an iterative search algorithm is comprised of the following two main components.

Compilation Time: This is the time spent by the compiler as it applies optimization phases to the current function, file, or program to generate the output code. Although often a minor component of the total search time in the general case, compilation time becomes significant for very large functions due to both the time required to apply each phase and typically longer phase sequences. In particular, compilation time is the only component of the search time for unexecuted functions, which the search algorithm optimizes purely for reduced code size.

Execution/Simulation Time: This is the component of the search time that is spent executing or simulating the program to measure the dynamic performance of the code produced by the current phase sequence. As mentioned earlier, in typical cases, this is the major portion of the search time.

We decided to instead report repeatable counts for these two components since we believe these counts provide more meaningful information than the actual wall clock times.

Current implementations of function-level searches explore the space of each function individually and independently of the re-

maining functions in the program. Therefore, each program execution/simulation is only able to reveal performance information regarding the current function. Thus, for a program with n distinct functions, a function-based search strategy may result in up to n times more program executions than a program-based approach.

Figure 5 shows the number of program executions/simulations required during individual function, file, and program level search algorithms. To maintain a uniform compilation time for the current experiments, we use a constant sequence length during our genetic algorithms for all functions in a single application. This length is selected to be twice the maximum length of *active* phases applied by the batch compiler over all functions in the program. Note that the selected sequence length for any benchmark is still about 5-10 times smaller than the number of phases *attempted* by the batch compiler for most functions. The phase sequence evaluated during our genetic algorithm may contain unsuccessful (dormant) phases interspersed with active phases, and the selected sequence length allows maximum opportunity to the genetic algorithm to construct more effective sequences.

The number of program executions shown in Figure 5 was directly affected by the number of executed functions in each application. It is easy to see that the number of program-based executions was less than the number of file-based executions. Likewise, the number of file-based executions was exceeded by the number of function-based executions. However, one can see that the average was skewed by the results for *ispell*, which had a significantly greater number of executed functions and hence a greater number of program executions.

A more meaningful measure is to compare against the number of executions for the function-level approach without avoiding executions for redundant phase sequences. The baseline number of executions in this case would be 4000*n, where n is the number of functions invoked one or more times during the program's execution and 4000 represents the maximum number of unique instances of functions, which is 20 chromosomes (sequences) for 200 generations. This measure allows each benchmark result to be weighted the same, regardless of the number of functions executed in the program. Thus, we can see from Figure 6 that a program-based search strategy requires only about 59% of the number of executions, on average, compared to those required for function-based searches. Again, file-based approaches achieve a middle ground and perform close to 84% as many program executions, on average, as those performed by an individual function approach. The results for the benchmark *tiff* are an exception, where the function-based search actually requires fewer executions than a corresponding program-based approach. Further analysis reveals that *tiff* has very few executed functions (four) with the largest among them dominating

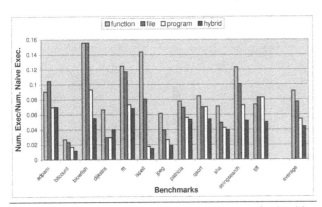

Figure 6. Ratio of program simulations during genetic algorithm searches to number of simulations using the function approach with no redundant sequences

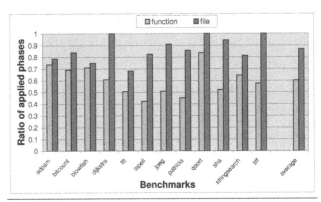

Figure 7. Ratio of (number of phases applied during *function* and *file* level search)/(number of phases applied during *program*-level search)

the number of executions count. In such cases, the inherent randomness in the GA search can produce such anomalies. For similar reasons, the *adpcm* requires the most executions with its file-based search approach. *adpcm* has only one executed function in each of its two files, and this slight increase in the number of executions during the file-based search can also be attributed to the genetic algorithm taking a different path through the search space. We can also see that a file-based strategy degenerates to a program-level approach (and performs the same number of executions) for single file benchmarks, namely, *dijkstra*, *qsort*, and *tiff*.

The other, and typically smaller, component of the search time during an iterative algorithm is the compilation time required to apply the optimization phases. In our earlier results comparing the number of program executions presented in Figures 5 and 6, all algorithms use a uniform sequence length for each benchmark, which is twice the maximum batch sequence length. However, the additional flexibility available in function (and file) based approaches can allow the genetic algorithm to use a distinct sequence length for each function (or file) in the program. Thus, searches for smaller functions can now work with smaller sequence lengths, thereby reducing the compilation overhead is such cases.

To quantify the reduction in the number of applied phases, we conducted a set of experiments that employ custom sequence lengths for each function during a function-based search, and each file during file-based search. The sequence length selected is twice the batch active sequence length of each function for function-level searches, twice the length of the longest active sequence among the functions in each file during file-level searches, and twice the length of the longest active sequence for all functions during program-level searches. The results of this study, illustrated in Figure 7, show that function-based searches only need to apply about 60% of the number of phases, on average, compared to the number applied during a program-based search. A similar comparison for file-based searches reveals a drop in the number of phases applied to 87%, on average, as compared to the program-based searches. The performance numbers of the best code generated by function and file level searches with variable sequence lengths remained the same.

Thus, the results described in this section enable us to make the following conclusions that were never reported earlier (to the best of our knowledge):

1. Function-level searches for the most effective optimization phase sequence produce better performing code than a program-level search. Additionally, based on the program layout, file-

based searches are also more effective at producing better code than a program-based approach.

2. The finer granularity of function (and file) based search strategy, allows this approach to typically reach better performance even during the earlier iterations of the search process.

3. The major drawback of finer granularity searches is the large number of additional program executions/simulations required over a program-based strategy, which often dominate the search time. However, function-based approaches can save some compilation time by using variable sequence lengths per function, and thus applying fewer number of phases than a program-based approach that needs to employ a single sequence length corresponding to the largest function in each program.

7. Hybrid Search Strategy

In the previous section we showed that both function and program based searches have their respective advantages and drawbacks. A file-based strategy can provide a middle ground, and, most importantly, may be the finest granularity available for search strategies implemented outside the compiler. In this section we propose and evaluate a new search strategy that encompasses and leverages the best features of both function and program based iterative search approaches.

Current implementations of function-based search approaches isolate the evaluation of each function from the remaining functions in the program. As a consequence of this isolated evaluation, a function-based search can require up to n times more program executions than a corresponding search over the entire program, where n is the number of functions in the program. Instead, our new *hybrid* search strategy is a function-based approach that performs the searches for all n functions simultaneously. Our hybrid search strategy delays program simulations for the performance estimation of individual functions, until all (executable) functions in the entire program also require a performance evaluation or have completed their search. The individual function performance achieved by distinct phase sequences for each function can now be evaluated in a single program simulation. Although obvious in hindsight, it should be noted that this search strategy, to the best of our knowledge, has never been attempted in the past.

This hybrid search strategy can be best described using the pseudo code in Figure 8. The outlined hybrid search strategy achieves all the advantages of both function and program-based search techniques. In fact, the hybrid strategy, in most cases, requires even fewer program simulations than the program-based approach. Both the hybrid and program-based strategies conserve search time by overlapping the evaluations of multiple individual functions in one program execution. However, a program-based approach applies the same phase sequence to all functions in a *synchronized* manner. Therefore, it requires program execution whenever *any* function updated by the current phase sequence needs to be evaluated for performance. As the algorithm in Figure 8 shows, the searches for individual functions in a hybrid search strategy proceed unsynchronized, and a function is passed only when it requires evaluation. Thus, in contrast to a program-based approach, a hybrid search strategy performs its executions only when *all* functions whose searches have not yet been completed in the program need performance evaluation.

```
DO
    FOR each function in program DO
        IF function search still incomplete THEN
            DO
                determine next compilation settings
                    for this function;
                compile function with these settings;
            UNTIL function is not redundant OR
                    function search is complete
        ENDIF
    END FOR
    get results of each function by
        simulating program once;
UNTIL number of search generations completed
    for all functions in program;
```

Figure 8. Algorithm for hybrid search approach

This further saving in the number of executions/simulations can be observed from Figure 6, which shows the number of program simulations relative to the number required for the function-level approach when not avoiding redundant sequences during each of four different search strategies, *function, file, program,* and *hybrid.* Thus, a function-level hybrid strategy requires about 48% fewer program simulations, on average than the program-level approach and only about 4% of the total simulations as compared to a naive function-level approach.

Most importantly, the hybrid approach is able to leverage all the advantages that are inherent in the flexibility allowed by a finer granularity search approach. Thus, our hybrid strategy uses customized sequence lengths for individual functions, producing the savings in compilation times illustrated earlier in Figure 7. Figure 3 compares the performance of the hybrid search approaches using variable sequence lengths with the performance of the earlier three search strategies. As we had observed earlier, the reduced sequence lengths for smaller functions do not produce any degradation in the performance of the code generated by the best sequence. [4] Finally, Figure 4 compares the average performance over all benchmarks during each iteration of a hybrid search, function-level search, file-level search, and program-level search. This figure again confirms that a hybrid-based search shows performance characteristics similar to a function-level approach.

8. Future Work

In the future, we plan to further investigate three issues related to the study presented in this paper. First, our current results demonstrate that customizing the phase sequence over finer program lev-

els can lead to greater performance benefits. In this study we selected an individual function as the finest granularity for conducting the phase sequence search. Instead, in the future, we would like to lower the granularity further, and explore the most effective phase sequence for individual *loops* within a single function, and quantify the resulting performance benefit over the entire program. Similar to our current work, we will also devise additional search strategies to limit the number of program executions during loop-level searches for effective phase sequences.

In addition to genetic algorithms, researchers investigating the phase ordering and phase selection problems have incorporated various other heuristic, evolutionary, and statistical mechanisms during their phase sequence searches, including simulated annealing, hill-climbing, orthogonal arrays, fractional factorial design, logistic regression, as well as other custom approaches. Likewise, we plan to conduct our experiments using other search mechanisms to assess if our current results regarding the performance benefits and search time improvements transcend other heuristic and statistical mechanisms.

Finally, we also plan to evaluate the use of a cluster of processors to reduce the search time. It will also be interesting to study how the various search mechanisms lend themselves to parallelism on multi-core or multi-processor machines. The most effective and fastest search strategy will likely be one where individual phase sequences or individual functions are able to be evaluated independently on separate processors. We believe that the techniques presented in this paper can be extended to further enhance the search time on multi-processor machines.

9. Conclusions

Phase ordering and phase selection are important problems in compiler optimization research, and are especially relevant to the area of performance and cost-constrained embedded systems. Iterative searches for the most effective phase sequences are typically conducted at the *function* or *entire program* level. This paper describes the first study to compare the performance benefits and costs of searches conducted at these two levels. We conclude that the finer granularity of function-level searches allows the search algorithm to find better customized phase sequences over smaller code units, resulting in enhancing the overall program performance in most cases, but at a significant cost in search overhead. We further introduced and evaluated a *file*-level search strategy that can provide the finest granularity searches for mechanisms implemented outside the compiler.

Previously, a major concern with function-level searches was the additional search overhead due to the number of program executions/simulations increasing linearly with the number of functions in the program. To alleviate this concern, we introduced a new *hybrid* search strategy that conducts all function-level searches simultaneously, and reduces the number of program executions/simulations to the number required for the function having the most nonredundant sequences in the program. We demonstrated that a hybrid search strategy can reduce the number of program executions to be even less than the number required by a program-based approach, while retaining the performance benefits and compilation time savings of the function-based approach. Thus, our hybrid search strategy using a variable sequence length achieves the best advantages of function and program level searches.

Acknowledgments

We thank the anonymous reviewers for their constructive comments and suggestions. This research was supported in part by NSF grants CNS-0615085 and CNS-0915926.

---

[4] The slight average performance improvement of hybrid search over function-based search is, most likely, due to a different random path selected by the genetic algorithm during the hybrid approach.

References

[1] F. Agakov, E. Bonilla, J. Cavazos, B. Franke, G. Fursin, M. F. P. O'Boyle, J. Thomson, M. Toussaint, and C. K. I. Williams. Using machine learning to focus iterative optimization. In *CGO '06: Proceedings of the International Symposium on Code Generation and Optimization*, pages 295–305, Washington, DC, USA, 2006.

[2] L. Almagor, K. D. Cooper, A. Grosul, T. J. Harvey, S. W. Reeves, D. Subramanian, L. Torczon, and T. Waterman. Finding effective compilation sequences. In *LCTES '04: Proceedings of the 2004 ACM SIGPLAN/SIGBED Conference on Languages, Compilers, and Tools for Embedded Systems*, pages 231–239, 2004. ISBN 1-58113-806-7.

[3] M. E. Benitez and J. W. Davidson. A portable global optimizer and linker. In *Proceedings of the SIGPLAN'88 Conference on Programming Language Design and Implementation*, pages 329–338. ACM Press, 1988. ISBN 0-89791-269-1.

[4] F. Bodin, T. Kisuki, P. Knijnenburg, M. O'Boyle, , and E. Rohou. Iterative compilation in a non-linear optimisation space. Proc. Workshop on Profile and Feedback Directed Compilation.Organized in conjuction with PACT'98, 1998.

[5] G. E. P. Box, W. G. Hunter, and J. S. Hunter. *Statistics for Experimenters: An Introduction to Design, Data Analysis, and Model Building.* John Wiley & Sons, 1 edition, June 1978. isbn:0471093157.

[6] D. Burger and T. Austin. The SimpleScalar tool set, version 2.0. *SIGARCH Comput. Archit. News*, 25(3):13–25, 1997.

[7] J. Cavazos and M. F. P. O'Boyle. Method-specific dynamic compilation using logistic regression. In *OOPSLA '06: Proceedings of the 21st annual ACM SIGPLAN conference on Object-oriented programming systems, languages, and applications*, pages 229–240, 2006. ISBN 1-59593-348-4.

[8] K. D. Cooper, P. J. Schielke, and D. Subramanian. Optimizing for reduced code space using genetic algorithms. In *Workshop on Languages, Compilers, and Tools for Embedded Systems*, pages 1–9, May 1999. URL citeseer.ist.psu.edu/cooper99optimizing.html.

[9] K. D. Cooper, A. Grosul, T. J. Harvey, S. Reeves, D. Subramanian, L. Torczon, and T. Waterman. Acme: adaptive compilation made efficient. In *LCTES '05: Proceedings of the 2005 ACM SIGPLAN/SIGBED conference on Languages, compilers, and tools for embedded systems*, pages 69–77, 2005. ISBN 1-59593-018-3.

[10] G. Fursin, A. Cohen, M. O'Boyle, and O. Temam. Quick and practical run-time evaluation of multiple program optimizations. pages 34–53, 2007.

[11] G. Fursin, C. Miranda, O. Temam, M. Namolaru, E. Yom-Tov, A. Zaks, B. Mendelson, E. Bonilla, J. Thomson, H. Leather, C. Williams, and M. O. Boyle. Milepost gcc: machine learning based research compiler. GCC Summit, 2008. http://www.milepost.eu/.

[12] J. R. Goodman and W.-C. Hsu. Code scheduling and register allocation in large basic blocks. In *ICS '88: Proceedings of the 2nd international conference on Supercomputing*, pages 442–452, 1988. ISBN 0-89791-272-1.

[13] M. R. Guthaus, J. S. Ringenberg, D. Ernst, T. M. Austin, T. Mudge, and R. B. Brown. MiBench: A free, commercially representative embedded benchmark suite. *IEEE 4th Annual Workshop on Workload Characterization*, December 2001.

[14] M. Haneda, P. M. W. Knijnenburg, and H. A. G. Wijshoff. Generating new general compiler optimization settings. In *ICS '05: Proceedings of the 19th Annual International Conference on Supercomputing*, pages 161–168, 2005.

[15] M. Haneda, P. M. W. Knijnenburg, and H. A. G. Wijshoff. Automatic selection of compiler options using non-parametric inferential statistics. In *PACT '05: Proceedings of the 14th International Conference on Parallel Architectures and Compilation Techniques*, pages 123–132, Washington, DC, USA, 2005. IEEE Computer Society. ISBN 0-7695-2429-X.

[16] K. Hoste and L. Eeckhout. Cole: Compiler optimization level exploration. In *accepted in the International Symposium on Code Generation and Optimization (CGO 2008)*, 2008.

[17] T. Kisuki, P. Knijnenburg, M. O'Boyle, F. Bodin, , and H. Wijshoff. A feasibility study in iterative compilation. In *Proceedings of ISHPC'99, volume 1615 of Lecture Notes in Computer Science*, pages 121–132, 1999.

[18] T. Kisuki, P. Knijnenburg, , and M. O'Boyle. Combined selection of tile sizes and unroll factors using iterative compilation. In *Internation Conference on Parallel Architectures and Compilation Techniques*, pages 237–246, 2000.

[19] P. Kulkarni, W. Zhao, H. Moon, K. Cho, D. Whalley, J. Davidson, M. Bailey, Y. Paek, and K. Gallivan. Finding effective optimization phase sequences. In *Proceedings of the 2003 ACM SIGPLAN Conference on Languages, Compilers, and Tools for Embedded Systems*, pages 12–23. ACM Press, 2003. ISBN 1-58113-647-1.

[20] P. Kulkarni, S. Hines, J. Hiser, D. Whalley, J. Davidson, and D. Jones. Fast searches for effective optimization phase sequences. In *Proceedings of the ACM SIGPLAN '04 Conference on Programming Language Design and Implementation*, pages 171–182, Washington DC, USA, June 2004.

[21] P. Kulkarni, D. Whalley, G. Tyson, and J. Davidson. Exhaustive optimization phase order space exploration. In *Proceedings of the Fourth Annual IEEE/ACM International Symposium on Code Generation and Optimization*, pages 306–308, March 26-29 2006.

[22] P. Kulkarni, D. Whalley, G. Tyson, and J. Davidson. In search of near-optimal optimization phase orderings. In *LCTES '06: Proceedings of the 2006 ACM SIGPLAN/SIGBED conference on Language, compilers and tool support for embedded systems*, pages 83–92, New York, NY, USA, 2006. ACM Press. ISBN 1-59593-362-X.

[23] P. A. Kulkarni, S. R. Hines, D. B. Whalley, J. D. Hiser, J. W. Davidson, and D. L. Jones. Fast and efficient searches for effective optimization-phase sequences. *ACM Transactions on Architecture and Code Optimization*, 2(2):165–198, 2005. ISSN 1544-3566.

[24] P. A. Kulkarni, D. B. Whalley, and G. S. Tyson. Evaluating heuristic optimization phase order search algorithms. In *CGO '07: Proceedings of the International Symposium on Code Generation and Optimization*, pages 157–169, Washington, DC, USA, 2007. IEEE Computer Society. ISBN 0-7695-2764-7.

[25] B. W. Leverett, R. G. G. Cattell, S. O. Hobbs, J. M. Newcomer, A. H. Reiner, B. R. Schatz, and W. A. Wulf. An overview of the production-quality compiler-compiler project. *Computer*, 13(8):38–49, 1980. ISSN 0018-9162.

[26] M. Mitchell. *An Introduction to Genetic Algorithms.* Cambridge, Mass. MIT Press, 1996.

[27] Z. Pan and R. Eigenmann. Fast and effective orchestration of compiler optimizations for automatic performance tuning. In *CGO '06: Proceedings of the International Symposium on Code Generation and Optimization*, pages 319–332, Washington, DC, USA, 2006. IEEE Computer Society. ISBN 0-7695-2499-0.

[28] S. Triantafyllis, M. Vachharajani, N. Vachharajani and D. I. August. Compiler optimization-space exploration. In *Proceedings of the International Symposium on Code Generation and Optimization*, pages 204–215. IEEE Computer Society, 2003. ISBN 0-7695-1913-X.

[29] S. R. Vegdahl. Phase coupling and constant generation in an optimizing microcode compiler. In *Proceedings of the 15th Annual Workshop on Microprogramming*, pages 125–133. IEEE Press, 1982.

[30] D. Whitfield and M. L. Soffa. An approach to ordering optimizing transformations. In *Proceedings of the second ACM SIGPLAN symposium on Principles & Practice of Parallel Programming*, pages 137–146. ACM Press, 1990. ISBN 0-89791-350-7.

[31] M. Zhao, B. Childers, and M. L. Soffa. Predicting the impact of optimizations for embedded systems. In *LCTES '03: Proceedings of the 2003 ACM SIGPLAN Conference on Language, compiler, and tool for embedded systems*, pages 1–11, New York, NY, USA, 2003. ACM Press. ISBN 1-58113-647-1.

[32] M. Zhao, B. R. Childers, and M. L. Soffa. A model-based framework: An approach for profit-driven optimization. In *Proceedings of the International Symposium on Code Generation and Optimization*, pages 317–327, Washington, DC, USA, 2005. ISBN 0-7695-2298-X.

An Efficient Code Update Scheme for DSP Applications in Mobile Embedded Systems

Weijia Li , Youtao Zhang

Computer Science Department,University of Pittsburgh,Pittsburgh, PA 15260
{weijiali,zhangyt}@cs.pitt.edu

Abstract

DSP processors usually provide dedicated address generation units (AGUs) to assist address computation. By carefully allocating variables in the memory, DSP compilers take advantage of AGUs and generate efficient code with compact size and improved performance. However, DSP applications running on mobile embedded systems often need to be updated after their initial releases. Studies showed that small changes at the source code level may significantly change the variable layout in the memory and thus the binary code, which causes large energy overheads to mobile embedded systems that patch through wireless or satellite communication, and often pecuniary burden to the users.

In this paper, we propose an update-conscious code update scheme to effectively reduce patch size. It first performs incremental offset assignment based on a recent variable coalescing heuristic, and then summarizes the code difference using two types of update primitives. Our experimental results showed that using update-conscious code update can greatly improve code similarity and thus reduce the update script sizes.

Categories and Subject Descriptors D.3.4 [*Processors*]: Code generation, Compilers, Incremental compilers, Interpreters, Optimization; K.6,3 [*Software Management*]: Software maintenance

General Terms Algorithms, Design, Experimentation

Keywords Incremental coalescing simple offset assignment (IC-SOA), Incremental coalescing general offset assignment (ICGOA), context-aware script, context-unaware script

1. Introduction

Mobile embedded systems such as PDAs and cell phones widely integrate DSP processors to support multimedia applications that process audio, video and communication signals. DSP processors strive to achieve low-cost, low-power, and low-latency processing of digital signals by integrating specially designed and optimized architectural components. For example, a dedicated address generation unit (AGU) can perform parallel address computation in *register-indirect-automatic* addressing mode. With *register-indirect-automatic* addressing, the memory address is stored in an address register (AR) whose value can be automatically updated

within a small range before or after the memory access. The access incurs no extra cost. As a comparison, the *base-register-plus-offset* addressing requires two instruction words on 16-bit DSP processors e.g. AT&T DSP16xx [12]. By carefully allocating variables in the memory, DSP compilers can generate efficient code with compact size and improved performance.

The problem of assigning variables in memory was formulated by Bartley [2] and Liao *et al.* [13] as simple offset assignment (SOA) when there is only one AR, and general offset assignment (GOA) when there are multiple ARs. Many heuristic algorithms have been proposed in the literature to reduce the code size and improve the performance [14, 24, 1, 22, 3, 9, 15, 26, 16, 21]. To keep low execution overhead and better performance, many DSP applications are optimized and then released in binary format.

DSP applications running on mobile embedded systems often need to be updated after their initial releases. Bug fixes are the most common need due to the increasing complexity of modern embedded applications. Another need is to upgrade the current application with new features. For example, the map service on iPhone currently has no voice instructions [7], a very useful functionality that might be added in the future.

Although it is possible to patch or upgrade the code by directly connecting the mobile system to a server e.g. using a USB cable, there are situations where using wireless or even more expensive satellite communication is the only choice. For example, people may be traveling or working in a wild field, and thus do not have wired access to the server or the Internet. Updating code through wireless communication tends to incur both energy overhead and pecuniary burden. For example, it consumes 1000 times more energy to communicate one bit than to execute one instruction under certain settings [18]. As another example, many wireless data plans charge per KByte fee if the traffic is beyond the monthly quota. Since mobile embedded systems can be recharged when users return to the home, the energy efficiency goal focuses more on reducing the amount of transmitted data, even at the cost of executing slightly more instructions.

It is challenging to achieve cost-efficient DSP code update through wireless communication. Although transmitting a *diff*-based update script instead of the complete new binary is an effective approach to reduce the overall communication overhead [23, 10, 5], studies showed that using existing update oblivious compilers, a small change at the source code level may result in significant binary changes [18]. Several schemes have been proposed to achieve energy efficiency in updating sensor code after deployment [23, 18]. However, they are not directly applicable to updating DSP code. A big difference between wireless sensors and mobile systems is that it is almost impossible to recharge sensor battery while periodically recharging mobile systems is very common. Preserving energy is much more critical in wireless sensor networks, e.g. running low quality code may draw more energy in the long run. For the compilation scheme to minimize update script size in [18], Li *et al.* proposed an update-conscious compilation approach to reduce update script size on systems that perform *base-register-plus-offset* addressing. This approach tries to improve the register allocation similarity when generating the new version, so that the update script is small. Unfortunately, for the embedded systems that intensively access memory through *register-indirect* addressing and use post-/pre- incremental automatic AR update, both the register allocation changes and the data allocation changes can cause instruction updates. Thus, this scheme is not applicable to the DSP applications.

In this paper, we propose an update-conscious offset assignment approach for minimizing *diff*-based script sizes in updating DSP applications through wireless or satellite communication. In particular, we observed that generating a better offset assignment plays an important role in determining the code size and performance of DSP applications. In a case study of different versions of a real DSPstone program, we found that the offset assignment might be significantly different after small changes at the source code level. We developed an incremental variable coalescing heuristic to improve code similarity before and after the update, and then designed two types of scripts to summarize the code difference using context-unaware and context-aware primitives respectively. We implemented and evaluated the proposed incremental offset assignment scheme. In the experiments, we observed that incremental assignment with context-aware update primitives greatly reduces the update script size for medium sized changes.

The remainder of the paper is organized as follows. Section 2 discusses the background. The update-conscious offset assignment scheme and update script generation are elaborated in Section 3 and 4 respectively. We extend the scheme to GOA in Section 5. The experiments are discussed and analyzed in Section 6. Section 7 discusses the related work and Section 8 concludes the paper.

2. Background

2.1 Auto addressing on DSP processors

The *address generation unit* (AGU) on DSP processors assists the address computation in parallel. For the most frequently used auto addressing instructions i.e. post- and pre- address increment/decrement instructions, no explicit addressing instruction is needed when the address distance of two consecutive memory accesses is smaller than two; otherwise an extra instruction is needed to update the address register (as shown in Figure 1). Extra addressing instructions increase code size and slow down the execution. Since allocating variables to different locations in memory affects the address distance of adjacent accesses, different offset assignment heuristics have been proposed to minimize the number of extra addressing instructions e.g.[13, 2, 14, 24, 1, 22, 3, 9, 15, 26, 16, 21].

The problem of assigning variables in memory was formulated as simple offset assignment (SOA) when there is only one AR, and general offset assignment (GOA) when there are multiple ARs.

Offset distance	1st memory access	2nd memory access
0	no	no
1	post	no
1	no	pre
2	post	pre
> 2	addr. update instr.	no
> 2	no	addr. update instr.

Figure 1. Addressing modes between two adjacent memory instructions.

2.2 Offset assignment with variable coalescing

In this paper we propose our scheme based on a recently proposed effective offset assignment heuristic using variable coalescing [26, 21]. The *coalescing simple offset assignment* (CSOA) scheme [21] builds up two auxiliary graphs: (i) an *access graph* in which each vertex denotes a variable, and the edge weight denotes the frequency of adjacent accesses of the two corresponding variables; (ii) an *interference graph* in which each vertex indicates a variable, and an edge between two vertices indicates the live ranges of these two variables overlap and these cannot be allocated into the same memory location.

The offset assignment problem is modeled as finding the maximum weight path cover on the access graph [13]. Since many variables have short live ranges, they can be allocated to the same location in memory. CSOA iteratively chooses an edge in the *access graph* and adds it to the maximum weight path, or coalesces two vertices that do not interfere with each other. The decision is made based on the cost/benefit equations of each choice.

3. Update-Conscious Offset Assignment

3.1 A motivational example

Figure 2 illustrates the motivation to design an update-conscious SOA. It requires two and six words respectively with and without variable coalescing. The one with variable coalescing requires no extra addressing instructions as the reduction of memory usage increases the likeliness of two adjacent memory accesses being close enough to avoid explicit addressing instructions.

After a small update of the code, i.e. the third instruction is changed (Figure 2(d)), recompiling the code using CSOA generates a very different variable coalescing result (Figure 2(h)). The memory layout difference further translates to selecting different addressing instructions at each memory access (Figure 3). Out of seven updated instructions, four of them are due to the data allocation change, i.e. column 5 in Figure 3. As a comparison, keeping these variables in their original positions requires two instructions to be updated, i.e. column 7 in Figure 3.

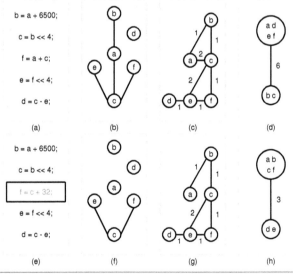

Figure 2. A motivational example: (a) the original C code segment; (b) the original interference graph; (c) the original access graph; (d) the offset assignment result using CSOA [21]; (e) the C code after a simple update; (f) the new interference graph; (g) the new access graph; (h) the new assignment using CSOA.

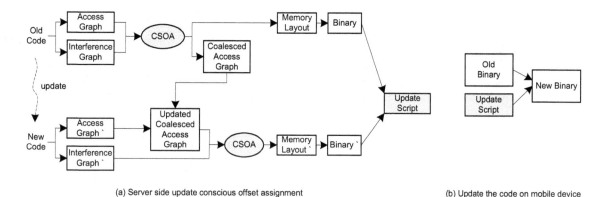

(a) Server side update conscious offset assignment   (b) Update the code on mobile device

Figure 4. An overview of Incremental Coalescing Offset Assignment (ICSOA) -based code update scheme.

	Access sequence	Original code	Update-Oblivious		Update-Conscious	
			code	update	code	update
0	a	•++	•	diff**	•++	
1	b	•	•		•	
2	b	•	•		•	
3	c	•--	•	diff	•	diff
4	→ a*	•++		diff		diff
5	c	•--	•	diff	•--	
6	f	•	•		•	
7	f	•	•++	diff**	•	
8	e	•++	•--	diff**	•++	
9	c	•--	•++	diff**	•--	
10	e	•	•		•	
11	d	•	•		•	

*: This access only exists in the old version.
**: The instruction that needs to be updated, due to data allocation changes.
•++: An instruction with post-increment addressing.
•- -: An instruction with post-decrement addressing.
The old version memory layout is "slot 0: a, d, e, f; slot 1: b, c"
The memory layout for GCC result is "slot 0: a, b, c, f; slot 1: d, e".
The memory layout for UCC result is "slot 0: a, d, e, f; slot 1: b, c".

Figure 3. Update script comparison between two versions using CSOA.

3.2 Incremental coalescing simple offset assignment (ICSOA)

To minimize the update script, we propose to perform update-conscious code updates through incremental coalescing SOA (ICSOA) (Figure 4). When a DSP application undergoes a small update, the change does not greatly affect the binary code. On the server side, ICSOA reads in the old access graph and its interference graph, and strives to generate a new memory layout that minimizes the update script. On the mobile system side, only the update script needs to be downloaded. With simple interpretation, the mobile system regenerates the new binary and/or the new memory layout.

The pseudo code of ICSOA is shown in Algorithm 1. It first builds the access graphs before and after the code update, performs the CSOA algorithm, retrieves the coalesced variable assignment in CAG_1, updates the new access graph AG_2, resolves possible conflicts when applying the old layout to the new code, and calls CSOA again to find the new offset assignment.

Function update_access_graph(). It combines the access graph result of the old version (CAG_1) and the newly generated access graph (AG_2), into a new access graph (AG_{NEW}). We build AG_{NEW} based on CAG_1, by adding new variable nodes and removing un-

---

Algorithm 1 Incremental Coalescing-Based SOA (ICSOA)

Input: AS_1, AS_2: access sequences before and after update;
    IG_1, IG_2: interference graphs before and after update;
Output: the offset assignment.
1: $AG_1 \leftarrow$ Build access graph using AS_1;
2: $AG_2 \leftarrow$ Build access graph using AS_2;
3: $CAG_1 \leftarrow$ CSOA(AG_1, IG_1);
4: $AG_{NEW} \leftarrow$ update_access_graph(CAG_1, AG_2);
5: resolve_conflicts(AG_{NEW}, IG_2);
6: $CAG_2 \leftarrow$ CSOA(AG_{NEW}, IG_2);
7: Return offset assignment based on CAG_2;

---

used nodes, so that AG_{NEW} not only represents the updated access sequence but also keeps all the coalescing offset assignment result from the old version. Using AG_{NEW} instead of AG_2 as the offset assignment input helps to improve the offset assignment similarity with the previous version, and reduces the patch transmission overhead. However, when the code change is relatively big, the energy saved by improving code similarity may be offset by the code quality loss. For this reason, when combining the graphs, *update_access_graph()* evaluates the number of accesses of each old variable in the new code, and extracts it from its coalescing group if the variable has more new or updated accesses than the unchanged ones. The intuition is to extract the variables from their old coalescing groups only if it can bring explicit benefits. A new node is introduced for each extracted variable. Empty group nodes will be removed from AG_{NEW}. At the end, the function adjusts the weights of impacted access edges accordingly to finish the update.

Function resolve_conflicts(). Due to code update, two variables that are coalesced in the old assignment may interfere with each other. We identify this as a *conflict* and call *resolve_conflicts()* to resolve it.

The function first orders the variables in each coalescing group, by the factor

$$\frac{Num_{local\_itfs}}{Num_{local\_acs}}.$$

Here, Num_{local_itfs} represents the number of interferences between the variable and the other group members, and Num_{local_acs} represents the number of adjacent accesses with other group members. The function then extracts the interfering variables with a higher factor one by one until all the interferences in the group are resolved. By doing so, the variables that create more interferences but have less adjacent accesses with others are extracted first from the coalescing group.

For each variable chosen to be extracted from the coalescing group, the function splits the live range (i.e. conflict range) into to two subranges, the original part and the newly extended part. We use the old variable name to represent the original subrange, and introduce a *patch variable* for the extended subrange. To ensure semantic correctness, we insert a'=a or a=a' to move the value between the subranges. The insertion involves memory copy and tends to incur large overhead. We will evaluate its impact in the experiments.

For the example in Figure 2, ICSOA combines the coalesced offset assignment (Figure 2(d)) and the new access graph (Figure 2(f)). Figure 5(a) shows the updated access graph. As there is no conflict between the access graph and interference graph, ICSOA outputs the same coalesced assignment (Figure 5(c)). In this example, the script generated from ICSOA is 71% smaller than that of recompilation using CSOA.

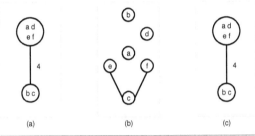

Figure 5. An example of ICSOA scheme: (a) AG_{NEW}, the updated access graph; (b) IG_2, the new interference graph; (c) the final offset assignment.

4. Code Update Script

After generating the new binary, our scheme summarizes its difference from the old binary in an update script that consists of a sequence of updating primitives specifying how to generate the new code on mobile devices (Figure 6). The primitives can be categorized to context-unaware or context-aware primitives, according to whether it will pass the updated memory layout to the remote devices.

4.1 Context-unaware script

The update script is generated by comparing the new and old binaries at the instruction level. To simplify the comparison, we link the unmodified code blocks in the old and new code, and then use the context-unaware primitives to specify how to update the changed code blocks.

4.1.1 Simple context-unaware primitives

There are four *simple primitives*: *insert*, *replace*, *copy* and *remove*. Both *insert* and *replace* primitives have a one-byte opcode and n-byte data or instructions to be inserted/replaced to the new code. The *copy* and *remove* primitives take one byte each and specify the size of data/instructions that need to be copied or removed.

To regenerate the new binary, the script interpreter on remote devices maintains two instruction pointers — one points to the old code and the other points to the last instruction that has been generated in the new code. The *insert* primitive inserts the instructions in its data part into the new code, and moves the pointer in the new code to the end. The *replace* primitive does the same thing to the new code but also moves the pointer in the old code for the same distance. The *copy* primitive reads the instructions from the old code, and moves both pointers.

Primitive		Format and Operation	Size (bytes)
context-unaware	insert	`000x xxxx` `data` ... `data` number of bytes to be inserted	1 + number
	replace	`001x xxxx` `data` ... `data` number of bytes to be replaced	1 + number
	copy	`010x xxxx` number of bytes to be copied	1
	remove	`011x xxxx` number of bytes to be removed	1
	insert _access	`100x xxxx` `data` ... `data` number of bytes to be inserted	1+number
context-aware	copy _slot	`110x xxxx` number of data slots to be copied	1
	insert _slot	`101x xxxx` `variable` ... `variable` number of data slots to be inserted	1+number
	shift _slot	`111x xxxx` `start_slot` `offset` number of consecutive unchanged slots	3

Figure 6. Code update primitives.

4.1.2 Advanced context-unaware primitives

When inserting a new memory access between two existing accesses, we need two *update* primitives and one *insert* primitive, as shown in Figure 7(d). Since the update primitives only modify the addressing modes, a compact way to express them is to include the memory address difference in the script and let the mobile devices generate the correct addressing modes for the related instructions. Thus we introduce an *advanced context-unaware primitive – insert_access*.

The *insert_access* primitive is similar to the *insert* primitive, except that its data field is specified as follows:

$$[operation, \delta_{diff}]$$

where δ_{diff} represents the address difference between the locations accessed by the current instruction and the preceding instruction respectively. In the example (Figure 7(c)), the new access is *c* (*located in memory slot 0*), and the preceding memory access is *a* (*located in memory slot 1*), so δ_{diff} is -1. Since it is the add operation that accesses *c* in the new instruction, the update primitive is

$$insert\_access \quad 1 \quad [ADD, -1].$$

Rewriting the update script of the example, using the *insert_access* primitive, the script size is reduced by 50% (Figure 7(e)).

To maintain the correct program semantics, the interpreter has to know the memory locations accessed before and after the inserted instruction, and generate the correct addressing modes for these instructions. It is achieved by temporarily buffering each affected instruction, and updating its addressing mode when the memory location to be accessed in the next instruction is known.

4.2 Context-aware script

In our experiments, we observed that binary changes at several places may be caused by one memory layout change. For example, assuming variable a appears in several places in the code and is relocated to a new memory location, we may generate a script with multiple update primitives each of which summarizes an instruction level change. Instead, if the script interpreter on mobile devices can

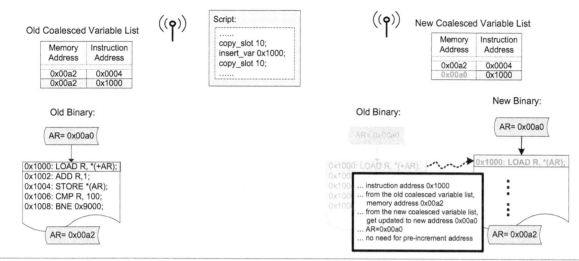

Figure 8. Context-aware code retrieval (The left shows the server side, and the right shows the mobile device side updates).

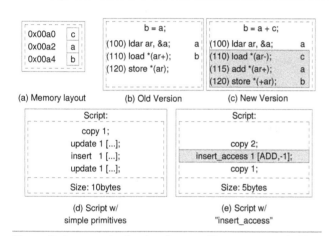

Figure 7. An example showing the use of *insert_access* primitive: (a) data allocation for both versions; (b) the original code; (c) the modified code; (d) update script using simple primitives; (e) update script using advanced primitives.

decode DSP instructions, and identify all its uses, then it is possible to send one "relocate a" primitive instead of individual instruction update.

We call the binary instructions that are inserted, removed, or changed due to the offset assignment changes as *Addressing Mode Change* (AMC) instructions. The motivation of developing *context-aware primitives* is to reduce the transmission of AMC instructions, and let the mobile devices construct them by themselves. Compared to the *insert_access* primitive, context-aware primitives are designed to update the code in more than one place.

4.2.1 Context-aware primitives

In order to update the AMC instructions automatically, the offset assignment changes (rather than affected instructions) need to be transmitted. Figure 6 lists the *context-aware* update primitives that we use to specify the memory layout change. We only consider the allocation of scalar variables in this paper. Each memory location contains one variable or multiple coalesced variables ([21, 26]).

copy_slot. This primitive copies multiple memory slots from the old offset assignment to the new assignment. There are two pointers pointing to the new and old assignments respectively. They are updated to the next slot with this primitive.

insert_var. This primitive adds a list of variables to the current memory slot in the old assignment. The related slot with the added variables is then copied to the new assignment. The insertion can be caused by adding a new variable, or by moving an existing variable from another location. The latter implicitly has the variable removed from the old location, which is omitted to keep the script compact.

shift_slot. This primitive represents the case that multiple slots may be grouped and shifted from the old assignment to the new assignment. The *shift_slot* primitive specifies the number of slots that need to be shifted, the starting point of the shift, and the shift offset.

4.2.2 Context-aware code retrieval

After receiving the update script, each sensor interprets the *context-aware primitives* to generate the new memory layout, and then interprets the *context-unaware primitives* to construct basic blocks by inserting, removing, or updating certain instructions on top of the old binary version. The interpreter fixes the addressing mode of each instruction in a basic block according to the new memory layout, and then writes the completed block into the flash.

However, it may require additional information to fix the addressing modes on the mobile device side. As shown in Figure 8, CSOA coalesces multiple variables — both a and e, in one memory location 0x00a2, a code update may re-allocate e to 0x00a0 while keeping a in the same memory slot. This complicates the code update as some accesses to 0x00a0 should be updated while others should not.

Figure 8 illustrates our solution to this problem. We use an implicit pointer to track the current memory slot when copying from the old layout to the new layout. "*insert_var* 0x1000" inserts e into the current slot, i.e. 0x00a0. Here variable e is represented using its instruction address 0x1000. A record can be found in the coalesced variable list indicating this mapping, and will be updated to reflect to the re-allocation.

To update the addressing mode in the new code, a query is sent to the coalesced variable list, from which we know this instruction accesses 0x00a0 instead of 0x00a2. Since AR contains 0x00a0 when entering the basic block, there is no need for pre-increment. Similar decisions are made for other instructions in the basic block and ensure the exiting AR contains 0x00a2.

From this discussion, the context-aware interpreter needs the following information to fix the addressing modes:

- A coalesced variable list to distinguish each of coalesced variables; and
- The AR values when entering and exiting each basic block.

4.2.3 Auxiliary data structures

To correctly update the code with a memory layout change, e.g. a is assigned to a different memory location, we need to locate all of a's uses and ensure the AR contains the correct address when accessing a. Conceptually, this can be done by a relocation table. Unfortunately a traditional relocation table [10] identifies all the places that the binary code accesses the memory. Since DSP code relies heavily on offset assignment and accesses the memory frequently, adopting a traditional relocation table would generate a table linear to the size of the binary code. Instead, in this paper we introduce the following two lightweight auxiliary data structures to enable relocatable DSP code.

Coalesced variable list. The coalesced variable list is designed to differentiate the coalesced variables in one memory location. If a memory location contains only one variable, then we do not allocate any entry in the list. If multiple variables are coalesced and stored in the same memory location, we allocate the entries as follows.

Memory Address	Instruction Address
0x00a2	0x0004
0x00a2	0x1000

Figure 9. Coalesced variable list.

Since the coalesced variables have their accesses spread in the code, we group consecutive definitions/uses that access the same variable and allocate one entry to each group. This is done based on the code text without considering the control flow, or the variable live range etc. For example, if the live ranges of two coalesced variables overlap due to linear layout of control structures such as branches, then we allocate one entry for each segment. As shown in Figure 9, each entry contains two fields: the memory slot address, and the starting instruction address of each code text segment.

For example, variable a and e share the same memory location 0x00a2. The live ranges of a and e are [0x0000,0x0004] and [0x0010,0x1000] respectively. Figure 9 illustrates its coalesced variable list. Given a memory access to 0x00a2, we can easily differentiate whether it is accessing a or e.

The original coalesced variable list is preloaded on the mobile devices before deployment. The updates to the coalesced variable list is transmitted with the code update script. The coalesced variable list update primitives will be discussed later.

AR in/out value list. As we discussed before, we need the AR in and out values for each basic block in order to generate the correct addressing modes on the mobile device side. We choose to construct the list rather than building the control flow graph on demand to reduce the memory and complexity overheads. This table contains the starting, ending addresses, the address register's entering, exiting values and the successive basic block(s) of each basic block, as shown in Figure 10.

Index	Starting Address	Ending Address	AR In	AR Out	Successive Basic Blocks
10	0x1000	0x1008	0x00a0	0x00a2	20

Figure 10. The AR in/out value list.

The original list is preloaded on the mobile devices before deployment. The context-aware interpreter automatically generates the new list while generating the new binary code.

The AR out value of a basic block may affect the addressing mode of its successive basic blocks. The situation becomes more complicated if there are multiple predecessors (or successors). Synchronization needs to be done among these predecessors (or successors), which may cascadingly affect other instructions in those basic blocks. To simplify the code update on mobile device side, the server explicitly sends out the AMC instructions that follow an inserted/updated/removed instruction, and those that are the last instruction of a basic block.

5. General Offset Assignment

In this section, we discuss our update-conscious offset assignment scheme in the presence of multiple address registers.

5.1 Coalescing general offset assignment (CGOA)

To compile a DSP application using k address registers, the CGOA scheme [21] first partitions all variables into k different sets. Variables in the same set use the same address register throughout the code. After partitioning the variables, the access graph and interference graph can be partitioned accordingly. The CSOA scheme is then applied to each access graph to generate the offset assignment for that address register. The overall offset assignment is the combination of individual assignments.

A brief discussion of variable partition is as follows. For each variable, CGOA computes a global interference number that is the number of interferences between this variable and all other variables. CGOA sorts the variables in decreasing order of their global interference numbers, and processes the variables iteratively. To decide which set a variable should be inserted, CGOA also computes the local interference number of this variable, i.e. the number of interferences with all the variables in each partition. CGOA assigns the variable to the partition with the lowest local interference number.

The objective of variable partition is to minimize the interference among variables assigned to the same set, and to increase the chances of variable coalescing in CSOA.

5.2 Incremental coalescing general offset assignment (ICGOA)

Our incremental variable coalescing based general offset assignment (ICGOA) scheme works as follows. It first divides the variables that exist in the old code into partitions based on their global interference numbers in the old code. It then sorts the new variables according to the decreasing order of their global interference numbers in the new code. ICGOA assigns new variables to the partitions according to their local interference numbers, similar to CGOA. After the variable partitioning, ICSOA is applied to each variable set to generate the offset assignment.

5.3 Update scripts

When generating the update script using only context-unaware primitives, there is no difference between ICSOA and ICGOA schemes.

When using context-aware primitives, we need to enhance the auxiliary data structures to handle each variable independently. Since variables in the coalesced variable list are sorted according to their memory addresses, and those using the same address register are grouped together, we only need to add a one-byte flag to terminate each group. That is, we need extra $k-1$ bytes for the architecture with k address registers. In addition we add information to the AR in/out value list to capture the entering/exiting values of each address register. The update does not significantly increase the script size as the auxiliary data structures are preloaded, and only the modified sections are transmitted. With enhanced auxiliary data structures, ICGOA processes each address register independently similar to ICSOA as we discussed in preceding sections.

6. Experiments

6.1 Settings

We have implemented our proposed update-conscious ICSOA/ICGOA algorithms. We chose the Lance Compiler[11] to convert the source code (C code) into intermediate representations (IRs) from which the access sequence and interference graph are extracted. We selected the DSPstone[4] benchmark suite that is widely used to measure the performance of DSP compilers. We adopted CSOA-Offsetstone[20] as the baseline CSOA and implemented ICSOA on top of it.

We created the code update benchmarks using three methods:
i). compare two official releases;
ii). manually insert code changes to the application;
iii). automatically insert code changes to the application.
Then we generated the new binary using either CSOA/CGOA or ICSOA/ICGOA, and the update script using different scripting schemes. We evaluated their effectiveness based on code quality and code similarity.

6.2 Software update overhead

We manually made changes to two functions from DSPstone — the encoding/decoding verification function (*verify.c*) and the matrix multiplication function (*matrix1.c*). We modified these functions and, according to the impact on the existing code, categorized the changes into small and medium changes, according to the number of affected instructions (cases 1 to 5 in Figure 11).

In addition, one function may have different versions in DSP-stone, such as the multiplication function *matrix.c* which has two versions, and the ADPCM standard implementation *opt_adpcm.c* which has four versions. We selected the *main* function in *matrix.c*, as well as the *speed_control* function in *opt_adpcm.c* as our benchmarks. The three manually generated test cases are divided into medium and large categories (cases 6 to 8 in Figure 11).

We evaluated the impact as the number of variable interferences that are added by the code update, and whether these new interferences conflict with existing variable partitioning result. An interference conflict happens when two coalesced variables (in the old assignment) have overlapped live ranges and thus cannot be coalesced anymore.

Figure 12 compares the software update overhead for CSOA and ICSOA. We used three script formats to do the comparison.

- *Simple context-unaware script* that uses only the first types of context-unaware primitives;

- *Advanced context-unaware script* that uses all types of context-unaware primitives;

- *Context-aware script* that uses both context-unaware and context-aware primitives.

Using the same script generator with ICSOA, the update script size can be reduced by 32%. This is because that the update-aware scheme follows the variable coalesces and offset assignment of the old code. The generated code has better code similarity to the old version in terms of both offset assignment and instruction addressing mode. In Test-Case 1, the code update is very small such that the difference between the old and new offset assignments is not big. We did not see much benefit using ICSOA over CSOA.

When comparing different script generators, we observed that between the two *context-unaware* schemes, the advanced *context-*

Test Case	Category	Function	Description
1	small	verify.c	Update **one basic block** to create the interference between two variables that are **not coalesced** in the original version.
2	medium	verify.c	Update **one basic block** to create the interference between three variables that are **coalesced** in the original version.
3	medium	verify.c	Expand the live ranges of three variables to **cross basic blocks**.
4	medium	matrix1.c	Shrink the live range of the one variable and Expand the live range of another variable within on basic block. **Over ten interferences** are updated.
5	medium	matrix1.c	Shrink the live ranges of the two variables and Expand the live ranges of another two variables within on basic block. **Over ten interferences** are updated.
6	medium	matrix1.c ⇒matrix2.c	Move two iterations out of the loop.
7	medium	speed_control 1 ⇒2	Seven temporary variables are introduced to hold the value of the comparison results.
8	large	speed_control 2 ⇒3	Multiple global variables are combined into a structure. The reference to the variables are changed due to this change.

Figure 11. Experimental benchmarks.

unaware script generator produces a smaller script due to its usage of the *insert_access* primitive. When there is no variable access insertion but contains removal or update in the code update, the two script generators produce the same script i.e. Test-Case 4 and 5.

The *context-aware* script generator produces smaller scripts when the code update is medium. Instead of sending individual instruction differences, it just sends out the data allocation differences, from which each node generates the new binary by itself i.e. Test-Case 4 and 5. We see a significant script size reduction by using this scheme. Adopting context-aware script tends to incur large complexity i.e. Test-Case 1 and 3 where we see a small script size increase due to the complexity to specify the offset assignment change. When the code has significant changes e.g. Test-Case 8 introduces 32% code changes, the old and new code segments are mixed such that the benefit from keeping the old data offset assignment diminishes.

GOA script size comparison. When there are multiple ARs, Figure 13 compares CGOA and ICGOA schemes with the different script generators.

When there are more ARs, recompiling the program results in large changes in both the variable partition and offset assignment. For Test-Case 3, CGOA with context-aware script has larger size than that with simple script. This is because that the significant variable partition change and requires more primitives to specify the new offset layout.

In conclusion, ICSOA/ICGOA is preferred when there are medium changes while recompilation is preferred when the change is small or big.

6.3 Code quality

In this paper we evaluated the static code quality i.e. the number of instructions in the new binary produced by CSOA and ICSOA schemes. An alternative approach is to evaluate the dynamic code quality i.e. the runtime instruction counts with given execution

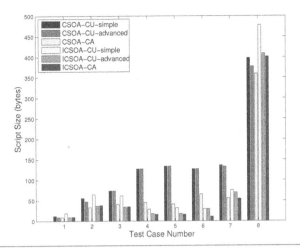

Figure 12. Script size comparison between CSOA and ICSOA (Single address register).

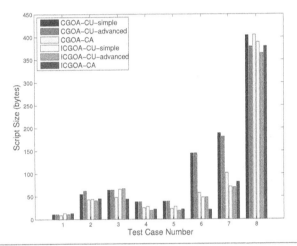

Figure 13. Script size comparison between CGOA and ICGOA (Double address register).

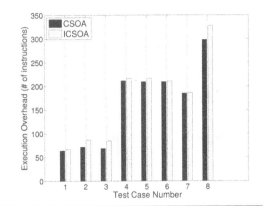

Figure 14. Code quality comparison between CSOA and ICSOA.

Test	CSOA				ICSOA			
Case#	T1	T2	T3	T4	T1	T2	T3	T4
1	0	7	1	0	0	7	2	0
2	1	7	9	0	0	8	12	3
3	1	7	7	0	0	10	12	6
4	4	24	0	0	0	24	2	1
5	4	22	0	0	0	24	2	1

Figure 15. Execution overhead breakdown.

Figure 3; (2) adding addressing mode change instructions. The first type update does not change the instruction number as no extra instruction is added, but for the second type, one extra instruction is added per change.

To study the code quality, we divide the overhead into four categories as follows. T1-T3 shows how efficient the offset assignment algorithm is; and T4 shows how the extra patch affects the final result.

- T1: AR loading instructions removed from the old code;
- T2: AR loading instructions inserted into the old code;
- T3: AR loading instructions inserted into the new code;
- T4: ALU instructions inserted into the new code.

Comparing columns T1 and T2 of both CSOA and ICSOA in Figure 15, we found that CSOA generates less binary instructions for the unchanged IR part. It removes more AR loading instructions, and inserts less such instructions. For the new code part, CSOA generates less AR loading instructions. When performing complete recompilation, CSOA uses the new access sequences and variable interferences of the whole function, and thus can generate the better offset assignment.

Column T4 shows the number of ALU instructions generated by compiling the new assembly code. Since ICSOA needs to add patch variables to remove the interferences due to overlapped live ranges, it adds several "move" instructions in the code, which causes more T4 type instructions.

GOA performance comparison. For the test case 3 that has the largest code quality difference, we increased the number of available ARs, and found that with more available ARs, the code quality difference is reduced, as shown in Figure 16. The extra instruction number drops from 20% to 6% when the address register number is increased from 1 to 4. This is because with more ARs, the variables are partitioned into smaller sets. The software update tends to create less new interference and needs fewer patch variables. Fewer interferences result in less overhead in ICSOA.

profiles. Although the latter provides more accurate evaluation, as we discussed in the introduction section, embedded mobile systems can periodically recharge the battery, so the execution overhead is less critical compared to its the communication overhead.

As shown in Figure 14, ICSOA produces about the similar number of instructions as CSOA. On average, the binary generated by ICSOA is 10% larger than the binary generated by CSOA. And for the worst test case, i.e. Test-Case 3, the binary generated by ICSOA is 23% larger than CSOA. Because the ICSOA scheme incrementally does the data allocation based on the *coalesced access graph* of the old version, the old variable coalescing result is kept in the new version to improve code similarity. As a result, the code generated by ICSOA is not as efficient.

To better understand the code quality difference between two approaches, Figure 15 shows the breakdown of the execution overhead. We separated the new code at the intermediate representation (IR) level into the changed and unchanged parts. We then create their mapping to the binary level code segments.

Due to the change to offset assignment, the same IR instructions may be different in the old and new code. The change could be categorized into two types: (1) updating the addressing mode of the related binary instructions, such as the first memory access in

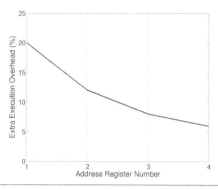

Figure 16. Code quality comparison with multiple ARs.

6.4 Random code insertion

We next inserted changes randomly into a file (*verify.c*) to study the robustness of our proposed scheme. The inserted code involves the use of both existing and new variables. The ratio of these two types is 1:1, and the sizes of the inserted/changed code range from 5% to 60% of the original code. Given an update percentage, we randomly generated 500 test cases and reported the average.

The script size comparison is shown in Figure 17. For all three types of the script generation schemes, incremental compilation scheme reduces more of the update script size and thus the software update transmission overhead. However, the results show that we achieved the maximum script size reduction when the update percentage is between 10% and 40%. This is because ICSOA benefits more when most of the update is caused by the data allocation changes rather than new/updated instruction operations. When the update percentage is too big, i.e. larger than 40%, most changes are new or updated instructions. When the update percentage is too small, i.e. smaller than 20%, the data allocation table is less likely to change even with recompilation. Thus, the benefits from ICSOA are limited.

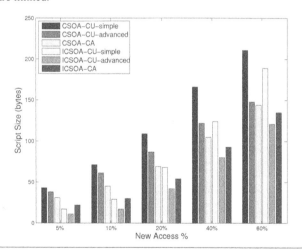

Figure 17. Script size comparison between recompile and incremental-compile (scattered random new code insertion).

The code quality is compared in Figure 18. Larger code update percentage, i.e. over 40%, has more live range extension of old variables, which produces more patch variables and instructions. Thus, the code produced by the recompilation scheme has a larger number of T4 type instructions; the code generated by the ICSOA scheme has a worse execution performance.

From Figure 18 and Figure 17, we conclude that when the code update percentage is between 20% and 40%, using the update-conscious offset assignment scheme can save about 30% of the

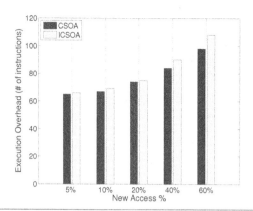

Figure 18. Code quality comparison between recompile and incremental-compile (scattered random new code insertion).

transmission overhead, assuming that context-unaware advanced script is used, with about 2% extra instruction execution.

From the experimental results, we can also see that the context-unaware scheme works better with the incremental compilation scheme, and the context-aware scheme works better with the re-compilation scheme. This is because that the context-aware scheme trades updating individual instructions for setting up the auxiliary data structures and letting the sensors to construct these updates. Thus, when we recompile the new version, a relatively large number of instructions are changed due to the data allocation differences, so the context-aware scheme can gain more benefit by saving those updates. On the other hand, when we use the incremental compilation technique, the saving is not great enough to balance the spending in setting up the data structures, therefore, the context-unaware scheme is more beneficial.

7. Related work

7.1 Software patching in resource constrained embedded systems

Software patching has become an integral part of software development, and is particularly important for systems that patch their code through wireless communication e.g. wireless sensor networks, and mobile embedded systems.

There have been efforts to design energy efficient post-deployment code dissemination in wireless sensor networks. Early schemes focused more on the protocol design and usually disseminated the entire new code [25, 6]. Recent schemes widely adopted the *diff*-based strategy. Reijers *et al.* [23] proposed simple update primitives to summarize the difference between new and old binaries, and disseminate the update script instead of the complete new code. Since without having the prior knowledge of code structure, Jeong *et al.* adapted the *rsync* algorithm to generate hashes of fixed code blocks from which the update script can be derived. Li *et al.* proposed update-conscious register allocation and data allocation techniques for applications using *base-register-plus-offset* addressing mode [18].

Patching code at higher semantic levels tends to generate smaller update script. Levis *et al.* showed that the code size is very short when they are represented using virtual machine instructions. Marron *et al.* proposed to produce separate object files for TinyOS components linked by the sensor [19]. Dunkels *et al.* further proposed a dynamical linker for this system [5]. Koshy *et al.* proposed to relocated modules and generate the binary using a remote linker [10]. A drawback of releasing code not in the binary format is the increased runtime overhead, which might not be acceptable for tightly resource-constrained embedded systems.

We need algorithms that support efficient binary code update as DSP code is often highly optimized or even hand tuned to ensure performance and is released only in binary format. The update-conscious offset assignment algorithm in this paper is, to the best of our knowledge, the first such algorithm for DSP processors.

7.2 Offset assignment problem on DSP processors

Allocating variables to memory on DSP processors was formulated as offset assignment problem by Bartley et al. [2] and Liao et al. [13]. Liao et al. modeled the problem as finding the maximum weight path cover (MWPC) of the access graph [13]. Leupers et al. extended their work by proposing a *tie-breaking* heuristic in building access graphs and a variable partition heuristic for GOA [14]. Atri et al. improved the heuristic with an incremental SOA algorithm [1]. Sudarsanam et al. presented their algorithm [24] when the hardware supports auto addressing range [-L,+L]. Rao et al. proposed to reorder variables accessed in operations with commutative operands [22]. Choi et al. coupled offset assignment with code scheduling to minimize addressing instructions [3]. Kandemir et al. proposed more aggressive intra- and inter- statement transformation for reordering access sequences [9]. A genetic algorithm (GA) based algorithm was proposed by Leupers et al. [15] to handle multiple registers with addressing range [-L,+L]. Leupers constructed the Offsetstone benchmark suite [20] and conducted empirical comparison of major assignment heuristics [16]. A more comprehensive bibliography can also be found at this website [20].

Zhuang et al [26] and Ottoni et al. [21] independently developed algorithms to optimize offset assignment based on variable coalescing — variables that are not alive simultaneously can be allocated in the same memory location. They reported around 70% stack size reduction for both SOA and GOA. Our scheme is orthogonal to existing offset assignment heuristics and explores the offset algorithm space from a new direction.

8. Conclusions

In this paper we proposed an efficient code update scheme for achieving the best tradeoff between minimized update script size, compact binary size, and the runtime performance. Our study showed that, due to DSP code being closely coupled to data layout in memory, it is effective to perform incremental offset assignment such that the code similarity of the new and old code can be improved.

Acknowledgment

This work is supported in part by NSF CNS-0720595, NSF CAREER CCF-0641177. The authors thank anonymous reviewers for their constructive comments.The authors thank Dr. Jiang Zheng for the early discussion of the idea, and anonymous reviewers for their constructive comments.

References

[1] S. Atri, J. Ramanujam, and M. Kandemir, "Improving Offset Assignment for Embedded Processors," In *Languages and Compilers for High-Performance Computing*, S. Midkiff et al. (eds.), LNCS, Springer, 2001.

[2] D.H. Bartley, "Optimizing Stack Frame Accesses for Processors with Restricted Addressing Modes," In *Software: Practice and Experience*, 22(2):101–110, 1992.

[3] Y. Choi, and T. Kim, "Address Assignment Combined with Scheduling in DSP Code Generation," In *Design Automation Conference*, 2002.

[4] DSPStone Benchmark Suite, *http://www.iss.rwth-aachen.de/Projekte/Tools/DSPSTONE.*

[5] A. Dunkels, N. Finne, J. Eriksson, and T. Voigt, "Run-Time Dynamic Linking for Reprogramming Wireless Sensor Networks," In *ACM International Conference on Embedded Networked Sensor Systems*, pp. 15–28, 2006.

[6] J. W. Hui, and D. Culler, "The Dynamic Behavior of a Data Dissemination Protocol for Network Programming at Scale," In *the 2nd ACM Conference on Embedded Networked Sensor Systems*, 2004.

[7] iPhone manual. http://www.apple.com.

[8] J. Jeong, and D. Culler, "Incremental Network Programming for Wireless Sensors," In *International Conference on Sensor and Ad Hoc Communications and Networks*, 2004.

[9] M. Kandemir, M. J. Irwin , G. Chen and J. Ramanujam, "Address Register Assignment for Reducing Code Size," In *the 12th International Conference on Compiler Construction*, 2003.

[10] J. Koshy, and R. Pandey, "Remote Incremental Linking for Energy-Efficient Reprogramming of Sensor Networks," In *European Workshop on Wireless Sensor Networks*, pp. 354–365, 2005.

[11] Lance Compiler *http://www.lancecompiler.com/.*

[12] P. Lapsley, J. Bier, A. Shoham, and EA Lee, "DSP Processor Fundamentals: Architectures and Features," Berkeley Design Technology, Inc., 1996.

[13] S. Liao, S. Devadas, K. Keutzer, S. Tjiang, and A. Wang, "Storage Assignment to Decrease Code Size," In *ACM Transactions on Programming Language and Systems*, 18(3):235-253, 1996.

[14] R. Leupers, and P. Marwedel, "Algorithms for Address Assignment in DSP Code Generation," In *International Conference on Computer Aided Design*, pp. 109-112, 1996.

[15] R. Leupers and F. David, "A Uniform Optimization Technique for Offset Assignment Problems," In *International Symposium on System Synthesis*, pp. 3–8, 1998.

[16] R. Leupers, "Offset Assignment Showdown: Evaluation of DSP Address Code Optimization Algorithms," In *the 12th International Conference on Compiler Construction*, 2003.

[17] P. Levis, and D. Culler, "Mate: A Tiny Virtual Machine for Sensor Networks," In *International Conference on Architectural Support for Programming Languages and Operating Systems*, pp. 85–95, 2002.

[18] W. Li, Y. Zhang, J. Yang, and J. Zheng, "UCC: Update-conscious Compilation for Energy Efficiency in Wireless Sensor Networks," In *ACM SIGPLAN Conference on Programming Language Design and Implementation*, 2007.

[19] P. J. Marron, M. Gauger, A. Lachenmann, D. Minder, O. Saukh, and K. Rothermel, "FlexCup: A Flexible and Efficient Code Update Mechanism for Sensor Networks," In *European Workshop on Wireless Sensor Networks*, pp. 212–227, 2006.

[20] OffsetStone Benchmark Suite, *http://www.address-code-optimization.org.*

[21] D. Ottoni, G. Otoni, G. Unicamp, and R. Leupers, "Offset Assignment Using Simultaneous Variable Coalescing," In *ACM Transactions on Embedded Computing Systems*, 5(4):864-883, 2006.

[22] A. Rao, and S. Pande, "Storage Assignment Optimizations to Generate Compact and Efficient Code on Embedded DSPs," In *ACM SIGPLAN Conference on Programming Language Design and Implementation*, pp. 128-138, 1999.

[23] N. Reijers, and K. Langendoen, "Efficient Code Distribution in Wireless Sensor Networks," In *International Workshop on Wireless Sensor Network Architecture*, pp. 60–67, 2003.

[24] A. Sudarsanam, S. Liao, and S. Devadas, "Analysis and Evaluation of Address Arithmetic Capabilities in Custom DSP Architectures," In *Design Automation Conference*, pp. 287–292, 1997.

[25] Crossbow Technology Inc. "Mote In-Network Programming User Reference," 2003.

[26] X. Zhuang, C. Lau, and S. Pande, "Storage Assignment Optimizations through Variable Coalescence for Embedded Processors," In *the International Conference on Languages, Compilers, and Tools for Embedded Systems*, 2003.

Elastic Computing: A Framework for Transparent, Portable, and Adaptive Multi-core Heterogeneous Computing

John R. Wernsing, Dr. Greg Stitt

University of Florida
Department of Electrical & Computer Engineering
Gainesville, FL, USA
wernsing@ufl.edu, gstitt@ece.ufl.edu

Abstract

Over the past decade, system architectures have started on a clear trend towards increased parallelism and heterogeneity, often resulting in speedups of 10x to 100x. Despite numerous compiler and high-level synthesis studies, usage of such systems has largely been limited to device experts, due to significantly increased application design complexity. To reduce application design complexity, we introduce elastic computing – a framework that separates functionality from implementation details by enabling designers to use specialized functions, called elastic functions, which enable an optimization framework to explore thousands of possible implementations, even ones using different algorithms. Elastic functions allow designers to execute the *same application code* efficiently on potentially any architecture and for different runtime parameters such as input size, battery life, etc. In this paper, we present an initial elastic computing framework that transparently optimizes application code onto diverse systems, achieving significant speedups ranging from 1.3x to 46x on a hyper-threaded Xeon system with an FPGA accelerator, a 16-CPU Opteron system, and a quad-core Xeon system.

Categories and Subject Descriptors J.6 [*Computer-Aided Engineering*]: Computer-aided design (CAD).

General Terms Performance, Design

Keywords elastic computing; heterogeneous architectures; multi-core; FPGA; speedup

1. Introduction

The power bottleneck caused by increasing clock frequencies has led to a trend towards increased parallelism, most notably with multi-core microprocessors [13][15][28], in addition to increased diversity via heterogeneous processing resources specialized for different tasks. Such heterogeneity often includes accelerators such as field-programmable gate arrays (FPGAs) and graphics processing units (GPUs), which numerous studies have shown to achieve 10x to 100x speedups over microprocessors for many applications [5][11][18]. Due to these significant performance improvements, the combination of multi-cores and heterogeneity,

referred to as *multi-core heterogeneous systems* for simplicity, is becoming increasingly common in domains ranging from low-power embedded systems [6][28][32], to high-performance embedded computing [16][31], to high-performance computing (HPC) systems [4][24].

Although multi-core heterogeneous systems provide significant improvements, effective use of such systems has mainly been limited to experts due to an increase in application design complexity. Numerous approaches have aimed to reduce design complexity for such systems by hiding low-level details using improved compilation [9] and high-level synthesis [12][26]. Similarly, new languages have been introduced to ease parallel programming [2][3][7].

Although these previous approaches have had some impact on productivity, a fundamental limitation of previous work is the specification of an application as a single implementation. Much prior work [10][27] has shown that different implementations of the same application often have widely varying performances on different architectures, which we refer to as the *implementation portability problem*. For example, a designer implementing a sorting function may use a merge-sort or bitonic-sort algorithm to create an FPGA implementation but a quick-sort algorithm to create a microprocessor implementation. Furthermore, this problem extends beyond efficiency for a particular architecture. Different algorithms operate more efficiently for different input sizes [23], different amounts of resources [8], and potentially any other runtime parameter. Although existing tools can perform transformations to optimize an implementation, *those transformations cannot convert between algorithms* (e.g., quick-sort into merge-sort), which is often required for efficiency on a particular device. Thus, even with improved compilers, synthesis tools, and languages, efficient application design for multi-core heterogeneous systems will still require significant designer effort, limiting usage to device and algorithm experts.

To address these limitations, we propose a complementary approach, referred to as *elastic computing*, which enables transparent and portable application design for multi-core heterogeneous systems, while also enabling adaptation to different runtime conditions. Elastic computing, shown in Figure 1, is a framework, combining standard application code – potentially written in any language – with a library of specialized *elastic functions*, an *implementation planning* tool, and an *elastic computing system* runtime environment. As shown in Figure 1(a), elastic functions specify multiple implementations of the same functionality, possibly including calls to other elastic functions, which enables implementation planning to explore and even generate thousands of new implementations specialized for different situations such as

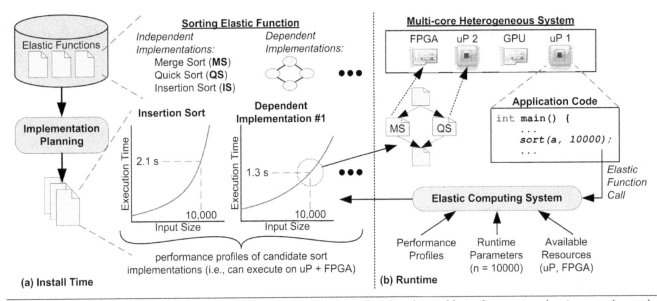

Figure 1. An overview of *elastic computing*, which is enabled by (a) *elastic functions* that enable *implementation planning* to explore and even generate different implementations specialized for parameters such as input size, available resources, etc. (b) When an executing application calls an elastic function, the *elastic computing system* selects the quickest implementation based on the current runtime parameters and available resources. Note that no changes to the application code are required to use different resources.

different input sizes, resource combinations, and potentially even remaining battery life, current power consumption, etc. Note that the naming convention used in this paper is to refer to an algorithm using hyphened form (e.g., merge-sort) and the corresponding implementation using proper noun form (e.g., Merge Sort).

One key advantage of elastic computing is the complete separation of functionality from implementation details. As shown in Figure 1(b) for a sorting example, the application designer simply calls an elastic sorting function without specifying how that sort is implemented. Instead, the elastic function call invokes the elastic computing system which analyzes runtime parameters and selects the most efficient implementation for the current situation by using performance profiles previously determined during implementation planning. Thus, without any effort or knowledge of the architecture, the application designer in this example is able to execute a sorting implementation that elastic computing automatically specializes for the current architecture, taking advantage of the FPGA as well as a microprocessor. While previous work has shown such optimization for specific systems, applications, and languages, to our knowledge, elastic computing is the first generalized technique that potentially enables invisible optimization of any application for any system.

Elastic computing is largely intended to enable mainstream application designers, who often lack the skills required for programming specialized devices, to take advantage of such devices with minimal effort. Of course, for elastic computing to be widely used, an elastic function library must be provided to these application designers. We envision that such a library could be created for different domains, with implementations being provided by device vendors (e.g., Xilinx, Nvidia) interested in attracting a new market of users, third parties (e.g., Rapidmind [20]), or even by open-source efforts. As opposed to only improving productivity of mainstream application designers, elastic computing also provides mechanisms that make implementation design of elastic functions less complex than existing multi-core heterogeneous design. A complete discussion of possible usage scenarios is discussed in Section 6.

The paper is organized as follows. Section 2 discusses related work. Section 3 defines elastic functions. Section 4 discusses implementation planning. Section 5 describes the elastic computing system. Section 6 summarizes elastic computing usage scenarios, advantages, and limitations. Section 7 presents experimental results.

2. Related Work

The implementation portability problem was addressed by Grattan [10], who introduced codesign-extended applications that specified multiple implementations of a function, which enabled a compiler to explore multiple possibilities for hardware and software implementations. Although that approach achieved improvements in portability and efficiency, application designers had to manually specify multiple implementations, resulting in decreased productivity. With elastic computing, for cases where an appropriate elastic function is provided, application designers do not specify any implementation details and instead simply call elastic functions, with efficient implementations of those functions determined by the elastic computing system.

Previous work on adaptable software also shares similarities with elastic computing. FFTW (Fastest Fourier Transform in the West) [8] is an adaptive implementation of FFT that tunes an implementation by composing small blocks of functionality, called codelets, in different ways based on the particular architecture. OSKI (Optimized Sparse Kernel Interface) [29] is a similar library of automatically-tuned sparse matrix kernels. ATLAS [30] is a software package of linear algebra kernels that are capable of automatically tuning themselves to different architectures. Such approaches are essentially examples of manually created elastic functions for particular devices. PetaBricks [1] consists of a language and compiler that enables algorithmic choice, but restricts parallelizing decisions to static choices. Qilin [17] can dynamically determine an effective partitioning of work across heterogeneous resources, but targets data-parallel operations. Elastic computing aims to provide a general framework that enables any elastic

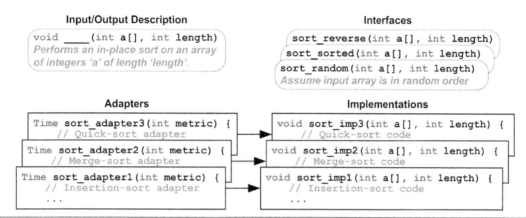

Figure 2. Components of an example sorting elastic function.

3. Elastic Functions

Elastic functions form the basis of elastic computing by hiding implementation details, allowing the application designer to simply call the elastic function and rely on the elastic computing system to make all of the implementation decisions. As shown in Figure 2 for a sorting example, elastic functions consist of four components: an *input/output* description, a set of *interfaces*, a set of *implementations,* and an *adapter* for each implementation.

The input/output description defines the input and output parameters for the elastic function, similar to a C-function prototype. Although not used by the elastic computing system, the input/output description also includes a semantic description of the parameters. For example, in Figure 2, the input/output description specifies that the function accepts two parameters, the first parameter being a pointer to an integer array which should be sorted in-place, and the second parameter being the size of the array.

Elastic function interfaces are function prototypes that are exposed to standard programming languages, which enable an application designer to invoke an elastic function. Unlike standard functions, elastic functions provide one or more interfaces that enable the application designer to inform the elastic computing system of specific assumptions. For example, because different sorting implementations have different performances based on the characteristics of the input data (e.g., randomly distributed, mostly sorted), interfaces enable the designer to describe those characteristics so that the elastic computing system can make better implementation selection decisions. As shown in Figure 2, the elastic function can provide a separate interface for sorting randomly distributed data, in which case the elastic computing system may select a Quick Sort implementation, in addition to an interface for sorting mostly sorted data, in which case the elastic computing system may select an Insertion Sort implementation. Each interface is invoked identically (i.e., adheres to the same input/output description).

The main difference between standard functions and elastic functions is that elastic functions define one or more possible implementations, each of which adheres to the input/output description. We categorize the implementations into two groups: *independent implementations* and *dependent implementations*. Independent implementations are binary executables for a specific combination of resources, which can be created using any language or compiler/synthesis tool. For example, a sorting elastic function may have independent implementations that rely on different algorithms (e.g., quick-sort, insertion-sort, merge-sort) and different resource combinations (e.g., microprocessor, FPGA, GPU, microprocessor+FPGA, microprocessor+GPU).

Dependent implementations are defined similarly to independent implementations, but also internally call one or more elastic functions (i.e., the implementation *depends* on functionality provided by other elastic functions). For each elastic function call in the dependent implementation, the elastic computing system selects a corresponding implementation at runtime, which may be dependent or independent. For example, a dependent implementation of a *Sort* elastic function may internally rely on elastic functions for *Split*, *Merge*, and *Sort*. By referring to other elastic functions, dependent implementations effectively create degrees of freedom that enable the elastic computing system to create completely new implementations for different situations. Dependent implementations also have the advantage of specifying explicit task-level parallelism.

Each implementation additionally provides an adapter that allows implementation planning to configure the input parameters of the implementation, as described in detail in the following section.

4. Implementation Planning

Implementation planning analyzes elastic function implementations and the execution resources of the system to determine a "plan" that identifies the most efficient implementation of each elastic function for all combinations of resources, input parameters, and interfaces. Such planning is necessary to minimize the runtime overhead of implementation selection in the elastic computing system, which is discussed in Section 5. Implementation planning executes when the elastic computing framework is installed on a system, when the elastic function library changes (e.g., new implementations are added), or when new resources are added to a system (e.g., adding an FPGA board).

Implementation planning outputs a *performance profile* for every valid combination of elastic function interface, execution resources, and implementation. The performance profile consists of a set of statistically significant points, referred to as *significant points*, that represent execution times for different input parameters, which the elastic computing system can use to estimate the

```
ImplementationPlanning( e_library, resources )
begin
  do
    foreach Combination r of resources
      foreach Interface e in e_library
        foreach Implementation i that supports e
          a = i.GetAdapter();
          profiles[r,e,i] = a.CreateProfile(r,e);
        endfor;
      endfor;
    endfor;
  loop until AllProfilesStabilized(profiles);
  return profiles;
end;
```

Figure 3. High-level steps of implementation planning.

execution time of an implementation for any combination of input parameters via linear interpolation. Specifically, the performance profile represents a two-dimensional plot with an abstraction referred to as the *metric* on the X-axis and execution time on the Y-axis. Implementation planning internally uses the metric as an abstract representation of the input parameters to an implementation. The adapter for each implementation provides a mapping between metric and input parameters. For example, one possible adapter for an Insertion Sort implementation may map the metric value to the size of the sort. In this example, the estimated execution time for any invocation of the Insertion Sort can be found by simply looking up the Y-value (i.e., execution time) in the performance profile when the X-value (i.e., metric) is equal to the size of the sort. More complicated adapter mappings are discussed in Section 4.1.

By comparing the performance profiles of multiple implementations for an elastic function interface, the elastic computing system can determine the fastest overall implementation for a given combination of execution resources and input parameters. For example, Figure 1 demonstrates a sorting elastic function with several possible implementations (e.g., Insertion Sort, Merge Sort, Quick Sort). For simplicity, the example assumes that the adapter maps input size directly to metric. The call to the **sort**() from the application code specifies that a sort for 10,000 elements is required. The elastic computing system uses the performance profiles for each of the implementations, evaluated at a metric of 10,000, to estimate the execution time of each implementation. The elastic computing system then selects the implementation with the fastest estimated execution time, a dependent implementation in this case, and initiates its execution on the available execution resources. Note that this is just one example and different input parameters, implementations, or execution resources could affect the decision.

Figure 3 shows the high-level steps of the implementation planning algorithm. The input to the algorithm is a library of elastic functions (**e_library**) and the resources available on the system (**resources**). For each iteration of the innermost loop, the algorithm first obtains the implementation's adapter to convert the profiled metric values to the input parameters (Section 4.1), and then creates a new performance profile using that adapter for a specific combination of elastic function interface and execution resources, using a heuristic described in Section 4.2. For dependent implementations, the profiles of other implementations may affect the performance of the current implementation. As a result,

the outermost loop repeats the profiling process until all the profiles stabilize, as described in Section 4.3. Section 4.4 discusses limitations of the algorithm.

4.1 Adapter

One challenge is that implementation planning must create performance profiles for any type of implementation and elastic function interface. Different implementations require different types and amounts of resources to execute, and every implementation has varying requirements on its input and output parameters. Some implementations may even require allocation and initialization of secondary data structures (e.g., a sorting implementation expecting an array of integers as input). Additionally, different elastic function interfaces may require different types of parameter initializations (e.g., populating an array with randomly distributed data as opposed to mostly sorted data). Abstracting these implementation and elastic function interface details are the purpose of the adapter.

The implementation planner relies solely on an abstract value, referred to as the metric, to represent the input parameters for any implementation. The adapter internally provides mappings between the metric and input parameters. The adapter also provides functionality to empirically measure the execution time of an implementation for a given metric value. Specifically, the implementation planner can call the adapter passing in a metric value. The adapter internally performs any necessary initialization to execute the implementation, maps the metric value to corresponding input parameters, and then executes the implementation while measuring its execution time. The adapter then returns the resulting execution time, which the heuristic can use to locate the significant points and construct the performance profile, as described in Section 4.2.

The complexity of the adapter itself depends mostly on the difficulty of creating a mapping between input parameters and the metric. Many implementations can have their execution time predominantly dictated by a single input parameter. For example, the size of the input array predominantly determines the execution time for an Insertion Sort implementation. In these cases, an adapter design would typically map the metric directly to that input parameter (e.g., map the metric to be the size of the sort) and have the remaining parameters appropriately populated (e.g., allocate an array of randomly distributed data to be sorted). For more complicated implementations, other techniques such as algorithmic complexity analysis can be used to determine a mapping. Algorithmic complexity analysis takes advantage of an in-depth understanding of the factors involved in the algorithm's execution time to find an appropriate metric mapping. For example, one algorithm to implement circular convolution results in a complexity analysis of $\Theta(|a|*|b|)$, that is the execution time is proportional to the product of the two input operands. An obvious direct mapping in this case is not possible as the size of both operands significantly affect the execution time of the implementation. However, if it is assumed that the proportionality factor in the complexity analysis remains approximately constant, then one possible adapter for this algorithm would be to map the metric to be the length of one of the operands and to fix the length of the second operand to be one. The reverse mapping from input parameters to metric would then be to set the metric equal to the product of the lengths of the two input parameters. This mapping works as the product is the same. For example, if the performance profile specifies that convolving 1,000,000 elements (mapped to metric) and 1 element (constant) takes 2 seconds, then the estimated execution time for convolving 1,000 elements and 1,000 elements should also be approximately 2 seconds.

To maximize prediction accuracy, the adapter should ideally meet specific assumptions made by the performance profile creation heuristic. First, the heuristic assumes that execution time is non-decreasing with increasing metric. Second, the heuristic assumes that execution time changes smoothly with small metric changes (i.e., no abrupt jumps). Lastly, the heuristic assumes that for a specific metric value, execution time is distributed normally amongst a constant mean. The closer the adapter meets these assumptions, the more accurate the resulting performance profile will be. However, even if the adapter does not perfectly meet any of these assumptions, the resulting profile is typically still usable albeit with reduced accuracy.

4.2 Performance Profile Creation

This section describes a heuristic for creating a performance profile for a single implementation on a given set of resources. Creating the performance profiles is one of the main challenges of implementation planning because unlike previous performance prediction work [14][25], each profile must predict performances for all combinations of input parameters.

The basic operation of the heuristic is to generate the performance profile by locating the metric value of each significant point based on prediction parameters discussed in the next paragraph. The heuristic estimates the location of significant points by empirically measuring the execution time of the implementation at several metric values, a process we refer to as *sampling*, and then analyzing sets of nearby samples using linear regression analysis.

The prediction parameters are defined when the elastic function library is installed, enabling different systems to tune the heuristic for specific devices. The first prediction parameter, which we refer to as $\alpha\%$, specifies the maximum allowed percent error of the performance profile. If it is assumed that execution time is non-decreasing with increasing metric, then spacing the significant points $\alpha\%$ apart, as illustrated in Figure 4, limits the maximum percent error for any point in between the significant points to be $\alpha\%$. The second prediction parameter, which we refer to as $\beta\%$, specifies the level of required confidence in the location of each significant point. Specifically, the parameter specifies the maximum percent width allowed for a confidence interval relative to its location. For example, if the linear regression analysis specifies that the execution time for a specific metric is 5 ± 1 seconds, which is also equal to $5\pm20\%$ seconds, the accuracy would not be deemed sufficient if $\beta\%$ was less-than 20%. The third prediction parameter is the confidence level used for confidence interval calculations. The last prediction parameter is the range of metric values for which the heuristic should generate the performance profile. The range of metric values may be different for every implementation.

Figure 4 illustrates the detailed operation of the heuristic. First, the heuristic starts at the smallest metric value, referred to as m_0, and collects enough samples at that metric value to be able to determine the execution time, referred to as t_0, for that metric within $\beta\%$ accuracy. The resulting (m_0, t_0) point is the first significant point of the performance profile. Second, the heuristic increments the execution time of the previous significant point (henceforth referred to a t_{n-1}) by $\alpha\%$ to determine the execution time of the current significant point ($t_n = t_{n-1} + \alpha\%$). Third, the heuristic identifies a subset of the samples, out of all the samples it has taken thus far, on which to perform a linear regression analysis for determining if it already knows the metric value of the current significant point (i.e., what m_n would yield an execution time of t_n) within the required $\beta\%$ accuracy. One way to pick this subset would be to consider only samples with an execution time between t_{n-1} and t_{n+1} (a more robust approach is discussed in the

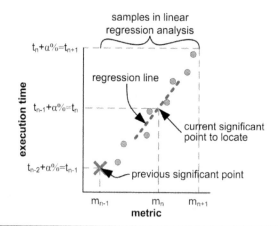

Figure 4. Illustration of performance profile generation.

following paragraph). Fourth, if there are not enough samples to determine the current significant point, the heuristic measures another sample and the process repeats. One way the heuristic could determine the metric value to sample would be to randomly pick a metric within the range between m_{n-1} and the metric of the first sample that has an execution time greater than t_{n+1} (a more robust approach is discussed in the next paragraph). Lastly, once the heuristic has enough samples to determine the current significant point within $\beta\%$ accuracy, the heuristic appends the significant point (m_n, t_n) to the performance profile and the process repeats with the next significant point. The heuristic completes once the linear regression analysis reveals that the current significant point would have a metric value greater-than the upper bound.

The procedure of selecting samples for the linear regression analysis, used in steps three and four of the previous discussion, made the assumption that samples are non-decreasing with increasing metric, which is generally not true as there is often some variance in execution time. A more robust approach is to not filter out samples based on their execution time alone, but instead filter based on the regression of the samples. To perform this filtering, the heuristic first sorts all of the samples in ascending metric order, finds the first sample with a metric greater-than or equal to the previous significant point's metric (m_{n-1}), and inserts that sample into a set S. Second, the heuristic inserts the next two samples, in sorted increasing metric order, also into S. Three samples are initially required to avoid a non-trivial linear regression analysis. Third, the heuristic performs a linear regression analysis on the samples in S and calculates the execution time that the regression line has for the largest metric in S, which is also the last sample in S as the samples are sorted. Fourth, if this calculated execution time is less-than t_{n+1} then the heuristic adds the next sample to S, also in increasing metric order, and repeats. Lastly, if the calculated execution time is greater-than or equal to t_{n+1} then the process is complete. By filtering based on the regression, the susceptibility of the heuristic to the variance inherent in the execution time of individual samples is reduced and the entire process becomes more robust.

Although a complete evaluation of the performance profile creation heuristic is outside the scope of this paper, we summarize the results as follows. In a test involving twelve different implementations having a variety of time complexities, with prediction parameters set to $\alpha\% = \beta\% = 5\%$, the heuristic on average required only 374 samples and created a performance profile with an average estimation error of 5.84% (calculated using 250 random combinations of input parameters for each implementation).

In fact, five of the twelve implementations had a prediction error of less than 1%, with only one of the implementations having an error of greater than 12%. Additionally, the tests showed that when the prediction parameters were set to $\alpha\% = \beta\% = 50\%$ (a 10x increase in allowed error), the average number of samples dropped to 52, resulting in a 6x speedup of the heuristic, yet the average estimation error increased only to 6.1%.

4.3 Performance Profile Stabilization

Because dependent implementations internally call elastic functions, their performance profiles are dependent on the performance profiles of the fastest implementation of each called elastic function. This interdependence results in performance profiles that may improve (i.e., are unstable) after every iteration of the implementation planning algorithm. For example, if an updated performance profile reveals a quicker implementation for sorting 10,000 elements, this would improve the execution time and change the resulting performance profile for any dependent implementation of any elastic function that happens to internally call a sort for 10,000 elements.

Implementation planning iterates until the performance profiles show no improvement, which we refer to as profile stabilization. An upper bound on the number of iterations required for stabilization is equal to the deepest call-stack achievable by the dependent implementations (regardless of which elastic functions are actually called). In practice, the profiles often stabilize after only a few iterations due to dependent implementations being used only to parallelize the elastic function, and independent implementations being used to actually perform the computation on individual resources. As a result, the dependent implementation call stack is only a few levels deep reflecting only the partitioning required by the elastic function. For the evaluated applications, the profiles stabilized after only three iterations.

4.4 Limitations

The main limitations of the implementation planning algorithm correspond to difficulties in creating an effective adapter for an implementation. First, an implementation must provide a way to map a metric to input parameters. Implementations that are not deterministic or exhibit widely varying execution times are not suitable. Second, architecture specific effects may reduce the accuracy of the performance profiles. Cache flushing, data alignment, and CPU pre-emption will add a level of variation to execution time measurements. However, in most cases these variations are relatively small and can be ignored. Third, some performance profiles will have reduced accuracy for corner cases. Corner cases are small subsets of input parameter combinations to an implementation that force the execution time to not follow the general trend. For example, a Quick Sort implementation exhibits an algorithmic time complexity of $O(n \log n)$ for randomly distributed data but $O(n^2)$ for already sorted data, where 'n' is the number of elements to sort. In this case, a performance profile generated using randomly distributed data would have a large percent error if used to estimate the execution time for sorting already sorted data. However, elastic computing alleviates the affect of corner cases by enabling the designer to specify usage assumptions, such as by having separate interfaces for sorting randomly distributed data and sorting mostly sorted data.

5. Elastic Computing System

The elastic computing system, illustrated in Figure 5, serves two main purposes. First, when an application invokes an elastic function, the elastic computing system analyzes the current available resources and invocation parameters of the elastic function, and then selects the fastest implementation based on the performance profiles from implementation planning. Second, the elastic computing system provides runtime services (e.g., resource allocation, device abstraction, and communication), to support the implementations until the elastic function is complete.

The elastic computing system is invoked whenever an application or a dependent implementation calls an elastic function via one the function's interfaces. When an application calls an elastic function, the elastic computing system will by default allocate all available resources to that elastic function, although the application designer has the option to explicitly state which resources to use. When a dependent implementation calls an elastic function, the implementation itself allocates a subset of its resources to use for that call.

With the combination of the elastic function invocation parameters, the list of resources, and the corresponding interface used by the application, the elastic computing system determines the fastest implementation for the current situation. The elastic computing system determines the fastest implementation for an elastic function by computing the estimated execution time of each candidate implementation and selecting the fastest. Only the implementations that support the corresponding elastic function interface and that can execute on a subset of the available resources are considered (e.g., the elastic computing system cannot select an FPGA implementation if an FPGA is not available). For each of those implementations, the corresponding performance profile is used to estimate the execution time given the actual input parameters of the interface's invocation. If a performance profile does not contain a significant point that corresponds to the current invocation parameters, the elastic computing system uses linear interpolation to estimate the execution time.

After selecting the fastest implementation, the elastic computing system executes the implementation within its own execution context, which defines the group of resources allocated for that implementation. The resources are categorized into two types: primary and secondary. Primary resources are controlled by the elastic computing system and are instructed of which implementation to execute. With the current version of the elastic computing system, only CPU's can be primary resources, although the framework could be extended to consider other resources. Secondary resources (e.g., FPGA's) are associated with the execution context but are not directly controlled. Instead, the implementation itself, running on the primary resources, has the option to take control of any secondary resources within its same execution context (e.g., an implementation running on a CPU instructing an FPGA to perform some computation).

Before executing a selected implementation, the elastic computing system first sets up the execution context and then starts the implementation's execution on all of the primary resources. Each primary resource executes the same implementation. All of the invocation parameters are passed into the implementation, as well as an extra parameter that specifies the execution context. It is through the execution context parameter that the different instances of the implementation can communicate with each other. In this way, the implementation running on the primary resources are similar to a single-instruction-multiple-data (SIMD) function. Additionally, the execution context is similar to an MPI Communicator.

When dependent implementations internally invoke an elastic function call, the implementation has the option to partition the execution context into multiple sub-contexts. Each sub-context is independent of each other and can execute different elastic functions and/or pass different parameters. It is through this mechan-

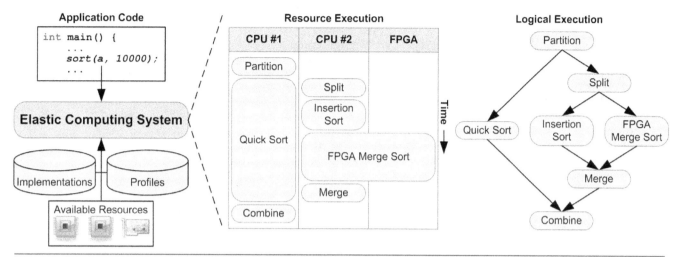

Figure 5. When an application executes an elastic function, the *elastic computing system* uses the performance profiles from implementation planning to select and execute the fastest implementation for the available resources and input parameters.

ism that the elastic computing system allows task-level parallelism.

The elastic function is complete when the outermost implementation finishes. At this point, the elastic computing system returns control to the originating application, which resumes execution.

Figure 5 illustrates an example of the elastic computing system, showing the independent implementations selected for a sorting elastic function (details regarding execution contexts and dependent implementations are omitted for brevity). When the application executes the **sort()** interface function, the interface invokes the elastic computing system, which searches for the fastest implementation for an input size of 10,000 and available resources consisting of two CPU's and one FPGA. The elastic computing system uses the performance profiles of the candidate implementations and determines that the fastest implementation is a dependent implementation. The dependent implementation first partitions the input using a CPU and then invokes two additional elastic sorting functions, executing in parallel, to sort the partitioned data. For one of those functions, the elastic computing system determines the fastest implementation is a Quick Sort implementation. For the other function, the elastic computing system selects another dependent implementation that first splits the data and then uses Insertion Sort running on a CPU and Merge Sort running on an FPGA to sort the split data. The elastic computing system then selects a Merge implementation to merge the results from the Insertion Sort and FPGA Merge Sort. Finally, the outer-most dependent implementation executes a Combine implementation to combine the results into the final sorted output. The logical execution, ignoring timing, is shown on the right side of the figure. Note that all of the information used to determine the fastest implementation is saved in the performance profiles from the implementation planning step.

6. Usage Scenarios

The main target for elastic computing is mainstream, non-device-expert application designers who are solely concerned with specifying functionality and often lack the expertise required to design efficient functions for multi-core heterogeneous systems. Motivating examples include domain scientists, such as computational biologists/chemists, who commonly write applications in C/Fortran and MPI, and would like to use multi-core heterogene-

ous systems without becoming experts in FPGA's, GPU's, etc. [21]. Although elastic computing improves upon previous approaches by using multiple implementations, assuming that appropriate elastic function libraries are available, application designers do not need to create these implementations. In the ideal case, application designers would use elastic functions in the same way as existing, widely-used function libraries.

Of course, there may be situations where new implementations need to be created either to target new hardware or provide new functionality. Elastic computing aids the development of new implementations by providing an environment for implementation execution and allowing an implementation to call existing elastic functions. As discussed in Section 5, the elastic computing system provides communication and resource management features to the implementation. Additionally, as most implementations can be broken up into simpler steps (e.g., a convex hull implementation that internally relies on sorting), the implementation could be coded to internally call pre-existing elastic functions, thereby allowing even the individual steps to benefit from elastic computing. Lastly, elastic computing provides a framework for code reuse by allowing any developed implementation to be simply included as another implementation option for an elastic function. As a result, the more pervasive elastic computing becomes, the less often new implementations or elastic functions will need to be created.

We envision that elastic function libraries could potentially be created for different applications domains, where implementations (and corresponding adapters) of each elastic function are provided by several potential sources. Device vendors for specialized devices are one likely source for implementations, because by enabling transparent usage of their corresponding devices via elastic functions, those devices could potentially become useable by new markets (e.g., mainstream designers). For example, Xilinx could attract software designers by enabling transparent usage of their FPGA's via elastic function implementations for functionality common to specific domains. Third-party library designers such as Rapidmind [20], who already target specialized devices, could also provide implementations of elastic functions for numerous devices. Finally, open-source projects could potentially establish a standardized elastic function library that could be extended with implementations from all participants. In this situation, experts from different domains could provide implementations optimized for different situations and devices. With the ability of the elastic computing system to automatically identify fast implementations, mainstream application designers could transparently exploit an implementation specialized for any given situation without any knowledge of the actual implementation or situation.

6.1 Summary of Advantages

Transparency Elastic computing achieves transparency of implementation and architecture, enabling non-expert designers to take advantage of powerful multi-core heterogeneous systems. Elastic computing also achieves a more transparent integration into existing tool flows compared to new language approaches that have largely been resisted due to the inconvenience of modifying well-established tool flows. In most cases, taking advantage of elastic computing is a simple matter of replacing pre-existing function calls with their elastic function equivalents.

Portability Unlike existing applications, which without modifications typically do not improve in performance when executed on a system with more or different types of resources, elastic computing invisibly selects/creates implementations that can utilize extra resources to improve performance.

Adaptability Elastic computing can adapt the implementation of a function to runtime parameters and changes in resources. Elastic computing has the flexibility to take advantage of as many or as few computing resources as it deems would be most efficient. For embedded systems, elastic computing could be extended to automatically choose power-efficient implementations and avoid using certain computing resources when battery life is low. For space systems, elastic computing could potentially avoid using computing resources that have been flagged as being damaged or disabled. Previous work has implemented similar behavior manually, but has required significant designer effort and device expertise.

6.2 Summary of Limitations

The main limitation of elastic computing is that improvement in design productivity depends on the percentage of code that can be defined using elastic functions. Ideally, an elastic function library combined with vendor-provided implementations could provide most designers with the majority of functionality they require.

Potential limitations of implementation planning include the time required for implementation planning to complete and the accuracy of the resulting performance profiles. Implementation planning requires several executions of each implementation which may require a considerable amount of time, but this process is only required once for a system and can be amortized over its entire lifetime. Implementation planning creates performance profiles by empirically measuring the execution time of implementations executing on sample input data. The empirical measurements reflect system effects, such as cache size and memory latency, but cannot account for some run-time issues, such as non-representative input data and resource contention. However, these effects are normally not significant enough to affect run-time performance as the elastic computing system does not make decisions based on absolute execution time (i.e., "how long will this implementation take?") but only relative execution time (i.e., "which implementation is the fastest?"). None the less, reducing these errors is an on-going research challenge.

Another potential limitation is the runtime overhead of implementation selection by the elastic computing system. As shown in the results, the performance improvement of using an elastic function normally greatly outweighs the overhead of dynamically determining its implementation. For elastic functions that require

a very short execution time, the elastic computing system will likely immediately decide on an independent implementation, requiring the overhead of only a single implementation selection. None the less, repeated calls to elastic functions with extremely quick execution times could be dominated by the implementation selection overhead. For these cases, future work focuses on compile-time analysis of the source code to replace those elastic function calls with a pre-selected implementation, eliminating all runtime overhead.

7. Experiments
7.1 Experimental Setup

To perform elastic computing experiments, we developed the described implementation planning and elastic computing system tools in addition to several elastic functions. In total, over 11,000 lines of C++ code were required.

We implemented a *Sort* elastic function, in addition to nine others described later, with the following independent implementations: static size-2/3/4 sort network, in-place/out-of-place insertion-sort, heap-sort, quick-sort, and an FPGA-based in-place/out-of-place merge-sort. The following dependent implementations were also created: in-place/out-of-place parallel/serial merge-sort (i.e., two sorts followed by merging the results) and in-place/out-of-place parallel/serial quick-sort (i.e., a partition followed by two sorts). To enable these dependent implementations, we also created independent implementations for elastic functions to perform a partition (first-step of a quick-sort implementation) and a merge (last-step of a merge-sort implementation). All microprocessor-based code was written in C++ and compiled using g++ 3.4.4 with –O3 optimizations. All FPGA-based code was written in VHDL and compiled using Xilinx ISE 9.2i.

We evaluated the elastic computing framework on three diverse systems. The first was a 3.2 GHz hyper-threaded Intel Xeon microprocessor with a Nallatech H101-PCIXM FPGA accelerator [24], which has a Xilinx Virtex IV LX100. The second was a 2.4 GHz 16-CPU AMD Opteron 880 system (8 dual-core microprocessors) with no FPGA's. The third was a 2.4 GHz quad-core Intel Xeon also with no FPGA's.

All results represent total execution time, including elastic computing overhead, communication times, etc. The only overhead not included is the configuring of the FPGA with the bitfile, as all VHDL code was compiled into a single bitfile that was pre-loaded at application startup. The baseline comparisons were written using hand-optimized serial code to represent a fair alternative to using elastic functions when targeting an arbitrary system. To ensure accuracy, each result is the average of several executions.

7.2 Results

Figure 6 illustrates the portability advantages of elastic computing for the *sort* elastic function with an input of 4,194,304 elements, running on the 16-CPU Opteron system. The baseline is a Quick Sort function running on a single CPU. As more resources are allocated, the elastic function automatically takes advantage of the additional computing power without any coding changes, resulting in a speedup of over 4x for 16 CPU's.

Figure 7 illustrates similar advantages of several elastic functions for embedded systems, each of which includes microprocessor and FPGA-based independent implementations, running on the Xeon/Nallatech system. *Sort* is the previously described sort elastic function with an input of 4,194,304 elements. *Prewitt* performs Prewitt edge detection on a 640x480 pixel image. *Conv* (convolution) convolves a 1 million length vector with a 256 length vector, with each element being single-precision floating-point. *MM* (matrix multiply) multiplies two 1024x1024 matrices

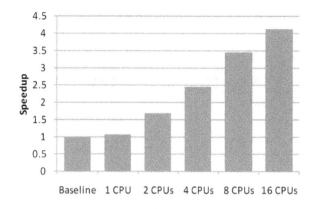

Figure 6. Portability of a *Sort* elastic function, illustrated by increasing speedup when allocated additional resources.

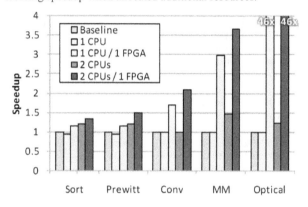

Figure 7. Speedups illustrating elastic computing portability for several elastic functions running on a hyper-threaded Intel Xeon system with a Nallatech H101-PCIXM FPGA accelerator.

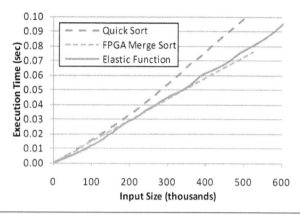

Figure 8. Elastic computing adaptability for a hyper-threaded Intel Xeon system with a Nallatech H101-PCIXM FPGA accelerator, showing that for all input sizes, elastic computing achieves the best (or near best) implementation.

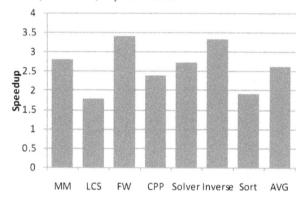

Figure 9. Elastic computing speedup on a quad-core Intel Xeon system for several elastic functions, compared to serial baselines.

using single-precision floating-point. *Optical* (optical flow) creates a two-dimensional match statistic map for a 17x17 template in a 640x480 pixel image. In all cases, elastic computing enables the application to gain significant speedup, ranging from 1.3x to 46x, by transparently taking advantage of the multiple cores and FPGA. The large 46x speedup of the *Optical* implementation is due to the FPGA exploiting a significantly larger amount of parallelism compared to the other examples.

Figure 8 illustrates the adaptability of elastic computing by comparing the performance between the independent implementations of sort and the elastic function. The results are shown across different input sizes running on the Xeon/Nallatech system. For all possible input sizes, elastic computing either achieved the fastest implementation or had a minimal overhead. For input sizes greater than 512k, elastic computing significantly out-performed the individual implementations. Note that the FPGA Merge Sort implementation only supports input sizes less than 512k elements due to limited on-board memory; however, the elastic function can still make use of it with larger input sizes by relying on dependent implementations to partition larger input sizes into multiple sub-sorts.

Figure 9 illustrates speedups of several additional elastic functions, chosen from graph analysis, computational geometry, and linear algebra, running on the quad-core Xeon system, compared to serial baselines. For each elastic function, we created a parallel independent implementation. *MM* (matrix multiply) multiplies

two 1000x1000 matrices using single-precision floating-point. *LCS* (longest common subsequence) determines the longest common subsequence between two 2,500 character strings. *FW* (Floyd-Warshall) finds the shortest path between 1,000 vertices in a weighted directed graph. *CPP* (closest-point pair) determines the closest pair of points from 1,000,000 points in a two-dimensional space. *Solver* solves a system of 1,000 linear equations. *Inverse* inverts a 1000x1000 floating point matrix. *Sort* is the previously described sorting function with 4,194,304 elements. In all cases, elastic computing transparently selected/created parallel implementations for each elastic function, resulting in speedup that ranged from 1.8x for *LCS* to 3.4x for *FW*, achieving an average speedup of 2.6x.

Note that although these speedups were obtained by using extra resources, the significance of elastic computing is that *no coding modifications were required to use those resources*. To our knowledge, no previous study has shown improved performance for such diverse systems without manual code modifications.

8. Conclusions

In this paper, we introduced a framework for elastic computing that is capable of separating functionality from implementation details, allowing application designers to more easily exploit the performance potential of multi-core heterogeneous systems. With elastic computing, the application designer simply specifies functionality in terms of elastic functions, which the elastic computing framework converts into specialized implementations through a combination of implementation planning and the elastic computing system. We evaluated elastic computing on three diverse systems, showing that the framework invisibly achieved speedup (no coding changes were required) for different resource amounts. Furthermore, we showed that elastic computing can adapt to run-time parameters, such as input size, achieving performance significantly better than the individual implementations, even with the overhead of the elastic computing system. Overall, elastic computing achieved significant speedup, ranging from 1.3x to 46x, without any changes to the application code and without any designer effort. Future work includes evaluation of different resources (e.g., GPU's), reduction of run-time overhead for elastic function calls with input parameters partially known at compile-time, and implementation planning for power consumption.

Acknowledgments

This research was supported by the National Science Foundation (CNS-0914474).

References

[1] J. Ansel, C. Chan, Y.L. Wong, M. Olszewskim, Q. Zhao, A. Edelman, and S. Amarasinghe. PetaBricks: A Language and Compiler for Algorithmic Choice. Proceedings of the ACM SIGPLAN Conference on Programming Language Design and Implementation (PLDI), 2009, pp. 38-49.

[2] B. Chamberlain, D. Callahan, and H. Zima. Parallel Programmability and the Chapel Language. International Journal of High Performance Computing Applications, Vol. 21, Issue 3, August 2007, pg. 291-312.

[3] W. Chen, D. Bonachea, J. Duell, P. Husbands, C. Iancu, and K. Yelick. A Performance Analysis of the Berkeley UPC Compiler. Proceedings of the International Conference on Supercomputing (ICS), 2003, pg. 63-73.

[4] Cray, Inc. Cray XT5 System. 2008. http://www.cray.com/Products/XT/Product/Technology.aspx.

[5] A. DeHon. The Density Advantage of Configurable Computing. Computer, Vol. 33, Issue 4, April 2000, pp 41-49.

[6] ElementCXI, Inc. ECA-64. http://www.elementcxi.com/productbrief.html.

[7] A. Fin, F. Fummi, and M. Signoretto. SystemC: A Homogenous Environment to Test Embedded Systems. Proceedings of the International Workshop on Hardware/Software Codesign (CODES), 2001, pp 17-22.

[8] M. Frigo and S. Johnson. FFTW: an Adaptive Software Architecture for the FFT. Acoustics, Speech and Signal Processing. Proceedings of the IEEE International Conference on Acoustics, Speech, and Signal Processing, 1998, pp. 1381-1384.

[9] M. Girkar and C. Polychronopoulos. Extracting Task-Level Parallelism. ACM Transactions on Programming Languages and Systems (TOPLAS), Vol. 17, Issue 4, July 1995, pp. 600-634.

[10] B. Grattan, G. Stitt and F. Vahid. Codesign-Extended Applications. IEEE/ACM International Symposium on Hardware/Software Codesign (CODES), 2002, pp. 1-6.

[11] Z. Guo, W. Najjar, F. Vahid, and K. Vissers. A Quantitative Analysis of the Speedup Factors of FPGAs over Processors. Proceedings of the International Symposium on Field Programmable Gate Arrays (FPGA), pp. 162-170, 2004.

[12] S. Gupta, N. Dutt, R. Gupta, and A. Nicolau. SPARK: A High-Level Synthesis Framework for Applying Parallelizing Compiler Transformations. Proceedings of International Conference on VLSI Design (VLSI), 2003.

[13] H. Peter Hofstee. Power Efficient Processor Architecture and the Cell Processor. Proceedings of the International Symposium on High Performance Computer Architecture (HPCA), 2005, pg. 258-262.

[14] B. Holland, K. Nagarajan, C. Conger, A. Jacobs, and A. George. RAT: a Methodology for Predicting Performance in Application Design Migration to FPGAs. Proceedings of the Workshop on High-Performance Reconfigurable Computing Technology and Applications (HPRCTA), pp 1-10, 2007.

[15] Intel Quad-Core Xeon. 2008. http://www.intel.com.

[16] L. Lewins and K. Prager. Experience and Results Porting HPEC Benchmarks to MONARCH. Proceedings of Workshop on High Performance Embedded Computing (HPEC), 2008.

[17] C. Luk, S. Hong, and H. Kim. Qilin: Exploiting Parallelism on Heterogeneous Multiprocessors with Adaptive Mapping. Proceedings of the IEEE/ACM International Symposium on Microarchitecture (MICRO), 2009, pg. 45-55.

[18] M. Macedonia. The GPU Enters Computing's Mainstream. IEEE Computer, Vol. 36, No. 10, October 2003, pp. 106-108.

[19] I. McCallum. Intel QuickAssist Technology Accelerator Abstraction Layer (AAL) 317481-001US. 2007. http://download.intel.com/technology/platforms/quickassist/quickassist_aal_whitepaper.pdf.

[20] M. D. McCool. Data-parallel programming on Cell BE and the GPU using the Rapidmind development platform. In GSPx Multicore Applications Conference, 2006.

[21] S. Merchant, B. Holland, C. Reardon, et al. Strategic Challenges for Application Development Productivity in Reconfigurable Computing. Proceedings of the IEEE National Areospace and Electronics Conference (NAECON), 2008.

[22] K. Morris. FPGAs in Space: Programmable Logic in Orbit. FPGA and Structured ASIC Journal, August, 2004.

[23] D. Musser. Introspective Sorting and Selection Algorithms. Software: Practice and Experience, Vol. 27, Issue 8, 1999, pp. 983-993.

[24] Nallatech Inc. Nallatech PCIXM FPGA accelerator card, 2008. http://www.nallatech.com/?node_id=1.2.2&id=41.

[25] G. R. Nudd, D. J. Kerbyson, E. Papaefstathiou, S. C. Perry, J. S. Harper, and D. V. Wilcox. Pace—A Toolset for the Performance Prediction of Parallel and Distributed Systems. International Journal of High Performance Computing Applications, Vol. 14, No. 3, 2000, pp. 228-251.

[26] L. Semeria, K. Sato, and G. De Micheli. Synthesis of Hardware Models in C with Pointers and Complex Data Structures. IEEE Transactions of Very Large Scale Integration Systems (TVLSI), Vol. 9, Issue 6, December 2001, pp. 743-756.

[27] G. Stitt, F. Vahid, and W. Najjar. A Code Refinement Methodology for Performance-Improved Synthesis from C. Proceedings of the IEEE/ACM International Conference on Computer-Aided Design (ICCAD), 2006, pp. 716-723

[28] Tilera Tile64 Processor Family. 2008. http://www.tilera.com/products/processors.php.

[29] R. Vuduc, J. Demmel, and K. Yelick. OSKI: A Library of Automatically Tuned Sparse Matrix Kernels. Journal of Physics, June 2005.

[30] R. Whaley and J. Dongarra. Automatically Tuned Linear Algebra Software. Proceedings of ACM/IEEE Conference on Supercomputing (SC), 1998, pp. 1-27.

[31] J. Williams, A. George, J. Richardson, K. Gosrani, and S. Suresh. Fixed and Reconfigurable Multi-Core Device Characterization for HPEC. Proceedings of Workshop on High-Performance Embedded Computing (HPEC), 2008.

[32] Xilinx Inc. Virtex IV FX devices, 2008. http://www.xilinx.com/products/silicon_solutions/fpgas/virtex/virtex4/index.htm.

Integrating Safety Analysis into the Model-based Development Toolchain of Automotive Embedded Systems

Matthias Biehl   Chen DeJiu   Martin Törngren

Embedded Control Systems, Royal Institute of Technology (KTH), Stockholm, Sweden

{biehl,chen,martin}@md.kth.se

Abstract

The automotive industry has a growing demand for the seamless integration of safety analysis tools into the model-based development toolchain for embedded systems. This requires translating concepts of the automotive domain to the safety domain. We automate such a translation between the automotive architecture description language EAST-ADL2 and the safety analysis tool HiP-HOPS by using model transformations and by leveraging the advantages of different model transformation techniques. Through this integration, the analysis can be conducted early in the development process, when the system can be redesigned to fulfill safety goals with relatively low effort and cost.

Categories and Subject Descriptors D.2.6 [*Programming Environments*]: Integrated Environments

General Terms Design, Reliability, Languages

Keywords Safety Analysis, Model-based Development, Architecture Description Language, Tool Integration

1. Introduction

An increasing number of industrial systems are provided with new functionalities and enhanced performance enabled by embedded systems. In many cases, the corresponding applications are increasingly safety related, exemplified by automotive driver assistance systems and industrial robots operating without safety barriers. Facing the challenge of developing increasingly advanced safety-critical systems, the automotive industry has a growing demand for the seamless integration of safety analysis tools into the model-based development toolchain for embedded systems. Such an integrated solution will allow iterative and incremental development of safety critical systems and is a step towards fulfilling the demands of the upcoming standard for safety-critical road vehicles, ISO-CD-26262.

Safety is a cross-cutting system property that has to be considered from the start and throughout the development of the system. Safety engineering is an iterative process. It starts with determining safety-critical aspects, procedes with identifying the causes of failures and deriving the safety requirements and concludes with developing safety solutions.

Integrating safety analysis into the development of automotive embedded systems requires translating concepts of the automotive domain to the generic safety and error analysis domain. We assume a model based development process where automotive concepts are represented by the EAST-ADL2 architecture description language, which supports system design on multiple levels of abstraction. The concepts of the error analysis domain are represented by the safety analysis tool HiP-HOPS.

We automate the translation from EAST-ADL2 to HiP-HOPS by using model transformations. We leverage the advantages of different model transformation techniques by decomposing the translation into two distinct phases, and using an appropriate technique for each phase: A phase for conceptual mapping between the domains followed by a phase for representing the output in the desired concrete syntax.

With the resulting tight integration of the safety analysis tool and the model-based development environment, the automotive safety engineer can perform the safety analysis repeatedly on refined models with minimal effort. This is compliant with the iterative design activities requiring to invoke the analysis after each change in the system design.

The remainder of this work is organized as follows. Section 2 introduces the technology we use in our approach. Section 3 explains our approach for safety analysis tool integration. Section 4 focuses on the model transformation of the approach. By means of a comprehensible case study we demonstrate in section 5 how the integrated safety analysis can be used. We present related work in section 6 before we conclude in section 7.

2. Technology

In this section we introduce the technology we depend on when integrating tool-based safety analysis into an automotive model-based development process.

2.1 Model Transformations

Model transformations play a key role in model-based software development. Model transformations describe the relationship between models, more specifically the mapping of information from one model to another one. These model transformation descriptions are interpreted by a model transformation engine. The *model transformation engine* produces the output model based on the transformation description and information from the input model. A model transformation involves two models: a source model and a target model, where source and target model can have the same or different metamodels. Model transformations use concepts of the metamodels in their descriptions. Thus they are general enough to describe the mapping for any model specified with the same metamodel. Model transformations are also used in generative programming [3], where they are called generators.

In the following we introduce a classification scheme for model transformations.

We can distinguish model transformations with respect to the creation of the target: *Model-to-model transformations* directly create elements of the target model. Each element in the source model maps to a specific element in the target model. *Model-to-text transformations* on the other hand create arbitrary, unstructured text. Each source element maps to an arbitrary fragment of text. This kind of transformation is also called model-to-code transformation or code transformation.

Model transformations can change the amount of detail presented in the model. They either introduce new details, reduce the amount of detail or leave it unchanged: *Refinement transformations* (vertical transformations) produce the target model by adding details to the source model. A change in the metamodel might be necessary for this step. This kind of transformation is the most common form. *Abstraction transformations* (vertical transformations) produce the target model by reducing the amount of detail. *Translation transformations* (horizontal transformations) produce the target model by expressing the same information found in the source model in a different language. The degree of detail stays the same. Translations are also called horizontal transformations.

We can differentiate model transformations according to the metamodels used in the transformation. *Endogenous* transformations map between the same metamodel. *Exogenous* transformations map between different metamodels.

Model transformations can be written using different languages. We can classify transformations according to the type of model transformation languages they use. *Declarative transformation languages* describe preconditions of the transformation and the according change with a postcondition. *Graph transformations* are described in this way, where a left-hand-side is the precondition and the right-hand-side is the postcondition. *Operational transformation languages* describe the transformation as a sequence of actions.

2.1.1 Model Transformation Engine openArchitecureWare (OAW)

OAW integrates a number of tools for model transformations into a coherent framework [6]. Among other tools, the OAW provides a workflow specification language and the transformation language Xpand. The workflow language is used to control the transformation process and to specify the sequence of transformations between the different models. The Xpand transformation language is a template-based, imperative language for model-to-text transformations. OAW is distributed as a plugin of the Eclipse platform and is able to process models that are conform to the EMF (Eclipse Modeling Framework).

2.1.2 Model Transformation Engine ATL

The ATLAS Transformation Language (ATL) is a hybrid model transformation language [7]. It includes both declarative and imperative constructs and supports both programming styles. However, the preferred style is declarative, which allows a cleaner and simpler implementation for simple mappings. However, imperative constructs are provided so that some mappings that are too complex to be handled declaratively can still be specified. An ATL transformation program is composed of rules that describe how to create and initialize the elements of the target models. The language is specified both as a metamodel and as a textual concrete syntax.

ATL is integrated in the Eclipse development environment and can handle models based on EMF. In this project we chose ATL for its ability to process UML models which are annotated with the UML extension mechanism for profiles, so we are able to process models that are conform to the EAST-ADL2 profile.

2.2 EAST-ADL2

EAST-ADL2 is an architecture description language for the development of automotive embedded systems [2]. It can be used to describe hardware (electronics), software and the environment (mechanics) of an embedded system. The goals of modeling with EAST-ADL2 are to handle complexity and improve safety, reliability, cost, and development efficiency through model-based development. A primary feature of EAST-ADL2 is its capability to structure a model into different abstraction levels. All these levels describe the same system, but on different levels of abstraction and from different viewpoints. Each level is associated with a different stage of the development process. EAST-ADL2 is an information model, connecting different views of the system. The views are influenced by the different engineering traditions and backgrounds in automotive industry. Control engineers focus on the functional view, the design view is often preferred by software engineers. This concept allows functional decomposition, supports analysis activities, design activities, implementation of software and hardware components and variability management.

EAST-ADL2 specifies a domain model, which is implemented as a UML profile depending on UML and SysML. Using the EAST-ADL2 profile for UML, it is possible to create EAST-ADL2 models in any UML design tool, i.e. the Eclipse-based Papyrus UML tool.

2.3 HiP-HOPS

Creating the FMEA (Failure Modes and Effects Analysis) and the FTA (Fault Tree Analysis) by hand is a very laborious and error-prone task, hindering the safety design process. However, safety considerations should be built into the design right from the start and an iterative safety analysis needs to be performed during the design. HiP-HOPS (Hierarchically Performed Hazard Origin and Propagation Studies) can support such an iterative safety design by automating FTA and FMEA and even combining the results. This analysis data can also be the basis for an optimization of the security and reliability of the system. HiP-HOPS expects a model describing the topology of the system (components and their subcomponents) including information about how individual components can fail as well as how failures are propagated. Among other functionalities, HiP-HOPS creates local fault trees, combines them to a system fault tree and calculates a minimum cutset [9].

3. Tool Integration

To establish the link between EAST-ADL2 system modeling tools and safety analysis tools, they have to be integrated. In his seminal work, Wasserman identifies five different aspects of tool integration [14]:

- control integration: tools can interoperate
- data integration: tools can exchange data
- presentation integration: tools have a unified GUI
- platform integration: a common platform provides services as a basis for integration
- process integration: the SW development processes can be integrated

In the following we evaluate how these five aspects can be realized for the integration of safety analysis into model-based development.

Process integration cannot be done by software itself, but depends on personal preferences, company culture and development organization. Automation of safety analysis has several advantages: It makes safety analysis easy, it is readily available and allows the engineers to obtain a thorough and quick analysis of their design. This fast feedback based on analysis results allows engineers to perform more micro iterations in the development process, where each iteration refines and improves the previously built model. The safety analysis is integrated in a the development and more specifically in the safety analysis process. This process is aligned to upcoming ISO-CD-26262 standard and described in an EPF (Eclipse Process Framework) model for EAST-ADL2.

The Eclipse platform provides a framework for platform and presentation integration. We use it by implementing our tool as an Eclipse plugin. We extend the graphical user interface of Eclipse by adding menus to invoke safety analysis for a given EAST-ADL2 model. This ensures seamless integration in the UML modeling environment and keeps the overhead for safety analysis experienced by the user as low as possible and thus allows for an iterative safety development process.

Control integration is realized by parameterizing and executing the model transformation engines and the safety analysis tool from within the developed plugin.

Data integration in this context is concerned with the transformation of modeling data. We transform from an EAST-ADL2 representation to a HiP-HOPS representation, while preserving the semantics. State of the art data integration for model-based development is supported by powerful model transformation engines and languages. Different transformation languages and engines are available, each of them solving a particular problem especially well. This is why the next section is dedicated to chosing the right model transformation language.

4. Translation from EAST-ADL2 to HiP-HOPS

Integrating safety analysis into the development of automotive embedded systems requires data integration. This can be achieved by translating concepts of the automotive domain to the error analysis domain. In the context of this work the automotive concepts are represented by the architecture description language EAST-ADL2 including its dependability model and the concepts of the error analysis domain are represented by the safety analysis tool HiP-HOPS. We need to expose the information of the EAST-ADL2 error models to HiP-HOPS in its native input format.

4.1 Model Transformation

We automate the translation between EAST-ADL2 and HiP-HOPS using model transformations. Model transformation languages are domain specific languages for extracting information from models, for building and for manipulating models. Model transformation languages, paradigms and engines have been classified in [4] and [8]. Different model transformation languages have their strengths and weaknesses in solving particular types of tasks [4]. A challenge is choosing the right tool for the model transformation task at hand.

We have identified the following fundamental requirements for the model transformation engine used in our solution.

- Needs to be able to process UML models which have a UML profile applied, in our case this is the EAST-ADL2 profile

- Needs to produce text output, not a model

- Needs to be maintainable, the source code needs to be compact and reusable, since both EAST-ADL2 and HiP-HOPS evolve

- Needs to integrate as a plugin into the modeling environment

The model transformations we have looked at, do not fulfill all requirements at once. For instance we could not find an engine that allows us to produce text output and process the EAST-ADL2 profile. For this reason, we decompose the model transformation into two specialized transformations. Each of the two transformations fulfills the requirements partially, but the two transformations together fulfill all requirements.

4.2 Transformation Design

We leverage the advantages of different model transformation techniques by splitting the translation into two distinct phases and using an appropriate model transformation technique for each phase. Each phase has a distinct purpose and tackles a different concern.

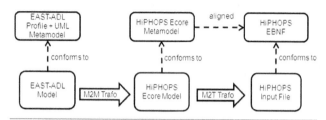

Figure 1. Transformation Design

(1) Semantic Mapping Transformation: The first transformation step is a model-to-model transformation and is called M2M Trafo in figure 1. It transforms an EAST-ADL2 model that was created in the Papyrus UML modeling environment into an intermediate model. The structure of the intermediate model resembles the HiP-HOPS grammar, so it is close to the structure of the desired output. This stage performs the semantic mapping between the domains of EAST-ADL2 and that of HiP-HOPS. However, this stage is not concerned with the actual representation of the data.

(2) Representation Transformation: The second transformation step, called M2T Trafo in figure 1, takes the intermediate model and creates the input file for the HiP-HOPS program. This step is mainly concerned with the representation of the information according to the concrete syntax required by HiP-HOPS.

We will discuss both transformations in more detail in sections 4.4 and 4.5. There we use the scheme for classifying model transformation introduced in section 2.1 to determine the type of each of the two transformations and to choose a transformation engine fitting the properties of that particular transformation.

4.3 Involved Models and Metamodels

Three different models are involved in this model transformation. An EAST-ADL2 model, an intermediate HiP-HOPS model and the final HiP-HOPS file. The EAST-ADL2 model serves as the initial source model, and is conform to the EAST-ADL2 metamodel. The HiP-HOPS file is the final outcome of the transformation and conforms to the HiP-HOPS grammar. We discuss the metamodels separately in the following sections.

4.3.1 EAST-ADL2 Error Model

EAST-ADL2 models created in the Eclipse-based Papyrus UML tool have a metamodel that is a composition of several separate metamodels. This metamodel consists of the UML metamodel and the EAST-ADL2 profile definition. These artifacts are combined by the Eclipse framework to the EAST-ADL2 metamodel. However, this combined metamodel is not an autonomous entity or file. This complicates the model transformation and limits the choice of model transformation engines.

The EAST-ADL2 domain model contains concepts for modeling the anomalies of a system in a so called error model, which describes the failure semantics of a system by relating the occurrences of internal errors and the propagations of such errors [2]. These error modeling constructs are separated from the constructs used for the nominal system definition, to clearly separate their different natures: error models are purely descriptive while nominal models are prescriptive and may be used for code generation.

The domain model of the EAST-ADL2 error modeling concepts is illustrated in figure 2. In the following we introduce the core concepts. The ErrorModelType metaclass represents the container for maintaining the information relating to the anomalies of a system, function, software component, or hardware device. The ErrorModelPrototype metaclass describes an instance of an ErrorModelType. Even though these concepts are similar to the concepts for nominal behavior, the decomposition of the system into ErrorModelTypes is kept separate from the nominal decomposition into FunctionTypes. This makes it possible to have either totally aligned or separate topologies in error modeling than in the targeted nominal architecture, depending on the needs for error analysis. An ErrorPropagationLink describes how failures in one component can propagate to other components.

4.3.2 HiP-HOPS Ecore Metamodel

Due to the decomposition into two separate transformations we introduced an intermediate model which connects the two transformations (see figure 1). The intermediate model is conform to a HiP-HOPS Ecore metamodel that is aligned to the HiP-HOPS grammar. It is conform to the Ecore metametamodel. The HiP-HOPS Ecore metamodel is depicted in figure 3.

At its core, the HiP-HOPS Ecore metamodel is a hierarchical decomposition into systems and components, where a system can contain components, which contain an implementation, which can contain another system. Thus hierarchical systems of any depths can be built recursively. Components and systems can be annotated with failure data, i.e. how failures propagate through the systems and where they originate from.

4.4 Semantic Mapping Transformation

The purpose of the semantic mapping transformation is to map concepts from EAST-ADL2 to HiP-HOPS in a way that preserves the semantics of the original model, even though the structure of the model must be changed heavily. EAST-ADL2 models and HiP-HOPS models are structurally different. This can be demonstrated by the following example. EAST-ADL2 follows the concepts of declaring types first and referencing to the declaration from each point of use. In HiP-HOPS on the other hand, the declaration and usage of a type is coupled, types are declared at the same point as they are used. Thus the declarations have to be inlined into every point of usage, when transforming from EAST-ADL2 to HiP-HOPS. Table 1 lists the detailed mapping between EAST-ADL2 concepts and HiP-HOPS concepts. In Figure 4 we show the part of this transformation that maps ErrorModelPrototypes of EAST-ADL2 to Components of the HiP-HOPS Ecore Metamodel.

According to the classification scheme introduced in section 2.1 the representation transformation can be classified as an exogeneous, horizontal, model-to-model transformation. Model-to-model transformations are well suited for our semantic mapping transformation, because both input and output are models. Mapping patterns can be described by relational and declarative transformation languages in a concise manner. Our solution leads to relatively short source code for the solution. We selected the ATLAS Transformation Language (ATL), a language that allows a choice of relational and imperative constructs. It furthermore allows processing of models that have a profiled metamodel, i.e. a metamodel that consists of a metamodel and a profile description. In our case the EAST-ADL2 metamodel consists of the UML metamodel and the EAST-ADL2 profile.

4.5 Representation Transformation

The purpose of the representation transformation is the generation of a textual description based on the intermediate model. According to section 2.1 the representation transformation can be classified as an endogeneous, horizontal, model-to-text transformation.

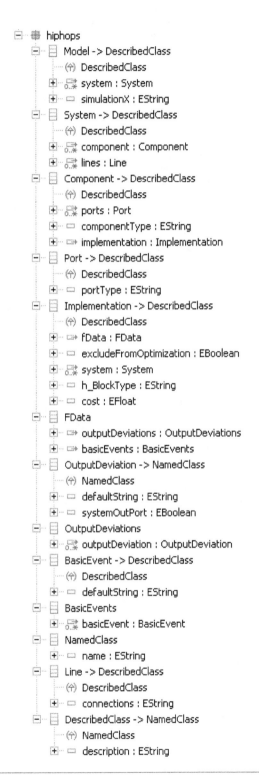

Figure 3. HiP-HOPS Ecore metamodel

EAST-ADL2 Pattern (Source)	EAST-ADL2 Type	HiP-HOPS Pattern (Target)
ErrorModelType	ErrorModelType	System
ErrorModelType.errorConnector	ErrorPropagationLink	System.Lines
ErrorModelType.parts	ErrorModelPrototype	System.Component
ErrorModelPrototype.type.errorPort	ErrorPort	System.Component.Ports
ErrorModelPrototype	ErrorModelPrototype	System.Component.Implementation
ErrorModelPrototype.type. errorBehaviorDescription.internalErrorEvent	ErrorEvent	System.Component. Implementation.FData.basicEvent
ErrorModelPrototype.type. errorBehaviorDescription.failureLogic	String	System.Component. Implementation.FData.outputDeviation
ErrorModelPrototype.type	ErrorModelType	System.Component. Implementation.System (recursion)

Table 1. Semantic mapping between EAST-ADL2 and HiP-HOPS

Textual representations can be generated particularly well with model-to-text transformation languages. We choose the Xpand language of OpenArchitectureWare. Xpand is a template-based model transformation language, which incorporates the output in the form of templates into the control structure. Figure 5 shows a part of this transformation, that creates a textual representation of the intermediate model, that can serve as input to HiP-HOPS.

The intermediate model is designed to have structure which is aligned to HiP-HOPS. No structural changes are required in this transformation. The focus is on serializing the model as text. When serializing a graph structure to text, as done here, the choice of exploration strategy is important, as it dictates the order of the output. We explore the intermediate model using a depth first exploration strategy.

4.6 Benefits of the Chosen Decomposition

In this section we discuss the benefits of this solution.

- Our solution separates two different concerns of the transformation from EAST-ADL2 to HiP-HOPS: (1) the semantic mapping between the domains of EAST-ADL2 and that of HiP-HOPS and the (2) details of the concrete syntax of the HiP-HOPS input file.

- Each transformation is a separate, self-contained module, which can be developed, changed and tested independently. This decomposition into two separate transformations allows us to parallelize the work on the two transformations and reduce development time. It also allows the two transformations to evolve independently without affecting each other, e.g. a change in the HiP-HOPS grammar will only affect the representation transformation.

- As discussed in the section on data integration, different transformation engines have different strengths which can be played out for different concerns. The solution allows us to select an appropriate tool for each concern.

- Since we chose appropriate tools for each steps, the resulting model transformation source code is very concise, resulting in a maintainable codebase.

5. Case Study

To demonstrate how the safety plugin works, we have created a hierarchical system model in EAST-ADL2 with a focus on the system's comprehensibility. The model is depicted in figure 6 and contains three functions. While F1 and F3 are atomic functions, F2 contains two subcomponents, a primary component F21 and a standby component F22, where the later takes over if the primary fails.

```
rule recursiveErrorModelPrototypeRule{
    from
        emp : east!ErrorModelPrototype
    to
        _components: hiphops!Component (
            implementation <- _implementation,
            ports <- _ports,
            name <- emp.base_Property.name
        ),
```

Figure 4. Example: part of the semantic mapping transformation in ATL

```
«DEFINE ComponentRule FOR Component-»
    Component (
        Component type "«componentType»"
        Name "«name»"
        Description "«description»"
        «EXPAND PortRule FOREACH ports-»
        «EXPAND ImplementationRule FOR implementation-»
    )
«ENDDEFINE»
```

Figure 5. Example: part of the representation transformation in OAW Xpand

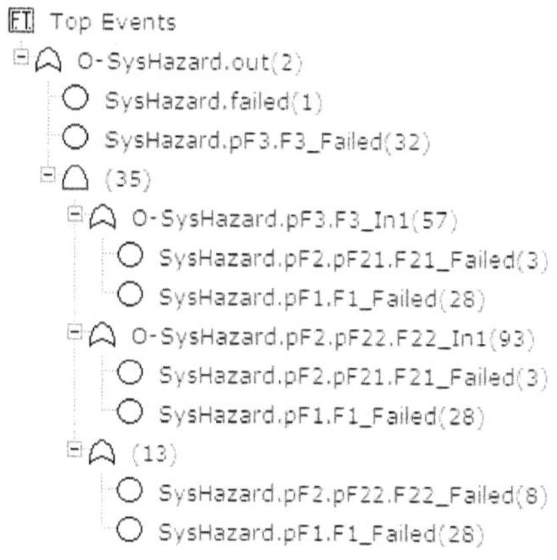

Figure 7. Fault tree of the hot standby system of figure 6

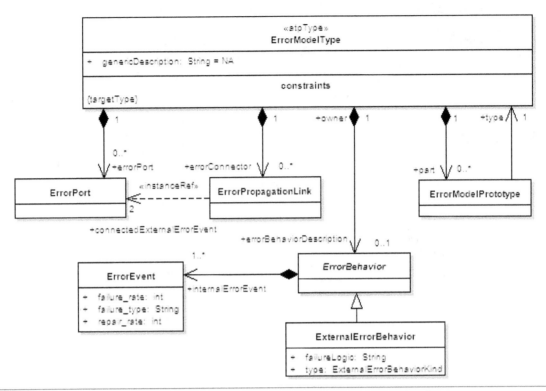

Figure 2. Domain Model of the EAST-ADL2 Error Modeling Concepts

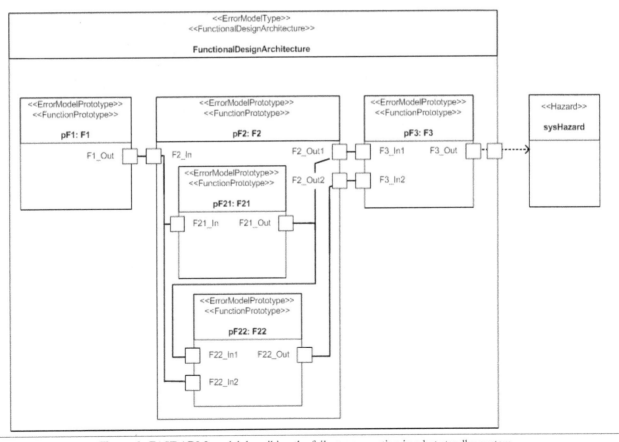

Figure 6. EAST-ADL2 model describing the failure propagation in a hot standby system

This pattern is called hot standby. It consists of a primary component and a standby component, that is ready to take over if the primary fails. The pattern is applied in reliability engineering as a failover mechanism to improve the reliability and safety of a system. The result of the safety analysis shows, how this pattern affects the outcome of the safety analysis.

We run our automated model transformation for the model depicted in figure 6. The EAST-ADL2 model is transformed into the HiP-HOPS language, as described in section 4.2. HiP-HOPS subsequently performs the analysis based on the transformed data and presents the results in various ways. The results can be represented as minimal cutsets, FMEA tables or fault trees. A fault tree of the system in figure 6 is depicted in figure 7.

The results of the safety analysis need to be interpreted by a safety engineer. Depending on the current stage of development, the engineer can use this information either to create and refine safety requirements or to adjust his design. He can do this e.g. by increasing redundancy, if a higher level of reliability is desired, or reducing the cost by removing unnecessary redundancy.

6. Related Work

The need to bridge the gap between the safety and system design disciplines has been identified in several domains. Integration in general covers the need to align processes, tools and the competences of the developers. The focus here is on model and tool integration between system design models (which may refer to structure and/or behavior at different abstraction levels) and safety analysis models such as failure modes and effects analysis and fault tree analysis models. Earlier work that has addressed this gap includes:

- As part of the SETTA project, Papadopoulos et al. annotate Matlab/Simulink models with FMEA information and provide an export for fault-tree generation [10].

- In the ESACS project and its follow up project ISAAC this gap was identified and addressed by providing tools, such as Statemate Magnum and Scade, to perform automated safety analysis starting from a system design model.

- Dumas et al. [5] perform model transformations between AADL, the Architecture and Analysis Description Language, and the analysis tool AltaRica [1].

- Price et al. [12] focus on safety analysis of electrical systems for cars. They explain the tradeoff between numerical and qualitative analysis and point out the importance of continuous safety analysis as opposed to snapshot analysis. While this work focuses mainly on electrical system, our approach can be used for electrical systems, software systems, or a combination of the two.

- The integration of HiP-HOPS and EAST-ADL2 has been attempted in the ATESST research project [13]. This resulted in a monolithic Java program where the code for data integration, control integration and presentation integration was mixed, resulting in low maintainability. In this work we specifically addressed these shortcomings by separating the different integration issues and by designing a transformation that leverages state-of-the-art model transformation technology and at the same time separates mapping concerns from representation concerns.

- A recent project that is based on all these advances and that has the ambition to provide multi-domain solutions, is the CESAR project [11].

7. Conclusion and Future Work

In this work we have shown how we integrated the safety analysis tool HiP-HOPS into the automotive model-based development toolchain based on EAST-ADL2. We used different model transformation techniques to translate the relevant information from the automotive domain to the safety analysis domain. This link enables early safety analysis.

Currently our analysis supports fault tree analysis for models of either hardware or software. We work on supporting fault tree analysis that considers the propagation of failures between hardware and software. This will allow us to analyze e.g. the effects of hardware failures on the software and how the software can handle them.

Acknowledgments The research presented in this article was supported by funding from the 7th Framework Programme of the European Community under grant agreement no. 224442.

References

[1] M. Boiteau, Y. Dutuit, A. Rauzy, and J. P. Signoret. The altarica dataflow language in use: modeling of production availability of a multistate system. *Reliability Engineering & System Safety*, 91(7), 2006.

[2] D. Chen, R. Johansson, H. Lönn, Y. Papadopoulos, A. Sandberg, F. Törner, and M. Törngren. Modelling support for design of safety-critical automotive embedded systems. In *Computer Safety, Reliability, and Security, Lecture Notes in Computer Science SAFECOMP2008*, 2008.

[3] K. Czarnecki and U. W. Eisenecker. *Generative Programming: Methods, Tools, and Applications*. Addison-Wesley, Boston, 2000.

[4] K. Czarnecki and S. Helsen. Feature-based survey of model transformation approaches. *IBM Systems Journal*, 45(3):621–645, 2006.

[5] X. Dumas, C. Pagetti, L. Sagaspe, P. Bieber, and P. Dhaussy. Vers la génération de modèles de sûreté de fonctionnement. *Revue des Nouvelles Technologies de l'Information*, RNTI-L-2:157–172, 2008.

[6] S. Efftinge, P. Friese, A. Haase, C. Kadura, B. Kolb, D. Moroff, K. Thoms, and M. Voelter. openarchitectureware user guide. Technical report, openArchitectureWare Community, 2007.

[7] F. Jouault, F. Allilaire, J. Bézivin, and I. Kurtev. ATL: a model transformation tool. *Science of Computer Programming*, 72:31–39, June 2008.

[8] T. Mens and P. Van Gorp. A taxonomy of model transformation. *Electr. Notes Theor. Comput. Sci*, 152:125–142, 2006.

[9] Y. Papadopoulos and J. A. McDermid. Hierarchically performed hazard origin and propagation studies. In M. Felici, K. Kanoun, and A. Pasquini, editors, *SAFECOMP*, volume 1698 of *Lecture Notes in Computer Science*, pages 139–152. Springer, 1999.

[10] Y. Papadopoulos, J. A. McDermid, R. Sasse, and G. Heiner. Analysis and synthesis of the behaviour of complex programmable electronic systems in conditions of failure. *Reliability Engineering and System Safety*, 71(3):229–247, 2001.

[11] C. P. Partners. Cesar project, 2010. URL http://www.cesarproject.eu.

[12] C. J. Price, N. A. Snooke, and S. D. Lewis. A layered approach to automated electrical safety analysis in automotive environments. *Computers in Industry*, 57(5):451–461, 2006. doi: 10.1016/j.compind.2006.02.001. URL http://dx.doi.org/10.1016/j.compind.2006.02.001.

[13] J. Shi, D. Chen, and M. Törngren. Case studies on integrating simulink, uml and safety analysis through model transformations. Technical report, KTH, Mechatronics Lab, 2007.

[14] A. I. Wasserman. Tool integration in software engineering environments. In F. Long, editor, *Software Engineering Environments, International Workshop on Environments Proceedings*, number 467 in Lecture Notes in Computer Science, pages 137–149. Springer-Verlag, September 1989.

Sampling-based Program Execution Monitoring

Sebastian Fischmeister

Department of Electrical and Computer Engineering
University of Waterloo
sfischme@uwaterloo.ca

Yanmeng Ba

Department of Electrical and Computer Engineering
University of Waterloo
yba@uwaterloo.ca

Abstract

For its high overall cost during product development, program debugging is an important aspect of system development. Debugging is a hard and complex activity, especially in time-sensitive systems which have limited resources and demanding timing constraints.

System tracing is a frequently used technique for debugging embedded systems. A specific use of system tracing is to monitor and debug control-flow problems in programs. However, it is difficult to implement because of the potentially high overhead it might introduce to the system and the changes which can occur to the system behavior due to tracing.

To solve the above problems, in this work, we present a sampling-based approach to execution monitoring which specifically helps developers debug time-sensitive systems such as real-time applications. We build the system model and propose three theorems to determine the sampling period in different scenarios. We also design seven heuristics and an instrumentation framework to extend the sampling period which can reduce the monitoring overhead and achieve an optimal tradeoff between accuracy and overhead introduced by instrumentation. Using this monitoring framework, we can use the information extracted through sampling to reconstruct the system state and execution paths to locate the deviation.

Categories and Subject Descriptors   D.2.5 [*Software Engineering*]: Testing and Debugging—tracing

General Terms   Theory, Algorithms, Experimentation

Keywords   sampling, monitoring, tracing, debugging, embedded system

1. Introduction

Debugging is an important procedure in embedded software development, because between 30 to 50 percent of the development cost is spent on testing and debugging (Bouyssounouse and J.Sifakis 2005; Gallaher and Kropp 2002). We define a software defect as "An incorrect step, process, data definition or result." (IEE 1990). While testing is the process of revealing failure by showing the presence of software defects, debugging starts after testing and is the process of locating and removing the defects. Because of the increase of system and software complexity, good debugging

methods for embedded software become increasingly important. Software instrumentation is a popular technique for software-based debugging and tracing. System monitoring can effectively detect faults of programs running in the system. However, both instrumentation and monitoring introduce overhead to the execution of the program.

Our approach to bound the cost of monitoring is to sample the program at a fixed rate to collect adequate and necessary information about the execution at runtime. Besides, we develop several algorithms to strategically insert markers to the program to reduce the overhead introduced by the instrumentation. We thus propose a sampling-based monitoring mechanism which allows the developer to extract information from the system under test to determine the execution path of programs with an optimal tradeoff between accuracy and overhead. The execution trace contains the execution path of the last run and helps to find the location of software defects. Our work targets embedded, time-sensitive systems, and provides a framework for reconstructing system state and execution paths. A typical debugging session in our work flow consists of the following steps:

1. **Detect the presence of software defect.** Using traditional testing methods such as unit tests (Elbaum et al. 2009) or white/blackbox tests (Kirani et al. 1994), the developer determines that the tested software deviates from its specification.

2. **Budget resources for monitoring.** A good practice when developing embedded systems is to define a specific budget for debugging overhead. The available budget determines the monitoring precision as it affects the sampling period.

3. **Prepare program for monitoring.** The developer uses our algorithms to instrument the program with markers for sampling-based monitoring.

4. **Collect traces.** The developer runs the instrumented system. A monitor periodically collects data from the markers and other system state and transmits them to the developer workstation.

5. **Reconstruct execution.** Once the instrumented system crashes or the developer stops the execution, the framework permits reconstructing the execution path from the sequence of samples to locate the software defect in the code.

The advantages of our approach are as follows: Compared with continuous monitoring, our sampling-based technique can greatly reduce the overhead introduced. Since the sampling rate is fixed, we can estimate and bound the overhead and impact on the system under test. Also, our approach can easily be combined with data-tracing methods. There are, however, several issues to be solved regarding sampling-based approaches:

First, we need to balance between overhead and correct reconstruction of the control flow. On one hand, we want to gather enough information to be able to reconstruct the execution path;

on the other hand, monitoring should have only modest impact on the program. Second, we need to address the problem of how many markers should be used. Each marker requires memory, so we want to use as few markers are possible. Third, we need to devise an instrumentation algorithm that efficiently uses the available markers. Using markers well can reduce the number of required markers to achieve the target sampling period.

This paper makes several contributions to the issues mentioned above:

- We provide a formal framework that permits quantitative reasoning of many aspects involved in sampling-based mechanisms.

- We propose the optimality from both vertex and the whole control-flow graph perspectives.

- We provide theorems for termination conditions of instrumentation algorithms with an unlimited number of markers and with exactly one marker.

- We validate the general approach by proposing and comparing several algorithms for inserting markers into programs.

- We investigate interference among markers and propose tailored algorithms to compensate for this interference.

- We discuss a number of observations and insights from the development of the algorithms.

Besides debugging, sampling-based execution monitoring can also be used in performance profiling of software systems. Combined with tracing, it can give performance engineers a sufficiently detailed analysis of the system with relatively low overhead (Metz et al. 2005), such as event relationships in time and reconstructing the dynamic behavior of a software system. In addition, sampling-based execution monitoring can be applied to code coverage testing (Shye et al. 2005) which finds the code exercised by a particular set of test input. Moreover, sampling-based execution monitoring can be a feasible and efficient technique for reducing the overhead while collecting profile information (Lee and Zilles 2008).

In our paper, following a discussion about several traditional approaches, we firstly describe the problem targeted and then build our system model (Section 3) which served as the theoretical foundation for the whole paper. Secondly, we propose two theorems which provide the termination conditions of instrumentations in different scenarios and give the corresponding examples to explain them (Section 4). We then proceed and propose a BFS-based algorithm which calculates the sampling period (Section 5). We analyze the interference between instrumentations in Section 6. With the interference and the proper model, we proceed to experiment with different algorithms (Section 7) and interpret the results (Section 8). By drawing conclusions we close the paper in Section 9 and outline future work.

2. Related Works

Debugging techniques have been around since the early programming stages and come in different flavors. In hardware-based debugging, boundary scan testing (also named as JTAG) (Chun and Lim 2005) targets systems with limited resources and space for debugging. This method provides the ability to run the program and halt it at any given time which is undesirable in real-time system because of the timing constraints. With the higher integration of SoC and the increase of software complexity, logic analyzers become expensive for debugging, because of the high frequency and the increased number of ports required by large systems. ARM CoreSight is an On-chip debug technology for streaming data off the chip (Orme 2008). However, it suffers from limited bandwidth on the trace port (e.g., not all program counter values can be streamed off chip) and is only available on a limited number of chips.

Instrumentation is usually used to collect program profile and run-time information for various testing/debugging and analysis applications, such as detecting program invariants, dynamic slicing and alias analysis (Kumar et al. 2005), to monitor and track the program behavior (Biberstein et al. 2005). However, it introduces considerable overhead to the execution of the program. Researchers have proposed several methods to reduce the cost of instrumentation overhead (Kumar et al. 2005; Arnold and Ryder 2001; Misurda et al. 2005). Software instrumentation collects information of program execution by inserting instrumentation statements which might print out program location or variable values (Titzer and Palsberg 2005). Instrumenting *printf* statements is a naive approach which is tedious and inflexible. It might also result in "probe effect".

Software failure is expensive (IEE 2005) and system monitoring is one method to detect faults before they become failures (Jiang et al. 2009). There are some different flavors of system monitoring. Metric-correlation models use correlations among management metrics in software systems to detect bugs and localize their cause (Jiang et al. 2009). By posing queries, a software-based framework was proposed to monitor the state and performance of running programs (Cheung and Madden 2008). Structural monitoring determines which program entities, such as statements, branches and data-flow or control-flow relationships, are executed (Santelices and Harrold 2007). Previous research has developed efficient monitoring methods for states and branches (Ball and Larus 1992, 1994) which insert various counters into the program executed. An efficient branch-based monitoring approach is DUA (definition-use associations) (Frankl and Weyuker 1988; Hutchins et al. 1994), which results in additional overhead (Santelices and Harrold 2007).

One use for software instrumentation is to monitor control-flow. From the perspective of when to instrument the program, there are usually two types of software instrumentations: the static instrumentation insert the instrumentation code to the program before it executes, while the dynamic instrumentation instruments the program when it is running. The most commonly used static binary instrumentation tool is ATOM (Srivastava and Eustace 2004), which was implemented by extending OM and provides a framework for building a customized program analysis tools. For dynamic binary instrumentation, Pin provided by Intel is a valid option. Pin (Luk et al. 2005) follows the model of ATOM, but it does not instrument an executable statically by rewriting it, but rather adds the code dynamically while the executable is running. However, by instrumenting the executable with extra code, these software instrumentation methods might change the timing of the execution of the program unexpectedly and unpredictably, thus they are not soundly applicable to the real-time systems where timing has the top priority. Related work investigated software-support perspectives (Ball and Larus 1994) and hardware-based approach (Zhang et al. 2005). Meanwhile, monitoring control-flow is especially expensive, and there is little work done so far to characterize or bound its cost.

There are already several works that apply the concept of sampling into program debugging: using random sampling in statistical debugging to isolate bugs (Liblit et al. 2005); debugging programs given sampled data from thousands of user runs (Zheng et al. 2006); a sampling infrastructure for gathering information from a large number of executions (Liblit et al. 2003). These works focused on using the sampling concept to gather run-time information from program executions in workstation softwares.

3. System Model & Terminology

This work concentrates on multi-process single-threaded applications like the ones found in background/foreground systems. This structure dominates the embedded software domain due to its maintainable structure and efficient resource utilization (Labrosse 2002; Fischmeister and Lee 2007). Note that about 85 percent of all embedded systems use 8-bit or smaller architectures (Tennenhouse 2000).

We also assume that the system supports interrupts and has at least one high-precision timer as commonly found in microcontrollers. For example, the ATmega128 microcontroller has four timers.

3.1 Model Definition and Terminology

To analyze and reconstruct the execution path of the application, we convert a source program to a directed graph, representing the program's control flow, which is defined as the control-flow graph $G = \langle V, E \rangle$.

In G, each vertex ($v \in V$) represents a basic code block in a program. The entry vertex v_{en} is the start of the program. The exit vertex v_{ex} is the termination of the program. Edge $e := \langle v_s, v_d \rangle$ represents the specific transition from a source vertex v_s to a destination vertex v_d. It assumes that G is an *unweighed graph* with $e := \langle v_s, v_d \rangle = 0$, which means that the transition between two vertices requires no time.

We define the function $c : V \to \mathbb{N}$, which specifies the required execution time for a vertex v. For example, $c(v_0) = 10$ means that the basic code block at vertex v_0 requires 10 time units for its execution.

A path p is defined as a sequence of adjacent vertices $v_i \to v_{i+1} \to \ldots \to v_k$. The execution time of a path is the sum of the execution times of all vertices and is defined as $c_p(p) = \sum c(v_i)$ for all $v_i \in p$. An execution path r, which is a special p, is the actual path executed from the entry vertex v_{en} to the exit vertex v_{ex}.

Our approach periodically takes samples from the execution information and program state. In this context, we define a sample as a triple $s := \langle state, v, t \rangle$ where v represents the vertex sampled, t represents the time stamp when the sample is taken and $state$ represents the program state(e.g. the values of some variables) at that time stamp. The sampling period T is defined as the constant time interval Δt between two adjacent samples, that is, $T = \Delta t = t_{i+1} - t_i$ for two adjacent samples $s_i := \langle state_i, v_i, t_i \rangle$ and $s_{i+1} := \langle state_{i+1}, v_{i+1}, t_{i+1} \rangle$.

Furthermore, to evaluate the quality of the sampling period, we define the function $\text{pathfind}_t(v_i, v_j, \Delta t)$ with $\Delta t = t_j - t_i$ returning all possible paths between two vertices while Δt represents the execution time interval between v_i and v_j. We define the sampling period as *too long*, if multiple paths exist between two vertices of two samples, which is indicated by $|\text{pathfind}(v_i, v_j, \Delta t)| > 1$, where $v_i, v_j \in V$. We define a sampling period as *sufficient*, if only one path exists between two vertices.

The concept of *optimality* for the sampling period is formed with respect to both a vertex and a complete control-flow graph. If a sampling period of T is sufficient and a sampling period of $T + \epsilon$ is too long, then T is the optimal sampling period for the the starting vertex in the given control-flow graph. In other words: sampling after T permits only one path between the two samples and $T + \epsilon$ permits multiple. Stating this formally, starting from a specific node v_i, the sampling period T is said to be *optimal* for the node v_i, if $|\text{pathfind}_t(v_i, v_{next}, T)| = 1$ while $\left|\text{pathfind}_t(v_i, v'_{next}, T + \epsilon)\right| > 1$.

For the whole control-flow graph $G = (V, E)$, the *optimal* sampling period is the minimum of the *optimal* sampling periods

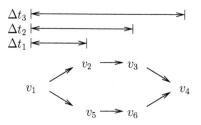

Figure 1. Different sampling periods for one control flow

of vertices in the control-flow graph. Thus, the *optimal* sampling period T_{opt} is defined as $T_{opt} = min(T_1, \ldots, T_k)$ where T_i is the *optimal* sampling period for $v_i \in V$ with $V = (v_1, \ldots, v_k)$.

Example 1. *Figure 1 shows an example of a control-flow graph, a starting vertex v_1, and several sampling periods $\Delta t_1 = 1$, $\Delta t_2 = 2$, and $\Delta t_3 = 3$. All basic blocks have the same execution time $c(v_i) = 1$. From our definitions, the sampling period Δt_1 is sufficient, since $|\text{pathfind}_t(v_1, v_2, \Delta t_1)| = |\text{pathfind}_t(v_1, v_5, \Delta t_1)| = 1$; Δt_2 is optimal, since $|\text{pathfind}_t(v_1, v_3, \Delta t_2)| = 1$ while $|\text{pathfind}_t(v_1, v_4, \Delta t_2 + 1)| = 2$; Δt_3 is too long, since $|\text{pathfind}_t(v_1, v_4, \Delta t_3)| = 2$.*

3.2 Markers

To increase the sampling period which will reduce the monitoring overhead, we introduce the concept of markers and extend a sample with state information. A marker can be a system element such as the program counter, very useful, because a vertex in the control-flow graph is a basic block in the source code. Besides, a marker can also be a newly introduced variable solely used for the purpose of monitoring the software. For the remainder of this paper, we will only use this extended sample and thus $s := \langle state, v, t \rangle$ where $state$ is also a tuple defined as $state := \langle m_1, \ldots, m_k \rangle$ with m_i representing a marker of a system state such as memory, processor word, I/O registers, or our introduced variables.

We thus refine the pathfind function as $\text{pathfind}_s(v_i, v_j, state_i, state_j, \Delta t)$ where $state_i$ and $state_j$ are the state elements of the corresponding samples. Using the function pathfind_s, a sampling period T is *optimal*, if $|\text{pathfind}_s(v_i, v_{next}, state_i, state_{next}, T_i)| = 1$ while $\left|\text{pathfind}_s(v_i, v'_{next}, state_i, state'_{next}, T_i + \epsilon)\right| > 1$.

As stated above, markers are special variables that can be used for extending the optimal sampling period. We introduce such new markers and increment their values at strategically well-placed locations. We give the following example to show how the markers work.

Example 2. *Figure 2 shows a program control flow. All basic blocks have the same execution time $c(v_i) = 1$.*

Without introducing a monitoring variable a, we use function $\text{pathfind}_t(v_i, v_j, \Delta t)$ to find the optimal sampling period. Starting from vertex v_1, there are three possible paths afterwards. If we take the sample after time 1, then $|\text{pathfind}_t(v_1, v_i, 1)| = 1$ with $i = 2, 3, 4$. However, if we take the sample after time 2, then $|\text{pathfind}_t(v_1, v_5, 2)| = 2$. Figure 3 shows this mechanism. Thus, the optimal sampling period for node v_1 is $T_1 = 1$. Applying the same mechanism, for every other vertex v_i with $i = 2, 3, 4, 5$ in the control-flow graph, the optimal sampling period T_i with $i = 2, 3, 4, 5$ is $4, 3, 3, 2$ respectively. Thus, for the whole control-flow graph $G = \langle V, E \rangle$, the optimal sampling period T_{opt} is 1.

Using the monitoring variable a, Figure 4 shows the resulting optimal sampling period. We will use function $\text{pathfind}_s(v_i, v_j, state_i, state_j, \Delta t)$ to select the optimal sam-

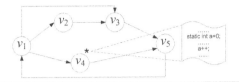

Figure 2. Control-flow graph with marker instrumented

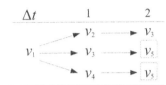

Figure 3. $\text{pathfind}_t(v_i, v_j, \Delta t)$

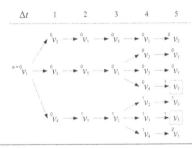

Figure 4. $\text{pathfind}_s(v_i, v_j, state_i, state_j, \Delta t)$

pling period. Starting from vertex v_1, the mechanism is shown in Figure 4. While $|\text{pathfind}_s(v_1, v_i, state_1, state_i, 4)| = 1$ with $i = 2, 3, 4, 5$ and state $:= \langle a \rangle$, $|\text{pathfind}_s(v_1, v_5, state_1, state_5, 5)| = 2$. Thus, for vertex v_1, the optimal *sampling period is 4. Applying the same mechanism, for every other vertex v_i with $i = 2, 3, 4, 5$ in the control-flow graph, the* optimal *sampling period T_i with $i = 2, 3, 4, 5$ is $7, 6, 6, 5$ respectively. Thus, for the whole control-flow graph $G = \langle V, E \rangle$, the* optimal *sampling period T_{opt} is 4. Compared with the previous example, introducing marker a increases the* optimal *sampling period T_{opt} by a factor of 4.*

4. Theoretic Optimum

By using markers we can increase the sampling period without losing any essential information about the execution paths. We call the process of inserting such markers into vertices instrumentation.

An important problem is to understand the limitations of such marker-based instrumentation. We therefore provide theorems to find the theoretic sampling period and decide termination conditions.

We require two additional definitions for the theorems. A pathpair *pp* can be defined as two paths which have the same entrance vertex and the same exit vertex with their exit vertices overlapping in time, but no other vertices between the entrance vertex and the exit vertex overlap in time. That is, $|\text{pathfind}_s(v_{en}, v_{ex}, state_{en}, state_{ex}, \Delta t_{ex})| = 2$ while $|\text{pathfind}_s(v_{en}, v_{next}, state_{en}, state_{next}, \Delta t_{next})| = 1$, where $0 < \Delta t_{next} < \Delta t_{ex}$. A path set is defined as a set of paths of which any two paths constitute a pathpair as defined above.

Lemma 1. *In a pathpair pp, a path which starts from the entrance vertex v_{en} and ends at any other vertex except the exit vertex v_{ex} is unique. Formally,*

$|\text{pathfind}_s(v_{en}, v_{next}, state_{en}, state_{next}, \Delta t)| = 1$, *where $v_{next} \in V_{pp}$ and $v_{next} \neq v_{ex}$.*

From the definition of a pathpair, we can draw the following conclusion:

Lemma 2. *(Optimal Vertex Sampling Period)*
In a control-flow graph, all pathpairs starting at vertex v_i constitute a vector $PP_{v_i}\langle pp_1, pp_2, \ldots, pp_k, \ldots, pp_m \rangle$, with each pathpair starting at time t_{ien} and ends at time t_{kex}, with $k = 1, 2, \ldots, m$. The optimal sampling period of this v_i is defined as $T_{opt_i} = \min |(t_{kex} - t_{ien})| - \epsilon$, with $k = 1, 2, \ldots, m$.

Therefore, to calculate the theoretic optimal sampling period, it is essential to find pathpairs for every vertex in the control-flow graph. We propose the following approach to find pathpairs starting from v_i: we construct an array of vertex states ordered by time; starting from v_i, we search v_i's child vertices and their corresponding states; then, we compare the state of child vertex v_j with that of v_k in the state array. If they meet the pathpair conditions, we will say that the path which starts from v_i and ends at v_j and the path which starts from v_i and ends at v_k constitute a pathpair; if the conditions are not met, we will treat that child vertex as a father vertex, add it to the state array after sorting and continue to search for pathpair.

Theorem 1 (Optimal Sampling Period). *For a control-flow graph with N vertices, the optimal sampling period of the whole graph is the minimum sampling period of all sampling periods for all vertices. Formally, $T_{opt} = min(T_{opt_1}, \ldots, T_{opt_N})$.*

By choosing a proper strategy to find the vertices which are instrumented with markers and thus making the states of overlapping exit vertices different, we can extend the pathpair and therefore increase the sampling period. However, the number of markers to instrument with is limited. With increasing the number of markers, the following situation would occur: After the number of the markers reaches a certain value, no matter how to instrument the vertices with markers, we can not extend pathpair any further. In other words, we cannot increase the sampling period any more. In this situation, regardless how many markers are available, we can no longer distinguish the two paths in the pathpair. Obviously, we should terminate the instrumentation process at this point. We propose the following theorem to draw this termination condition:

Theorem 2 (Pathpair Termination). *For two paths p_1 and p_2 in a pathpair, if they meet the following conditions:*

- *they have the same vertices with the same number of appearances but possibly different order in time respectively*
- *the states of the corresponding vertices are the same*

we can no longer instrument vertices with markers to differentiate these two paths, thus reach the theoretical optimum sampling period for this pathpair.

Proof. We use "reductio ad absurdum" to prove our theorem. Suppose that when reaching a pathpair with its two paths (p_1 and p_2) violating the above conditions in Theorem 2. For example, the two paths have different vertices between them or the two paths have exactly the same vertices but the numbers of their appearances in these two paths differ. We assume that the sampling period $T_{falseopt}$ we get here is the theoretic optimum sampling period. However, if we instrument the distinct vertices of the two paths or the identical vertices having different numbers of appearances in two paths with markers, we can still extend this pathpair and form a new pathpair whose sampling period is larger than $T_{falseopt}$. This contradicts the assumption that $T_{falseopt}$ is the theoretic optimum sampling period, because we can still distinguish these two paths. In this way, we can prove that our theorem is correct. □

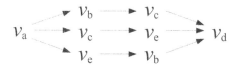

Figure 5. Scenario when theoretical optimum is reached using only one marker

When a pathpair satisfies the condition in Theorem 2, we can terminate the instrumentation process since we can no longer distinguish the two paths through instrumenting vertices with markers.

Theorem 3 (Single Marker Termination). *The instrumentation of a path set with a single marker is essentially an SAT problem.*

Proof. For a path set of n paths, there are $N = C_n^2$ pathpairs which share the same entrance and exit vertices. For a pathpair pp_k, all the vertices except the entrance and exit vertices constitute an internal vertices set Ω_k. In Ω_k, all vertices that can be used to instrument with markers constitute the set Φ_k, with all the other vertices which can not be instrumented constituting the set Ψ_k. Apparently, $\Omega_k = \Phi_k + \Psi_k$. When $cond_k = (v_{k1} \vee v_{k2}\vee,\ldots,\vee v_{kj}) \wedge (\overline{v_{kj+1}} \vee \overline{v_{kj+2}}\vee,\ldots,\vee \overline{v_{kj+m}})$, with $\Phi_k = \{v_{k1},\ldots,v_{kj}\}$ and $\Psi_k = \{v_{kj+1},\ldots,v_{kj+m}\}$, is satisfiable, we can distinguish the two paths in pathpair k.

The theoretical optimum for a graph using only one marker is reached, when we get to a path set, where $\Upsilon = cond_1 \wedge cond_2 \wedge \ldots \wedge cond_N$ can never be satisfied. $\square$

Example 3. *As shown in Figure 5 we get to a path set $S = \{p_1, p_2, p_3\}$ with $p_1 = v_a \rightarrow v_b \rightarrow v_c \rightarrow v_d, p_2 = v_a \rightarrow v_c \rightarrow v_e \rightarrow v_d$ and $p_3 = v_a \rightarrow v_e \rightarrow v_b \rightarrow v_d$. For pathpair $pp_{12} = \{p_1, p_2\}$, the two paths p_1 and p_2 can be distinguished using only one marker, because $cond_{12} = (v_b \vee v_e) \wedge \overline{v_c}$ is satisfiable. So do pathpairs $pp_{13} = \{p_1, p_3\}$ and $pp_{23} = \{p_2, p_3\}$, with $cond_{13} = (v_c \vee v_e) \wedge \overline{v_b}$ and $cond_{23} = (v_b \vee v_c) \wedge \overline{v_e}$ satisfiable. However, $cond_{12}, cond_{13}$ and $cond_{23}$ can not be satisfied at the same time using only one marker, in other words, $\Upsilon = cond_{12} \wedge cond_{13} \wedge cond_{23}$ can never be satisfied. At this point, we reach the theoretic optimum using only one marker.*

5. Calculating the Sampling Period

From Theorem 3, we know that calculating the theoretical optimum for a path set using one marker is actually an NP-hard problem. However, in practice, we encounter pathpairs much more often than path set as the likelihood is quite small for three or more paths to have the same entry and exit vertices with the same time span. Thus, it is both practical and important to develop an algorithm that has a polynomial runtime complexity to calculate the sampling period for pathpairs.

Given a control-flow graph $G = \langle V, E \rangle$, to calculate the optimal sampling period for a vertex in the pathpair, we propose the following algorithm based on the breath-first-search(BFS) (Cormen et al. 2001) to implement $pathfind_s$.

This algorithm is based on breadth-first search (BFS). Firstly, we pick a starting vertex $vertex$ by setting its $state$ as OPEN. We also build a set V_{open} which contains all vertices that are adjacent to vertex $vertex$ and set it to OPEN as well. In set V_{open}, we choose the vertex which has the least execution time t_{min} as the next starting vertex v_{next} to move to. At the same time, we update the sampling period by increasing it by t_{min} and the execution time of all vertices in set V_{open} by decrementing them by t_{min}. We build another set V_{toopen} which contains all the vertices that are both adjacent to and reachable from v_{next}. At last, we check

```
Vertex v := ⟨state, time⟩,
Edge e := ⟨v_src, v_dst, cond, updates⟩
for all v ∈ V do
    v.state ⟸ CLOSED
end for
v_en.state ⟸ OPEN
tResult ⟸ 0
V_toopen ⟸ {}
V_open ⟸ {}
loop
    if V_open is empty then
        for all v ∈ V_toopen do
            v.state ⟸ OPEN
        end for
        V_open ⋃{v|v ∈ V and v.state = OPEN}
        V_toopen ⟸ {}
    end if
    t_min ⟸ min(v.time) of all v ∈ V_open
    v_next ⟸ v where v ∈ V_open with v.time = t_min
    tResult ⟸ tResult + t_min
    for all v in V_open do
        v.time ⟸ v.time - t_min
    end for
    for all e ∈ E with e.v_src = v_next and eval(e.cond) = T do
        if e.v_dst.state = OPEN and e.v_dst.time > 0 then
            break from loop
        else
            create state for e.v_dst and execute updates (e.updates) on this state
            V_toopen ⟸ V_toopen ⋃ e.v_dst
        end if
    end for
    v_next.state ⟸ CLOSED
end loop
return tResult - 1
```

Algorithm 1: Find optimal sampling period for a vertex

the set V_{toopen}. If it contains a vertex whose $state$ is OPEN and execution time is greater than zero, we say the optimum sampling period for that vertex is reached and return the current sampling period as $optimum$. If not, we repeat the above procedure until we reach the $optimum$ conditions stated above.

Since the algorithm uses BFS, the runtime complexity for our algorithm is $O(|V| + |E|)$.

6. Instrumenting Control Flows

As stated above, in order to increase the sampling period, we introduce markers into the control-flow graph. In this section, we present our instrumentation approaches, analyze the related issues caused by the instrumentation and give our strategies to resolve these issues.

6.1 Increment VS Assignment

Instrumentation algorithms can use markers in different ways. One method is to increment the value of the marker each time the marker is hit. The other assigns absolute number to the marker. We provide the following two examples to prove that neither of these two options is better than the other.

Figure 5 shows a path set. By adding the marker with a different assignment to the last vertex before the exit vertex (e.g., $v_c \leftarrow a = 1$, $v_e \leftarrow a = 2$ and $v_b \leftarrow a = 3$) in each path, we can distinguish these three paths in a sample taking at v_d. However, according to Theorem 3, we cannot distinguish these three paths by increment-based marker methods. Thus, the assignment-based marker method can instrument cases that the increment-based one cannot.

Figure 6 shows another case. We can instrument v_4 or v_7 with increment-based markers and distinguish the two paths in pathpair

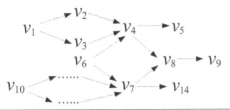

Figure 6. Scenario where increment works but not assignment

$pp_{(6,8)}$. However, since v_4 and v_7 are also the exit vertices of two other pathpairs $pp_{(1,4)}$ and $pp_{(10,7)}$, instrumenting these two vertices by assignments renders any previous instrumentations invalid, because several paths will share the same marker value and can invalidate another instrumentation at a later point. As shown, if we use increment instead, we will be able to solve this problem and distinguish the paths. Thus, the increment-based method can instrument cases that the assignment-based method cannot.

Since each method can instrument at least one case that the other cannot instrument, both methods have their justification as they can instrument different sets of control-flow problems.

6.2 Interference

Greedy instrumentation suffers from the problem that the instrumentation at a subsequent step may influence the instrumentations of previous steps. This can happen in either a direct or an indirect way. In *direct interference*, the subsequent instrumentation adds a marker to a vertex which is already part of a previous pathpair or path set and this breaks the original instrumentation for that particular pathpair. In *indirect interference*, the subsequent instrumentation adds a marker to a vertex which reveals a new pathpair with a shorter time span. The following two examples show these effects.

Example 4 (Direct interference). *We assume a control-flow graph, a greedy instrumentation strategy with only one available marker, and that each vertex has an execution time of one time step. Figure 7(a) shows the initial state of a pathpair $pp_{(1,4)}$. Any greedy strategy will pick either v_2 or v_5 to instrument with a marker. Here we assume that the strategy picks v_2 as shown in Figure 7(b).*

v_5 is also part of another pathpair $pp_{(6,11)}$ with a longer time span as shown in Figure 7(c). In this example, there will be a problem, if the greedy strategy picks v_5 in the subsequent instrumentation step instead of v_{10}, v_7, or v_8. By instrumenting v_5, it breaks the original instrumentation for pathpair $pp_{(1,4)}$, since both paths in pathpair $pp_{(1,4)}$ are then instrumented and can not be distinguished from each other.

Example 5 (Indirect interference). *We make the same assumptions as that in Example 4. As shown in Figure 8, the greedy algorithm first discovers the pathpair $pp_{(1,4)}$ and instruments v_5 to distinguish the two paths. By instrumenting v_5, the greedy algorithm also distinguishes the pathpair $pp_{(6,11)}$, so the algorithm will not notice it—we now call it hidden—and instead see the pathpair $pp_{(12,14)}$ as the next pathpair with the shortest time span. If the algorithm now instruments v_8, the hidden pathpair will cause a decrease in the sampling period.*

While a greedy algorithm can eliminate direct interference—see our SAT-based algorithms—eliminating indirect interference is hard, because it requires the algorithm to search for hidden pathpairs with all possible marker configurations.

6.3 Algorithms

We design seven different greedy algorithms (strategies) to find a suitable instrumentation. In our algorithms, the potential candidate

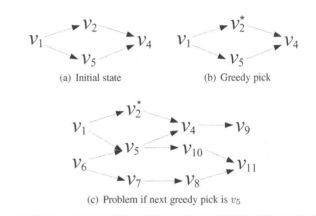

(a) Initial state   (b) Greedy pick

(c) Problem if next greedy pick is v_5

Figure 7. The problem of interference during greedy instrumentation

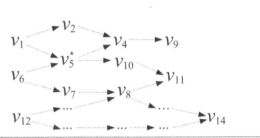

Figure 8. The indirect interference caused by greedy pick

vertex to instrument with markers to distinguish the two paths in a pathpair is the one that is distinct in either of the two paths or is contained in both paths but has different numbers of appearances.

The seven strategies can be divided into three categories:

- Degree-Based: The algorithms make decisions based upon the largest or smallest sum of in-degree and/or out-degree of the vertices in the context of the whole directed graph.

- Frequency-Based: The algorithms make decisions based upon the the occurrence frequency in the pathpair, such as the most or least frequently occurring vertex.

- SAT-Based: The algorithms transform the instrumentation into an SAT problem and compute a solution to find the instrumentation. The weighted SAT algorithm tries to combine the frequency-based with the SAT-based ideas.

7. Experimental Method

To validate the theorems and the concepts of this work, we build an instrumentation engine that instruments control flow graphs. The engine provides the framework to test different heuristics but also computes the theoretic optimum following Theorem 2. The outputs are the instrumentation vertices, the required execution time, and the resulting sampling period.

Our inputs are realistic and statistically significant. The input data consist of 5 000 control flow graphs which model typical C program flows (Thorup 1998). We generate these control flows with a customized version of Task Graphs For Free (Dick et al. 1998). Regarding the SAT-based heuristic, we implement it using a sat solver called SAT4J (09: 2009a) in our instrumentation engine. One experiment run works as follows: we select a control flow graph, a heuristic (or the optimum algorithm), and the number of available markers and pass these values to the instrumentation engine. The engine computes the input control-flow graph and

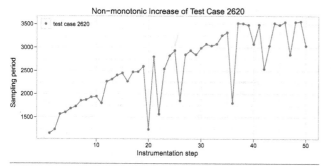

Figure 9. Example of interference of greedy instrumentation

returns the sampling period, vertex to instrument, and the required execution time. Since the computational work is quite intensive, we perform our simulation through the Canadian super computing cluster called SHARCNET (09: 2009b) collecting about 3.2 million instrumentation data points from up to 50 instrumentation steps, seven strategies, and several multi-marker configurations.

Our data successfully pass these integrity checks: (1) the execution time of the heuristic increases with the number of instrumentation steps, (2) no sampling period found by a heuristic is greater than the optimal sampling period, and (3) on average, the sampling period increases with the increase in the number of instrumentation steps.

The data distribution differs from a normal distribution (Shapiro-Wilk normality test for the data series varies around $p = 1^{-15}$). Thus, we rely on median values and testing procedures free of the normality assumption.

7.1 Instrumentation Performance Metric

To compare the performances of the algorithms, we take the maximum sampling period achieved in each run per algorithm and sum them up; see Eq. (1). This metric is robust against direct and indirect interference outlined in Section 6.2.

$$P = \sum max(T_i) \qquad (1)$$

7.2 Monotonicity Metric

Interference in the greedy instrumentation algorithms has an unpleasant effect on the monotonicity of the algorithms: a subsequent instrumentation may decrease the sampling period. This is contrary to what the user expects as each instrumentation increases the overhead and thus should increment the sampling period. Figure 9 shows an example of this behavior.

We use the following monotonicity metric to evaluate the algorithms:

$$M = \frac{N}{\sum d_i} \qquad (2)$$

with

$$d_i = \begin{cases} 0 & \text{if } run_i - run_{i+1} \leq 0, \\ run_i - run_{i+1} & \text{otherwise} \end{cases}$$

In the metric, we use d_i to denote the decrement between two instrumentation steps run_i and run_{i+1}, if the sampling period of one instrumentation step run_i is greater than that of its subsequent instrumentation step run_{i+1}. $\sum d_i$ denotes the sum of decrements in the entire instrumentation steps for a test case. N denotes the number of the total instrumentation steps. This monotonicity describes the reciprocal of average decrement across the entire process of instrumentation steps for a test case using a specific strategy and

gives a general assessment of that strategy, since the decrement represents the interference introduced by instrumenting vertices with markers.

7.3 Execution time

We measure the execution time by comparing the time stamp when the execution of heuristic starts with the time stamp after the instrumentation step is completed. The sum of all these times for one run provides the total execution time for that run. While we will not be able to compare quantitative results, because of the heterogeneity of SHARCNET, we will draw conclusions based on similarity of the algorithms.

8. Results and Discussion

Following the experimental methods presented, we give our experiment results which are sound and show statistically integrity. We also discuss the results and give the corresponding interpretation.

8.1 Instrumentation Performance

We follow the recommended guidelines for multiple testing (Benjamini and Hochberg 1995). We check that all input data for calculating the performance metric have roughly the same shape (single bell-like shape with a cut-off left tail) for all algorithms. The instrumentation performance differs significantly among the algorithms (Kruskal-Wallis Rank Sum Test returns $p = 2^{-6}$). Using a Bonferroni correction for multiple testing among our algorithms, we test an individual algorithm with a $p \leq \frac{0.05}{91}$ to be accepted.

Figure 10 shows the result of the performance measurements for up to 50 instrumentation steps and compares it with the theoretic maximum achievable following Theorem 3. The higher the performance value, the better. For the single-marker algorithms—the right part of the figure—the degree-based algorithms outperform the others except the 'max impact' algorithm. We use the Wilcoxon rank sum test with continuity correction and it shows that the differences among the degree-based algorithms are insignificant while it shows a difference between all degree-based algorithms and the 'min impact' as well as the SAT-based algorithms. An interesting point is that the SAT-based algorithms perform significantly worse than any of the other algorithms. Part of this is, because bad early decisions in the SAT algorithm cannot be undone by a later instrumentation. While, for example, the degree-based algorithms may break a previous instrumentation and causes direct interference, the SAT-based ones cannot do this, because they preserve all previous instrumentations.

Using multiple markers improves the performance and asymptotically approaches the optimum. The middle part of Figure 10 shows the 'max impact' algorithm with different markers. Since 'max impact' performs similarly to other degree-based algorithms, if we were using a different algorithm, it would result in the same data. The gains achieved with low marker increases are significant. However, once the number of markers grows beyond ten, the results no longer differ using the Wilcoxon rank sum test with the adjusted significance level.

8.2 Monotonicity

Besides instrumentation performance, we also investigate monotonicity by the monotonicity metric defined in Section **??**. Figure **??** shows the monotonicity of all heuristics normalized to SAT. The higher the monotonicity value, the better. The left part of the figure shows the results of using only one marker. We use the same statistical test procedures as mentioned above to establish statistical significance. The SAT-based algorithms clearly outperform all other algorithms. The reason is that the SAT-based heuristics always carry forward the previous pathpairs and thus guarantee that a

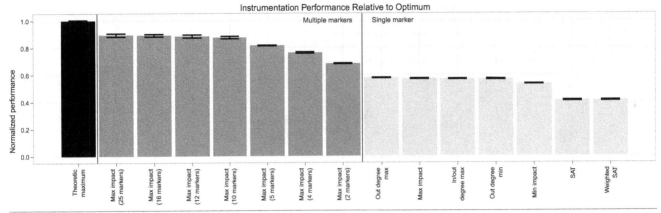

Figure 10. Instrumentation performance of all algorithms.

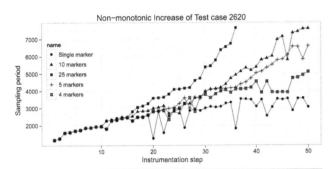

Figure 12. Improving monotonicity with multiple markers

subsequent instrumentation avoids interfering with a previous one. The remaining monotonicity only originates from indirect interference. We can also conclude that in general approximately 20% of the interference in the instrumentation is indirect interference while 80% is direct interference.

Using multiple markers, we try to: (1) increase the achieved sampling period, and (2) improve monotonicity. We try to increase the sampling period, because if one marker is no longer sufficient (Theorem 3), we can use another marker until we hit the optimum for pathpairs (Theorem 2). Figure 10 shows that we have achieved this. We also hoped to improve monotonicity by reducing the interference between subsequent instrumentation steps. Whenever we switch to a new marker, we avoid interfering with a previous instrumentation. The results are quite surprising.

The right part of Figure 11 shows monotonicity with multiple markers. While using multiple markers improves the monotonicity of the heuristics, the improvements are still rather limited, and at some point become insignificant in general. However, individual cases can benefit significantly, as Figure 12 shows. The SAT-based heuristics still shows a better overall monotonicity than the 'max impact' heuristic with 25 markers.

8.3 Execution Time

We use SHARCNET to compute the results and collected the execution time of each instrumentation step. Based on the differences in the available computation time and platforms on SHARCNET, the results are purely informal and allow us to draw only conclusions when we can justify them algorithmically. For example, the weighted SAT algorithm bases on the SAT algorithm and uses a timeout to bound the execution time. Its execution time is about three orders of magnitudes greater than the SAT-based test. How-

ever, the complexity of the weighted SAT algorithm yields no improvement as seen in the performance and monotonicity analysis before.

9. Conclusion

Determining the execution path of a program helps locate bugs in a program. However, for real-time systems the developer needs to bound the instrumentation overhead.

In our paper, we proposed a framework for sampling-based monitoring to determine the execution path of the program and analyzed different algorithms for instrumenting a control-flow graph. We defined the system model and proposed two theorems based on it to determine when to stop instrumentation. While all heuristics worked to increase the sampling period, the degree-based heuristics outperformed the SAT-based ones, but the SAT-based ones achieved a higher monotonicity. Through normalized comparison, SAT-based heuristic proved to be superior to others in terms of monotonicity based on which we further concluded that only 20% of interference was from indirect interference.

We showed how to increase the sampling period by using multiple markers. However, this method had limitation in that overusing markers did not pay off as much as we expected in the long run.

The presented work fills the first pieces in a holistic framework for sampling-based execution monitoring. There is room for optimization by improving the algorithms to achieve both longer sampling periods and better monotonicity. However, we also need to investigate decision criteria when to switch markers before moving on to industrial case studies.

10. Acknowledgements

We would like to thank Byoung-gi Lee for his help with implementing the test case generator based on Task Graphs For Free. We would also like to thank the SHARCNET, Canada's shared hierarchical academic research computing network, that permitted us to use their vast computing resources for simulations. This research was supported in part by NSERC DG 357121-2008 and ORF RE03-045.

References

IEEE Standard Glossary of Software Engineering Terminology. *IEEE Std 610.12-1990*, Dec 1990.

SAT4J. web page, Oct 2009a. www.sat4j.org.

SHARCNET: Shared Hierarchical Academic Research Computing Network. web page, Oct. 2009b. www.sharcnet.ca.

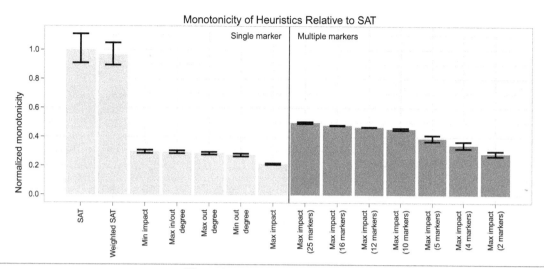

Figure 11. Monotonicity of heuristics

M. Arnold and B. G. Ryder. A framework for reducing the cost of instrumented code. In *PLDI '01: Proceedings of the ACM SIGPLAN 2001 conference on Programming language design and implementation*, pages 168–179, New York, NY, USA, 2001. ACM. ISBN 1-58113-414-2. doi: http://doi.acm.org.proxy.lib.uwaterloo.ca/10.1145/378795.378832.

T. Ball and J. R. Larus. Optimally profiling and tracing programs. In *POPL '92: Proceedings of the 19th ACM SIGPLAN-SIGACT symposium on Principles of programming languages*, pages 59–70, New York, NY, USA, 1992. ACM. ISBN 0-89791-453-8. doi: http://doi.acm.org.proxy.lib.uwaterloo.ca/10.1145/143165.143180.

T. Ball and J. R. Larus. Optimally profiling and tracing programs. *ACM Trans. Program. Lang. Syst.*, 16(4):1319–1360, 1994. ISSN 0164-0925. doi: http://doi.acm.org.proxy.lib.uwaterloo.ca/10.1145/183432.183527.

Y. Benjamini and Y. Hochberg. Controlling the false discovery rate: A practical and powerful approach to multiple testing. *Journal of the Royal Statistical Society. Series B (Methodological)*, 57(1):289–300, 1995. ISSN 00359246. URL http://www.jstor.org/stable/2346101.

M. Biberstein, V. C. Sreedhar, B. Mendelson, D. Citron, and A. Giammaria. Instrumenting annotated programs. In *VEE '05: Proceedings of the 1st ACM/USENIX international conference on Virtual execution environments*, pages 164–174, New York, NY, USA, 2005. ACM. ISBN 1-59593-047-7. doi: http://doi.acm.org.proxy.lib.uwaterloo.ca/10.1145/1064979.1065002.

B. Bouyssounouse and J.Sifakis, editors. *Embedded Systems Design: The ARTIST Roadmap for Research and Development*, volume 3436 of *LNCS*. Springer, first edition, May 2005.

A. Cheung and S. Madden. Performance profiling with endoscope, an acquisitional software monitoring framework. *Proc. VLDB Endow.*, 1 (1):42–53, 2008. doi: http://doi.acm.org.proxy.lib.uwaterloo.ca/10.1145/1453856.1453866.

I. Chun and C. Lim. Es-debugger : the flexible embedded system debugger based on jtag technology. *Advanced Communication Technology, 2005, ICACT 2005. The 7th International Conference on*, 2:900–903, 0-0 2005. doi: 10.1109/ICACT.2005.246099.

T. H. Cormen, C. E. Leiserson, R. L. Rivest, and C. Stein. *Introduction to Algorithms*. MIT Press, second edition, 2001.

R. Dick, D. Rhodes, and W. Wolf. Tgff: task graphs for free. In *Hardware/Software Codesign, 1998. (CODES/CASHE '98) Proceedings of the Sixth International Workshop on*, pages 97–101, Mar 1998. doi: 10.1109/HSC.1998.666245.

S. Elbaum, H. N. Chin, M. Dwyer, and M. Jorde. Carving and replaying differential unit test cases from system test cases. *Software Engineering, IEEE Transactions on*, 35(1):29–45, Jan.-Feb. 2009. ISSN 0098-5589. doi: 10.1109/TSE.2008.103.

S. Fischmeister and I. Lee. *Handbook on Real-Time Systems*, chapter Temporal Control in Real-Time Systems: Languages and Systems, pages 10–1 to 10–18. Information Science Series. CRC Press, 2007.

P. Frankl and E. Weyuker. An applicable family of data flow testing criteria. *Software Engineering, IEEE Transactions on*, 14(10):1483–1498, Oct 1988. ISSN 0098-5589. doi: 10.1109/32.6194.

M. Gallaher and B. Kropp. The Economic Impacts of Inadequate Infrastructure for Software Testing. National Institute of Standards & Technologg Planning Report 02–03, May 2002.

M. Hutchins, H. Foster, T. Goradia, and T. Ostrand. Experiments of the effectiveness of dataflow- and controlflow-based test adequacy criteria. In *ICSE '94: Proceedings of the 16th international conference on Software engineering*, pages 191–200, Los Alamitos, CA, USA, 1994. IEEE Computer Society Press. ISBN 0-8186-5855-X.

Learning From Software Failure. IEEE Spectrum, September 2005.

M. Jiang, M. A. Munawar, T. Reidemeister, and P. A. Ward. System monitoring with metric-correlation models: problems and solutions. In *ICAC '09: Proceedings of the 6th international conference on Autonomic computing*, pages 13–22, New York, NY, USA, 2009. ACM. ISBN 978-1-60558-564-2. doi: http://doi.acm.org.proxy.lib.uwaterloo.ca/10.1145/1555228.1555233.

S. H. Kirani, I. A. Zualkernan, and W.-T. Tsai. Evaluation of expert system testing methods. *Commun. ACM*, 37(11):71–81, 1994. ISSN 0001-0782. doi: http://doi.acm.org/10.1145/188280.188373.

N. Kumar, B. R. Childers, and M. L. Soffa. Low overhead program monitoring and profiling. In *PASTE '05: Proceedings of the 6th ACM SIGPLAN-SIGSOFT workshop on Program analysis for software tools and engineering*, pages 28–34, New York, NY, USA, 2005. ACM. ISBN 1-59593-239-9. doi: http://doi.acm.org.proxy.lib.uwaterloo.ca/10.1145/1108792.1108801.

J. J. Labrosse. *MicroC OS II: The Real Time Kernel*. CMP Books, 2002.

E. Lee and C. Zilles. Branch-on-random. In *CGO '08: Proceedings of the sixth annual IEEE/ACM international symposium on Code generation and optimization*, pages 84–93, New York, NY, USA, 2008. ACM. ISBN 978-1-59593-978-4. doi: http://doi.acm.org.proxy.lib.uwaterloo.ca/10.1145/1356058.1356070.

B. Liblit, A. Aiken, A. X. Zheng, and M. I. Jordan. Bug isolation via remote program sampling. In *PLDI '03: Proceedings of the ACM SIGPLAN 2003 conference on Programming language design and implementation*, pages 141–154, New York, NY, USA, 2003. ACM. ISBN 1-58113-662-5. doi: http://doi.acm.org.proxy.lib.uwaterloo.ca/10.1145/781131.781140.

B. Liblit, M. Naik, A. X. Zheng, A. Aiken, and M. I. Jordan. Scalable statistical bug isolation. In *PLDI '05: Proceedings of the 2005 ACM*

SIGPLAN conference on Programming language design and implementation, pages 15–26, New York, NY, USA, 2005. ACM. ISBN 1-59593-056-6. doi: http://doi.acm.org.proxy.lib.uwaterloo.ca/10.1145/1065010.1065014.

C.-K. Luk, R. Cohn, R. Muth, H. Patil, A. Klauser, G. Lowney, S. Wallace, V. J. Reddi, and K. Hazelwood. Pin: building customized program analysis tools with dynamic instrumentation. In *PLDI '05: Proceedings of the 2005 ACM SIGPLAN conference on Programming language design and implementation*, pages 190–200, New York, NY, USA, 2005. ACM. ISBN 1-59593-056-6. doi: http://doi.acm.org/10.1145/1065010.1065034.

E. Metz, R. Lencevicius, and T. F. Gonzalez. Performance data collection using a hybrid approach. In *ESEC/FSE-13: Proceedings of the 10th European software engineering conference held jointly with 13th ACM SIGSOFT international symposium on Foundations of software engineering*, pages 126–135, New York, NY, USA, 2005. ACM. ISBN 1-59593-014-0. doi: http://doi.acm.org.proxy.lib.uwaterloo.ca/10.1145/1081706.1081729.

J. Misurda, J. A. Clause, J. L. Reed, B. R. Childers, and M. L. Soffa. Demand-driven structural testing with dynamic instrumentation. In *ICSE '05: Proceedings of the 27th international conference on Software engineering*, pages 156–165, New York, NY, USA, 2005. ACM. ISBN 1-59593-963-2. doi: http://doi.acm.org.proxy.lib.uwaterloo.ca/10.1145/1062455.1062496.

W. Orme. *Debug and Trace for Multicore SoCs*. ARM, September 2008. http://www.arm.com/pdfs/CoresightWhitepaper.pdf.

R. Santelices and M. J. Harrold. Efficiently monitoring data-flow test coverage. In *ASE '07: Proceedings of the twenty-second IEEE/ACM international conference on Automated software engineering*, pages 343–352, New York, NY, USA, 2007. ACM. ISBN 978-1-59593-882-4. doi: http://doi.acm.org.proxy.lib.uwaterloo.ca/10.1145/1321631.1321682.

A. Shye, M. Iyer, V. J. Reddi, and D. A. Connors. Code coverage testing using hardware performance monitoring support. In *AADEBUG'05: Proceedings of the sixth international symposium on Automated analysis-driven debugging*, pages 159–163, New York, NY, USA, 2005. ACM. ISBN 1-59593-050-7. doi: http://doi.acm.org.proxy.lib.uwaterloo.ca/10.1145/1085130.1085151.

A. Srivastava and A. Eustace. Atom: a system for building customized program analysis tools. *SIGPLAN Not.*, 39(4):528–539, 2004. ISSN 0362-1340. doi: http://doi.acm.org/10.1145/989393.989446.

D. Tennenhouse. Proactive computing. *Commun. ACM*, 43(5):43–50, 2000. ISSN 0001-0782. doi: http://doi.acm.org/10.1145/332833.332837.

M. Thorup. All structured programs have small tree width and good register allocation. *Inf. Comput.*, 142(2):159–181, 1998. ISSN 0890-5401. doi: http://dx.doi.org/10.1006/inco.1997.2697.

B. L. Titzer and J. Palsberg. Nonintrusive precision instrumentation of microcontroller software. In *LCTES '05: Proceedings of the 2005 ACM SIGPLAN/SIGBED conference on Languages, compilers, and tools for embedded systems*, pages 59–68, New York, NY, USA, 2005. ACM. ISBN 1-59593-018-3. doi: http://doi.acm.org.proxy.lib.uwaterloo.ca/10.1145/1065910.1065919.

T. Zhang, X. Zhuang, S. Pande, and W. Lee. Anomalous path detection with hardware support. In *CASES '05: Proceedings of the 2005 international conference on Compilers, architectures and synthesis for embedded systems*, pages 43–54, New York, NY, USA, 2005. ACM. ISBN 1-59593-149-X. doi: http://doi.acm.org.proxy.lib.uwaterloo.ca/10.1145/1086297.1086305.

A. X. Zheng, M. I. Jordan, B. Liblit, M. Naik, and A. Aiken. Statistical debugging: simultaneous identification of multiple bugs. In *ICML '06: Proceedings of the 23rd international conference on Machine learning*, pages 1105–1112, New York, NY, USA, 2006. ACM. ISBN 1-59593-383-2. doi: http://doi.acm.org.proxy.lib.uwaterloo.ca/10.1145/1143844.1143983.

Cache Vulnerability Equations for Protecting Data in Embedded Processor Caches from Soft Errors

Aviral Shrivastava

Compiler and Microarchitecture
Laboratory, Arizona State University,
Tempe, AZ 85281, USA
aviral.shrivastava@asu.edu

Jongeun Lee *

High Performance Computing
Laboratory, Ulsan National Institute of
Science and Technology, South Korea
jlee@unist.ac.kr

Reiley Jeyapaul

Compiler and Microarchitecture
Laboratory, Arizona State University,
Tempe, AZ 85281, USA
reiley.jeyapaul@asu.edu

Abstract

Continuous technology scaling has brought us to a point, where transistors have become extremely susceptible to cosmic radiation strikes, or soft errors. Inside the processor, caches are most vulnerable to soft errors, and techniques at various levels of design abstraction, e.g., fabrication, gate design, circuit design, and microarchitecture-level, have been developed to protect data in caches. However, no work has been done to investigate the effect of code transformations on the vulnerability of data in caches. Data is vulnerable to soft errors in the cache only if it will be read by the processor, and not if it will be overwritten. Since code transformations can change the read-write pattern of program variables, they significantly effect the soft error vulnerability of program variables in the cache. We observe that often opportunity exists to significantly reduce the soft error vulnerability of cache data by trading-off a little performance. However, even if one wanted to exploit this trade-off, it is difficult, since there are no efficient techniques to estimate vulnerability of data in caches. To this end, this paper develops efficient static analysis method to estimate program vulnerability in caches, which enables the compiler to exploit the performance-vulnerability trade-offs in applications. Finally, as compared to simulation based estimation, static analysis techniques provide the insights into vulnerability calculations that provide some simple schemes to reduce program vulnerability.

Categories and Subject Descriptors C.4 [*PERFORMANCE OF SYSTEMS*]: Fault tolerance; C.3 [*SPECIAL-PURPOSE AND APPLICATION-BASED SYSTEMS*]: Real-time and embedded systems

General Terms Design, Measurement, Reliability, Theory

Keywords cache vulnerability, static analysis, soft errors, code transformation, compiler technique, embedded processors

1. Introduction

Soft errors are becoming an ever important concern for electronic system designs manufactured in deep sub-micrometer fabrication technologies. Soft errors are transient faults caused due to several sources, such as static noise in digital circuits, interconnect coupling, charge sharing noise etc., but radiation particle strikes are responsible for more transient faults than all the other causes combined [30]. Soft errors are especially important for embedded systems which may be used inside humans, close to humans, in financial, medical, and security transactions, and even in hostile and enemy territory, where there is a critical need for dependable information. Although the soft error rate in embedded devices such as handhelds is about once-per-year today, due to its exponential growth rate with technology generations, it is expected to reach alarming levels of once-per-day in about a decade [13].

Inside a processor, memory elements are most susceptible to soft errors, not only because they are typically the largest structures by area and transistor count, but also because there is no logical and temporal masking of soft errors in memories, and they operate on lower voltage swings [5, 9, 17, 31]. In fact, according to [18], more than 50% of soft errors happen in memories. Lower levels of memories (farther from processor) can be relatively easily protected using ECC (Error Correcting Code) based techniques, but protecting memories closer to the processor (i.e., L1 caches) results in high overheads. Previous research [16, 23] has shown that implementing SEC-DED (Singe-Error Correction and Double-Error Detection) can increase L1 cache access latency by up to 95%, power consumption by up to 22%, and area cost by up to 18%. Even if the performance overhead could be hidden, the power and area overheads cannot. Moreover, due to high degree of process variations, SEC-DED in caches is increasingly being used in covering up for manufacturing defects, leaving only parity checking for many cache blocks. The other option of implementing double-bit error correction has extremely high overheads [1, 21]. Another popular approach is to use write-through L1 caches. Write-through L1 caches ensure at least two copies of the latest data, therefore, they drastically reduce the vulnerability of data in caches, but it greatly increases the memory traffic between the processor and the lower levels of memory. Consequently, they are not desirable for multi-core and multi-processor systems [12].

This paper explores an orthogonal solution space for protecting data in caches - through software techniques. We observe that data is vulnerable to soft errors in the cache only if it will be read by the processor, and not if it will be overwritten. Basic code transformations like loop interchange, loop fusion, and data layout transformations like array interleaving, and array placement can change the read/write pattern of variables in the cache, and therefore should have significant effect on the vulnerability of data in the cache.

In order to demonstrate the effect of code transformations on vulnerability and to motivate for the need for techniques to ana-

---

* Corresponding Author

LCTES'10, April 13–15, 2010. Stockholm, Sweden.
Copyright © 2010 ACM 978-1-60558-953-4/10/04. . . $10.00

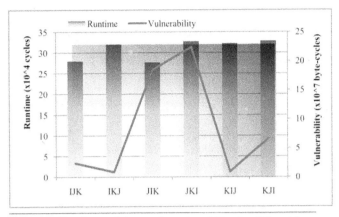

Figure 1. Runtime and data cache vulnerability for different loop orders of matrix multiplication. **Observation 1:** Variation in vulnerability = 96%, Variation in runtime = 16%. **Observation 2:** Loop order IJK has low runtime and low vulnerability. **Observation 3:** Runtime and vulnerability do not follow the same trend.

lytically estimate vulnerability, we perform a simple experiment of loop interchange on the matrix multiplication kernel. The application involves three 2D arrays of 32x32 words, and data cache of 1KB size, 32-byte block, direct-mapped, with write-back, and write-allocate policies. L1 data cache vulnerability is measured using cycle-accurate simulation. Figure 1 shows the vulnerability and runtime results for all six loop orders.

The **first observation** from the graph is that there is a much greater variation in vulnerability (96%, from JKI to IKJ) than in runtime (16%, from KJI to JIK). This shows that there is an interesting trade-off between vulnerability and runtime – in the sense that vulnerability can be significantly reduced at low runtime overhead.

The **second observation** we make from this graph is that IJK loop order has low runtime, and low vulnerability. In fact as compared to the least runtime loop order, JIK, we increase runtime by less than 1%, while reducing the data-cache vulnerability by more than 4X. This motivates for the need of finding such design/execution points, which simultaneously optimize runtime and vulnerability.

Our **final observation** from the graph is that the trend of runtime and vulnerability is not dependent, and cannot be derived from one another. This is a little counter-intuitive since to a first order of approximation, increase in runtime should imply an increase in the vulnerability, since the data spends more time in the cache. However, vulnerability depends on many other factors including program's data access pattern, cache parameters, and data placement.

Therefore, to be able to find design/execution points which are good both in terms of runtime and vulnerability, we need a scheme to estimate the vulnerability of data in caches. Only cycle-accurate simulation based techniques are known to estimate cache vulnerability. While they can certainly be used (e.g. in our motivating example) to explore some code transformations, and optimize for vulnerability and runtime, however there are limitations. Cycle-accurate simulation is very slow (only a few Kilo instructions-per-second [4]), and the design space for some compiler transformations can be very large. For example, using cycle-accurate simulation to explore design space for array placement for even a 32 x 32 matrix multiplication will take months on a 2 GHz dual-core processor system. Thus there is a need for efficient techniques to estimate cache vulnerability of programs.

To this end, in this paper, we develop analytical techniques to estimate data vulnerability in caches. In spite of analytic techniques

being efficient, they provide insights which can be used to develop simpler techniques to approximate; which is another critical limitation of simulation based techniques.

This paper makes several key contributions:

- Demonstrate that code transformations can significantly affect vulnerability of program loops. Often, it is possible to trade-off little performance loss for significant vulnerability reduction.

- Develop static analysis to accurately estimate vulnerability of affine loops. This includes making suitable approximations to trade-off accuracy of vulnerability estimation to computational complexity.

- Realizing that vulnerability estimation is complex, we show how our understanding from analytical vulnerability calculations can be used much more simply.

2. Related Work

Solutions to mitigate the impact of soft errors are being sought after at all levels of computer design e.g., careful selection and screening of materials [2], SOI fabrication technologies [6], increasing the transistor size, adding passive capacitance, or changing the transistor types with threshold voltage shifts, adding gated resistors [29], partially protected caches [15], software duplication [28], to triple modular redundancy [25].

As opposed to hardware techniques, software techniques reserve the advantages of *flexibility* of application, and therefore the overheads thereof. Indeed, the most important benefit of software schemes is as a last-minute fix. For example, if it is required to improve the system reliability after system design, then only software techniques may be easily applicable. Most existing software approaches that attempt to improve reliability and mitigate the effect of soft errors are based on some form of program duplication [8, 11, 22, 28], and therefore incur severe power and resource overhead. This work is fundamentally different from all those previous software approaches – we study code transformations that will improve the reliability of application programs – without re-executing any instruction of the program. Therefore our techniques can have much less power, performance, and resource overheads.

Caches are one of the most vulnerable microarchitectural components in the processor and several techniques have been developed to reduce failures due to soft errors in caches, e.g. [3, 15, 20, 32], however the effect of code transformations, and in general compilers has not been evaluated. While there has been recent work in developing compiler techniques for register file protection [14, 35], there are no compiler approaches to mitigate the impact of soft errors in caches. Vulnerability [19] is the measure of failure rate of caches, and only simulation-based techniques are known to estimate it [32]. The ability to estimate the vulnerability for any given code is fundamental to not only driving, but even developing any compilation technique to optimize for vulnerability, and in general, simulation based techniques are not usable. This underscores the need for more efficient techniques to estimate vulnerability of data in caches.

This paper proposes a static analysis to estimate program analysis, and our approach builds upon cache miss analysis [10]. While there is a more general approach [7] to model reuses in Presburger arithmetic [26], we use the reuse-vector based approach [34], since it is much more tractable. We use the Omega library [26] to perform polygon union and intersection operations and Polylib [24] to count the number of points in the polygons containing vulnerable iterations.

3. Background

3.1 Program Model

As is common with many static loop analysis techniques (e.g., [7, 10]), we consider a single loop nest, whose loop bounds and array index expressions are defined by affine functions of the enclosing loop indices. We also assume that all the load/store references inside a nest correspond to only the array references. Scalars can be analyzed as single element arrays. We use reuse vectors to find the last access, which further requires that references generate memory addresses in a uniform manner. In this paper we consider only perfectly nested loops and assume that the loop body has no conditional statement other than the loop itself. We also assume that memory accesses are made only through array references and arrays do not overlap (no alias). In practice, however, the constraints in our program model are not too restrictive. [10] showed by an empirical study, that most of the runtime-wise important loop nests in standard benchmark suits, like SpecFP are amenable to these analysis constraints.

3.2 Architecture Model

The basic architecture modeled here is a uni-processor model with a single-level, data cache hierarchy. It will be possible to extend the analysis to multi-level cache hierarchies, but, lower level of caches are relatively easily and routinely protected through ECC-based hardware techniques. We assume a direct-mapped cache with write-allocate policy, implying that if the processor writes to a cache block, and the cache block is not present in the cache, it is brought into the cache before writing on it.

3.3 Terminology

A **Reference** is a static memory read or write operation in the program whereas an *access* refers to a dynamic instance of a reference [10]. In the example illustrated in Figure 2 (a), $R_a = a[j]$, and $R_b = b[i]$ are references. For $N = 4$, each of them is invoked 16 times, and each invocation is an access.

The iterations of an n-level nested loop can be represented by an n-dimensional convex polytope $\mathcal{I} \subset \mathcal{Z}^n$ bounded by the loop bounds, called **Iteration Space** (outermost loop index being the first element in the vector). Each point in an iteration space represents an *iteration* of the loop nest. Similar to Chatterjee et al. [7] we augment each iteration with reference ID to represent *access* (IDs are given in the order in which they will be accessed in the loop of interest). We then define the **Access Space** as $\mathcal{A} = \{(\vec{j}, R) \mid \vec{j} \in \mathcal{I}, R \in \mathcal{R}\}$, where $\mathcal{R}$ is the set of IDs for all references. In the example, the access space of reference R_a is shown by the 4×4 grid of points in the light square, while that of R_b is shown by the points in the dark square in Figure 2 (b).

Like iterations, accesses are ordered. An access $(\vec{j}, R)$ precedes another access $(\vec{k}, S)$ if $(\vec{j}, R)$ is lexicographically less than $(\vec{k}, S)$, or $(\vec{j}, R) \prec (\vec{k}, S)$. [1] We use access and iteration interchangeably when considering only one reference.

The mapping from an iteration to memory address for a reference is called it's *access function*, $AF_R : \mathcal{I} \to \mathcal{Z}$, and the set of all possible memory addresses accessed is the **Memory Space** of the program. Figure 2 (c) shows the memory space of the program, where both arrays have 4 elements. Array a starts from the origin, and array b starts immediately after it ends. The access function of reference R_a is $AF_{R_a}(i, j) = S_a + j$, where $S_a = 0$ is the starting address of the array a in the memory. To model caches, we note

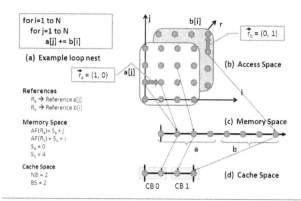

Figure 2. Access Space and Access Relations: **(a)** $R_a = a[j]$ is a reference, while each instance of it when the program executes is an access. **(b)** 16 points in the $i \times j$ space denotes the iteration space, and 2 sets of these points, one for reference R_a and one for R_b constitute the access space. **(c)** Accesses $(0, 1, R_a)$ and $(1, 1, R_a)$ have a *reuse relation* since they access the same memory address. **(d)** Accesses $(2, 2, R_a)$, and $(3, 3, R_b)$ access the same cache block, therefore they have a *conflict relation*, while accesses $(1, 1, R_a)$ and $(2, 2, R_a)$ are *unrelated* since they access different cache blocks.

that data is organized as blocks in caches. The *cache block* function CB gives the cache block number for a memory address. Thus $CB : \mathcal{Z} \to \mathcal{Z}$. The set of block numbers is called **Cache Space**. For a direct mapped cache, $CB(n) = (\frac{n}{CS})\%BS$, where CS is the cache size, and BS is the block size of the cache. In the example in Figure 2 (d), the cache has 2 blocks, each of size 2 elements.

Every pair of memory accesses have either a *reuse relation*, a *conflict relation*, or are *unrelated*. Two accesses have a **reuse relation** if they access the same memory address. In Figure 2, the access $(0, 1, R_a)$ and $(1, 1, R_a)$ access the same address in memory (corresponding to the location of $a[1]$, therefore they have a *reuse relation*. Given a memory access, $\vec{a} = (\vec{j}, R)$, any access $(\vec{k}, S)$ that has reuse relation with it is called a *reuse access* of $\vec{a}$, and $\vec{k}$ is called a *reuse iteration* of $\vec{j}$. Of particular interest is the last reuse access $\vec{a}$, and which is just the latest of reuse accesses among those that precede $\vec{a}$. Reuse vectors are used to succinctly capture last reuse access for references [34]. The reuse vector for R_a is $\vec{r_a} = (1, 0)$, and the reuse vector for reference R_b is $\vec{r_b} = (0, 1)$.

Two accesses have a **conflict relation** if they access different memory address, but the same cache block. In Figure 2, access $(2, 2, R_a)$ and $(3, 3, R_b)$ access different memory addresses, $a[2]$, and $b[3]$ respectively, but access the same cache block, $CB1$. Therefore accesses $(2, 2, R_a)$ and $(3, 3, R_b)$ conflict with each other. Finally, if both the memory addresses and the cache blocks of two accesses are different, then the two accesses are **unrelated**. In Figure 2, accesses $(1, 0, R_a)$ and $(2, 2, R_a)$ are unrelated, since they access different cache blocks.

In the absence of aliasing (e.g., the arrays are non-overlapping, the references are always accessed by their true names), there is no reuse between accesses of different references. However, there still may be conflicts between accesses of different references. Finally, if cache block size is equal to one element, there is just one reuse vector per reference to an array.

4. Cache Miss Equations

Any memory access that has a preceding reuse access but has no conflict access between itself and its last reuse access must result in a cache hit. Conversely, a conflict access between the two accesses

---

[1] **Note:** The lexicographical size of a vector $\vec{v}$, denoted by $\|\vec{v}\|$ and simply called *size*, is defined as the number of points that are lexicographically less than $\vec{v}$ in the iteration space. Greater/smaller/minimum is also in the lexicographical sense.

to the same address will cause a cache miss in a direct-mapped cache. Thus in order to identify cache hits and misses, we need to know only two things: i) last reuse access, and ii) whether a conflicting access exists or not.

Finding conflicts among accesses is easy. We know that two accesses $(\vec{j}, R)$, and $(\vec{k}, S)$ conflict iff $CB(AF_R(j)) = CB(AF_S(k))$. Finding the last reuse access is a little tricky. First lets assume that there is only one reference to an array, and there is only one reuse vector per reference. Then for the reference R, we assume that $\vec{r}$ is the reuse vector, then by definition of reuse vectors, if some memory address is accessed in iteration $\vec{j}$, then it was last accessed in iteration $(\vec{j} - \vec{r})$, and both access the cache block $CB(AF_R(j))$. Now by our definition of cache miss, there will be a miss iff, some other reference, say S, accesses the same cache block in iterations $(\vec{j} - \vec{r})$ through $\vec{j}$. This is captured in the Cache Miss Equation:

$$CME_R^S(\vec{j}, \vec{k}, \vec{r}) := (CB(AF_R(\vec{j})) = CB(AF_S(\vec{k})))$$
$$\wedge ((\vec{j} - \vec{r}) \prec \vec{k} \prec \vec{j}) \tag{1}$$

It states that the reference R will experience cache miss at iteration $\vec{j}$ along the reuse vector $\vec{r}$, due to another reference S in iteration $\vec{k}$, iff they access the same cache block. If the equality is satisfied for any value of $\vec{k}$, there is a cache miss at iteration $\vec{j}$. Now we can collect the iterations in which miss occurs:

$$MI_R^S(\vec{r}) = \{\vec{j} \in \mathcal{I} \mid \exists \vec{k} \in \mathcal{I}, CME_R^S(\vec{j}, \vec{k}, \vec{r})\} \tag{2}$$

MI_R^S is the set of all iterations $\vec{j}$ in which there is a cache miss for accesses of reference R due to a conflict with another reference S, along the reuse vector $\vec{r}$.

Till now we have only considered misses because of one other reference S. If there are multiple references, then there will be a miss at iteration $\vec{j}$, if there is a conflicting access due to any of the other references. Therefore,

$$MI_R(\vec{r}) = \bigcup_{S \in \mathcal{R}} MI_R^S(\vec{r}) \tag{3}$$

$MI_R(\vec{r})$ will be the set of all iterations $\vec{j}$ at which a cache miss occurs due to a conflict with *any* other reference (except another reference to the same array) by conflicting with the reuse due to reuse vector $\vec{r}$.

Now if there are multiple references to the same array, then it will result in multiple reuse vectors. There can be more than one reuse vectors, even if the cache block size is more than one element. In that case, there is spatial reuse [10]. When there are multiple reuse vectors, then, a cache miss will occur at iteration $\vec{j}$, if there is a cache miss due to the smallest reuse vector. Noting that if there is a miss due to smallest reuse vector, then even the longer reuse vectors must suffer a cache miss, we can simply use the intersection operator. Therefore,

$$MI_R = \bigcap_i MI_R(\vec{r_i}) = \bigcap_i (\bigcup_{S \in \mathcal{R}} MI_R^S(\vec{r_i})) \tag{4}$$

MI_R will contain the set of all iterations $\vec{j}$ at which a cache miss occurs for accesses of reference R due to any reuse vector, and any other reference. All the misses in the loop is then just a collection of misses of each reference.

5. Cache Vulnerability and Challenges in Estimation

Cache vulnerability (CV) is defined as the number of vulnerable bits in the cache, summed over the duration of a program execution, measured in byte-cycles. A bit is vulnerable if a soft error in it can destroy *architecturally correct execution* [19] of the processor.

Any bit that is going to be overwritten is not vulnerable. Any bit in the data array that is protected with parity bit is not vulnerable if the cache block is clean and the bit is going to be accessed while the block remains clean. This is because a clean block can be simply invalidated if an error is detected in it. We assume, that all lines are protected by a parity bit, and therefore clean lines are not vulnerable.

Only cycle-accurate simulation based schemes are known for cache vulnerability estimation. While simulation based techniques are time consuming, they can be used in extremely embedded applications, where neither the program flow, or the data changes. However, if the data and its size can change, then simulation based techniques are of little help. In addition, the design space of some code transformations and data layout optimizations is so large, that exhaustive simulation is infeasible. Thus, except for in extremely embedded systems, an efficient technique to estimate data cache vulnerability is needed to decide on code transformations and data layout optimizations. An analytical model to estimate cache vulnerability offer the additional advantage of insights that we gain, and can then be utilized either apply these technique more to a different architecture/data set. In addition, it also provides a systematic and more informed mechanism to trade-off accuracy for the analysis time.

We build our cache vulnerability estimation technique similar to cache miss equations, but estimating cache vulnerability is far more complicated than cache misses. Cache miss equations estimate the number of cache misses, which is a subset of the cache accesses to the same data. In comparison, cache vulnerability is the sum of "time duration" between two consecutive accesses to the same data, when the second access is a read, and the data that was accessed was dirty. The two main complications in vulnerability estimation, as compared to estimating cache misses are: i) Notion of "time" between accesses, and ii) More information about the accesses, e.g., whether the accesses is a read or write, the knowledge of whether the data was "dirty" at the time of access.

While the second problem is simpler (in theory) and can be solved by adding more detailed information about references, the first is a fundamentally challenging problem. To compute cache misses, fundamentally for every access we only define a **Boolean function** $AM: \mathcal{A} \rightarrow \{0, 1\}$ from the access space indicating whether there was a miss at the access. The misses in the program are then just specified as a subset of the access space, i.e., $Miss = \{\vec{a} \mid AM(\vec{a}) = 1, \vec{a} \in \mathcal{A}\}$. While enumerating the elements of $Miss$ is doubly exponential [7], the number of cache misses can be found in polynomial time by simply counting the number of elements in the set [10].

In contrast, to compute cache vulnerability, we need to define an **Integer function** $AV: \mathcal{A} \rightarrow \mathcal{Z}$ which captures the vulnerability of the data since it was last accessed. The program vulnerability can then be computed by adding the vulnerabilities of each access, i.e., $Vul = \sum_{\vec{a} \in \mathcal{A}} AV(\vec{a})$. One of the main challenges in computing cache misses is of converting the integer function into sets, such that the total vulnerability can be computed by finding the number of elements in a set.

Other practical challenges in vulnerability estimation is that analysis at iteration granularity is required, as compared to estimating cache misses in which analysis at cache access granularity suffices. Furthermore, since the dirty information in caches is maintained at a block level of granularity, a whole block is considered vulnerable if any single bit in it is vulnerable. This makes modeling cache vulnerability at word or byte granularity challenging. This is because, a word may be vulnerable even if there are no access to it at all – it can be vulnerable if the blocks containing them are dirty!

Finally, even if we can exactly compute CV by considering all these factors, such a model is likely to be very complicated (as we

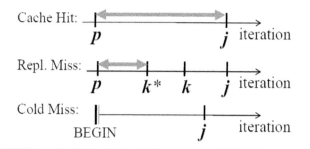

Cache Hit:

p j iteration

Repl. Miss:

p k^* k j iteration

Cold Miss:

BEGIN j iteration

Figure 3. Access Vulnerability is the vulnerability from the last accumulated from the last access to the same data. **Cold Miss:** The vulnerable duration for the first access is 0. **Cache Hit:** The vulnerable duration is the length of the smallest reuse vector. **Cache Miss:** The vulnerable duration is the distance from the previous access to the first interfering access.

will see in the paper), so as to jeopardize its practical use. Thus, an important challenge in vulnerability estimation is also to be able to make trade-off between modeling complexity and modeling accuracy, so that we can develop a relatively simple, yet accurate model of cache vulnerability.

6. Cache Vulnerability Equations

6.1 Access Vulnerability

Unlike cache misses, which is an "event", vulnerability is computed as an "interval", or "duration". The key idea in computing vulnerability is to associate it with each access. The *Access Vulnerability*, $AV: \mathcal{A} \to \mathcal{Z}$ of an access $\vec{a} = (\vec{j}, R)$ is the vulnerability of the datum at the memory location $MF_R(\vec{j})$, since it was last accessed. If $\vec{a}$ is the first access to the data, then the datum is not considered vulnerable, or $AV(\vec{a}) = 0$. Similarly, if if this access is a write access, then it is not considered vulnerable. The reason is, that the datum is overwritten, and any error in it since the last access is inconsequential. Also if if the datum was not dirty at the time of access, then the datum is not considered vulnerable. This is because we assume that parity protection will detect the error, and the correct value can be read from the lower levels of memory, which we consider protected (through use of ECC or any other scheme).

The access vulnerability is non-zero only when the the the access is a "read", and the datum was dirty at the time of access. However, the value of vulnerability depends on whether the access is a cache hit or a miss. If the access is a cache hit, then the datum was vulnerable for the whole duration from the last access to this access. Suppose that R is the only reference to the array, and it has only one reuse vector $\vec{r}$. Then the datum that is accessed by $\vec{a} = (\vec{j}, R)$ was last accessed by $\vec{b} = ((\vec{j} - \vec{r}), R)$. If the access $\vec{a} = (\vec{j}, R)$ is a cache hit, then the datum was vulnerable for the whole duration from $(\vec{j} - \vec{r})$ through $\vec{j}$, i.e., $AV(\vec{a}) = ||\vec{r}||$ (shown in Figure 3). However, if the access $\vec{a} = (\vec{j}, R)$ is a cache miss, then this datum was replaced by a conflicting access, say $\vec{c} = (\vec{k}, S)$, at iteration $\vec{k}$. Therefore, the datum was in the cache only from iteration $(\vec{j} - \vec{r})$ through $\vec{k}$. After this, from iteration $\vec{k}$ through $\vec{j}$, the datum was in the lower levels of memory, which we consider "protected". Therefore, $AV(\vec{a}) = ||\vec{k} - (\vec{j} - \vec{r})||$. However, even in the case when there are only two references, and only a single reuse vector per reference, the other reference may access and conflict more than once between accesses $\vec{b}$ and $\vec{a}$. In this case, we must consider only the distance from the last access $(\vec{j} - \vec{r})$ to the first access that interferes $\vec{k}^* = min(\vec{k})$. All these cases are illustrated in Figure 3.

6.2 Representing Integer Function

A central problem in CV modeling is how to represent the integer function AV. Recall that AM is a Boolean function, which can be easily represented as a set. Our solution is to augment the vector $\vec{j}$ in (2) with a scalar c, and let c take on all integer values less than the vulnerability l: $\{(\vec{j}, c) \mid 0 \le c < l = ||\vec{k}^*|| - ||\vec{p}||, \cdots\}$. Essentially we diversify each $\vec{j}$ exactly l times, so that we can get the total vulnerability simply by counting the elements of the set. However, still it is not obvious how to express $\vec{k}^*$. Since $\vec{k}^*$ is the earliest conflict iteration we would like to say $\vec{k}^* = min\{\vec{k}\}$, or $\vec{k}^* \le \vec{k}, \forall \vec{k}$. However, $\vec{k}$ is already qualified with existential quantifier ($\exists$), and moreover adding universal quantifier ($\forall$) causes the equation to be only a general Presburger formula and not a simpler Diophantine equation, greatly increasing the complexity.

We resolve this problem by counting *nonvulnerability* instead, i.e., the size of a reuse vector minus the vulnerability. Thus we first calculate *vulnerability capacity*, and subtract nonvulnerability from it to compute real vulnerability.

Access vulnerability AV_r of reference r with only one reuse vector $\vec{v}$:

$$ANV_R^S(\vec{r}) = \{(\vec{j} \in \mathcal{I}, c) \mid \exists \vec{k} \in \mathcal{I},$$
$$0 \le c < ||\vec{j}|| - ||\vec{k}||, \text{CME}_R^S(\vec{j}, \vec{k}, \vec{r})\} \quad (5)$$

$$ANV_R(\vec{r}) = \bigcup_S ANV_R^S(\vec{r}) \quad (6)$$

$$AV_R = ||\vec{r}|| \cdot |\mathcal{I}| - |ANV_R(\vec{r})| \quad (7)$$

Working with nonvulnerability also makes it easier to consider multiple references, as shown in (6). Further, read-hit iterations are automatically taken care of in this formula; for a hit iteration $\vec{j}$, (5) returns null since no $\vec{k}$ exists, and (7) returns the correct value. However, cold miss iterations should be excluded, which is not done by the formula.

6.3 Multiple Reuse Vectors

The formula (5)–(7) has two limitations: incorrect handling of cold miss iterations, and considering only a single reuse vector. Those two limitations are closely related and can be solved at once by extending the concept of reuse vector with *domain*. In our formulation as well as in CME, reuse vectors serve the purpose of limiting the search space for conflict miss to the previous m iterations, where m is given by the size of a reuse vector. Ideally, m should be given by the last reuse iteration (LRI). However, exact computation of LRI is intractable in the general case, but most often it can be found from reuse vectors. A reuse vector $\vec{r}$ of reference R is derived from

$$MF_R(\vec{j} - \vec{r}) = MF_R(\vec{j}) \quad (8)$$

which suggests $\vec{j} - \vec{r}$ is a possible LRI of $\vec{j}$. In order for that to be the case, two conditions must be met: i) $\vec{r}$ should be valid on $\vec{j}$ for (8), ii) there should be no smaller reuse vector valid on $\vec{j}$. We call the set of iterations where a reuse vector is valid for (8), the *domain* of the reuse vector. Certainly, domain can be defined for any reuse vector.

While there can be iterations that are not included in any domain (they are cold miss iterations), we can easily find the smallest reuse vector for any iteration that is included in at least one domain. Given a set of reuse vectors $\{\vec{r}_i\}$ sorted in their sizes, i.e., $\vec{r}_1 \prec \vec{r}_2 \prec \cdots$, and the corresponding set of domains $\{\mathcal{D}_i\}$, we define *differential domains*, $\{\mathcal{P}_i\}$, as follows.

$$\mathcal{P}_i = \mathcal{D}_i - \mathcal{D}_{i-1} - \cdots - \mathcal{D}_1 \quad (9)$$

Differential domain $\mathcal{P}_i$ is the set of iterations in which $\vec{r}_i$ is the smallest reuse vector. Clearly, differential domains are mutually disjoint, and do not include any cold miss iteration. Now we can easily extend (5)–(7).

$$ANV_R^S(\vec{r}_i, \mathcal{P}_i) = \{(\vec{j} \in \mathcal{P}_i, c) \mid \exists \vec{k} \in \mathcal{I}, \exists n \in \mathcal{Z},$$
$$0 \le c < ||\vec{j}|| - ||\vec{k}||, \text{CME}_R^S(\vec{j}, \vec{k}, \vec{r}_i, n)\} \quad (10)$$

$$ANV_R(\vec{r}_i, \mathcal{P}_i) = \bigcup_S ANV_R^S(\vec{r}_i, \mathcal{P}_i) \quad (11)$$

$$AV_R = \sum_i \left(||\vec{r}_i|| \cdot |\mathcal{P}_i| - |ANV_R(\vec{r}_i, \mathcal{P}_i)| \right) \quad (12)$$

6.4 Access Type and Cache block State

So far we have considered how to model the effect of cache hit/miss on CV. Now we consider how to model the effect of read vs. write difference. AV_R in (12) is accurate for read accesses. For write accesses we need to exclude vulnerability due to hit accesses, which we call *hit-nonvulnerability*. Hit-nonvulnerability, HNV_R:

$$HNV_R = \sum_i ||\vec{r}_i|| \cdot |HI_R(\vec{r}_i, \mathcal{P}_i)| \quad (13)$$

$$HI_R(\vec{r}_i, \mathcal{P}_i) = \mathcal{P}_i - MI_R(\vec{r}_i) \quad (14)$$

where $MI_R(\vec{v}_i)$ is calculated by (2)–(3).

Modeling cache block state is less obvious than access type. Exact modeling requires looking even beyond LRI ($= \vec{j} - \vec{r}$) for any write to the same memory block, with the search space expanded up to the next conflict access. Compared to the formulation developed so far, which needs to find only one conflict iteration ($\vec{k}$), this new modeling requires two more (write reuse, the next conflict), which will greatly impact the complexity. Fortunately, for loops with uniformly-generated references we have a much simpler rule. Among uniformly-generated references we can define a total order from their leading/trailing relationship. For instance, in a i-j loop nest, $A[i][j]$ trails $A[i+2][j+3]$ at the distance of $[2,3]$, which is in fact one of the reuse vectors of $A[i][j]$. We consider that a reference accesses only clean blocks if it does not follow a write reference. The other references are considered to access dirty blocks. We understand that this simple rule is only an approximation and is not always correct. However, it can be very easily applied and yet highly accurate if a write reference has no group reuse or the group reuse vector is small, which is the case in many loops including matrix multiplication.

6.5 Post-access Vulnerability

Our access vulnerability can account for only the portion of CV that becomes certain by the last access to each memory block. After the last access, there can be no more reuse but only zero or more conflict accesses. If a conflict access exists, the vulnerable interval extends to the first conflict access; otherwise, the vulnerable interval extends to the end of the program (provided that the block is dirty). Thus we need to find out i) the set of iterations in which the last accesses (per memory block) are made, and ii) the lengths of vulnerable intervals.

First, given a reference R, the set $\mathcal{P}_*$ of iterations for last accesses can be found from the *ranges*, $\{\mathcal{R}_i\}$, of reuse vectors, $\{\vec{r}_i\}$. Range is defined similarly to domain except that $-\vec{v}$ is replaced with $+\vec{v}$ in (8). Then it follows from the definition that $\mathcal{P}_*$ is the set of iterations that are not included in any range, or $\mathcal{P}_* = \mathcal{I} - \mathcal{R}_1 - \mathcal{R}_2 - \cdots$. Second, the vulnerable interval is either $|\mathcal{I}| - ||\vec{j}||$ or $||\vec{k}^*|| - ||\vec{j}||$, whichever is the smaller, where $\vec{k}^*$ is the earliest of, if any, future conflict iterations. Again we use nonvulnerability to find this interval. Post-access vulnerability of

---

Algorithm 1 Find access vulnerability of all references

1: **for all** $R \in \mathcal{R}$ that can access dirty cache blocks **do**
2:     integer (vulnerability of R): $V_R \leftarrow 0$
3:     Find all the reuse vectors $\vec{r}_i$ and their domains $\mathcal{D}_i$
4:     **for all** i in the increasing order of $||\vec{r}_i||$ **do**
5:         Find $\mathcal{P}_i$ from $\{\mathcal{D}_i\}$
6:         **for all** $S \in \mathcal{R}$ **do**
7:             Find $ANV_R^S(\vec{r}_i, \mathcal{P}_i)$ /* CME extended for CV */
8:         **end for**
9:         integer: $ANV_R(i) \leftarrow |\cup_S ANV_R^S(\vec{r}_i, \mathcal{P}_i)|$
10:         $V_R \leftarrow V_R + ||\vec{r}_i|| \cdot |\mathcal{P}_i| - ANV_R(i)$
11:     **end for**
12:     **if** R is a write reference **then**
13:         Compute HNV_R using CME
14:         $V_R \leftarrow V_R - HNV_R$
15:     **end if**
16: **end for**

---

reference R is $PV_R = |U_R| - |PNV_R|$, where $U_R = \{(\vec{j} \in \mathcal{P}_*, c) \mid 0 \le c < |\mathcal{I}| - ||\vec{j}||\}$ and PNV_R, the post-access nonvulnerability, is the union of all the post-access nonvulnerabilities PNV_R^S from different references S. Finally, $PNV_R^S = \{(\vec{j} \in \mathcal{P}_*, c) \mid 0 \le c < |\mathcal{I}| - ||\vec{k}||, \exists \vec{k} \in \mathcal{I}, \exists n \in \mathcal{Z}, \text{CME'}_R^S(\vec{j}, \vec{k}, n)\}$, where CME' is CME with $(\vec{j}, R) \prec (\vec{k}, S)$ substituting for the original range constraint.

6.6 Implementation and Complexity

Algorithm 1 lists the procedure to compute access vulnerability for all references in a loop (post-access vulnerability can be computed similarly). The core of this procedure is writing extended CMEs (line 7) and counting the integer points in them (line 9). CME, extended or not, is a set of constraints that specify a polytope possibly using existential quantifier, and counting integer points in such a polytope can be done in polynomial time using the *barvinok* library [33], which is based on *PolyLib* [24]. However, further complication comes from the union operation in between (line 9), which exists in CME as well. There are several ways to handle unions. A simple method is to convert unions into intersections (intersections pose no problem) using the inclusion-exclusion property ($|A \cup B| = |A| + |B| - |A \cap B|$), which has unfortunately an exponential complexity. Another way is to use Pugh's method of converting unions into disjoint unions [27]. Counting the number of integer points is repeated for each reuse vector (line 4) and for each reference that can access dirty cache blocks (line 1). In our current implementation the complexity is dominated by the handling of union operator, and is $O(c \cdot N \cdot 2^{|\mathcal{R}|})$, where c is the average time for handling unions, and N is the total number of reuse vectors of references that can access dirty blocks.

7. Experiments

7.1 Vulnerability and Runtime Trade-off

Here we demonstrate through simulation, that interesting trade-off exists between vulnerability and runtime of applications. At the first glance, it seems that as the runtime increases, the vulnerability of the program should also increase, and therefore they are closely coupled. While this is true in general, there is a very significant impact of the access pattern on the cache behavior, significantly changing the amount of vulnerable data present in the cache, and therefore this direct coupling may not be realized. We show this by experimenting on several loop transformations. We collected important loop kernels from the SPEC 2000 and multimedia benchmark suites. We modified the SimpleScalar [4] simulator to com-

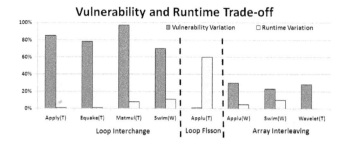

Figure 4. Runtime vs. Vulnerability: Opportunities to greatly reduce vulnerability at little performance cost exist.

Loop order	Analytical			Simulation			
	CV(li)	#CM	ACV	CV(li)	#CM	CV(bc)	RT(c)
ikj[†]	2071	538	**1321**	2071	538	**1.71M**	**41.2K**
kij	5488	788	2874	5488	788	4.67M	45.9K
ijk*	6744	418	2669	6744	**418**	**5.07M**	**39.0K**
kji	15163	1746	7377	15163	1746	16.71M	68.5K
jik	33852	598	8816	33852	598	22.59M	42.5K
jki	32341	1544	11732	32341	1544	33.06M	65.4K
Corr.	1.000	1.000	.995			—	

Table 1. Vulnerability results for mmult, N=12. Legend - CV: cache vulnerability, CM: cache miss, ACV: adjusted CV, RT: runtime, (li): line-iteration, (bc): byte-cycle, and (c): cycle.

pute the data cache vulnerability. The sim-outorder simulator has been parameterized to model a simple in-order embedded processor with $L1$ data cache of size $32KB$, direct mapped, with 32 byte cache block size, and 25 cycle miss penalty. The benchmarks are compiled with gcc(version 2.95.3) using the '-O' option to ensure that the compiler does reschedule the loops.

Figure 4 plots the variation in the runtime and vulnerability of the $L1$ data cache for three popular loop and data transformations, loop interchange, loop fusion, and array interleaving. For each transformation, we find the setting that results in the minimum vulnerability and the setting that results in the maximum vulnerability. The vulnerability variation is then computed as difference in the vulnerabilities of these configuration divided by the vulnerability in the maximum vulnerability setting. The runtime variation is also computed using the minimum and maximum vulnerability settings. For example, for loop interchange on matrix multiplication, Figure 1 shows, that the maximum vulnerability loop order is JKI, and the minimum vulnerability loop order is IKJ. The runtime and vulnerability variations are computed for these configurations. For loop fission there are only two setting, either the loops are fused, or they are separate (fission). Similarly there are two settings for the array interleaving case, either all the arrays are separate, or all the arrays in the loop are interleaved.

Next to application names the letter, T or W, in parentheses indicates the direction of variation; vulnerability and runtime move in the opposite directions (trade-off or T) or in the same direction (win-win or W). In about half the applications (particularly for loop interchange), we observe trade-off relationship between vulnerability and runtime, typically with much less variation in runtime (46% vulnerability variation vs. 16% runtime variation, on average). This means that for some applications we can greatly reduce vulnerability while affecting performance very little, reconfirming our motivation for cost-effective soft error approaches by compilers. In a win-win situation, on the other hand, we can get automatic vulnerability reduction by choosing performance-optimal loop transformations.

Clearly the percentage variation in runtime and vulnerability is sensitive on the relative size of the application data and cache size and other cache and memory parameters. For example, if the cache is extremely small, and all accesses miss, then will be little impact of loop orders on either cache misses, or the vulnerability. Similarly, if the cache is quite large, and there are only capacity misses, then again there will be no variation in the runtime and vulnerability of the loops. However, in general, we expect the variation in vulnerability to be much more magnified than the variation in the runtime, due to the multiplicative effect of misses in vulnerability computation. To exploit vulnerability-runtime trade-offs, techniques to estimate vulnerability are required, and efficient techniques (like Cache Miss Equations for performance) will be needed if we want the compiler to make these trade-offs automatically.

7.2 Model Validation

To validate our static analysis as well as to demonstrate its effectiveness and usefulness in program optimization we use the matrix multiply loop kernel. Our static analysis is performed using an automated analysis flow, which first derives reuse vectors and their domains from application description, then generates vulnerability equations, and finally calculates cache vulnerability using an integer-point counting engine. Simulation is performed using the SimpleScalar cycle-accurate simulator [4]. In all our experiments we assume that the L1 data cache is write-back and direct-mapped, with 32-byte line size. The cache size is set to 1~4 KBytes depending on the application's memory footprint. Small cache sizes are chosen not only to model embedded systems but also to induce frequent cache misses, which will create more variety in the number of cache misses and cache vulnerability, and thus make it more challenging to predict the cache behavior.

Loop interchange is a well-known loop optimization that changes the order of loops in a loop nest. Since it can completely reorder the memory accesses in a loop, loop interchange can greatly affect cache vulnerability as well as cache misses. As we will see in our experimental results, there is usually much greater variation in cache vulnerability than in the number of cache misses. Moreover, the loop order with the least number of cache misses is not always the one with the lowest cache vulnerability. This suggests that in order to address reliability issues, compilers should specifically target vulnerability reduction rather than just cache miss reduction.

Table 1 compares the cache vulnerability of mmult (matrix multiplication) computed by our static analysis and by simulation. The adjusted cache vulnerability (ACV) is calculated using the number of cache misses (#CM) predicted by the CM equations [10] with modifications due to domains. The rows are sorted in the increasing order of simulation CV in byte-cycles (7th column). The last row lists the correlation coefficient between each column on the analytical side and the corresponding column on the simulation side, with ACV corresponding to CV in byte-cycles on the simulation side.

First, we can see that the second column (analytical CV in line-iterations) exactly matches the fifth column (CV in line-iteration from simulation). Mmult has nontrivial access pattern in that all three references have different pairs of spatial and temporal reuse vectors. Thus this validation result gives some assurance of our CV equations. In the table, we also observe that the number of cache misses predicted by the CM equations, with modifications due to domains, is 100% accurate as compared to simulation. Finally, the ACV numbers also closely follow the simulation results, with a very high correlation.

Besides the basic validation results, there are interesting points to observe from the table. First, the CV variation is much higher than CM variation or RT (runtime) variation. Cache vulnerability, as measured in byte-cycles from simulation, varies from 1.71M to 33.06M, or more than 19 times, whereas the number of cache misses and runtime vary by mere 3.2 and 1.7 times respectively.

Loop order	Analytical			Simulation			
	CV(li)	#CM	ACV	CV(li)	#CM	CV(bc)	RT(c)
ikj[†]	3622	2173	**3055**	3622	2333	**3.19M**	92.3K
ijk[*]	9892	1462	5230	10778	**1574**	**9.25M**	79.4K
kij	10221	2653	6520	8988	2773	10.47M	99.1K
kji	26150	3658	13575	26103	3801	35.79M	130.3K
jik	63882	1564	18549	53568	1692	49.15M	82.9K
jki	66581	3438	24793	57827	3565	81.88M	127.1K
Corr.	.9978	.9998	.9919			—	

Table 2. Vulnerability results for mmult, N=14. Legend - CV: cache vulnerability, CM: cache miss, ACV: adjusted CV, RT: runtime, (li): line-iteration, (bc): byte-cycle, and (c): cycle.

Therefore the effect of compiler optimizations for cache vulnerability can be greater than for cache misses. Second, the loop order for the minimum RT is not the same as the one for the minimum CV. The original loop order, which is marked with an asterisk in the first column, has minimum CM and consequently minimum runtime as well. However, if we choose another loop order, marked with a dagger, the cache vulnerability can be reduced by almost three times while the runtime is increased by only 5.7% (The minimum-CV loop-order can be correctly predicted by our analysis as shown in the table). Please note that the cache vulnerability in byte-cycles already takes into account the effect of increased runtime; therefore, the three times reduction in CV is the real reduction that we can expect to see in the soft error rate of the data array of L1 data cache. The above two points strongly suggest the need and scope of compiler optimizations to reduce cache vulnerability, which has been neglected in traditional loop optimizations focusing on cache misses only. Our static analysis can be an important first step toward compiler optimizations for cache reliability.

A potential weakness of our technique, as it relies on reuse vectors to simplify the equations, is the inaccuracy of reuse vectors and their domains. The prediction of reuse vectors on the last reuse access can become less accurate at the boundary of the iteration space. In our first example where $N = 12$, the iteration space is divided by the cache line size in all its dimensions (a cache line contains exactly four array elements of double word each). If we change N to 14, the boundary effect starts to appear, which is shown in Table 7.2. In the table we notice that even the CM equations start to disagree with simulation although the overall correlation is very high. Comparing Columns 2 and 5 (CV in line-iterations), our CV equations tend to be more accurate in low CV region while it amplifies in high CV region. Our CV analysis sometimes loses on the details but it accurately captures the overall trend. Most importantly, the ordering in the adjusted CV exactly matches the ordering in the simulation CV in byte-cycles. Again in this example, we observe the same pattern that the loop order for minimum CM is different from that of minimum CV, and there is much more to gain in terms of cache vulnerability if we can make a little trade-off in terms of runtime.

7.3 Analytical Optimization Case Study

Many loop transformations significantly affect cache vulnerability, often much more than cache misses. While our cache vulnerability equations can be used to accurately compute the total cache vulnerability of a loop nest, and thus can guide compiler optimizations, evaluating the equations is not always easy due to the limitations of back-end tools. Here we showcase alternative use cases of our cache vulnerability equations, using data placement.

7.3.1 Array Placement

In loops, array placement can dramatically affect the number of cache misses and cache vulnerability. There are two ways to change

```
for ( i = 0 ; i < N ; i++ )
  for ( j = 0 ; j < N ; j++ ) {
    A_{j,i+1} = f_1(P_{j,i+1}, P_{j,i}, U_{j,i+1})
    B_{j+1,i} = f_2(P_{j+1,i}, P_{j,i}, V_{j+1,i})
    C_{j+1,i+1} = f_3(V_{j+1,i+1}, V_{j+1,i}, U_{j+1,i+1},
             U_{j,i+1}, P_{j,i}, P_{j,i+1}, P_{j+1,i+1}, P_{j+1,i})
    D_{j,i} = f_4(P_{j,i}, U_{j,i+1}, U_{j,i}, V_{j+1,i}, V_{j,i})
  }
```

Figure 5. Calc1 loop from swim (after loop interchange).

array placement. Intra-variable padding increases row sizes to reduce cache conflicts (both self and cross), which increases memory footprint. Inter-variable padding, or array placement adds unused space between arrays, or changes the base addresses of arrays, to reduce cache conflicts between different arrays. We use array placement to demonstrate the effectiveness of analytical optimization on cache vulnerability.

Figure 5 shows an abstract version of a loop nest from swim after loop interchange (detail is omitted to avoid copyright infringement). Hereafter we refer to the loop-interchanged loop as the original loop. This loop involves 7 arrays and many more references with very complex access patterns. Exhaustive exploration of array placement parameters for such a loop is prohibitive. For a very small 1KB cache, and even after restricting the base addresses to the cache line boundary (=32B), the design space has still $(2^5)^6 = 2^{30}$ combinations. Instead, we can quickly find optimal points exploiting the intuition provided by our CV equations.

Our CV equation has two parts. It first computes the total vulnerability *capacity* and then subtracts nonvulnerability from it. Often the total vulnerability capacity is not affected by base addresses. Therefore our goal is to maximize nonvulnerability by changing base addresses. Nonvulnerability is proportional to the distance between the current iteration and the earliest conflict iteration after the previous reuse. In other words, maximum nonvulnerability occurs if a dirty cache line is evicted immediately after it is accessed, which agrees with the intuition. However, since frequent cache conflict will increase runtime, which negatively impacts cache vulnerability, our strategy is to evict as soon as possible those dirty cache lines that will *not* be accessed for a long time.

In our original loop in Figure 5, dirty cache lines are generated only by the four LHS (left-hand side) references. We can evict those lines by creating conflicts between each of them and any of the ensuing accesses. Let us use write accesses for that, since write misses generally incur less penalty. Then we have a chain of conflicts like this: $A_{j,i+1} \rightarrow B_{j+1,i} \rightarrow C_{j+1,i+1} \rightarrow D_{j,i}$. The last reference $D_{j,i}$ can be made to have conflict with one of the read references in the next iteration.

To derive formulas let us assume that all the arrays are initially placed at offset zero modulo the cache size, and that we can independently control the offset μ_X of each array X. Note that this can be implemented very easily without losing optimality. Let us also assume $\mu_A = 0$. Then the above chain of conflicts gives the offsets of the other three arrays. For instance, between A and B:

$$Addr(A_{j,i+1}) \equiv Addr(B_{j+1,i})$$
$$\Leftrightarrow \quad \mu_A + jM + (i+1) \equiv \mu_B + (j+1)M + i$$

where $\equiv$ is equality under modulo on the cache size and M is the size of each row (assuming every array has the same row size).

For the last reference, we must consider the next iteration, which can be either the next j-iteration or the next i-iteration. For each case we can set up a different array to have conflict with $D_{j,i}$. We explore three choices.

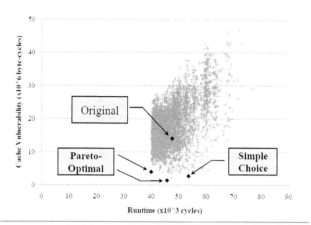

Figure 6. Cache vulnerability and runtime reduction through array placement.

Loop	CV (bc)	%reduc.	RT (c)	%incr.
Original (loop-interchanged)	14.08M	–	47.7K	–
Simple choice	2.69M	80.9%	53.6K	12.4%
Pareto-optimal 1	1.36M	90.3%	45.8K	–3.9%
Pareto-optimal 2	3.92M	72.1%	40.0K	–16.2%

Table 3. Array placement optimization results for swim

(1) Simple choice: Using $U_{j,i+1}$ and $P_{j,i}$

$$Addr(D_{j,i}) \equiv Addr(U_{j,i+1})|_{j=j+1}$$
$$\Leftrightarrow \quad \mu_D + jM + i \equiv \mu_U + (j+1)M + (i+1)$$

and

$$Addr(D_{j,i})|_{j=N-1} \equiv Addr(P_{j,i})|_{i=i+1,j=0}$$
$$\Leftrightarrow \quad \mu_D + (N-1)M + i \equiv \mu_P + (i+2)$$

Figure 6 plots CV and runtime results from simulation for random offsets (5000 instances). It also shows the CV and runtime for the original loop, which is about the center of the distribution. For parameters we use $N = 14$ and $M = 16$, and the cache size is set to 1KB. Compared to the original loop, our simple choice can reduce CV by more than 80%, which further validates our static vulnerability model. However the runtime is significantly increased. Although it is not surprising given that we have tried only to reduce CV, it suggests that cache misses should be considered in order to get truly optimal parameters.

(2) Pareto-optimal: To contain the runtime increase problem we resort to traditional CM reduction methods such as [10]. The key idea is to make the read references conflict as little as possible. Close examination of the offsets determined by the simple choice reveals that $\mu_U = \mu_C$ and $\mu_V = \mu_A$, which creates unnecessary conflicts and increases runtime. The latter is because we did not set any constraint on μ_V, which defaulted to zero, and the former is by chance. To improve the situation we set up a different reference $V_{j+1,i}$ to have conflict with $D_{j,i}$ along the j-loop, and used either $P_{j,i+1}$ or $P_{j+1,i}$ to have conflict along the i-loop, which gives two sets of parameters. Then the remaining free array U is assigned an offset that is farthest away from all the other arrays. The simulation results for these sets of parameters are shown in Figure 6 (marked as Optimal). Both points are pareto-optimal, and reduces CV by up to 90% or runtime by up to 16% compared to the original loop. Table 3 summarizes the exploration results.

8. Summary

To combat the threat of soft errors, techniques have been developed at all abstractions of processor design. Software schemes are particularly useful since they provide flexibility of application and therefore overheads, and can be applied in current or even previous generation processors, and most importantly, are irreplaceable as a last-minute fix. Caches are the most "vulnerable" component in the processor, and traditional ECC-based techniques are getting used up in manufacturing errors, and effectively only parity protection remains. While there exist some microarchitectural techniques to reduce cache vulnerability, there are no compiler based techniques. This is chiefly owing to the lack of efficient schemes to estimate cache vulnerability – for which only simulation based techniques are known. This paper develops analytical techniques to efficiently and statically estimate cache vulnerability of programs, opening the doors for compiler techniques to trade-off power and performance for reliability. Our experiments demonstrate that often it is possible to trade-off a little performance for a significant vulnerability reduction by simple code transformations. In addition, we demonstrate how the insights from vulnerability calculations can be used to innovate simple practical schemes to reduce program vulnerabilities.

Acknowledgments

This research was partially funded by grants from National Science Foundation CCF-0916652, Microsoft Research, Raytheon, SFAz, Stardust Foundation, Korea Research Foundation Grant funded by the Korean Government(MOEHRD) (KRF-2007-357-D00225) and the 2009 Research Fund of the UNIST (Ulsan National Institute of Science and Technology).

References

[1] A. Agarwal, B. Paul, and K. Roy. Process variation in nano-scale memories: failure analysis and process tolerant architecture. pages 353–356, Oct. 2004.

[2] R. Baumann, T. Hossain, S. Murata, and H. Kitagawa. Boron compounds as a dominant source of alpha particles in semiconductor devices. In *Anual proceedings of IEEE symposium on Reliability Physics*, pages 297–302, 1995.

[3] J. A. Blome, S. Gupta, S. Feng, and S. Mahlke. Cost-efficient soft error protection for embedded microprocessors. In *CASES '06: Proceedings of the 2006 international conference on Compilers, architecture and synthesis for embedded systems*, pages 421–431, New York, NY, USA, 2006. ACM Press. ISBN 1-59593-543-6. doi: http://doi.acm.org/10.1145/1176760.1176811.

[4] D. Burger and T. M. Austin. The simplescalar tool set, version 2.0. *SIGARCH Comput. Archit. News*, 25(3):13–25, 1997. ISSN 0163-5964. doi: http://doi.acm.org/10.1145/268806.268810.

[5] Y. Cai, M. T. Schmitz, A. Ejlali, B. M. Al-Hashimi, and S. M. Reddy. Cache size selection for performance, energy and reliability of time-constrained systems. In *ASP-DAC '06: Proceedings of the 2006 Asia and South Pacific Design Automation Conference*, pages 923–928, Piscataway, NJ, USA, 2006. IEEE Press. ISBN 0-7803-9451-8. doi: http://doi.acm.org/10.1145/1118299.1118507.

[6] E. Cannon, D. Reinhardt, M. Gordon, and P. Makowenskyj. SRAM SER in 90, 130 and 180 nm bulk and SOI technologies. *Reliability Physics Symposium Proceedings, 2004. 42nd Annual. 2004 IEEE International*, pages 300–304, April 2004.

[7] S. Chatterjee, E. Parker, P. J. Hanlon, and A. R. Lebeck. Exact analysis of the cache behavior of nested loops. *SIGPLAN Notices*, 36(5):286–297, 2001. ISSN 0362-1340. doi: http://doi.acm.org/10.1145/381694.378859.

[8] L. Chen and A. Avizienis. N-version programming: A fault-tolerance approach to reliability of software operation. In *Twenty-Fifth*

International Symposium on Fault-Tolerant Computing, pages 113–119, Jun 1995.

[9] J. Gaisler. Evaluation of a 32-bit microprocessor with built-in concurrent error-detection. *Fault-Tolerant Computing, International Symposium on*, 0:42, 1997. ISSN 0731-3071. doi: http://doi.ieeecomputersociety.org/10.1109/FTCS.1997.614076.

[10] S. Ghosh, M. Martonosi, and S. Malik. Cache miss equations: an analytical representation of cache misses. In *ICS '97*, pages 317–324, 1997. ISBN 0-89791-902-5. doi: http://doi.acm.org/10.1145/263580.263657.

[11] M. A. Gomaa and T. N. Vijaykumar. Opportunistic transient-fault detection. *SIGARCH Comput. Archit. News*, 33(2):172–183, 2005. ISSN 0163-5964. doi: http://doi.acm.org/10.1145/1080695.1069985.

[12] L. Hung, M. Goshima, and S. Sakai. Mitigating soft errors in highly associative cache with cam-based tag. pages 342–347, Oct. 2005. doi: 10.1109/ICCD.2005.76.

[13] S. Kayali. Reliability considerations for advanced microelectronics. In *PRDC '00: Proceedings of the 2000 Pacific Rim International Symposium on Dependable Computing*, page 99, Washington, DC, USA, 2000. IEEE Computer Society. ISBN 0-7695-0975-4.

[14] J. Lee and A. Shrivastava. Static analysis to mitigate soft errors in register files. In *Design, Automation and Test in Europe Conference and Exhibition, 2009. DATE '09.*, pages 1367–1372, April 2009.

[15] K. Lee, A. Shrivastava, I. Issenin, N. Dutt, and N. Venkatasubramanian. Mitigating soft error failures for multimedia applications by selective data protection. In *CASES '06: Proceedings of the 2006 international conference on Compilers, architecture and synthesis for embedded systems*, pages 411–420, New York, NY, USA, 2006. ACM. ISBN 1-59593-543-6. doi: http://doi.acm.org.ezproxy1.lib.asu.edu/10.1145/1176760.1176810.

[16] J.-F. Li and Y.-J. Huang. An error detection and correction scheme for rams with partial-write function. In *Memory Technology, Design, and Testing, 2005. MTDT 2005. 2005 IEEE International Workshop on*, pages 115–120, Aug. 2005. doi: 10.1109/MTDT.2005.16.

[17] P. Liden, P. Dahlgren, R. Johansson, and J. Karlsson. On latching probability of particle induced transients in combinational networks. In *Fault-Tolerant Computing, 1994. FTCS-24. Digest of Papers., Twenty-Fourth International Symposium on*, pages 340–349, Jun 1994. doi: 10.1109/FTCS.1994.315626.

[18] S. Mitra, N. Seifert, M. Zhang, Q. Shi, and K. S. Kim. Robust system design with built-in soft-error resilience. *Computer*, 38(2):43–52, 2005. ISSN 0018-9162. doi: http://dx.doi.org/10.1109/MC.2005.70.

[19] S. Mukherjee, C. T. Weaver, J. Emer, S. K. Reinhardt, and T. Austin. Measuring architectural vulnerability factors. *IEEE Micro*, 23(6):70–75, 2003. ISSN 0272-1732. doi: http://doi.ieeecomputersociety.org/10.1109/MM.2003.1261389.

[20] S. S. Mukherjee, J. Emer, T. Fossum, and S. K. Reinhardt. Cache scrubbing in microprocessors: Myth or necessity? *Pacific Rim International Symposium on Dependable Computing, IEEE*, 0:37–42, 2004. doi: http://doi.ieeecomputersociety.org/10.1109/PRDC.2004.1276550.

[21] A. Nourivand, A. Al-Khalili, and Y. Savaria. Aggressive leakage reduction of srams using error checking and correcting (ecc) techniques. pages 426–429, Aug. 2008. doi: 10.1109/MWSCAS.2008.4616827.

[22] N. Oh, S. Mitra, and E. McCluskey. Ed4i: error detection by diverse data and duplicated instructions. *Computers, IEEE Transactions on*, 51(2):180–199, Feb 2002. ISSN 0018-9340. doi: 10.1109/12.980007.

[23] R. Phelan. Addressing soft errors in arm core-based designs. Technical report, ARM, 2003.

[24] polylib. URL http://icps.u-strasbg.fr/polylib. PolyLib – A library of polyhedral functions.

[25] D. K. Pradhan, editor. *Fault-tolerant computer system design*. Prentice-Hall, Inc., Upper Saddle River, NJ, USA, 1996. ISBN 0-13-057887-8.

[26] W. Pugh. The Omega test: a fast and practical integer programming algorithm for dependence analysis. In *Supercomputing '91: Proceedings of the 1991 ACM/IEEE conference on Supercomputing*, pages 4–13, New York, NY, USA, 1991. ACM. ISBN 0-89791-459-7. doi: http://doi.acm.org/10.1145/125826.125848.

[27] W. Pugh. Counting solutions to Presburger formulas: how and why. *SIGPLAN Notices*, 29(6):121–134, 1994. ISSN 0362-1340. doi: http://doi.acm.org/10.1145/773473.178254.

[28] G. A. Reis, J. Chang, N. Vachharajani, R. Rangan, and D. I. August. Swift: Software implemented fault tolerance. In *CGO '05: Proceedings of the international symposium on Code generation and optimization*, pages 243–254, Washington, DC, USA, 2005. IEEE Computer Society. ISBN 0-7695-2298-X. doi: http://dx.doi.org/10.1109/CGO.2005.34.

[29] L. R. Rockett Jr. Simulated SEU hardened scaled CMOS SRAM cell design using gated resistors. *Nuclear Science, IEEE Transactions on*, 39(5):1532–1541, Oct 1992. ISSN 0018-9499. doi: 10.1109/23.173239.

[30] K. Shepard, V. Narayanan, and R. Rose. Harmony: static noise analysis of deep submicron digital integrated circuits. *IEEE Trans. on CAD*, (8):1132–1150, 1999.

[31] P. Shivakumar, M. Kistler, S. W. Keckler, D. Burger, and L. Alvisi. Modeling the effect of technology trends on the soft error rate of combinational logic. *Dependable Systems and Networks, International Conference on*, 0:389, 2002. doi: http://doi.ieeecomputersociety.org/10.1109/DSN.2002.1028924.

[32] V. Sridharan, H. Asadi, M. B. Tahoori, and D. Kaeli. Reducing data cache susceptibility to soft errors. *IEEE Transactions on Dependable and Secure Computing*, 3(4):353–364, 2006. doi: http://doi.ieeecomputersociety.org/10.1109/TDSC.2006.55.

[33] S. Verdoolaege, R. Seghir, K. Beyls, V. Loechner, and M. Bruynooghe. Counting integer points in parametric polytopes using Barvinok's rational function. *Algorithmica*, 48(1):37–66, 2007. doi: 10.1007/s00453-006-1231-0.

[34] M. E. Wolf and M. S. Lam. A data locality optimizing algorithm. In *PLDI '91*, pages 30–44, 1991. ISBN 0-89791-428-7. doi: http://doi.acm.org/10.1145/113445.113449.

[35] J. Yan and W. Zhang. Compiler-guided register reliability improvement against soft errors. In *EMSOFT '05*, pages 203–209, 2005. ISBN 1-59593-091-4. doi: http://doi.acm.org/10.1145/1086228.1086266.

Resilience Analysis:
Tightening the CRPD bound for set-associative caches *

Sebastian Altmeyer   Claire Maiza (Burguière)   Jan Reineke[1]

Saarland University, Saarbrücken

{altmeyer, maiza, reineke}@cs.uni-saarland.de

Abstract

In preemptive real-time systems, scheduling analyses need—in addition to the worst-case execution time—the context-switch cost. In case of preemption, the preempted and the preempting task may interfere on the cache memory. This interference leads to additional cache misses in the preempted task. The delay due to these cache misses is referred to as the cache-related preemption delay (CRPD), which constitutes the major part of the context-switch cost.

In this paper, we present a new approach to compute tight bounds on the CRPD for LRU set-associative caches, based on analyses of both the preempted and the preempting task. Previous approaches analyzing both the preempted and the preempting task were either imprecise or unsound. As the basis of our approach we introduce the notion of *resilience*: The resilience of a memory block of the preempted task is the maximal number of memory accesses a preempting task could perform without causing an additional miss to this block. By computing lower bounds on the resilience of blocks and an upper bound on the number of accesses by a preempting task, one can guarantee that some blocks may not contribute to the CRPD. The CRPD analysis based on resilience considerably outperforms previous approaches.

Categories and Subject Descriptors D.2.4 [*Software Engineering*]: Software/Program Verification—Formal methods

General Terms Reliability, Verification

Keywords Cache-related Preemption Delay, LRU Caches, Timing Analysis

1. Introduction

In hard real-time systems, one needs to prove that all time-critical tasks meet their deadlines. Many task sets are only schedulable in a *preemptive* scheduling regime. For instance, high priority tasks

---

* This work was supported by ICT project PREDATOR in the European Community's Seventh Framework Programme under grant agreement no. 216008, by Transregional Collaborative Research Center AVACS of the German Research Council (DFG) and by ARTIST DESIGN NoE.

[1] Current address: Department of EECS, University of California, Berkeley, CA 94720, eMail: reineke@eecs.berkeley.edu

with short deadlines are often unschedulable in non-preemptive regimes.

However, in modern hardware architectures, preemption does not come for free. The preempting task may "disturb" the state of performance-enhancing features like caches, pipelines, etc. This disturbance may significantly increase the execution time of the preempted task once it is resumed. The additional execution time compared with non-preempted execution, including the additional execution time of the preempted task and the execution time of the scheduler in the operating system, is referred to as the context-switch cost. Schedulability analyses for preemptive systems require bounds on the worst-case execution times (WCET)[2] of tasks as well as on these context-switch costs.

In *cached* systems, the major part of the context-switch cost is due to additional cache misses in the preempted task: Memory accesses of the preempting task change the cache contents. As a consequence, accesses in the preempted task that would have been cache hits without preemption turn out to be misses. This part of the context-switch cost is commonly referred to as the *cache-related preemption delay* (CRPD). There are two main approaches to statically bound the CRPD:

* By analyzing the *preempted* task [8, 10, 17, 18]:
  Additional misses can only occur for memory blocks that are *useful* without preemption. A *useful cache block* (UCB) is a block that may be cached and that may be reused later, resulting in a cache hit. The number of such useful cache blocks is a bound on the number of additional cache misses due to preemption and can therefore be used to bound the CRPD independently of the preempting task.

* By analyzing the *preempting* task [10, 17–19]:
  The preempting task may only cause additional misses in the cache sets modified during its execution. The number of cache sets that memory blocks of the preempting task map to can therefore be used to bound the CRPD independently of the preempted task. However, for set-associative caches, the latter approaches have either been imprecise [6] or unsound [18] as shown in [6].

In this paper, we present a new approach to *precisely* and *soundly* bound the CRPD for set-associative caches, taking into account both the preempted and the preempting task. To this end, we introduce the notion of *resilience*, and a corresponding *resilience analysis* that determines how much "disturbance" by the preempting task a useful cache block may endure before becoming unuseful for the preempted task. The results of this analysis can then be combined with those of a simple analysis of the preempting task to determine a set of useful cache blocks that are guaranteed to *remain useful* after the preemption. Only cache blocks that are useful before pre-

---

[2] Considering non-preempted execution.

emption but that are not guaranteed to remain useful may contribute to the CRPD.

In our evaluation, resilience analysis improves on previous approaches by at least 28% and by 64% on average. Our new analysis is particularly useful in case of frequent preemptions by small tasks. Interrupt routines are typical representatives of this class.

2. Background & Related Work

In this section we introduce caches and the notions of useful cache blocks and evicting cache blocks. Then, we show that previous work on the computation of a bound on the CRPD by combining UCB and ECB for set-associative caches is either unsound or imprecise.

2.1 Caches

We will investigate CRPD computation for set-associative caches in the context of the Least-Recently-Used (LRU) policy, which is used, for instance, in the INTEL PENTIUM I and the MIPS 24K/34K. In the following description of LRU and later, we will use k for the associativity of the cache and c for the number of cache sets. The LRU policy replaces the least-recently-used element on a cache miss. It conceptually maintains a queue of length k for each cache set. Elements of the set are ordered from the most-recently-used to the least-recently used. In LRU each memory block can be associated with an age: the age of a memory block m is the number of other memory blocks that have been accessed since the last access to block m. In the case of LRU and associativity 4, $[b, c, e, d]$ denotes a cache set, where elements are ordered from most- to least-recently-used: the most-recently used element has age 0 (here: b) and the least-recently-used has age $k-1$ (here: d). If an element is accessed that is not yet in the cache (a miss), it is placed at the front of the queue. The last element of the queue, i.e., the least-recently-used, is then removed if the set is full. In our example, an access to f would thus result in $[f, b, c, e]$. The least-recently-used element d is replaced. Each element is aged by one and the age of element f is 0. Upon a cache hit, the accessed element is moved from its position in the queue to the front, in this respect treating hits and misses equally. Accessing c in $[f, b, c, e]$ results in $[c, f, b, e]$: the age of the elements that were younger than the accessed element (f and b) is incremented by one, the age of the elements that were older (element e) is not changed and the age of the accessed element c becomes 0.

2.2 Bounding the CRPD

The cache-related preemption delay denotes the additional execution time due to cache misses caused by preemption. Such cache misses occur, if the cache accesses of the preempting task cause eviction[3] of cache blocks of the preempted task that otherwise would be reused later. Therefore upper bounds on the CRPD can be derived from two directions: bounding the effect on the preempted task or bounding the impact of the preempting task.

Effect on the preempted task: For the analysis of the effect on the preempted task, Lee et al. introduced the notion of a *useful cache block* [8]:

Definition 1 (Useful Cache Block (UCB)). *A memory block m is called a* useful cache block *at program point P, if*

a) *m may be cached at P and*

b) *m may be reused at program point Q that may be reached from P without eviction of m on this path.*

----
[3] Such eviction does not necessarily happen during the execution of the preempting task. They can also occur during the execution of the preempted task but as a consequence of the preemption (see Figure 1(a)).

In the case of preemption at program point P, only the memory blocks that a) are cached and b) will be reused, may cause additional reloads. Hence, the number of UCBs at program point P gives an upper bound on the number of additional reloads due to a preemption at P. A global bound on the CRPD of the whole task is determined by the program point with the highest number of UCBs. However, due to imprecision in the UCB analysis, the number of UCBs per set may exceed the associativity of the cache. Still, the number of additional misses per set is limited to k:

$$\text{CRPD}_{\text{UCB}} = \sum_{s=1}^{c} \text{CRPD}_{\text{UCB}}^s \qquad (1)$$

where

$$\text{CRPD}_{\text{UCB}}^s = \text{CRT} \cdot min\{|\text{UCB}^s|, k\} \qquad (2)$$

where UCB^s denotes the set of UCBs mapping to cache set s and c is the number of sets. For a preemption at a specific program point, the whole CRPD is bounded by the sum of the CRPDs of all cache sets. For each set, the CRPD is bounded by the cache reload time (CRT), i.e., the time needed to load a cache block, times the minimum of the number of UCBs and the associativity (see [6]).

Note that the CRPD bounds denote the additional delay for one preemption. In case of several preemptions, the CRPD bound must be accounted for as often as preemption might occur.

Recently, Altmeyer and Burguiere introduced a new analysis of the effect on the preempted task: As some cache accesses are taken into account as misses as part of the WCET analysis, these accesses do not have to be accounted for a second time as part of the CRPD [4]. At a program point P a UCB is a *definitely-cached UCB* if it must be cached at P and along the path to its reuse. Using the notion of definitely-cached UCBs (DC-UCB), one computes the number of additional cache misses due to preemption that are not already taken into account as a miss by the WCET analysis. This number does not bound the CRPD but the part of the CRPD that is not already accounted for by the WCET analysis in the WCET bound. Thereby, the global bound on the WCET+CRPD can be significantly refined. The analysis presented in this paper can be used in both contexts—CRPD computed separately (based on the UCB notion introduced by Lee et al. [8]) or in combination with the WCET (DC-UCB).

Effect of the preempting task: The worst-case impact of a preempting task is given by the number of cache blocks this task may evict. Such evictions may occur during and after the preemption: accessing a cache set may have a deferred impact in case of set-associative caches, as we will illustrate shortly.

To analyse the effect of the preempting task, Tomiyama and Dutt introduced the concept of an *evicting cache block* [19]:

Definition 2 (Evicting Cache Blocks (ECB)). *A memory block of the preempting task is called an* evicting cache block, *if it may be accessed during the execution of the preempting task.*

As part of their CRPD computation, Tan et al. [18] use the number of ECBs as an upper-bound on the number of reloads:

$$\text{CRPD}_{\text{MIN\_ECB}} = \sum_{s=1}^{c} \text{CRPD}_{\text{MIN\_ECB}}^s \qquad (3)$$

where

$$\text{CRPD}_{\text{MIN\_ECB}}^s = \text{CRT} \cdot min\{|\text{ECB}^s|, k\} \qquad (4)$$

where ECB^s denotes the set of ECBs mapping to cache set s.

However, this function may underestimate the number of misses in several cases. Consider the CFG of Figure 1(a). Assume, all memory blocks map to the same cache set. Then, at the end of the execution of this basic block, the content of the 4-way set is given by $[b, a, 9, 8]$. Assume, furthermore, a preemption between two iterations of the loop and one block of the preempting task maps to

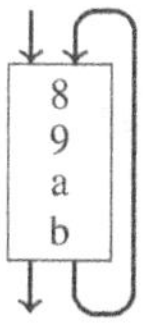

Without preemption:

ECBs $= \{e\}$

$[b, a, 9, 8] \xrightarrow{8} [8, b, a, 9] \xrightarrow{9} [9, 8, b, a] \xrightarrow{a} [a, 9, 8, b] \xrightarrow{b} [b, a, 9, 8]$ 0 misses

With preemption:

$[\mathbf{e}, b, a, 9] \xrightarrow{8^*} [8, \mathbf{e}, b, a] \xrightarrow{9^*} [9, 8, \mathbf{e}, b] \xrightarrow{a^*} [a, 9, 8, \mathbf{e}] \xrightarrow{b^*} [b, a, 9, 8]$ 4 misses

(a) Sequence of accesses where $\text{CRPD}_{\text{MIN_ECB}}$ ($= 1 \cdot \text{CRT}$) underestimates the CRPD ($= 4 \cdot \text{CRT}$)

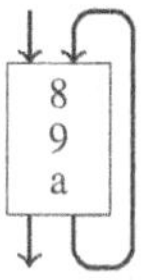

Without preemption:

ECBs $= \{e\}$

$[a, 9, 8, 7] \xrightarrow{8} [8, a, 9, 7] \xrightarrow{9} [9, 8, a, 7] \xrightarrow{a} [a, 9, 8, 7]$ 0 misses

With preemption:

$[\mathbf{e}, a, 9, 8] \xrightarrow{8} [8, \mathbf{e}, a, 9] \xrightarrow{9} [9, 8, \mathbf{e}, a] \xrightarrow{a} [a, 9, 8, \mathbf{e}]$ 0 misses

(b) Sequence of accesses where $\text{CRPD}_{\text{UCB\&ECB}}$ ($= 3 \cdot \text{CRT}$) roughly overestimates the CRPD ($= 0$). Note that CRPD_{TAN} ($= 1 \cdot \text{CRT}$) overestimates, too.

Figure 1. Evolution of the cache contents for LRU replacement. The first row shows the evolution of the cache contents for one iteration of the loop without preemption. The second row shows the evolution of the cache contents on the same sequence with preemption. The preempting task accesses block e. A * as in a^* indicates a miss.

this set: Using the formula presented above, only one additional miss is taken into account for this memory set ($min(1, 4) = 1$). However, the number of additional misses, four, is greater than the number of ECBs, one: All useful cache blocks are evicted and need to be reloaded. The cache blocks are not evicted during the execution of the preempting task but after the preemption during the execution of the preempted task. In this example, a valid upper bound is given, for instance, by the associativity whereas, the minimum between the number of ECBs and the associativity gives an underestimation of the CRPD.

Hence, instead of using the formula by Tan et al., a sound upper bound on the CRPD using ECB is given by:

$$\text{CRPD}_{\text{ECB}} = \sum_{s=1}^{c} \text{CRPD}^s_{\text{ECB}} \tag{5}$$

where

$$\text{CRPD}^s_{\text{ECB}} = \begin{cases} 0 & \text{if } \text{ECB}^s = \emptyset \\ \text{CRT} \cdot k & \textit{otherwise} \end{cases} \tag{6}$$

where ECB^s denotes the set of ECBs mapping to cache set s. The CRPD is bounded by the cache reload time times the associativity (k) of the cache in case at least one ECB maps to set s [6]. Note that in case of nested preemption the set of ECBs in the formula is the union of all ECB sets of the preempting tasks [17, 19].

In this paper, we focus on the CRPD computation for set-associative caches with LRU replacement using UCBs and ECBs. As shown in [6], for FIFO and PLRU replacement strategies, the CRPD cannot be bounded directly using UCB and ECB analyses. In the rest of the paper, we will investigate the CRPD computation for LRU only. In [6], Burguiere et al. sketched how to use the UCB analysis for LRU to bound the number of misses in case of preemption for FIFO and PLRU, by relative competitiveness [14]. The next subsection presents related work focusing on set-associative caches and the computation of a bound on the CRPD by combining UCB and ECB analyses.

Effect of the preempting task on the preempted task The results from the CRPD computation via UCB and via ECB can be combined by taking into account the minimum between the effect on the preempted task and the effect of the preempting task [6, 18]:

$$\text{CRPD}_{\text{UCB\&ECB}} = \sum_{s=1}^{c} min(\text{CRPD}^s_{\text{UCB}}, \text{CRPD}^s_{\text{ECB}}) \tag{7}$$

The CRPD computed in [18] takes into account Equation 4:

$$\text{CRPD}_{\text{TAN}} = \sum_{s=1}^{c} min(\text{CRPD}^s_{\text{UCB}}, \text{CRPD}^s_{\text{MIN_ECB}}) \tag{8}$$

Due to its use of $\text{CRPD}^s_{\text{MIN_ECB}}$ this formula is unsound. However, we list it in order to later compare our results to the ones obtained with it.

Equation 7 gives a bound on the CRPD that is sound but imprecise. Consider the example of Figure 1(b). As there is one ECB, the number of additional misses is bounded by the number of UCBs (three), which is lower than the number of ways (four). However, there are no additional misses due to this preemption: using Equation 7, the CRPD is overestimated; the formula is imprecise. Not every UCB may be evicted by a single ECB. Some UCBs *remain useful* under preemption. In the case of Figure 1(b), blocks 8, 9, and a remain useful under preemption. On the other hand, we strongly believe that Equation 7 is the best bound we can obtain by using *only* the numbers of UCBs and ECBs. A new analysis is necessary to combine the results of the UCB and ECB analyses considering the blocks that remain useful under preemption. For this purpose we introduce the notion of *resilience* in the following section.

Remark & notation Note that the computation of a bound on the CRPD for a whole set-associative cache is done by adding the bound on the CRPD for each set. For the sake of simplicity, in Section 3 and 4, we assume the cache to be fully-associative ($c = 1$). The extension to set-associative caches is then discussed in Section 5.

Table 2.2 presents the notation used in this paper. Note that, as we consider all types of caches (data and instruction), the set of UCBs can be different before and after a program point (see e.g. [4]).

$\mathbb{M}$	set of memory blocks
$\mathbb{P}$	set of all program points
k	associativity
c	number of sets
UCB^b_P	set of UCBs before program point P
UCB^a_P	set of UCBs after program point P
ECB	set of ECBs for a given preempting task

Table 1. Notation used within this paper.

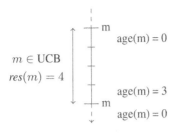

Figure 2. Illustration of a UCB m, with $res(m) = 4$. The cache associativity is 8. The dashes denote memory accesses.

3. The Notion of Resilience

The aim of our analysis is to derive a subset of the set of UCBs that cannot contribute to the cache-related preemption delay. To this end, we need to argue about the amount of "disturbance" caused by a preempting task and the "resilience" of the useful cache blocks. The amount of "disturbance" is given by the set of evicting cache blocks as presented in Section 2. The resilience $res(m)$ of a useful cache block m is the maximal disturbance, i.e., the maximal number of additional cache accesses (to different memory blocks) by the preempting task, such that m is still cached after preemption and remains cached until its next access. Hence, if the disturbance of the preempting task is less than or equal to the resilience, UCB m will remain useful after preemption and will not lead to an additional cache miss. *Resilience* is formally defined as follows:

Definition 3 (Resilience). *The resilience $res_P(m)$ of memory block m at program point P is the greatest l, such that all possible next accesses to m,*

a) that would be hits without preemption,
b) would still be hits in case of a preemption with l accesses at P.

The resilience of UCB m, $res_P(m)$ is l, if a preemption with up to l ECBs does not cause an additional miss to m: an access that would be a hit without preemption, would still be a hit under such a preemption. The resilience depends on the age of block m right before its next access. Consider the example in Figure 2 in which we assume the associativity to be 8. There are three memory accesses between the two accesses to m: before its reuse the age of m is 3. In an LRU-controlled cache with associativity 8, exactly those memory blocks with ages between 0 and 7 are cached. Thus, in the example, m could age by up to 4 ($3 + 4 = 7$) due to a preemption and still be cached at its reuse (see Figure 3). Between the two accesses to m, $res(m) = 4$.

So, at a program point P, the resilience of a block m is determined by the maximal age $max\text{-}age_P(m)$ of m at program points accessing m that can be reached from P without eviction of m:

$$res_P(m) = (k-1) - max\text{-}age_P(m). \qquad (9)$$

Consider Figure 4(a). The associativity is 8. The control flow first joins and then splits. The maximal age of 7 is obtained along the longest path, i.e., from the upper-left access to m to the lower-right access to m. Along this path, there are 7 different accesses between the two accesses to m. Thus, at all points along this path, $res(m) = 0$. The longest path starting from the lower-left access to m only contains 6 different accesses. Therefore from the lower-left access to the control flow join, the maximal age is 6. Similarly, the longest path to the upper-right access contains 5 different accesses.

If a memory block is not accessed along a path, then this path does not influence its resilience (Figure 4(b)) because of condition (a) of Definition 3. Similarly, if a memory access definitely

leads to a cache miss, then this access does not influence the memory block's resilience either (Figure 4(c)).

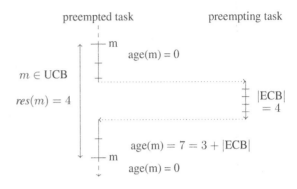

Figure 3. Illustration of a UCB m with $res(m) = 4$ remaining useful after a preemption with 4 ECBs (associativity $k = 8$).

Using bounds on the resilience, we compute a set of useful cache blocks that must remain useful under preemption with a given number of ECBs. Those blocks will not lead to additional misses due to preemption. The upper-bound on the CRPD can be refined by considering as additional misses under preemption only the UCBs that cannot be guaranteed to remain useful:

$$\text{CRPD-RES} = \text{CRT} \times |\overbrace{\underbrace{\text{UCB}}_{\text{may be useful}} \setminus \underbrace{\{m \mid res(m) \geq l\}}_{\text{must remain useful}}}^{\text{blocks that may have to be reloaded}}| \qquad (10)$$

In order to ensure the soundness of our results, we have to over-approximate the set of UCBs and to bound the number of ECBs from above, but underapproximate the resilience of the useful cache blocks. Only cache blocks, for which we can guarantee the "survival", can be safely excluded from the CRPD bound.

We can similarly refine the CRPD analysis results based on Definitely-Cached UCBs (see Section 2 and [4]). We just need to replace UCB by DC-UCB in Equation 10.

4. Resilience Analysis

How is the resilience computed? The resilience of a UCB m is determined by the maximal age $max\text{-}age(m)$ at all next hits to m without prior eviction. At each program point P, this maximal age can be split into two parts:

i) $ca_P^{\leftarrow}$, the maximal number of accesses from the last use of m to program point P, and

ii) $ca_P^{\rightarrow}$, the maximal number of accesses from program point P to the next hit to m,

both under the constraint that m is not evicted before its next reuse. We denote the two parts as the constrained ages $ca_P^{\leftarrow}$ and $ca_P^{\rightarrow}$ of m at P and employ two symmetric data-flow analyses on the control flow graph of the analyzed program to bound both parts from above: a forward analysis for the first (i) and a backward for the second part (ii). The maximal age is then bounded by the sum of both.

For the analysis[4] of the constrained age, ca, of a memory block, we only take those paths into account on which the constraint is satisfied[5]. Thus, ca of m does not necessarily overapproximate the

---

[4] The analysis of $ca^{\leftarrow}$ and $ca^{\rightarrow}$ only differ by the direction. Hence, we omit the direction in the following explanation.

[5] m is not evicted before its next reuse.

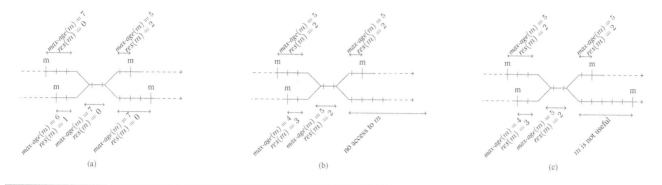

Figure 4. Resilience under several possible next accesses.

actual age of m. To be able to correctly update the constrained age ca, upon an access to a memory block, we also need to maintain an unconstrained bound on the age of the block. We denote this upper bound on the actual age by ua. To derive ua, we employ a *must* cache analysis [7].

Remember that we assume a fully-associative cache for this section. In case of a set-associative cache, the analysis is performed for each cache set.

The domain of the analysis is a tuple of two functions. The first function assigns each memory block a bound on its constrained age ca, and the second assigns a bound on its unconstrained age ua.

$$\mathbb{D} : \mathbb{D}_{ca} \times \mathbb{D}_{ua} \tag{11}$$

with

$$\mathbb{D}_{ca} : \mathbb{M} \to \{0, \ldots, k-1\} \tag{12}$$

and

$$\mathbb{D}_{ua} : \mathbb{M} \to \{0, \ldots, k-1, \infty\} \tag{13}$$

The age of a memory block m whose next access can still result in a hit is bounded by $k-1$. Older memory blocks are not cached. The next access to such blocks must be a miss. Hence, due to the constraint, the constrained age $ca(m)$ of a memory block m is at most $k-1$. Without the constraint, blocks may reach arbitrary ages $\geq k$, which we do not need to distinguish. In $\mathbb{D}_{ua}$, ages $\geq k$ are represented by ∞.

The join operator of the domain, invoked to combine flow information from different paths, is defined using a separate join-function for each element of the tuple:

$$\bigsqcup : \mathcal{P}(\mathbb{D}) \to \mathbb{D}$$

$$\bigsqcup D := (\bigsqcup_{ca} CA, \bigsqcup_{ua} UA) \tag{14}$$

where $CA := \{ca \mid (ca, ua) \in D\}$ and $UA := \{ua \mid (ca, ua) \in D\}$.
The join operator for the ca and ua are defined as follows:

$$\bigsqcup_{ca} : \mathcal{P}(\mathbb{D}_{ca}) \to \mathbb{D}_{ca}$$

$$\bigsqcup_{ca} CA := \lambda m. \max_{ca \in CA} ca(m) \tag{15}$$

$$\bigsqcup_{ua} : \mathcal{P}(\mathbb{D}_{ua}) \to \mathbb{D}_{ua}$$

$$\bigsqcup_{ua} UA := \lambda m. \max_{ua \in UA} ua(m) \tag{16}$$

In both cases, we bound the ages from above. Hence, we need to take the maximum of the bounds of all incoming data-flow values.

The transfer function, computing the update on the bounds, is defined using the following auxiliary functions t_{ca} and t_{ua}.

$$t_{ua} : \mathbb{D}_{ua} \times \mathbb{M} \to \mathbb{D}_{ua}$$

$$t_{ua}(ua, m) :=$$

$$\lambda m'. \begin{cases} 0 & m' = m \\ ua(m') & ua(m') \geq ua(m) \\ ua(m') + 1 & ua(m') < ua(m) \wedge ua(m') < k-1 \\ \infty & otherwise \end{cases}$$

$$\tag{17}$$

The inputs to t_{ua} are the upper bound on the age ua and the accessed memory block m. The age of the currently accessed memory block is zero. Older elements or elements of the same age as the accessed one remain unchanged. Only younger elements are aged by one. Note that $k-1$ is the maximal age of cached memory blocks. If $ua(m) = \infty$, m is not guaranteed to be cached.

The auxiliary function t_{ca} is similar to t_{ua}, yet it also takes unconstrained ages as inputs:

$$t_{ca} : \mathbb{D}_{ca} \times \mathbb{D}_{ua} \times 2^{\mathbb{M}} \times \mathbb{M} \to \mathbb{D}_{ca}$$

$$t_{ca}(ca, ua, \text{UCB}, m) :=$$

$$\lambda m'. \begin{cases} 0 & m' = m \vee m' \notin \text{UCB} \\ ca(m') & ca(m') \geq ua(m) \vee ca(m') = k-1 \\ ca(m') + 1 & ca(m') < ua(m) \end{cases}$$

$$\tag{18}$$

The inputs to t_{ca} are the bound on the constrained age ca, the bound on the unconstrained age ua, the set of UCBs at the specific program point and the accessed memory block m. Function t_{ca} defines the change of ca upon access to m given a specific set of UCBs. The update of ca is similar to the update of ua. In the first case, $ca(m') = 0$, if $m' = m$ or $m' \notin$ UCB. If $m' \notin$ UCB the constraint is not satisfied, i.e., the next access to m' may not be a hit. Then any bound would be correct and $ca(m') = 0$ is the best possible. Note that the bound on the constrained age ca may underapproximate the actual age. Hence, we need to consider $ua(m)$ as the upper bound on the age of the accessed element m. Under the constraint, that the next access to m' is a hit, it can never obtain an age greater than $k-1$, this explains the additional condition $ca(m') = k-1$ compared with the other transfer function.

The transfer function invokes t_{ca} and t_{ua} depending on the program point and the direction of the analysis. Remember that the forward analysis ($\to$) bounds the number of accesses from the last access to a memory block m to the current program point and the backward analysis ($\leftarrow$) from the current program point to the next access to m. The forward analysis invokes t_{ca} with incoming data-flow value ca, the memory block m_P accessed at P and the set of UCBs before P, UCB_P^b. The backward analysis considers the set of UCBs after the program point, UCB_P^a. In both cases, t_{ua} is invoked with ua and m_P.

$$T : \mathbb{D} \times \mathbb{P} \to \mathbb{D}$$

$$T^{\to}((ca, ua), P) := (t_{ca}(ca, ua, \text{UCB}_P^b, m_P), t_{ua}(ua, m_P)) \tag{19}$$

$$T^{\leftarrow}((ca, ua), P) := (t_{ca}(ca, ua, \text{UCB}_P^a, m_P), t_{ua}(ua, m_P)) \tag{20}$$

In case of data caches, the address of a memory access may be unknown statically. For instance, consider an array access within a loop. In such a case, only a non-singleton set of possible addresses for each memory access can be derived. The transfer function $\widehat{T}$ (for both, forward and backward analysis) is then defined by the join of the transfer function t applied to each element in the set of possible memory accesses ($\mathbb{M}_P$ is the set of memory blocks possibly accessed at P).

$$\widehat{T} : \mathbb{D} \times \mathbb{P} \to \mathbb{D}$$

$$\widehat{T}^{\to}((ca, ua), P) := \bigsqcup_{m \in \mathbb{M}_P} \{(t_{ca}(ca, ua, \text{UCB}_P^b, m), t_{ua}(ua, m))\} \tag{21}$$

$$\widehat{T}^{\leftarrow}((ca, ua), P) := \bigsqcup_{m \in \mathbb{M}_P} \{(t_{ca}(ca, ua, \text{UCB}_P^a, m), t_{ua}(ua, m))\} \tag{22}$$

Let $ca_P^{\to}$ be the result of the forward analysis and $ca_P^{\leftarrow}$ the result of the backward analysis before program point P. The maximal age $max\text{-}age$ is then bounded by the sum of both bounds limited to $(k-1)$:

$$max\text{-}age_P(m) \leq \min\{ca_P^{\to}(m) + ca_P^{\leftarrow}(m), k-1\} \tag{23}$$

Note that $k-1$ is the maximal age such that m is still cached at the next access. The resilience $res_P(m)$ of a memory block m before P is then given by Equation 9:

$$res_P(m) := (k-1) - max\text{-}age_P(m).$$

5. From Resilience to CRPD

The CRPD computation, based on the notion of resilience, has shortly been sketched in Section 3 for fully-associative caches and for a single program point only. In this section, we present the computation of the CRPD bound of a whole task, the extension to set-associative caches (with more than one set), an efficient approach to compute the CRPDs for given task sets, and the extension to multiple preemptions by multiple tasks.

In case of set-associative caches, the CRPD at program point P is given by the sum of the CRPDs of each set s:

$$\text{CRPD-RES}_P(\text{ECB}) = \sum_s \text{CRPD-RES}_P^s(\text{ECB}^s) \tag{24}$$

$$\text{CRPD-RES}_P^s(\text{ECB}_s) = \\ \text{CRT} \times |\text{UCB}_P^s \setminus \{m \mid res_P(m) \geq |\text{ECB}^s|\}| \tag{25}$$

where ECB^s and UCB_P^s denote the sets of elements from ECB/UCB mapping to cache set s.

The bound on the CRPD of the whole task is then determined by the maximum CRPD of all program points.

$$\text{CRPD-RES}(\text{ECB}) = \max\{\text{CRPD-RES}_P(\text{ECB}) \mid P \in \mathbb{P}\} \tag{26}$$

5.1 Computation of a sufficient set of preemption points

The drawback of this computation is that the set $(\text{UCB}_P^s \setminus \{m \mid res_P(m) \geq |\text{ECB}^s|\})$ has to be evaluated for each program point each time the CRPD is computed for another preempting task. Depending on the task size and the set of preempting tasks, this computation can be very time-consuming. Therefore, we present

a precomputation to speed up the instantiation by reducing the number of program points that need to be considered. To this end, we use a partial order on the program points, such that the CRPD only needs to be derived for a subset of all program points.

The partial order on CRPD-RES_P^s is defined by the point-wise comparison on the set of $(\text{UCB}_P^s \setminus \{m \mid res_P(m) \geq |\text{ECB}^s|\})$ for each possible input.

$$\text{CRPD-RES}_{P_1}^s \leq \text{CRPD-RES}_{P_2}^s \text{ iff } \forall l \in [0; k-1] : \\ |\text{UCB}_{P_1}^s \setminus \{m \mid res_{P_1}(m) \geq l\}| \leq \\ |\text{UCB}_{P_2}^s \setminus \{m \mid res_{P_2}(m) \geq l\}| \tag{27}$$

The partial order on CRPD-RES_P is then defined by the point-wise comparison on CRPD-RES_P^s for each cache-set s.

$$\text{CRPD-RES}_{P_1} \leq \text{CRPD-RES}_{P_2} \\ \text{iff } \forall s : \text{CRPD-RES}_{P_1}^s \leq \text{CRPD-RES}_{P_2}^s \tag{28}$$

The global CRPD bound must be assumed at one of the minimal program points in the partial order:

$$\mathbb{P}_{Max} = \{P \mid \neg \exists P' : \text{CRPD-RES}_P < \text{CRPD-RES}_{P'}\} \tag{29}$$

$$\text{CRPD-RES}(\text{ECB}) = \max\{\text{CRPD-RES}_P(\text{ECB}) \mid P \in \mathbb{P}_{Max}\} \tag{30}$$

5.2 Multiple preemptions

So far, we have presented the computation of bounds on the CRPD for a single preemption by a single task. However, schedulability analyses usually have to take into account multiple and nested preemptions. This can be preemptions by a single task or even by multiple different tasks. Nested preemptions can be easily handled by taking the union of the ECBs of all preempting tasks. In this section, we discuss the challenges that arise when bounding the CRPD for multiple preemptions and present an approach for our resilience analysis.

Why are multiple preemptions a challenge? Multiple preemptions, in particular by multiple preempting tasks, may "interact" to cause more additional misses than they would in "isolation". We say that two preemptions *interact* if there is a memory block m, s.t. there are two consecutive accesses to m that enclose the two preemptions. See Figures 5(a) and 5(b) for examples of interacting tasks T_1 and T_2 due to accesses to memory block m. We call preemptions that do not interact with any other preemption *isolated*. For direct-mapped (dm) caches, multiple—possibly interacting— preemptions do not pose additional problems. In direct-mapped caches, for all useful cache blocks m, $res(m) = 0$, i.e., each useful cache block is evicted by a single ECB. If two preempting tasks interact, they may only cause less misses than the sum of the misses of isolated preemptions by the two tasks. If the two preempting tasks access the same cache set (of associativity one) that contains a useful cache block they may cause at most one additional miss, while two isolated preemptions could cause up to two misses.

So, the CRPD caused by such preemptions is always bounded by the sum of the CRPDs the preemptions would cause in isolation. Let *Tasks* be the set of preempting tasks, $\text{CRPD}^{dm}(T)$ the cost of a single preemption by task $T \in \text{Tasks}$, and $\#p(T)$ the number of preemptions by task T. Then the total $\text{CRPD}^{dm}(\text{Tasks}, \#p)$ in a direct-mapped (dm) cache is bounded by:

$$\text{CRPD}^{dm}(\text{Tasks}, \#p) \leq \sum_{T \in \text{Tasks}} \#p(T) \cdot \text{CRPD}^{dm}(T). \tag{31}$$

This property is used in the analysis of multiple preemptions for direct-mapped caches [8, 16, 18].

However, this property does not hold for set-associative caches. The total CRPD caused by such preemptions may be higher than

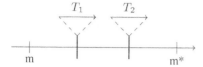

(a) Interacting preemptions by T_1 and T_2 between two subsequent accesses to m.

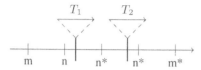

(b) Interacting preemptions by T_1 and T_2 between two subsequent accesses to m and between different accesses to n.

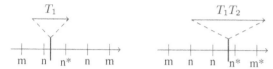

(c) Isolated preemptions by T_1 and $T_1 T_2$. The sum of the number of additional misses, $1 + 2 = 3$, bounds the number of additional misses in case of interacting preemptions, 3, by T_1 and T_2 as depicted in (b).

Figure 5. Different preemption scenarios with interacting and isolated preemptions. m and n denote memory accesses. A $*$ as in m^* indicates an additional miss due to one or more preemptions. In all scenarios, $|ECB(T_1)| = |ECB(T_2)| = 2$, $|ECB(T_1) \cup ECB(T_2)| = |ECB(T_1 T_2)| = 4$, and $res_P(m) = 3$, $res_P(n) = 1$ for all program points P.

the sum of the costs of preemptions by single tasks. Consider a useful cache block m that can be evicted by four evicting cache blocks but not by three. In our terms, $res(m) = 3$. If tasks T_1 and T_2 both access at most 2 memory blocks in the same set ($|ECB(T_1)| = |ECB(T_2)| = 2$), a preemption by T_1 alone or T_2 alone will not cause eviction of block m. However, if the task accessing m is preempted by both T_1 and T_2 between two accesses to m, i.e., the two preemptions interact, m may be evicted. Figure 5(a) illustrates this. Only upon the next use of m does the memory block "regain" its resilience. Even multiple preemptions by a single task may interact in such a way. While T_1 accesses at most 2 memory blocks in the same set, it may access different blocks in different executions. So several preemptions by T_1 may access more than 3 different blocks in the cache set of m and thereby evict it.

In general, it is therefore not sufficient to simply sum up the CRPD bounds obtained for individual isolated preempting tasks. Whether and to what extent this is possible depends on the CRPD analysis for the individual preemptions. Taking into account the $CRPD_{UCB\&ECB}$ as described in Section 2, one can compute a CRPD bound for set-associative caches as in Equation 31. This is because, $CRPD_{UCB\&ECB}$ does not tightly couple the analysis of the preempted and the preempting task. It does not take into account that certain blocks are too resilient to be evicted due to a particular preempting task. It assumes that blocks are evicted even if a single ECB maps to the same set, resembling the direct-mapped cache case. For CRPD bounds based on resilience summing up the CRPD bounds as in Equation 31 is not correct in general.

Bounds on the CRPD for multiple preemptions by a single task
Let the set of $ECB(T)$ overapproximate the set of memory blocks accessed by task T in *any* execution. Even if certain blocks may

not be accessed in the same execution of a task do they appear in $ECB(T)$. Using $ECB(T)$ in CRPD-RES($ECB(T)$) we already account for misses that may only occur due to several executions of T. Therefore, we can bound the total CRPD in set-associative (*sa*) caches caused by multiple preemptions by a single task in the following way:

$$\text{CRPD}^{sa}(\{T\}, \#p) \leq \#p(T) \cdot \text{CRPD-RES}(ECB(T)). \quad (32)$$

However, for multiple preemptions by multiple different tasks, this does not work as discussed in the previous section and as illustrated in Figure 5(a).

Bounds on the CRPD for multiple preemptions by multiple tasks
Our approach is to incrementally compute bounds on the CRPD for growing sets of preempting tasks. We start out with a single preempting task. Then, we keep adding preempting tasks, one at a time, maintaining an upper bound on the CRPD due to preemptions of the tasks that have been added so far.

In principle, any order of inserting the preempting tasks can be processed. However, the order has an influence on the precision of the resulting CRPD bound. Adding tasks in nonincreasing order of the number of preemptions simplifies the algorithm and promises to yield low bounds. In the following, we will assume w.l.o.g. that the preempting tasks $Tasks = \{T_1, T_2, \ldots\}$ are ordered in this way, i.e., $\#p(T_i) \geq \#p(T_{i+1})$ for all i.

Our algorithm is based on a slight generalization of the following insight:

$$\begin{aligned}\text{CRPD}^{sa}(\{T_1, T_2\}, \#p) \leq \ & \text{CRPD}^{sa}(\{T_1\}, \#p) \\ & + \text{CRPD}^{sa}(\{T_1 T_2\}, \#p')\end{aligned} \quad (33)$$

where $T_1 T_2$ denotes a task that is the sequential composition of T_1 and T_2 and $\#p'(T_1 T_2) = \#p(T_2)$.

Equation 33 says that we can compute a bound on the CRPD due to preemptions by T_1 and T_2 by adding up

1. a bound on the cost of the preemptions of T_1 in isolation, and

2. the cost of $\#p'(T_1 T_2) = \#p(T_2)$ preemptions by $T_1 T_2$.

Intuitively, the preemptions of T_2 may only interact $\#p(T_2)$ ($= \min\{\#p(T_1), \#p(T_2)\}$[6]) times with the preemptions of T_1. If a memory block may be evicted by an interaction of T_1 and T_2, it may also be evicted by the sequential composition $T_1 T_2$ of the two tasks. Figure 5(c) illustrates this.

Generalizing Equation 33 from pairs of preempting tasks to sets of preempting tasks yields the following:

$$\begin{aligned}\text{CRPD}^{sa}(\{T_1, \ldots, T_i\}, \#p) \leq \ & \text{CRPD}^{sa}(\{T_1, \ldots, T_{i-1}\}, \#p) \\ & + \text{CRPD}^{sa}(\{T_1 T_2 \ldots T_i\}, \#p')\end{aligned} \quad (34)$$

where $T_1 T_2 \ldots T_i$ denotes a task that is the sequential composition of $T_1, T_2, \ldots, T_i$ and $\#p'(T_1 T_2 \ldots T_i) = \#p(T_i)$.

Intuitively, the preemptions of T_i may only interact $\#p(T_i)$ ($= \min\{\#p(T_1), \ldots, \#p(T_i)\}$) times with the preemptions of $T_1, \ldots, T_{i-1}$. If a memory block may be evicted by an interaction of $T_1, T_2, \ldots, T_i$, it may also be evicted by the sequential composition $T_1 T_2 \ldots T_i$ of the set of tasks.

As the set of evicting cache blocks by $T_1 T_2 \ldots T_i$ is simply $\bigcup_{j=1\ldots i} ECB(T_j)$ we can use Equation 32 to bound the second summand of Equation 34 by $\#p(T_i) \cdot \text{CRPD-RES}(\bigcup_{j=1..i} ECB(T_j))$:

$$\begin{aligned}\text{CRPD}^{sa}(\{T_1, \ldots, T_i\}, \#p) \leq \ & \text{CRPD}^{sa}(\{T_1, \ldots, T_{i-1}\}, \#p) \\ & + \#p(T_i) \cdot \text{CRPD-RES}(\bigcup_{j=1..i} ECB(T_j))\end{aligned} \quad (35)$$

---

[6] Due to our assumption of a nonincreasing $\#p$-function.

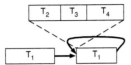

Figure 10. The execution of T_2, T_3, T_4 between the periodic execution of T_1 seen as a "preemption" of a cyclic T_1 task.

are executed between two instances of a task. Executions of other tasks between two instances of the same task can then be seen as preemptions at fixed program points. Additional misses due to such "preemptions" can then be accounted for as described in the previous sections. This idea is illustrated in Figure 10. It remains to evaluate the precision of this approach compared with that of [12].

7.2 Component-Wise Cache Analysis

Component-wise cache analysis [5, 13] tries to increase the scalability of cache analysis by analyzing components of a system independently. Instead of analyzing a function at every call site, it is only analyzed once, generating a summary of the "damage" on the cache state caused by the function. This summary is then applied to the cache states at every call site. Following such an approach one has to analyze library functions only once. Ballabriga et al. [5] recently increased the precision of component-wise cache analysis by deriving more precise summaries than Rakib et al. [13] who introduced the idea. Both [13] and [5] still have some limitations:

- They require the knowledge of relative positions of functions in the cache. This knowledge is only available after linking. If the relative positions are unknown, the two approaches would have to account for the *sum* of the "damages" caused by all different relative positions in the cache.

- If function pointers are employed it is not always statically known which function is called. In such cases, the above analyses again have to conservatively account for the *sum* of the "damages" done by all of the possible functions. If for instance, one function accesses cache sets 1 to 4 and the other function accesses the cache sets 5 to 8, the above analyses would have to account for "damage" in cache sets 1 to 8.

How can resilience analysis improve component-wise cache analysis? Instead of directly accounting for the damage done by the function that is called, one could first optimistically analyze a program ignoring the function calls. In a second step, one could then use the results of a resilience analysis to determine the maximal number of additional misses due to the function calls. If the relative positions of the called function and the caller are unknown, one could conservatively account for the maximal number of additional misses. This should be considerably more precise than accounting for the *sum* of the damages resulting from all possible relative positions. Similarly, for unresolved function calls due to function pointers.

8. Conclusions

Preemptive scheduling often offers increased schedulability at the cost of higher analysis complexity. Apart from schedulability analysis, timing analysis has to be extended to derive the context switch costs, and especially the cache-related preemption delay. The corresponding analyses for direct-mapped caches can be considered rather mature and precise. For set-associative caches, however, former analyses are either imprecise or unsound.

In this paper, we introduced a new CRPD analysis for LRU caches based on the notion of resilience. The resilience denotes how much disturbance by the preempting task, a cache block of the preempted one may endure, without eviction before its reuse.

We presented a data-flow analysis to derive the resilience of a cache block as well as the computation of CRPD bounds for single and multiple preemption based on this notion. The evaluation has shown that our analysis improves on former approaches by at least 28% and by 64% on average. Especially, for preemption due to small, but frequent tasks, such as interrupts, a strong improvement can be achieved.

As future work, we plan to evaluate our method for other cache configurations and in the presence of an RTOS.

References

[1] Mälardalen WCET benchmark suite. http://www.mrtc.mdh.se/projects/wcet/benchmarks.html.

[2] Papabench: a free real-time benchmark. http://www.irit.fr/recherches/ARCHI/MARCH/rubrique.php3?id_rubrique=97.

[3] B. Ackland, D. Anesko, D. Brinthaupt, S. J. Daubert, A. Kalavade, J. Knoblock, E. Micca, M. Moturi, C. J. Nicol, J. H. O'Neill, J. Othmer, E. Sackinger, K. J. Singh, J. Sweet, C. J. Terman, and J. Williams. A single-chip, 1.6 billion, 16-b mac/s multiprocessor dsp,. *IEEE Journal of Solid-state circuits*, 35(3):412–423, 2000.

[4] S. Altmeyer and C. Burguière. A new notion of useful cache block to improve the bounds of cache-related preemption delay. In *ECRTS '09*, pages 109–118. IEEE Computer Society, 2009.

[5] C. Ballabriga, H. Cassé, and P. Sainrat. An improved approach for set-associative instruction cache partial analysis. In *SAC '08*, pages 360–367, 2008.

[6] C. Burguière, J. Reineke, and S. Altmeyer. Cache-related preemption delay computation for set-associative caches: Pitfalls and solutions. In *WCET '09*, 2009.

[7] C. Ferdinand and R. Wilhelm. Fast and efficient cache behavior prediction for real-time systems. *Real-Time Systems*, 17(2/3):131–181, 1999.

[8] C.-G. Lee, J. Hahn, S. L. Min, R. Ha, S. Hong, C. Y. Park, M. Lee, and C. S. Kim. Analysis of cache-related preemption delay in fixed-priority preemptive scheduling. In *RTSS'96*, page 264. IEEE Computer Society, 1996.

[9] T. Lundqvist and P. Stenström. Timing anomalies in dynamically scheduled microprocessors. In *RTSS '99*, page 12. IEEE Computer Society, 1999.

[10] H. S. Negi, T. Mitra, and A. Roychoudhury. Accurate estimation of cache-related preemption delay. In *CODES+ISSS'03*. ACM, 2003.

[11] F. Nemer, H. Cassé, P. Sainrat, J. P. Bahsoun, and M. D. Michiel. Papabench: a free real-time benchmark. In *WCET '06*, Dagstuhl, 2006.

[12] F. Nemer, H. Cassé, P. Sainrat, and J. P. Bahsoun. Inter-task WCET computation for a-way instruction caches. In *SIES '08*, pages 169–176, 2008.

[13] A. Rakib, O. Parshin, S. Thesing, and R. Wilhelm. Component-wise i-cache behavior prediction. In *ATVA '04*, pages 211–229, 2004.

[14] J. Reineke and D. Grund. Relative competitive analysis of cache replacement policies. In *LCTES'08*, pages 51–60. ACM, June 2008.

[15] J. Reineke, B. Wachter, S. Thesing, R. Wilhelm, I. Polian, J. Eisinger, and B. Becker. A definition and classification of timing anomalies. In *WCET '06*, Dagstuhl, 2006.

[16] J. Staschulat and R. Ernst. Multiple process execution in cache related preemption delay analysis. In *EMSOFT '04*, pages 278–286. ACM, 2004.

[17] J. Staschulat and R. Ernst. Scalable precision cache analysis for real-time software. *ACM TECS*, 6(4):25, 2007. ISSN 1539-9087.

[18] Y. Tan and V. Mooney. Integrated intra- and inter-task cache analysis for preemptive multi-tasking real-time systems. In *SCOPES'04*, pages 182–199, 2004.

[19] H. Tomiyama and N. D. Dutt. Program path analysis to bound cache-related preemption delay in preemptive real-time systems. In *CODES '00*. ACM, 2000.

RNFTL: A Reuse-Aware NAND Flash Translation Layer for Flash Memory

Yi Wang[†], Duo Liu[†], Meng Wang[†], Zhiwei Qin[†], Zili Shao[†]* and Yong Guan[§]

[†]Department of Computing
The Hong Kong Polytechnic University
Hung Hom, Kowloon, Hong Kong
{csywang, csdliu, csmewang, cszqin,
cszlshao}@comp.polyu.edu.hk

[§]College of Computer and Information Management
Capital Normal University
Beijing, 100048, China
guanyong@mail.cnu.edu.cn

Abstract

In this paper, we propose a hybrid-level flash translation layer (FTL) called **RNFTL (Reuse-Aware NFTL)** to improve the endurance and space utilization of NAND flash memory. Our basic idea is to prevent a primary block with many free pages from being erased in a merge operation. The preserved primary blocks are further reused as replacement blocks. In such a way, the space utilization and the number of erase counts for each block in NAND flash can be enhanced. To the best of our knowledge, this is the first work to employ a reuse-aware strategy in FTL for improving the space utilization and endurance of NAND flash. We conduct experiments on a set of traces that collected from real workload in daily life. The experimental results show that our technique has significant improvement on space utilization, block lifetime and wear-leveling compared with the previous work.

Categories and Subject Descriptors D.4.2 [*Operating Systems*]: Storage Management—Secondary storage

General Terms Design, Experimentation, Measurement, Performance

Keywords Flash memory, endurance, space utilization, wear-leveling, reuse

1. INTRODUCTION

NAND flash memory is a widely used non-volatile storage device that provides small size, shock resistance and low power for both general-purpose and embedded systems. However, NAND flash has some constraints that impose challenges for its management. First, NAND flash suffers from out-of-place updates. An update (re-write) to existing data on a given physical location (known as a page) should be preceded by an erase operation on a larger region

* Zili Shao is the corresponding author

(known as a block). Second, NAND flash blocks have a limited erase lifetime. For example, in SAMSUNG K9F1G08U0C SLC (Single-Level Cell) NAND flash, one block has 100K erase counts, while the one in SAMSUNG K9G4G08U0A MLC (Multi-Level Cell) NAND flash has only 5K erase counts. A block becomes worn-out if its erase count reaches the limit [4]. Third, for some NAND flash management schemes, not all blocks in NAND flash get erased at the same rate, so the lifetime of specific blocks may decreases faster which would affect the usefulness of the entire flash memory. To overcome these constraints, it is very important to guarantee that erase or write operations be evenly distributed across all blocks (known as wear-leveling). This paper aims at enhancing the lifetime and space utilization of NAND flash without many modifications to existing designs. To achieve this, we propose a reuse-aware NAND flash translation layer to reduce the erase count of each block and evenly spread out erase operations.

NAND Flash is partitioned into blocks where each block usually contains 32 or 64 pages, and each block is further divided into multiple pages. Each page contains 512B or 2KB for data. There are three basic operations that can be performed on a NAND flash, *erase, write,* and *read*. A block is the smallest unit of erase operations, while a page is the minimum unit of read/write operations. According to the out-of-place specificity, data must be written to free pages. Consequently, NAND flash could run out of space after a number of write operations, and a reclaim operation known as garbage collection [7] is invoked to regenerate free space for NAND flash. To conceal these unfavorable characteristics, an intermediate software module called flash translation layer (FTL) is employed to emulate NAND flash as a block device [2]. The main role of FTL is to redirect logical addresses from the file system of a host into physical addresses in NAND flash, and maintains a mapping table to keep track of the mapping information. FTL not only supports address translation but also provides other useful components, such as garbage collector and wear-leveler, to optimize the space utilization and maintain the same level of wear for each block in NAND flash.

Since FTL plays an important role in NAND flash management, many studies for FTL have been conducted. According to the granularity of mapping unit, FTL designs can be mainly categorized into three types [10]: page-level mapping [5], block-level mapping [3, 6], and hybrid-level mapping [12]. The page-level FTL maps a logical page number into a corresponding physical page in NAND flash. It can provide good address translation time, less garbage collection overhead, and high space utilization but with significant memory requirement. On the contrary, the block-level FTL maps the logical block number into a physical block number, and requires much less mapping information. However, in block-level FTL, a logical page can only be written to a physical page with the designated page offset within a physical block. Thus, block-level FTL is not as good as page-level FTL in terms of the flexibility and space utilization. To overcome the shortcomings of the above two mapping schemes, hybrid-level FTL is proposed to balance the space overheads and flexibility. The technique proposed in this paper is based on hybrid-level FTL.

Hybrid-level FTL has been widely used, especially for large-scale flash storage systems [8]. Hybrid schemes have great improvement on the performance of FTL [3, 6, 9, 12, 14–16]. However, most of them use the same block reclamation method, known as merge, to erase both primary (data) and replacement (log) blocks at the same time. A merge operation usually collects valid pages scattered on two or more blocks (i.e., primary and replacement blocks) into one block to reclaim the other blocks. By applying such merge schemes, free pages within blocks are wasted, and unnecessary erase operations can also degrade the life span of each block in NAND flash. The statistical results provided in Section 4 show that up to 46% free pages in primary blocks are wasted during merge operations adopted by [9, 12, 15].

Lee et al. [13] introduce a hybrid-level FTL, *migration*, to reduce the block reclamation costs during merge operations. Their approach only erases replacement (log) blocks in merge operations, while the corresponding primary (data) blocks are not erased. However, a reserved primary block may permanently hold cold data, and its corresponding replacement block may be erased frequently due to update operations. Thus, the wear-leveling of their scheme can not be guaranteed and the lifetime of a primary block should be further enhanced. New techniques, therefore, are needed to address the endurance as well as wear-leveling issues in FTL management.

In this paper, we propose an efficient approach called **RNFTL (Reuse-Aware NFTL)** to enhance the endurance and space utilization of NAND flash. Different from the previous work, we employ a reuse strategy that effectively utilizes free pages inside un-erased primary blocks. Our basic idea is to prevent a primary block with free pages from being erased in a merge operation if the number of free pages is greater than a threshold. In other words, a primary block with many free pages will be preserved during merge operations such that we can effectively reduce the erase counts of blocks and enhance the endurance of NAND flash. In our technique, the un-erased primary block is considered as a dirty block and put into a dirty block list for further reusing as a replacement block to enhance the space utilization and wear-leveling. To the best of our knowledge, RNFTL is the first technique to apply the reuse strategy into the flash translation layer.

We conduct experiments on a set of traces collected from real workloads by DiskMon [1]. We compare our technique with a well-known implementation of block-level FTL (denoted by Original_NFTL hereinafter) [6] and a hybrid-level FTL (denoted by Revised_NFTL hereinafter) proposed by [15]. The experimental results show that our RNFTL technique can effectively improve the space utilization and reduce the average erase count of each block. For a 128MB NAND flash memory, our RNFTL can achieve an average reduction of 93.85% and 45.89% in block erase counts, and an average improvement of 94.11% and 46.28% in space utilization compared with Original_NFTL and Revised_NFTL, respectively. According to the experimental results, our RNFTL can not only improve the space utilization and endurance, but also the wear-leveling of NAND flash.

This paper makes the following contributions:

• We present for the first time a reuse-aware flash translation layer for improving the space utilization, endurance and wear-leveling of NAND flash.

• We demonstrate the effectiveness of our technique by comparing with representative techniques using a set of real traces.

The rest of this paper is organized as follows. Section 2 gives an overview of NAND flash architecture and the representative FTL implementations. Section 3 presents our RNFTL technique. Section 4 presents the experimental results. Section 5 concludes the paper and discusses future work.

2. BACKGROUND

In this section, we introduce the system architecture of NAND flash and the implementation of some representative FTL schemes. We first summarize the system architecture of NAND flash in Section 2.1. Then we revisit the implementation of well-known FTL schemes in Section 2.2. Finally, we present the motivation of this paper in Section 2.3.

2.1 NAND Flash System Architecture

A typical NAND flash storage system usually includes two layers, the Flash Translation Layer (FTL) and the Memory Technology Device (MTD) layer, as shown in Figure 1. The MTD layer provides primitive functions, such as read, write, and erase over flash memory. The FTL emulates the flash memory as block devices so that the file systems can access the flash memory transparently. The FTL usually provides three components: address translator, garbage collector, and wear-leveler. In FTL, address translator translates addresses between Logical Block Address (LBA) and Physical Block Address (PBA); garbage collector reclaims space by erasing obsolete blocks in which there exists invalidated data; wear-leveler is an optional component that distributes erase operations evenly across all blocks, so as to extend the lifetime of flash memory. In this paper, we propose a new FTL, called RNFTL, to improve the endurance and the space utilization of NAND flash.

2.2 The Implementations of FTL

In this section, we briefly introduce two representative implementations of FTL, Original_NFTL [3, 6] and Revised_NFTL [15]. A well known block-level FTL, denoted by Original_NFTL in this paper, was proposed by [3, 6]. In Original_NFTL, a logical block address (LBA) is divided by the number of pages in a block to obtain the virtual block address (VBA) and block offset, where the VBA is the quotient, and the block offset is the remainder of the division. A block-level mapping table maps the VBA into a physical block (known as *primary block*). And each primary block is associated with some physical blocks (known as *replacement block*). To facilitate the traversing for both read and write operations, the replacement blocks are maintained in a linked list. A write operation to an LBA is always done to a page in a primary block first, and subsequent update operations to the same LBA are made on the corresponding replacement block with the same block offset.

The space utilization of Original_NFTL can be degraded due to frequently update of the same LBA. To address this issue, an improved scheme, called Revised_NFTL in this paper, assigns each primary block with only one replacement block. The examples of Original_NFTL and Revised_NFTL are shown in Figure 2(a) and Figure 2(b), respectively. In the example, each block has 8 pages, and the request sequence of write (wr) and read (rd) operations are listed in Figure 2(c).

For Original_NFTL shown in Figure 2(a), the first three operations are written to the same LBA (17). Thus, the second and third

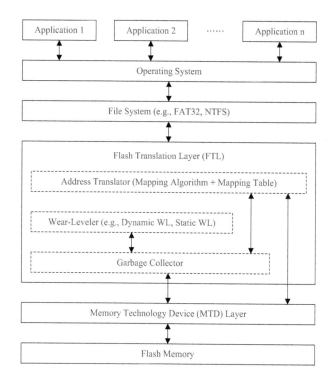

Figure 1. Illustration of system architecture for NAND flash.

write operations update the original content A by $A1$ and $A2$, respectively. As shown, two replacement blocks (#1 and #2) are allocated for these update operations and added into the linked list of the primary block #0. $A1$ is written to page 1 of the replacement block #1 with the same block offset of the primary block (the remainder of $\frac{17}{8}$). Likewise, replacement block #2 is further added into the linked list when $A1$ is updated by $A2$, and $A2$ is also written to the page with the same block offset 1 in replacement block #2. In this example, three replacement blocks are allocated in the linked list since LBA 20 is re-written by the content $C1$, $C2$, and $C3$ for three times. In Original_NFTL, the most recent copy of data ($A2$) is marked as valid while the old copies of data (A and $A1$) are still marked as valid.

For a read operation in Original_NFTL, it is traversed to find the most recent data (i.e., valid page) among the replacement blocks in the linked list. For a write operation, it is traversed to find the first free page with the same block offset in the replacement blocks. When there comes another re-write request and there is no free block for this request, the blocks on the longest linked list are merged into one block by copying the valid pages from the primary and replacement blocks to the last replacement block in the linked list, and the last replacement block becomes a new primary block. After a merge operation, the original primary block and replacement blocks except the last one are erased and become free blocks for further usage.

For Revised_NFTL shown in Figure 2(b), when a write operation is performed, the content of the write operation is first written to the page with the corresponding block offset in a primary block. Different from Original_NFTL, only one replacement block is assigned to each primary block to handle subsequent update operations, and the contents of the update operations are sequentially written to the replacement block. For instance, the contents for requests 17 and 20 are written into the replacement block sequentially, and the page with the most recent content ($A2$ and $C3$) is

marked as valid. The most recent copy of content can be found by reading the replacement block backwards. For example, the up-to-date content for LBA 20 is stored in page 4 of the replacement block #1. When a replacement block is full, a merge operation is performed. Valid pages in the replacement block and its associated primary block are copied into a new primary block while the old replacement and primary block are erased.

It is noticed that the space utilization of Revised_NFTL is better than that of Original_NFTL. As shown in Figure 2, the space utilization of Revised_NFTL is 50% (i.e., 8 pages are used among two blocks), while that of Original_NFTL is 25% (i.e., 8 pages are used among four blocks). Therefore, Revised_NFTL is widely used and combined with other FTL implementations [9, 12, 15].

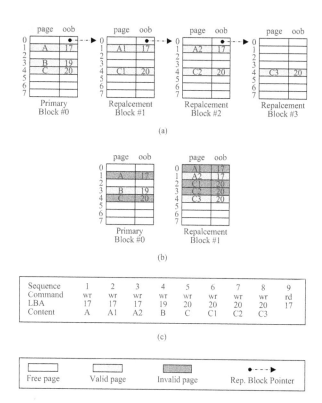

Figure 2. Illustration of representative FTL implementations. (a) Original_NFTL. (b) Revised_NFTL. (c) I/O request sequence.

2.3 Motivation

In Original_NFTL and Revised_NFTL, a primary block and its associated replacement block(s) are erased during a merge operation. However, many free pages may exist in the erased primary block, and thus, these unused free pages are wasted. Therefore, a merge operation in both of these representative FTL designs may not completely utilize all pages inside a primary block. In addition, the erasure of a primary block in a merge operation may also degrade the endurance of the primary block, and further influence the average lifetime of all blocks in NAND flash. These observations motivate us to propose an approach called **RNFTL (Reuse-Aware NFTL)** to effectively improve the space utilization, endurance and wear-leveling of NAND flash memory.

3. RNFTL – Reuse-Aware NFTL

In this section, we introduce our **RNFTL (Reuse-Aware NFTL)** approach to effectively improve the space utilization, endurance and wear-leveling of NAND flash. We first give an overview of RNFTL in Section 3.1. The detailed description of RNFTL is then presented in Section 3.2. Finally, we analyze some issues related to wear-leveling, extreme case and performance efficiency.

3.1 Overview

As mentioned earlier, our RNFTL is different from the previous work [9, 12, 15] that erase both primary and replacement blocks at the same time in merge operations. The basic idea of RNFTL is to preserve a primary block from being erased if there are many free pages inside the primary block. In our technique, each primary block only associates with one replacement block. We employ a reuse strategy to completely utilize all free pages inside a preserved primary block. To achieve this, we put the preserved primary blocks (dirty blocks) into a dirty block list, in which each dirty block will be further reused as a replacement block for a new primary block. By applying RNFTL, a primary block with many unused pages is reserved and reused as a replacement block to completely utilize all of its free pages. Therefore, the erase count of a primary block is reduced and all pages in a primary block are fully utilized. Consequently, the endurance and space utilization of all blocks can be enhanced. We show the detailed reuse strategy below.

3.2 The Reuse Strategy

In RNFTL, the reuse strategy is performed based on the number of free pages in a primary block. If there are a lot of free pages in a primary block, this primary block should not be erased during merge operations in order to fully utilize its space and reduce its erase count. On the other hand, if there only left one or two pages in a primary block, this primary block can be erased like the conventional scheme, since only one or two pages may not be valuable for reusing. Hence, we compare the actual free page ratio (the number of free pages to the number of total pages of a block), denoted by α, with a predefined threshold, denoted by μ, to decide whether or not to reuse a primary block during merge operations. Two cases are explained as follows:

- There remains many free pages in a primary block ($\alpha \geq \mu$): then this primary block is preserved and reused as a replacement block, the free pages in this primary block are completely utilized.

- There remains very few free pages in a primary block ($\alpha < \mu$): then we discard this primary block and erase it together with the replacement block.

In our technique, if a primary block is preserved for reusing, the valid pages in the primary and its corresponding replacement block are first copied into a new primary block. After that, the replacement block is erased and the valid pages in the preserved primary block is marked as invalid. Finally, the preserved primary block is considered as a dirty block and put into a **dirty block list** for reusing. If an update operation of the data in another primary block is issued, a replacement block is needed. In this case, a dirty block from the dirty block list is chose as a replacement block. If the dirty block list is empty, a new block from the free block list will become the new replacement block. In RNFTL, an update operation is traversed to find the first free page in the replacement block, and a read operation first finds the up-to-date data in the replacement block backwards.

An example of RNFTL is shown in Figure 3. In the example, the threshold μ is set as 30%, then a primary block will be reused if its free page ratio α is greater than or equal to 30%. Otherwise, it will be erased together with the replacement block during merge operations. As shown in Figure 3(a), for the first request (write request to LBA 17 with content A), block #0 is allocated from the free block list to use as a primary block. For the second request (write request to LBA 17 with content $A1$), as it writes to the same LBA as that of the first request, block #1 from the free block list is allocated and used as a replacement block of the primary block #0, and the page 1 in the primary block #0 is marked as invalid. Similarly, the requests 3 to 11 will first write to the primary block #0, and the updated content will be stored in the replacement block #1. After writing $C5$ (the request 12) to replacement block #1, the replacement block #1 becomes full, and a merge operation is issued. Block #2 is chosen from the head of a free block list to be a new primary block, and the valid pages with the up-to-date data ($A3$, B and $C5$) in primary block #0 and replacement block #1 are copied to a new block #2. Since the free page ratio α of the primary block #0 is 62.5% (5 free pages out of 8 pages in one block), it is greater than the threshold μ (30%). Therefore, the primary block #0 is considered as a dirty block and put into a dirty block list for further reuse. Figure 3(b) shows the reuse strategy. When the content E of LBA 25 in primary block #3 is updated by a write request $E1$ (the request 18), a replacement block is needed. So dirty block #0 in the head of the dirty block list shown in Figure 3(a) is selected as the new replacement block. Then $E1$ writes to the first free page in the replacement block #0 and this page (page 0) is marked as valid. Using the reuse strategy, free pages in the primary block are fully utilized. Consequently, the erase counts for blocks in the NAND flash can be further reduced, and the endurance and space utilization of all blocks can be improved.

3.3 The Analysis of RNFTL

This section provides an analysis of RNFTL, to show that how the wear-leveling and performance is enhanced. We first analyze the performance improvement of RNFTL over representative techniques for two special cases, frequent update and sequential write operations. Then we analyze the possibility to use the reused block as a new primary block. Finally, we will discuss the performance efficiency of our RNFTL scheme.

Frequent update and sequential write operations form two extreme cases for the write requests of NAND flash. Given a number of write requests N_{wr} to NAND flash, frequent update operations denote all N_{wr} write requests are with the same LBA (logical address). The content of this LBA will be updated for N_{wr} times. Sequential write operations denote each of the N_{wr} write requests is with different LBA. For sequential write operations, N_{wr} requests write to N_{wr} distinct pages, and thus no update is needed. In real applications, all the write requests for NAND flash are the combination of frequent update and sequential write operations. Therefore, we analyze the performance of our RNFTL and other representative schemes under these two extreme cases.

Table 1 shows the performance analysis of frequent update and sequential write operations. In this table, N_p denotes the number of pages in a block; N_{wr} denotes the number of write requests to NAND flash, and we assume N_{wr} is less than the number of blocks in a NAND flash; N_{blk} denotes the number of blocks needed for N_{wr} write requests; α_{pri} denotes the average free page ratio (the number of free pages to the number of total pages N_p of a block) of all primary blocks; α_{rep} denotes the average free page ratio of all replacement blocks; α_{avg} denotes the average free page ratio of all blocks (including primary and replacement blocks).

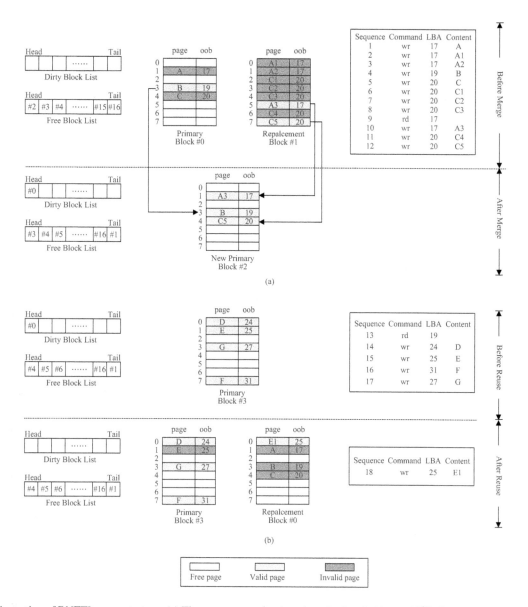

Figure 3. Illustration of RNFTL reuse strategy. (a) The merge operation based on the threshold $\mu = 30\%$. (b) The reuse strategy of RNFTL.

As shown in Table 1, our RNFTL can achieve significant improvement over Original_NFTL and Revised_NFTL in terms of the number of used blocks N_{blk} and the average free page ratio. For a frequent update operation, Original_NFTL will allocate a new replacement block with the same offset. Therefore, N_{wr} blocks are used for N_{wr} write requests, and each block only use one page. Revised_NFTL can fully utilize the replacement block, but each primary block only use one page. When the threshold μ is less than or equal to $(N_p-1)/N_p$, our RNFTL can fully utilize both primary and replacement blocks such that the erase counts of each block is reduced and the wear-leveling is enhanced. When the threshold μ is greater than $(N_p-1)/N_p$, RNFTL achieves the same performance as that of Revised_NFTL.

In terms of the number of used blocks N_{blk} for frequent update operations, the maximum improvement of our RNFTL over Original_NFTL is shown as follows:

$$(1 - \frac{\lceil (N_{wr}-2)/(N_p-1)\rceil + 1}{N_{wr}}) \times 100\% \qquad (1)$$

Similarly, the maximum improvement of our RNFTL over Revised_NFTL is:

$$(1 - \frac{\lceil (N_{wr}-2)/(N_p-1)\rceil + 1}{\lceil (N_{wr}-1)/N_p\rceil \times 2}) \times 100\% \qquad (2)$$

To quantitative analyze the maximum improvement of our RNFTL over representative schemes for frequent update operations, Table 2 shows the results with different size of NAND flash memory. For instance, RNFTL can save up to 96.77% and 48.39% blocks compared to Original_NFTL and Revised_NFTL, respectively. For the 64GB NAND flash, the maximum improvement

Table 1. The performance analysis of frequent update operations and sequential write operations.

		Original_NFTL	Revised_NFTL	RNFTL
Frequent Update Operations	N_{blk}	N_{wr}	$\lceil (N_{wr}-1)/N_p \rceil \times 2$	$\lceil (N_{wr}-2)/(N_p-1) \rceil + 1$
	α_{pri}	$\dfrac{N_p-1}{N_p}$	$\dfrac{N_p-1}{N_p}$	0
	α_{rep}	$\dfrac{N_p-1}{N_p}$	$\dfrac{(N_p-(N_{wr}-1)\bmod N_p)\bmod N_p}{\lceil (N_{wr}-1)/N_p \rceil}$	$\dfrac{N_p-N_{wr}\bmod(N_p-1)}{\lceil (N_{wr}-2)/(N_p-1) \rceil}$
	α_{avg}	$\dfrac{N_p-1}{N_p}$	$\left(\dfrac{N_p-1}{N_p}+\dfrac{(N_p-(N_{wr}-1)\bmod N_p)\bmod N_p}{\lceil (N_{wr}-1)/N_p \rceil}\right)/2$	$\dfrac{N_p-N_{wr}\bmod(N_p-1)}{\lceil (N_{wr}-2)/(N_p-1) \rceil + 1}$
Sequential Write Operations	N_{blk}	$\lceil N_{wr}/N_p \rceil$	$\lceil N_{wr}/N_p \rceil$	$\lceil N_{wr}/N_p \rceil$
	α_{pri}	$\dfrac{(N_p-N_{wr}\bmod N_p)\bmod N_p}{\lceil N_{wr}/N_p \rceil}$	$\dfrac{(N_p-N_{wr}\bmod N_p)\bmod N_p}{\lceil N_{wr}/N_p \rceil}$	$\dfrac{(N_p-N_{wr}\bmod N_p)\bmod N_p}{\lceil N_{wr}/N_p \rceil}$
	α_{rep}	0	0	0
	α_{avg}	$\dfrac{(N_p-N_{wr}\bmod N_p)\bmod N_p}{\lceil N_{wr}/N_p \rceil}$	$\dfrac{(N_p-N_{wr}\bmod N_p)\bmod N_p}{\lceil N_{wr}/N_p \rceil}$	$\dfrac{(N_p-N_{wr}\bmod N_p)\bmod N_p}{\lceil N_{wr}/N_p \rceil}$

Table 2. The maximum improvement in the number of used block N_{blk} of RNFTL versus Original_NFTL and Revised_NFTL.

	Improvement of RNFTL over Original_NFTL (%)	Improvement of RNFTL over Revised_NFTL (%)
128MB	96.75	48.04
256MB	96.77	48.24
64GB	96.77	48.39

is relatively close to that of NAND flash with size 128MB and 256MB. Therefore, in the experiments, we choose 128MB NAND flash memory to evaluate our RNFTL scheme.

For sequential write operations, each page of a primary block is written by sequential write operations with distinct LBA. As sequential write operations do not perform update operations, for Original_NFTL, Revised_NFTL and RNFTL, no replacement is needed and there are almost no free pages left in primary block. In such case, these three schemes achieve the same results. The last column in Table 1 shows the analysis for sequential write operations. As mentioned earlier, write requests in real applications are the mixture of frequent update and sequential write operations. In most cases, the probability of frequent update operations is much higher than that of sequential write operations [11]. Therefore, RNFTL can achieve significant improvement in space utilization and endurance of NAND flash on average. The experimental results in Section 4 depicts this fact.

The reuse strategy of RNFTL is to prevent a primary block with many free pages from being erased during merge operations and reuse it as a replacement block. From another point of view, a dirty block can also be reused as a primary block for further usage. However, such strategy may result in the performance degrading of wear-leveling. For example, in Figure 3, when a write operation to LBA 25 is issued, instead of using a dirty block as a replacement

block, the dirty block #0 in the dirty block list is assumed to be reused as a primary block. In this case, if there are several update operations on the same LBA (i.e., 25) are issued, then a new replacement block from free block list is allocated due to these updates. When this replacement block becomes full, the primary block #0 will be reused again without any changes. For the next time, if this dirty block #0 is reused in the same way as that in the above extreme case, it will not be erased permanently. Therefore, it can be predicted that the erase counts of some blocks are uneven and may result in poor endurance of the NAND flash. Due to this reason, our RNFTL reuses a dirty block as a replacement block to guarantee that all blocks get erased evenly.

A merge operation in flash translation layer is a time consuming task. During a merge operation, a series of copy and write operations are performed, and there follows a number of block erase operations. Different FTL implementations have different number of erase operations in a merge operation. For Original_NFTL, the number of erase operations (N_e) depends on the number of replacement blocks ($N_e \geq 2$). For Revised_NFTL, the number of erase operations equals to 2. For our RNFTL, the number of erase operations is either 1 or 2 according to the free page ratio α of a primary block and the predefined threshold μ. Therefore, the performance efficiency of these implementations is different due to the number of erase operations in each merge operation.

$$\eta = \frac{N_p}{N_e \times T_e + \dfrac{(N_{Rp}+1) \times N_p}{S_{rd}} + \dfrac{N_{Vp}+N_{Vr}}{S_{wr}}} \quad (3)$$

Equation 3 presents a general performance efficiency η of a merge operation for different FTL implementations. In this equation, N_p denotes the number of pages in a block; N_e denotes the number of erase operations in a merge operation; T_e denotes the time consumption to erase one physical block; N_{Rp} denotes the number of replacement blocks; N_{Vp} denotes the number of valid pages in the primary block ($N_{Vp} \leq N_p$); N_{Vr} denotes the number of valid pages (the pages with the up-to-date data) in the corresponding replacement block(s) ($N_{Vr} \leq N_{Rp} \times N_p$); S_{rd} denotes the speed of read for one physical page, and S_{wr} denotes the speed of write for one physical page.

In each merge operation, it has to read the OOB area of each page in both primary and replacement blocks to check if the page holds the valid data. Therefore, $(N_{Rp} + 1) \times N_p$ pages are read in a merge operation. For write operations, only valid pages with the up-to-date data are copied from the primary and replacement blocks to a new primary block. Therefore, there are $N_{Vp} + N_{Vr}$ write operations in a merge operation. As erase operation takes the longest time, to reduce the number of blocks for erasure can improve the performance efficiency. From Equation 3, we can see that the performance efficiency of Original_NFTL is the worst if it has more than two replacement blocks. And our RNFTL has a better efficiency than Revised_NFTL if primary blocks are reused. With the increasing of the threshold μ, the total number of erase counts accordingly increased. For traces collected from real workload in daily life, our experimental results show that we can reuse all primary blocks when μ is set as 20%.

4. PERFORMANCE EVALUATION

To evaluate the effectiveness of the proposed technique RNFTL, we conduct a series of experiments and present the experimental results with analysis in this section. We compare and evaluate our proposed RNFTL scheme over the representative flash translation layer schemes, Original_NFTL [3, 6] and Revised_ NFTL [15], in terms of two performance metrics: the number of block erase counts, and the ratio of block utilization. In this section, we first introduce the experimental setup. Then, we present the experimental results collected from our simulation framework. Finally, we give the analysis based on the experimental results.

4.1 Experimental Setup

Table 3. Experimental setup and trace characteristics.

Hardware	CPU	Intel Dual Core 2GHz
	Disk Space	200GB
	RAM	2GB
Simulation Environment	OS Kernel	Linux 2.6.17
	Flash Simulator	nandsim
	Flash Size	128MB
Trace	OS	Windows XP (NTFS)
	Trace Generator	DiskMon
	Applications	Web App, MSN, Word Excel, Power Point, Media Player, Emuler

Table 3 summarizes our experimental platform and trace characteristics. As shown, our approach is evaluated through a trace-driven simulation. The trace of data request was collected by running DiskMon [1] in Windows XP over a desktop with an Intel Pentium Dual Core 2GHz processor, a 200GB hard disk, and a 2GB DRAM. The trace data reflects the real workload of the system in accessing the hard disk for daily use, such as web surfing, document typewriting, downloading, movie playing and gaming.

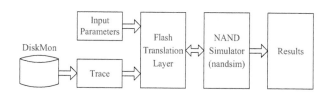

Figure 4. The framework of simulation platform.

The framework of our simulation platform, as shown in Figure 4, consists of two modules - a NAND flash simulator module (nandsim) providing basic read, write and erase capabilities; and a desired flash translation layer management scheme that can be executed on top of the NAND flash simulator. In our experiments, a 128MB NAND flash memory is configured in the NAND simulator module and employed as the investigation targets in our simulation platform. The traces along with various flash parameters, such as block size and page size are fed into our simulation framework. The block size, page size, number of pages in a block, and size of the OOB for each page are set as 16KB, 512 Bytes, 32, and 16 Bytes, respectively. Therefore, in our experiments, the 128MB flash memory has 8,192 physical blocks.

4.2 Endurance Improvement

To evaluate the improvement of endurance, we present the experimental results in terms of the block erase counts in this section. The experiments are conducted over a 128MB NAND flash with six distinct traces. The total numbers of block erase counts over different flash memory for Original_NFTL, Revised_NFTL, and our RNFTL are shown in Table 4. The results from Table 4 show that our RN-FTL technique significantly reduces the erase counts of each block compared with the other two schemes.

From the results in Table 4, compared with Revised_NFTL, our RNFTL technique can achieve an average reduction of 45.89% among these six traces, and a maximum reduction of 46.86% (Trace 5) in the number of erase counts for each block; When compared with Original_NFTL, our RNFTL technique can achieve an even better endurance improvement, i.e., an average reduction of 93.85% and a maximum reduction of 94.94% (Trace 3).

As the flash memory has a restricted number of times to perform block erase operations, the distribution of erase counts among the blocks will directly influence the endurance of the NAND flash memory. For demonstration purpose, we add a counter in the NAND simulator (nandsim) to calculate the number of block erase counts for each physical block. Figure 5 illustrates the distribution of the number of block erase counts for each block in 128MB NAND flash. The experimental results for Original_NFTL, Revised_NFTL, and RNFTL, are represented by the curve in each sub-figure based on different traces. For example, as shown in Figure 5(a), the distribution of the number of block erase counts for each block generated by Original_NFTL is in a wide range, which will adversely affect the flash endurance. On the contrary, with our RNFTL technique, we can obtain an even distribution of erase operations among all blocks as shown in Figure 5(a). It can be seen that Revised_NFTL can also evenly distribute erase operations among all blocks. However, the number of block erase counts in Revised_NFTL is nearly two times than our RNFTL. The other sub-figures in Figure 5 reflect the same fact for 128MB flash memory.

From the experimental results, we can see that, our RNFTL scheme can not only enhance the lifetime of each block but also improve the wear-leveling of all blocks in NAND flash memory.

Table 4. The number of block erase counts of RNFTL versus Original_NFTL and Revised_NFTL.

Trace	Scheme			RNFTL IMP Original_NFTL (%)	RNFTL IMP Revised_NFTL (%)
	Original_NFTL	Revised_NFTL	RNFTL		
Trace 1	178,341	29,702	16,692	90.64	43.80
Trace 2	407,251	42,388	22,928	94.37	45.91
Trace 3	2,131,643	201,294	107,964	94.94	46.37
Trace 4	1,232,670	116,522	62,500	94.93	46.36
Trace 5	1,163,539	134,446	71,438	93.86	46.86
Trace 6	5,559,222	583,256	314,859	94.34	46.02
Average				93.85	45.89

Table 5. The block utilization ratio of RNFTL versus Original_NFTL and Revised_NFTL.

Scheme	Trace	# of Free Pages	# of Valid Pages	# of Invalid Pages	Block Utilization Ratio(%)
Original_NFTL	Trace 1	5,225,282	481,630	0	8.44
	Trace 2	12,334,325	697,707	0	5.62
	Trace 3	64,850,240	3,362,336	0	4.93
	Trace 4	37,511,691	1,933,749	0	4.90
	Trace 5	35,002,665	2,230,583	0	5.99
	Trace 6	168,206,517	9,688,587	0	5.45
Revised_NFTL	Trace 1	427,040	33,341	490,083	55.07
	Trace 2	623,954	33,060	699,402	54.00
	Trace 3	2,992,523	127,534	3,321,351	53.54
	Trace 4	1,730,882	75,209	1,922,613	53.58
	Trace 5	2,019,203	64,710	2,218,359	53.07
	Trace 6	8,617,313	423,155	9,623,724	53.05
RNFTL	Trace 1	0	33,539	500,605	100.00
	Trace 2	0	25,015	708,681	100.00
	Trace 3	0	99,244	3,355,604	100.00
	Trace 4	0	62,141	1,937,859	100.00
	Trace 5	0	50,126	2,235,890	100.00
	Trace 6	0	413,446	9,662,042	100.00

4.3 Space Utilization Improvement

To evaluate the improvement of space utilization, we present the experimental results in terms of the block utilization ratio in this section. The block utilization ratio is defined as follows:

$$\frac{\text{valid pages} + \text{invalid pages}}{\text{valid pages} + \text{invalid pages} + \text{free pages}} \quad (4)$$

The block utilization ratio for Original_NFTL, Revised_NFTL and our RNFTL over 128MB flash memory are shown in Table 5. The results show that our RNFTL technique can completely utilize all free pages in each block for all of the six traces, i.e., the block utilization ratio of RNFTL is 100%. As shown in Table 5, compared with Revised_NFTL, our RNFTL technique can achieve an average improvement of 46.28% among these six traces, and a maximum reduction of 46.95% (Trace 6) in the block utilization ratio for NAND flash. When compared with Original_NFTL, our RNFTL technique can achieve an even better space utilization improvement, i.e., an average reduction of 94.11% and a maximum reduction of 95.10% (Trace 4).

4.4 Extra Overhead

In general, each page in a block has one of four different statuses, *free, valid, invalid,* and *error*. For Original_NFTL, after a valid page is updated by re-write operations, the status of this valid page is not changed to invalid. While on the other hand, for this condition, the status of such valid page is changed to invalid in our RNFTL scheme and Revised_NFTL. In the experiments, the predefined threshold μ of RNFTL is set as 20%. It means that, for a primary block, if more than 20% of its pages are free during a merge operation, our RNFTL technique will reuse this primary block instead of erasing it. Since our RNFTL approach reuses a primary block as a replacement block for further use, there will be no free pages when the reused blocks become full. In such a way, we can completely utilize each page of each block. On the other hand, as a garbage collection is a time-consuming operation, we can obtain enhanced endurance of the flash memory with less garbage collection operations. By postponing the trigger of the garbage collection, our technique greatly improves the overall performance.

In this section, we briefly discuss the performance overhead related to our RNFTL. The overhead of our RNFTL technique is that it builds up a list or a table, called *dirty block list*, to track the reused primary blocks. This dirty block list is stored in a predefined

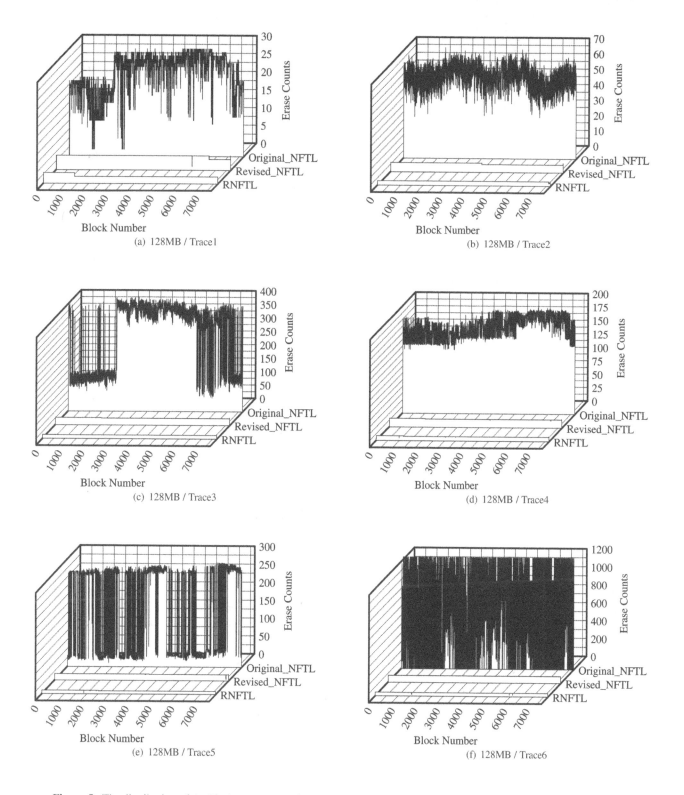

Figure 5. The distribution of the block erase counts in 128MB NAND flash memory over six traces from Trace 1 to Trace 6.

area in the flash memory. In our RNFTL, each primary block associates with only one replacement block. Therefore, at most half of the blocks in a flash memory can be allocated as replacement blocks. Then, the number of items in the dirty block list is at most half of the number of blocks in a flash memory. As each physical page can store multiple items, the size of the dirty block list is relatively negligible compared to the total size of the NAND flash. For example, a 1GB flash memory requires at most 1MB space for storing the table. Moreover, since our RNFTL scheme maintains the same read policy as that of Revised_NFTL, the read speed of our RNFTL is equivalent to that of Revised_NFTL. The sequential read in the replacement block of RNFTL and Revised_NFTL is slower than Original_NFTL, in which the data is read according to the block offset. However, our RNFTL can achieve significant improvement over Original_NFTL in terms of block erase counts and space utilization.

5. CONCLUSION AND FUTURE WORK

In this paper, we have proposed a reuse-aware NAND flash translation layer, called RNFTL, to exploit the advantages of the well-known FTL implementations in order to enhance the endurance and space utilization of the NAND flash memory. In our RNFTL, the performance improvement is achieved by preventing a primary block with many free pages from being erased during a merge operation. A reserved primary block is considered as a dirty block and put into a dirty block list for further usage. In RNFTL, we reuse a dirty block as a replacement block to improve the wear-leveling of NAND flash. We present quantitative analysis for RNFTL to show that how the performance is enhanced. We conducted experiments on a set of traces collected from real-life workloads. The experimental results show that our RNFTL technique can significantly reduce the number of block erase counts and enhance the space utilization of NAND flash compared with the previous work.

In the future, we will further study the mechanism of wear-leveling and garbage collection in NAND flash. As access pattern of applications may influence the the endurance and reliability of NAND flash, how to effectively identify the characteristics of access pattern of applications may also be a topic for us to explore.

6. Acknowledgment

We would like to thank the anonymous reviewers for their valuable feedback and improvements to this paper. The work described in this paper is partially supported by the grants from the Research Grants Council of the Hong Kong Special Administrative Region, China (GRF PolyU 5260/07E, GRF PolyU 5269/08E) and HK PolyU 1-ZV5S.

References

[1] DiskMon for Windows v2.01. *http://technet.microsoft.com/en-us/ sys-internals/bb896646.aspx*, 2010.

[2] Intel Corporation. Understanding the flash translation layer (FTL) specification. *http://developer.intel.com*, 2010.

[3] Memory Technology Device (MTD) Subsystem for Linux. *http://www.linux-mtd.infradead.org/*, 2010.

[4] SAMSUNG Corporation. SAMSUNG NAND flash. *http://www.samsung.com/global/business/semiconductor*, 2010.

[5] A. Ban. Flash file system. *US patent 5,404,485*, April 4, 1995.

[6] A. Ban. Flash file system optimized for page-mode flash technologies. *US patent 5,937,425*, August 10, 1999.

[7] L.-P. Chang and T.-W. Kuo. A real-time garbage collection mechanism for flash-memory stroage systems in embedded systems. In *Proceedings of the Eighth International Conference on Real-Time Computing systems and Applications (RTCSA '02)*, March 2002.

[8] L.-P. Chang and T.-W. Kuo. An efficient management scheme for large-scale flash-memory storage systems. In *Proceedings of the 2004 ACM symposium on Applied computing (SAC '04)*, pages 862–868, 2004.

[9] S. Choudhuri and T. Givargis. Performance improvement of block based nand flash translation layer. In *Proceedings of the 5th IEEE/ACM international conference on Hardware/software codesign and system synthesis (CODES+ISSS '07)*, pages 257–262, 2007.

[10] T.-S. Chung, D.-J. Park, S. Park, D.-H. Lee, S.-W. Lee, and H.-J. Song. A survey of flash translation layer. *J. Syst. Archit.*, 55(5-6):332–343, 2009.

[11] P.-C. Huang, Y.-H. Chang, T.-W. Kuo, J.-W. Hsieh, and M. Lin. The behavior analysis of flash-memory storage systems. In *Proceedings of the 2008 11th IEEE Symposium on Object Oriented Real-Time Distributed Computing (ISORC '08)*, pages 529–534, Washington, DC, USA, 2008.

[12] J. Kim, J. M. Kim, S. Noh, S. L. Min, and Y. Cho. A space-efficient flash translation layer for CompactFlash systems. *IEEE Transactions on Consumer Electronics*, 48(2):366–375, May 2002.

[13] J. Lee, S. Kim, H. Kwon, C. Hyun, S. Ahn, J. Choi, D. Lee, and S. H. Noh. Block recycling schemes and their cost-based optimization in nand flash memory based storage system. In *Proceedings of the 7th ACM & IEEE international conference on Embedded software (EMSOFT '07)*, pages 174–182, 2007.

[14] C. Park, W. Cheon, J. Kang, K. Roh, W. Cho, and J.-S. Kim. A reconfigurable ftl (flash translation layer) architecture for nand flash-based applications. *ACM Transactions on Embedded Computing Systems*, 7(4):1–23, 2008.

[15] C.-H. Wu and T.-W. Kuo. An adaptive two-level management for the flash translation layer in embedded systems. In *Proceedings of the 2006 IEEE/ACM international conference on Computer-aided design (ICCAD '06)*, pages 601–606, 2006.

[16] C.-H. Wu, T.-W. Kuo, and C.-L. Yang. A space-efficient caching mechanism for flash-memory address translation. In *Proceedings of the Ninth IEEE International Symposium on Object and Component-Oriented Real-Time Distributed Computing (ISORC '06)*, pages 64–71, 2006.

Author Index